The Making and Unmaking of a Saint

THE MAKING
AND UNMAKING
OF A SAINT

Hagiography and Memory
in the Cult of Gerald of Aurillac

MATHEW KUEFLER

PENN

UNIVERSITY OF PENNSYLVANIA PRESS

PHILADELPHIA

Published by
University of Pennsylvania Press
Philadelphia, Pennsylvania 19104-4112
www.upenn.edu/pennpress

Printed in the United States of America on acid-free paper
10 9 8 7 6 5 4 3 2 1

Library of Congress Cataloging-in-Publication Data

Kuefler, Mathew.
    The making and unmaking of a saint : hagiography and
memory in the cult of Gerald of Aurillac / Mathew Kuefler.
— 1st ed.
        p. cm. — (The Middle Ages series)
    Includes English translation of the Vita Geraldi brevior.
    Includes bibliographical references and index.
    ISBN 978-0-8122-4552-3 (hardcover : alk. paper)
        1. Gerald, of Aurillac, Saint, 855–909—Cult—History.
2. Odo, Saint, Abbot of Cluny, approximately 879–942.
Vita sancti Geraldi Auriliacensis. 3. Christian
hagiography—History—To 1500. 4. Christian
saints—France—Aurillac—Biography—Early works to
1800. I. Odo, Saint, Abbot of Cluny, approximately
879–942. Vita sancti Geraldi Auriliacensis. English.
II. Title. III. Series: Middle Ages series.
BX4700.G427K84 2014
270.3092—dc23
                                                    2013023877

For my mother

CONTENTS

NOTE ON NAMES

For place names, I use the modern English versions for well-known places, and the French or other vernacular versions of the historical names of the rest; if the modern name for a place has changed, I mention it in the notes. For personal names of individuals who lived in the Middle Ages, I use the modern English version, or the French version, if there is no common English name or obvious English equivalent, with the Latin in parentheses at first use if it is not obvious.

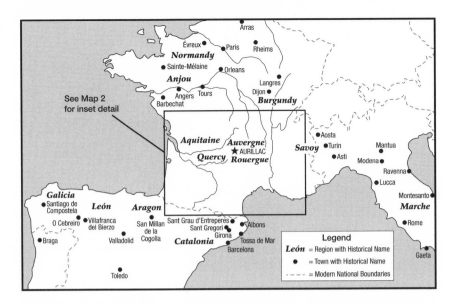

Map 1. Southwestern Europe.

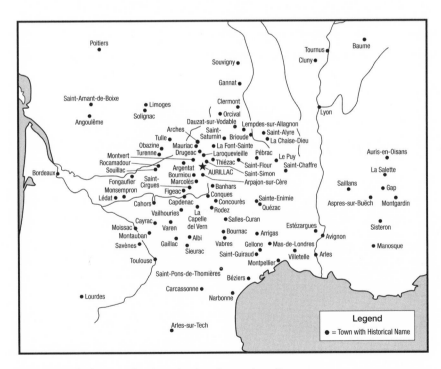

Map 2. Detail of Map 1, showing what is today southern France.

Hagiography, Memory, History

High up in the French Alps, near the end of a twisting mountain road that snakes farther and farther up a steep mountainside from the village of Auris-en-Oisans, sits the medieval chapel of Saint-Giraud. No record survives of its origins: its first mention dates from 1454, when the bishop of Grenoble stopped there on his visitation through the district.[1] It was never a parish church, and perhaps not a priory, although a sizable pile of stones next to the chapel hints that another structure, perhaps a residence, of which there is no historical recollection, once stood nearby. The chapel may be much older, since the bishop noted how deteriorated it appeared, and he ordered it restored. When I visited it in 2009 it showed only signs of decay—birds had even nested behind the altar. The chapel sits alone in its spectacular setting: abandoned, forgotten, silent (see fig. 1). No one with whom I spoke in the village could recall any event happening there, and no one knew anything about the Saint Gerald to whom the chapel was dedicated. The story of this little chapel is in many ways the story of Saint Gerald himself.

We know very little that is certain about Gerald of Aurillac. He was probably born in the middle of the ninth century and died in the early tenth.[2] He spent most of his life in the mountainous region of Auvergne in the center of what is now France, which was then part of a larger Frankish empire. He belonged to one of the families of landowners and warriors that would become Europe's nobility. He seems never to have married or had children, so before he died he left some or perhaps all of his wealth and lands to a monastery that he founded at the site that would become the modern city of Aurillac in the modern *département* of Cantal.

Within a generation of his death, Gerald was remembered as a saint. His piety and temperance in everyday life, his reputation for goodness and fair-mindedness, his chastity and pacifism, all contributed to his reputation—as

Figure 1. Chapel of Saint-Giraud, Auris-en-Oisans (*département* of Isère). Photo by the author.

did the reports of miracles he performed both during his lifetime and after his death. Within a century of his death the monastery he had founded and dedicated to Saint Peter and perhaps also to Saint Clement bore his name instead, as did a few dozen churches elsewhere, some in substantial towns like Limoges and Toulouse, others as far afield as Catalonia and Galicia. Without a formal process of canonization for saints yet in place, Gerald's saintly memory was crafted, disseminated, and preserved especially through the biographies, sermons, and prayers written about him—hagiographical writings that were carried across the south of France and as far as Paris and Normandy, Venice and Lombardy.

Gerald's status as a lay saint was highly unusual. His was an age in which Christian sanctity was mostly equated with the life of the cloister or cathedral.[3] It must have been difficult to imagine a lay male saint at a time when the basic features of manhood—eager participation in sex and violence—contravened Christian ideals so sharply. The result was a certain "anxiety" in relating Gerald's sanctity, as Stuart Airlie puts it.[4] Perhaps that anxiety took shape in the mind of the hagiographer, attempting to reconcile the values of the court to those of the cloister and offering a new model of lay holiness, as Barbara Rosenwein would have it.[5] Or perhaps it derived from Gerald himself, as Janet Nelson suggests, unable to come to terms with the requirements of a secular masculinity but unwilling to abandon his worldly life fully.[6]

In the end, it may have been that equivocation that "undid" Gerald's saintly memory. Other saints rose to prominence in the last centuries of the Middle Ages and beyond who exhibited a more inspiring or advantageous saintliness. The declining fortunes of the monastery of Aurillac also lost for Gerald the principal guardians of his memory. So forgotten was he in many of the places he had once been revered that new legends were crafted about him, tales at times vastly different from his original story. In the late nineteenth century, even as some revived Gerald's memory, his cult acquired new features in keeping with idealized recollections of the medieval past. That is the trajectory of this book.

In contrast to Gerald's obscurity among modern Catholic believers, the saint of Aurillac has attracted considerable scholarly attention, in part simply because there are only a handful of figures from the central Middle Ages for whom as rich a hagiographical tradition survives. The longer version of the *Vita Geraldi* (known to scholars as the *Vita prolixior*) has long been held to be the original version authored by Odo of Cluny in about 930; it has received the lion's share of academic interest. Recent scholarship has added a sermon for Gerald's feast day to the authentic writings of Odo. Relatively neglected is the briefer version of the *vita* (known as the *Vita brevior*), dismissed by most as uninteresting, overly condensed, and composed by some unknown and easily ignored forger in the late tenth century. Recently, additional miracle stories have been brought to light, composed no earlier than 972, and assigned to a second forger. Regrettably, these assumptions about dating and authorship are wrong, and I begin by correcting these errors, arguing that the briefer version of the *Vita Geraldi* belongs to Odo of Cluny, while the longer version, as well as the sermon and additional miracle stories, came from the hand of the infamous forger Ademar of Chabannes sometime in the 1020s.

Apart from these medieval texts, there is little else that survives from which to reconstruct the historical memory of Gerald of Aurillac. The monastic library at Aurillac that would have contained the best and most detailed records was sacked twice, at the hands of Aurillac's townspeople in 1233 and again by Protestant Huguenots in 1567. Further losses happened during the French Revolution. Only a handful of manuscripts survive from the medieval library.[7] Others survive elsewhere, especially at archives near the former priories that once belonged to the monastery of Aurillac, but there, too, little remains. The later chapters in this book, then, represent something of the challenge of reconstructing historical memory without much in the way of historical documentation—and a bit on the methods by which it might still be done.[8]

The complicated meanings attached to Gerald's sanctity are the heart of this book. Gerald's position between court and cloister placed him in the vanguard of a new broadening of saintly ideals for men: he was, insofar as we can tell, the first to be venerated as a saint for having lived a good life without having become a bishop or theologian, a monk or hermit, and his biographers both medieval and modern have pointed out this distinction.[9] There were other noble lay male saints who lived before Gerald and who were revered for their holiness, it is true, but the writings about these men mostly date from much later centuries, and many of them were also remembered as martyrs, so they serve to confirm rather than to challenge Gerald's precocity.[10] Nonetheless, the tensions within Gerald's model of sanctity are patent enough. On the one hand, one might see in Gerald the quintessence of the ethical code that all men of his era were exhorted to follow: to be both good Christians and good citizens.[11] On the other hand, Gerald's embrace of an ascetic lifestyle, his avoidance of sex, and reluctance to engage in battle were things that Carolingian piety would never have presumed.[12] Both of these assessments may be fair. Perhaps like all saints, Gerald was at once a model for others and inimitable.[13]

The two sides of Gerald's sanctity, his adoption of a monastic life while remaining outside the cloister and his renunciation of violence even while leading armies, served specific and important—if different, and historically contingent—needs for his hagiographers. Nonetheless, the placement of such equivocation within the legend of Gerald may have contributed to his undoing as a saint in the centuries after his death. After all, if a life lived in this world can be holy, why sacrifice oneself to an ascetic life? And if some forms of violence may be permissible to a good Christian, what others might also be? Gerald gave no easy answers to these questions. It is worth noting that the reshapings of Gerald's legend in modern times often functioned as correctives to this ambiguity, redirecting Gerald's memory into less uncertain channels.

This book is also, then, about the legacy that Gerald's medieval hagiographers left behind. Before popes took control of the canonization process in the late twelfth and early thirteenth centuries, hagiography provided a principal occasion for the commemoration of saints. Yet despite the subject's importance, it is not entirely clear how these writings should be read. Scholars once saw in legends about the saints the projection of a past society's heroic ideals.[14] Many are now increasingly reluctant to assume that saints' lives provide an unobstructed glimpse into any past society.[15] The elusiveness and even outright unreliability of medieval hagiography have been brought home in a singular manner in the career of Ademar of Chabannes, who plays a central role in this book. Ademar forged a set of documents that described the life of a saint who never lived with a status that he never held and a history of devotion to him that never happened, and did it so successfully that only in the twentieth century was the deception uncovered.[16]

In this book I offer my own readings of hagiography and religious art as well as new ways of thinking about the central role that individuals have played in the production of saints. I attempt, in particular, to restore to medieval hagiographers their proper role in the crafting of the historical memory of saints.[17] Jay Rubenstein laments the stereotype that medieval writers lacked "textual sophistication." Instead, he encourages us to conjecture how even in the Middle Ages the truism that "all biography to some extent is autobiography" still applies: "The narrative of a person's life grows out of beliefs of how a life ought to be lived, and a person's beliefs about how a life ought to be lived inevitably relate to that person's own life."[18]

Sadly, Rubenstein dismisses medieval hagiography from this consideration. According to him, hagiographers were too restricted in their ability to present a "sense of a 'self'" and their writings are formulaic and uninteresting.[19] Rubenstein might be forgiven for such an opinion, given his work on Guibert of Nogent, one of the most colorful and least conventional of medieval authors, but others have shared it. Paul Fouracre and Richard Gerberding, for example, conclude that medieval hagiography tended "to draw upon a common stock of conventions and to borrow wholesale from other texts, especially the Bible," to such an extent that its "language . . . does not reveal any layer of social reality different from that formally expressed," indeed, so much so "that it is almost impossible to find within it any sub-text of opposition or dissent."[20] Even while they admit to considerable variety and even originality in hagiographical texts, they assert that the conventions of the genre could not really be abandoned, since they were integral to the author's purpose in making the individual recognizable as a saint. For this reason, the truly unique elements had to be manipulated into standard shapes.[21]

Oddly, this dismissal seems to be a step back from the position that Fouracre had taken only a few years earlier when he admitted that there were conventions to hagiography, but argued that medieval hagiographers were also constrained from rote formulaicism by the living memories of the saint or a popular tradition, however dubiously founded.[22] He also noted that, since authors were free to choose some models over others, even "the manner in which each work drew upon the range of available conventions may in itself be revealing."[23] Indeed, he concluded that "the old was used to give legitimacy to the new," so the very conventions of hagiography might help to disguise what was most problematic within the life of the saint.[24]

Hagiography can indeed bear the weight of modern critical scrutiny, as I hope to show through the example of Saint Gerald. But it cannot be done by imputing to hagiographers an unvarying piety that effaces them as writers. Rather, we must see them as bringing to their writings the richness of their interior lives. My book thus seeks to answer Walter Pohl's call for postmodern readings of medieval manuscripts. Rather than pit the different textual traditions about Gerald against each other, trying to explain away variant readings, I wish to exploit, even relish the differences between them, a science that Pohl calls "textual archeology."[25] Through this, I hope to reveal the hagiographer behind the hagiography, and to challenge especially the notion that medieval hagiographers wrote only with the most transparently pious of intentions.

I have been particularly inspired by the work of Kathleen Ashley and Pamela Sheingorn on the cult of Sainte Foy of Conques. They call their study of medieval hagiography a "social semiotics" since they seek to understand each layer of Sainte Foy's legend through the texts about her, even when the authors of these texts were little known, or anonymous, and the historical contexts in which they were created and recreated are not well understood.[26] Amy Remensnyder, too, has written about Sainte Foy in ways equally important to me, especially for her demonstration, through religious articles preserved at Conques, that material objects might both safeguard pious memories and rechannel those memories in substantially new directions.[27]

Especially in the last chapter I make use of visual images of Saint Gerald: they have become an important modern means of remembering him. I speculate about the messages that these images may have carried to viewers, given what we know of the era in which they were crafted and displayed and what we can conjecture about those who revered these images.[28] Yet the ambiguity of any visual symbol is perhaps especially pronounced in religious art, which is intended first and foremost to facilitate transcendence through devotion beyond the specifics of the visual.[29] We can learn something of the intertextuality behind hagiographical art.[30] Accordingly, I have felt free to speculate about this religious imagery as communicating a shared awareness and articulating a group identity.

Writings and rewritings about saints, however plentiful or imaginative, embellished or censored, sophisticated or sensationalized, could not guarantee the preservation of social memory, and many are the saints whose memory was lost in the Middle Ages or beyond and who returned to "bones and ashes." The first abbess of the medieval monastery of Gandersheim in Saxony, for example, a woman named Hathumoda who lived about the same time as Gerald, was quickly forgotten and her cult neglected despite the *vita* written about her.[31] A number of recent studies have mapped out the recollections of a medieval saint's life through time, watching the ebb and flow of shifting social ideals and historical circumstances, although most have confined themselves to the evolution of a saint only to the end of the Middle Ages.[32] Tracing the evolution of Saint Gerald's cult through a thousand years of history provides a much broader scope within which to view such changes. Insofar as I know, such efforts have really only been attempted for the greatest of the Christian saints.[33] Still, "like all living organisms," Moshe Sluhovsky writes in his study of Saint Geneviève of Paris, "saints and their cults are born, live, succeed or fail, and—more often than not—die." He characterizes Geneviève as "a success story" because she "remained relevant" to many even as she was "made and remade by them"; Gerald was not.[34]

How Gerald suffered his fate, falling into obscurity and near nothingness, is in some ways a fundamental question of this book. How is a saint forgotten? Or, more precisely, how could the memory of a holy man like Gerald, buttressed with the official and tangible sanction of biographies and believers, statues and shrines, cease to be known, his stories cease to be told, and his monuments cease to be visited? The study of historical memory is much in vogue among scholars, but we are still struggling with how to analyze the loss of memory. Because we deal with so distant a past, medievalists are perhaps better acquainted than most with the ways in which memories are composed, recomposed, and sometimes left to decompose across time.[35] Still, new events are always cemented into place by fixing them within familiar patterns, and old traditions are bent and reshaped by new social realities.[36]

Lawrence Kritzman suggests that the study of the past, in revealing a world that no longer exists, whether real or imagined, through a glance that is either nostalgic or condescending, helps to reinforce our sense of being modern and our essential difference from what has come before us.[37] The study of Saint Gerald has accomplished that much for me, I readily admit, but it has also provided me with a wonderful opportunity to reflect on how much we are like the inhabitants of the past as well as how much we are no longer like them, perhaps more than we would often care to admit. I hope that in what follows I might provide my readers with the same unsettling experience.

Prolegomenon on the Dating and Authorship of the Writings about Gerald of Aurillac

Gerald of Aurillac is a familiar figure to scholars of the central Middle Ages, and his life has provided rare and intriguing glimpses into this era: its forms of individual piety, the relations between peasants and landowners, the methods of justice, and even the banality of violence. The traditional dating and attribution of the texts about Gerald of Aurillac are erroneous, however, and this error has had serious consequences for the conclusions that scholars have drawn from Gerald's biography. Most have accepted the opinion, established in the late nineteenth century, that Odo of Cluny wrote a detailed *vita* for Gerald of Aurillac in about 930 and that another and unknown monk of Aurillac composed an uninteresting and greatly abbreviated version shortly thereafter. This assumption needs to be corrected and a more reliable authorship and dating for the *Vita Geraldi* and the other writings about Gerald of Aurillac need to be established.

The Two Versions of the *Vita Geraldi*, One Real, One Forged

Two versions of the *Vita Geraldi* exist, both of which identify Odo of Cluny as their author. The more detailed version, in two books known as the *Vita Geraldi prolixior* (hereafter *Vita prolixior*), is the one much better known to scholars.[1] A much briefer version, the *Vita Geraldi brevior* (hereafter *Vita brevior*), is much less well known.[2] The longer version includes accounts of Gerald's death and of posthumous miracles, usually numbered as books 3 and 4 (as they are in the *PL*), although both are also titled in some early manuscripts, as will be explained below. In addition, an early sermon and a collection of additional miracle stories also survive.

The most damning evidence against Odo of Cluny's authorship of the longer version of the *Vita Geraldi* are the errors in it not found in the briefer version. Foremost among them is Gerald's misidentification as a count, repeated three times in the *Vita prolixior* but never once claimed in the *Vita brevior*. There is no other evidence for there ever having been a count in Aurillac, nor is there likely to have been one in Gerald's day, since there was a count already with jurisdiction over the area (he was William the Pious, count of Auvergne and duke of Aquitaine). The error was compounded through several episodes in which Gerald acted as a count, for example, hearing important judicial cases when he would not have had the authority to do so, which scholars have tried with some difficulty to explain.[3]

Most of the errors in the *Vita prolixior* are difficult to imagine as having been made by Odo of Cluny, writing at Aurillac within a generation of Gerald's death. The *Vita prolixior* claims that Gerald had been born "in the fort or town of Aurillac [*oppido vel villa Aureliaco*]" (1.1), something the *Vita brevior* does not, but there was no Aurillac in Gerald's day: the archeological record confirms that the town sprang up around the monastery that Gerald founded only after Gerald's death.[4] (The *Vita brevior* [1] says instead that Gerald was born on the border of Auvergne near Cahors and Albi; the *Vita prolixior* [1.1] oddly repeats this information, too, even though these towns are each over a hundred kilometers distant from Aurillac.) The church that Gerald is said to have erected at Aurillac, moreover, is described in the *Vita prolixior* (2.5) as having been "built in a round design [*arcuato schemate fabricare*]" and erected next to a church dedicated to Saint Clement that his father had built. The *Vita brevior* gives neither of these details. Yet the archeological evidence has revealed neither a rounded shape to the original church, nor foundations sufficient for a vaulted roof, as some have suggested the phrase should be understood, nor any evidence for a second nearby church structure, and scholars have struggled to reconcile this evidence with the claims made in the *Vita prolixior*. This first church would have been the one still standing when Odo was at Aurillac, so it is difficult to understand him as having made this mistake, although it is easy enough to imagine a later forger as having mistaken the second church there—a larger structure built later in the tenth century with a rounded apse—for the original.[5]

Among the errors in the *Vita prolixior* are a number of seeming anachronisms, not found in the *Vita brevior* and equally difficult to explain as Odo's. For example, this longer version (1.37) mentions an enemy of Gerald's, a man named Godfred, who is described as the count of Turenne, even though that title did not exist until the end of the tenth century. (One scholar concludes, oddly enough, that Odo "speaks through anticipation" in this comment, and another admits only that "the mention . . . cannot be taken literally."[6]) There are also allusions to the three social orders and language that replicates Peace of God proclamations found in the *Vita prolixior* but not in the *Vita brevior*, as will be discussed below, both of which have made Odo seem greatly ahead of his time. Yet these errors and anachronisms disappear if it is recognized that the *Vita prolixior* is a forgery.

The implications of such a reappraisal cannot be overstated. The *Vita prolixior*, a key source for the history of southern France in the central Middle Ages, must be read very differently. We can no longer expect to gain insight from it into either Odo of Cluny's mindset or that of the early Cluniac movement more generally, for example. In point of fact, as will be discussed in detail in Chapter 2, the model of lay holiness found in the *Vita prolixior* never sat all that comfortably with Odo's championing of the monastic ideal (and that praise is much more muted in the *Vita brevior*, where Gerald is presented as having assumed more of the rigors of the cloister).[7] We must also rethink most of what we learn from the details of the *Vita prolixior*, whether about piety or economic structures or social relations, since they were invented more than a century after his death.[8] Many of the most recent scholarly discussions of the *Vita prolixior* have taken place within the context of the debates over the transformations in France between the tenth and eleventh centuries that go by the name "la mutation de l'an mil"; its reappraisal forces a reassessment of these changes—although that is beyond the scope of this book.[9] What this book can do is to provide for Gerald of Aurillac a new and more reliable place in the history of the central Middle Ages through a more accurate understanding of the writings about him.

The Origins of the Scholarly Consensus

The scholarly opinion that the *Vita prolixior* was written first and by Odo of Cluny and that the *Vita brevior* was a later abridgement of it was definitively established by the Bollandist scholar, Albert Poncelet, in an article published in *Analecta Bollandiana* in 1895.[10] It is worth noting, though, that he wrote in rebuttal to the conclusions of Jean-Barthélemy Hauréau, who had questioned Odo's authorship of the *Vita prolixior*—the only scholar I have found thus far to have identified the *Vita brevior* as Odo's.[11] Hauréau's opinions bear repeating here. He considered it unlikely that Odo had authored both versions, although the prefaces of each version made the claim, since neither mentioned any alternative version even though they were supposed to have been dedicated and sent to the same individuals. Given that the oldest manuscript of the *Vita prolixior* Hauréau had seen was from the fifteenth century, while there were two manuscripts of the *Vita brevior* from the tenth century, he concluded that common sense dictated that the version in the older manuscripts was likelier to be the authentic one. The fact that only the preface to the *Vita brevior* mentioned how "the matter seemed unclear to me on account of its newness [*novitas*]" confirmed his opinion that this version was the earlier.[12]

Poncelet attempted to demolish Hauréau's conclusions in his own article. He noted that older manuscripts of the *Vita prolixior*, unknown to Hauréau, had since been located, the oldest from the eleventh century. (Nonetheless, the earliest extant manuscripts are still those of the *Vita brevior*.[13]) Oddly enough, Poncelet did not seek to undermine Hauréau's other arguments. Indeed, he admitted that the description of Gerald as *domnus* (lord) in the preface to the *Vita brevior* and the use of the term *beatus* (saint) in the preface to the *Vita prolixior* might indicate that the latter was the later version, written after the formalization of devotion to Saint Gerald.[14] He did not pursue this counterpoint further and did not attempt to refute it. (Yet the argument might be further honed, since the *Vita prolixior* often refers to Gerald as *sanctus* and *confessor* as well as *beatus* and begins and ends by pointing to Gerald's *sanctitas*. The *Vita brevior*, in contrast, refers to Gerald as *vir Domini* or *famulus Dei*, as well as the simpler *domnus Geraldus*, and only once, near the end of the preface, does the *Vita brevior* refer to Gerald as *beatus vir*. We must consider what these word choices mean: we are expected to believe that the later forger suppressed all mentions of Gerald as a saint and confessor within his text as he abridged the *Vita Geraldi*. It is far easier to believe that a later author added these references as he elaborated an earlier text where they were absent.) In a second concession, Poncelet noted that biblical citations were more closely followed in the *Vita prolixior* than in the *Vita brevior*, and while he admitted that it might seem likelier that a later author had corrected the original errors, he believed instead that this author had merely been uncareful.[15]

Poncelet had his own reasons for favoring the primacy of the *Vita prolix-ior*. He noted that Peter the Venerable, a twelfth-century abbot of Cluny, had quoted briefly from it, and he thought it unlikely that the monastery of Cluny would have had in its medieval library the forged rather than the authentic version.[16] (It is likeliest, however, that Cluny had both versions in its library, since found among its scattered manuscripts are a series of hybrid forms of the *Vita Geraldi* that borrow from both the *Vita prolixior* and the *Vita brevior*.[17]) For the most part, however, Poncelet's reasoning was highly speculative. Since the author of the *Vita prolixior* had included so many episodes not found in the *Vita brevior*, he concluded that "if this is a forger, one must admit that he worked to the utmost and with singular skill and impudence" in augmenting the text to such an extent, and that such a forger would have been "a deceiver of the first rank."[18] "One does not invent with-out a purpose," he added, and he could discern no compelling reason for the added episodes, although enhancing Gerald's saintliness would seem a rather obvious motivation.[19] He then compared specific incidents between the two versions that he believed confirmed the earlier composition of the *Vita prolix-ior*. For example, he considered it likelier that a story of Gerald's having been nearly tempted into sex with one of his serfs, found in the *Vita prolixior* but not in the *Vita brevior*, would have been suppressed in an effort to cover up embarrassing misconduct rather than added into a later account. In view of the fact that the *Vita brevior* noted how miracles were said to have occurred at Gerald's mother's tomb while the *Vita prolixior* did not, Poncelet thought it unlikely that an elaboration would have omitted such a detail, as Gerald's mother's sanctity could only have enhanced his own.[20] Poncelet also found the description of Gerald's secret tonsure more plausibly presented in the *Vita prolixior*, where it is said that Gerald always wore a hat to cover it—that is, hiding what he was doing, than in the *Vita brevior*, where it is said that Gerald pretended that he was going bald—that is, not hiding the tonsure but denying its true meaning.[21] There are other minor arguments in Poncelet's article, but the whole remains equally speculative. Poncelet himself admitted that "all of this is perhaps a matter of appreciation, of impression, and it might appear up to a certain point an explanation based on feelings [*une raison de sentiment*], that is to say, the worst sort of critical arguments."[22]

Because scholarship must always rely on the findings of others, and because the Bollandists have made such a reputation for themselves in the study of hagiography, Poncelet's assertions have been universally accepted. Stuart Airlie, for example, concluded that the *Vita brevior* was an abridged version of the *Vita prolixior* written "quickly" after it (but not hazarding a guess as to its author).[23] Paolo Facciotto also described Odo of Cluny as "certainly [or "confidently," *sûrement*] at the origin of the principal line of the *Vita Geraldi*."[24] Isabelle Rosé admits that the text of the *Vita Geraldi* "still presents a certain number of uncertainties," but concludes that "it is certain that the greatest part of the [*Vita prolixior*] was written by Odo of Cluny."[25] Anne-Marie Bultot-Verleyson has confirmed this scholarly consensus in her critical edition of the *Vita prolixior*, where she does not even consider the possibility that it might not be Odo's, but writes: "Poncelet has been able to establish on solid bases that the long version was truly the original work."[26] This confidence is unfounded, however; it is a house of cards.

The Basic Differences between the *Vita brevior* and the *Vita prolixior*

Even a cursory glance at the prefaces to the two versions should make Odo's authorship of both suspect. In that regard, the scholarly consensus is correct. Both were said to have been dedicated to Aimon (Aymo), abbot of the monastery of Tulle, and his brother Turpin (Turpio), bishop of Limoges, both of whom had insisted that Odo compose the *Vita Geraldi*. (Since Aimon was abbot of Tulle only between 929 and 931, after which he became abbot of the monastery of Limoges, Odo's authentic work must have been written between these years.)[27] The preface to the *Vita prolixior* implies erroneously that Odo had only stopped briefly at Saint Gerald's tomb at Aurillac during a visit to Tulle: "But when the occasion demanded that we should visit the monastic brotherhood of Tulle, it pleased us to make a detour to his tomb [*Sed cum causa insisteret ut Tutelensis coenobii fraternitatem inviseremus, ad sepulcrum ipsius intendere libuit*]" (1.*praef.*). The *Vita brevior*, in contrast, does not say this. In fact, Odo spent at least a few months at Aurillac reforming its monastery in late 928 or early 929, and almost certainly composed his version of the *Vita Geraldi* then or shortly after.[28] The simplest solution is to believe that the forger did not know that Odo had been abbot of Aurillac—it was not mentioned in Odo's own *vita*[29]—but knew that Odo had been briefly at Tulle and so invented something that seemed plausible enough. To accept that the preface to the *Vita prolixior* is genuine is to believe that Odo was somehow attempting to mislead about a much stronger connection to

Aurillac than his having merely once visited the place. Again, scholars have bravely argued around these details, suggesting that Odo made an initial journey to investigate Gerald's sanctity before becoming abbot there and decided to mention only the former visit in his preface. Making the reasoning and the chronology work for such a supposition, however, is incredibly awkward.[30]

Both the *Vita brevior* and the *Vita prolixior* share the same basic biographical details. Both begin with Gerald's holy ancestry, mentioning that he had two saints among his ancestors, Caesarius of Arles and Aredius of Saint-Yrieux, and that he enjoyed the most virtuous of parents who had received a sign from God regarding Gerald's future holiness even before he was born. Both versions continue with Gerald's upbringing, in which chronic illness in childhood prompted his father to train him for ecclesiastical office, although he was eventually healthy enough to take up his lands and secular responsibilities. According to both, Gerald was humble with the authority he wielded, slow to anger and violence, and accepted the derision of those who thought he acted too timidly. He was chaste and modest, forgoing marriage and all sexual relations, and even washing himself after nocturnal emissions. Both agree that he eventually conceived a desire to establish a monastery on his lands and enter monastic life himself, and that he approached a Bishop Gauzbert, who persuaded him to live the life of a monk and to tonsure himself secretly but to remain outwardly a layman. Both note that Gerald traveled to Rome where he made a formal bequest of his lands to Saint Peter, and then began collecting monks, though with some difficulty, since there were so few worthy individuals. Finally, both assert that Gerald's holiness was confirmed by his private devotions, and by the cures performed through him, despite his wishes, often with the water in which he washed his hands. Both versions follow an orderly progression from his secular responsibilities to his spiritual devotions, and finally to the miracles attributed to him.[31]

The differences between the two versions, however, far outweigh these similarities. One might consider, for instance, the ordering of the episodes recounted in each. Almost all of the episodes found in the *Vita brevior* are also included in the *Vita prolixior*, yet they are often rearranged. They can be contrasted as follows (and for the sake of convenience I use here, and throughout the book, numbers used in the *PL* edition of the *Vita prolixior* that Bultot-Verleysen's edition also provides and mostly follows):

Vita brevior episode:	*Vita prolixior* equivalent:
1 Gerald's ancestry, parents, and birth	1.1, 1.2, and 1.3
2 his childhood and adolescence	1.4 and 1.5
3 his adulthood and nonviolence	1.6, 1.7, and 1.8
4 his chastity and modesty	1.9, 1.10, and 1.34
5 his secular responsibilities	1.11 and 1.25
6 his daily life and care for the poor	1.11, 1.13, 1.14, 1.15, 1.17, 1.25, and 1.42
7 his semi-monasticism	2.2, 2.3, and 2.4
8 his pilgrimages and his monastery	2.6, 2.8, and 2.17
9 the healings with his wash water	2.10
10 the cure of a lame boy from Aurillac	2.11
11 the cures of a blind man from Solignac,	2.10
a woman with a blind son near Lucca,	2.20
and a blind girl near Argentat	2.13
12 the cure of a demonic woman	2.32
13 the miraculous crossing of a stream	2.18
14 his knowledge of a distant death	2.25
15 (his miraculous multiplying of one fish)	2.19
16 (the cure of a man's shattered knee)	2.33

Even if the episodes drawn from the life of Gerald demonstrate approximate parallels, many of the episodes from his life as well as the accounts of his miracles have been jumbled around from one version to the other; the changes hardly seem reasonable if coming from the same author. The *Vita prolixior* also includes episodes not found in the *Vita brevior*, including a lengthy description of Gerald's physical appearance (1.12) and of his clothing (1.16). It seems difficult to imagine a scenario in which the same author, having decided that such information was symbolically important, would omit it altogether from an abridgement—or even that a copyist abridging an original work would do so. This omission is especially incomprehensible since the additional passages are pointedly intended to convey a moral lesson. For example, the physical description of Gerald ends by noting that while he was extremely handsome, strong, and agile, he was still humble: "whereas, in contrast, they are culpable who, having little or nothing of themselves, swell [with pride]" (1.12).

Another noticeable dissimilarity between the two texts is the differing emphasis on Gerald's secular responsibilities. The *Vita brevior* lacks virtually all detail about such matters, mentioning them only in the broadest of terms. It refers to Gerald's "authority and his possessions by hereditary right" and then to his military duties only by saying that "a great need compelled him now and again to suppress with arms the violent men who plundered his estates and peasants excessively" (3). It notes also only in the vaguest way his "followers and . . . others who were subjected to his authority," that he "prosecuted those who were bold in assaulting peasants" (5), and that he "journey[ed] to the royal court" in order to "to take part in the assemblies of princes" (7). These six brief phrases are literally all that is said in the *Vita brevior* about Gerald's secular activities. Most conspicuously, the *Vita brevior* never refers to Gerald as a count. The *Vita prolixior*, in contrast, clearly gives this title to Gerald on three occasions, noting also that Gerald refused to commend himself to the duke of Aquitaine, "because he had recently taken to himself the advantages of a count [*favore comitis nuper usurpato*]" (1.32; see also 1.27 and 2.18). More importantly, the *Vita prolixior* lingers on the secular activities that Gerald performed as count: his role as a peacemaker in violent disputes (1.7–8) and as an honest-minded local judge (1.11, 1.17), even recalling the specifics of various cases he had judged (1.18–20). His amicable relations with peasants are detailed through a number of incidents (1.21–23), as are his dealings with other men of the nobility, both his social equals (especially with a certain count Ademar, 1.35–36, and with Ademar's brother Adelhelm, 1.38–39) and those above him on the social ladder, like Duke William of Aquitaine (1.32–34). The *Vita brevior*, in short, shows no interest whatsoever in Gerald's secular role, while the *Vita prolixior* is much keener to present him as a model of specific comital duties and relationships. This difference further belies the same hand at work in the two texts.

Even when the same basic information is given in both versions, the focus often shifts meaningfully between the one and the other. For example, the *Vita brevior* claimed that Gerald had been struck blind for one year for having been tempted, when an adolescent, to indulge in sex with a certain young woman, even though the desire was never consummated. Nothing is said about the encounter itself; instead, the emphasis is placed on the aftermath of the incident: Gerald decided to spend the night outdoors in the cold, "in order that the vast cold of winter might extinguish the flame of deformed desire" (4). The *Vita prolixior* provides a much more dramatic scene, high-lighting the incident itself: "He sent to the girl's father who informed him that he should come at night. . . . Having reached an agreement, he entered the lodging for the girl. Since it was cold, she stood facing the hearth. Indeed, already divine grace had looked upon Gerald: to him that same girl now looked so deformed that he would not believe her to be the one he had seen, until her father declared her to be the same one" (1.9).[32] No mention is made of the night spent outside. The *Vita prolixior* concludes by saying that Gerald "right away ordered her father to hand her over in marriage; and he gave her freedom, and he granted her a certain small estate" (1.9), implying that she had been his serf or slave, something not said or even implied in the *Vita brevior*. Again, it is difficult to see how the same author could make such drastic changes to his text, yet it is only one of several similar episodes. Expanding on the foundation of a monastery on Gerald's lands, the *Vita prolixior* includes another event not found in the *Vita brevior*: the collapse of the first foundations for the monastic church, requiring its reconstruction (2.4). It is difficult to understand why this detail would have been omitted even from an abridgement, if, as is concluded in the *Vita prolixior*, it demonstrated both the Devil's malice against Gerald and Gerald's holy perseverance.

Another real and telling difference between the two versions is how little the phrasing is repeated from one to the next. Medieval copyists were adept at abbreviating, most often by copying word for word, then skipping phrases, sentences, or even whole sections before jumping back to an original text. Indeed, several of the manuscripts of the *Vita Geraldi* demonstrate just such a formula for abbreviation, skipping from sentence one to sentence three, or omitting some sections while repeating others verbatim.[33] The relationship between the *Vita brevior* and the *Vita prolixior* is not like that at all, and there is virtually no copying of sentences or sections. Sometimes the *Vita brevior* even contains longer descriptions than the *Vita prolixior*: an odd thing in an abridgement. Both versions, for example, recount a miracle that involved Gerald while he was still in his mother's womb. The extensive rewording, shown below, from one version to the other, provides a typical example of the sorts of substantial differences between the two (for ease of comparison, phrases used in common are in boldface and words or roots of words used in both are in italics):

Vita brevior: Ante vero quam *nasceretur*, forte *vigilans* pater cum matre *vigilante iacebat*; et *cum nescio quid vicissim* loqueretur, *infans*

de utero praegnantis *emisit vocem, quam* uterque parens *audiv*it.
Ambo igitur *obstupesc*entes, *voc*ant *cubiculariam,* ut *adhibito lumine
disquir*eret *quonam* infans *sonu*isset. At illa, *cum lumine* veniens,
locum perscrutabatur. Et *cum nullum infantem adesse* testaretur,
infans secundo sonuit. **Et post modicum intervallum sonuit etiam
tertio, videlicet sicut recens natus vagire solet.** Jam **ignorare** non
poterant quod illa vox in matris alvo sonuerit; quod idcirco
mirum est quia, *disponente rerum* auctore *Deo,* **contra naturae
modum constat accidisse.** Quinto post haec die mater puerum
enixa est. (1)

Vita prolixior: Genetrix eius cum esset vicina partui—nono videlicet
die priusquam *nasceretur*—contigit ut cum suo viro *vigilanti vigilans*
ipsa *iaceret. Et* dum *nescio quid vicissim* sermocinarentur, *infans emisit
vocem quam* ambo *audi*erunt. Cum attoniti, quidnam esset *obstupesc*-
erent, neque **ignorare poterant, quod illa vox in alvo matris
sonuerit.** *Voc*at pater *cubiculariam,* et *quonam* ille *vagi*tus increpuerit,
adhibito lumine, iubet *disquiri. Cum* illa *nullum* omnino *infantem
adesse,* qui *vocem illam* ediderit similiter attonita prostestaretur, *infans*
iterum *secundo sonuit;* **et post modicum intervallum, sonuit etiam
tertio, videlicet sicut recens natus vagire solet.** Ter igitur *in* ventre
matris auditus est. Quod profecto tam *mirum est* quam et **contra
naturae modum constat accidisse.** Et quia non casu sed *disponente
rerum* ordinatore *Deo* factum est, forte iam *vox illa* presagabat quod
in huius mortalitatis clausura vitales actus erat habiturus. (1.3)[34]

Only three phrases are substantially repeated. One cannot help but note how
lengthy the episode is in the *Vita brevior:* almost as long as in the *Vita prolixior.* There are a number of minor differences even when phrases are otherwise
parallel: *in matris alvo* is replaced by *in ventre matris* in one sentence, and
disponente rerum auctore Deo is replaced by *disponente rerum ordinatore Deo*
in another. The first passage, moreover, concludes by saying that "five days
later, his mother brought forth her son," while the second begins with "on
the ninth day before he was born," changing not only the position of this
information within the passage, but also the time when the miracle happened. (Even the conclusion reached in the *Vita brevior,* that God can act
against nature if He wishes, is contradicted by a statement elsewhere in the
Vita prolixior, that God abhors what is unnatural, 1.21).[35]

The two versions also present a number of more subtle variations. They differ, for example, in their presentations of Gerald's miracle-working abilities, which is much more of a central feature to the *Vita prolixior* than to the *Vita brevior*. (The absence of miracle stories is a feature of tenth-century hagiography.[36]) The author of the *Vita brevior* had mentioned that water Gerald had used to wash his hands cured the sick, but seemed a bit skeptical or at least prepared to deal with skeptical readers, adding that a few specific examples could help make that claim seem "more believable [*magis credibile*]" (9) and having Gerald himself dismiss the alleged healings with his wash water as a "a deception from the devil [*illusio diabolica*]" (11). The miracles in the *Vita prolixior*, in contrast, are underlined in importance rather than minimized: many of the individuals involved are directed through visions and dreams to make use of Gerald's wash water, so their healings result from divine commands rather than the peculiarities of individual devotion (for example, 2.10 or 2.20). The few miracles mentioned in the *Vita brevior* have a distinctly biblical aura: Gerald healed a lame boy (10), cured two blind persons (11), exorcised a possessed woman (12), and fed his men with a small fish (15). The *Vita prolixior* includes all of the miracles contained in the *Vita brevior*, but adds a lively assortment of others: Gerald caused wine to flow from a spring in the ground (2.21). When Gerald's men complained that they had no fresh meat, a stag threw itself down from a cliff edge in front of them (2.27). On one occasion, a fish deliberately swam toward Gerald and his men and allowed itself to be caught in order to feed them (2.29); on another, a fish showed up miraculously on the dinner table of hermit who was entertaining Gerald (2.30). A man who boasted that he could jump onto a high boulder through magic found after Gerald made the sign of the cross that he could no longer do it (2.31). As this last example suggests, the miracles presented only in the *Vita prolixior* underscore the efficacy of ritual actions, like making the sign of the cross (2.31 and 2.32), being in the presence of relics (2.21 and 2.23), and sprinkling with water that has been blessed by priests (2.26). The stories often rely on the highly improbable, as when bandits in the Alps help Gerald and his men carry their baggage through the mountains rather than despoil them of it (2.17). These peculiar sorts of miracles can be found in many medieval hagiographical texts, so it is their absence from the *Vita brevior* even while they are repeated in great detail in the *Vita prolixior* that is most noteworthy, suggesting not only different authorship but also differing concepts of the miraculous.

Word usage confirms the many differences between the two versions. Granted, their overall lengths differ considerably and must affect the precision of the contrast; still, the different usage is remarkable. Most instructive are the descriptions of Gerald himself. The *Vita prolixior* is replete with references to the virtues that Gerald exhibited: his piety (*pius* and *pietas*, mentioned twelve times in relation to Gerald), his humility (*humilis* and *humilitas*, mentioned sixteen times), and especially his justice (*iustus* or *iusticia*, mentioned twenty-three times), as well as fewer references to his patience, his clemency, and his simplicity of heart. In contrast, the *Vita brevior* identifies different virtues as typifying Gerald: his modesty (*verecundia*), his respectability (*honestas*, noted twice), and his love of poverty (*paupertatis amor*). Gerald's humility and his piety are noted, as in the *Vita prolixior*, but when Gerald's piety is mentioned, the word *religio* is preferred, where the *Vita prolixior* used *pietas* (*vita plena religione*, 5, and *religiose*, 6), and in contrast to the attention paid in the *Vita prolixior* to Gerald's sense of justice, the *Vita brevior* says only once that "Gerald "lived soberly and justly and piously [*sobre et iuste et pie vixerat*]" (6; a quotation of Titus 2:12). The *Vita prolixior* makes repeated references to Gerald's soul (*anima*) and his spirit or mind (*animus*) as motivating his actions, but the *Vita brevior* never uses either term.

Overall, the vocabulary of the two texts is noticeably different. These differences are clear from religious[37] as well as from secular vocabulary, although the lack of interest in Gerald's secular duties in the *Vita brevior* helps to explain this last set of differences.[38] Even minor word choices less than consciously chosen also demonstrate differences. The *Vita prolixior* relies heavily on an eclectic range of words borrowed from Greek, for example, whereas the *Vita brevior* uses only two, *eleemosyna* and *eulogia*.[39] The *Vita prolixior* uses many more late Latin words (that is, those used by patristic writers or found in the Vulgate, but not attested in classical writers) than the *Vita brevior*.[40] The *Vita prolixior* makes abundant use of superlatives: to give but two of the numerous examples, the men of the Bible were "the holiest and most patient of men [*sanctissimi et patientissimi*]" (1.8), and "the most ingenious enemy was most heatedly inflamed [*versutissimus hostis acerrime succendebatur*]" against Gerald's chastity (1.9). The *Vita brevior* uses not a single one. All of these examples force the conclusion that these two versions of the *Vita Geraldi* could not have come from the same author.

Odo of Cluny and the *Vita brevior*

There is no good reason to dispute the attribution of one of the versions of the *Vita Geraldi* to Odo of Cluny. The earliest external reference to the *Vita Geraldi* dates from the early eleventh century, in the *Chronicon* (also called the *Historia*) by Ademar of Chabannes, who ascribed it to Odo, saying that "the most revered Odo produced the life [*vitam*] of Saint Gerald at the insistence of Turpin," but referring to it in the singular without mention of any other version, whether extended or abridged.[41] In his *Commemoratio abbatum basilicae sancti Martialis*, Ademar repeated this information.[42] These references do let us know that Ademar of Chabannes had read at least one or the other version of the *vita*, a fact that should be kept in mind. Two twelfth-century references to Odo's authorship of the *Vita Geraldi* also exist. The first is from an anonymous and brief chronicle of the abbots of Aurillac written sometime before 1119. It records that "Odo, the venerable third abbot of Aurillac and abbot of Cluny, when asked by Turpin, the bishop of Limoges, and Aimon, the abbot of Tulle, wrote down the life [*descripsit vitam*] of Saint Gerald."[43] The second, mentioned above, is by Peter the Venerable, abbot of Cluny, who wrote sometime after 1142 in his *De miraculis* that "For as our father, Saint Odo, wrote in the Life of the saintly man Gerald [*Vita sancti viri Geraldi*], 'visions in dreams are not always inconsequential,'" a quotation from the *Vita prolixior* rather than the *Vita brevior*, as Poncelet noted.[44] If both versions of the *Vita Geraldi* were written by Odo of Cluny at Aurillac, it should be said, neither the anonymous chronicler at Aurillac nor a successor abbot at Cluny apparently knew it, since both referred to the *Vita Geraldi* as a singular text. Still, these references provide evidence for linking at least one of the versions of the *Vita Geraldi* to Odo.

Throughout the *Vita brevior* the concerns of a man such as Odo are clear. Monastic reform is foremost among them. Gerald is said to have "collected together such monks as he was able to find" for his monastery at Aurillac (7), although he lamented that he was unable to find monks worthy of the name to inhabit it. He predicted nonetheless that his monastery would one day be filled with such men (8). Gerald's frequent prayer, his love for the scriptures, his fasting and silence at meals, his letting go of grudges, even his charity to the poor (5–7) gave him a semi-monastic lifestyle that borrowed freely from the Rule of Saint Benedict.[45] Gerald's personal dedication to Rome, where he traveled every other year on pilgrimage, also mirrored Cluniac ideals. Undeniably, Gerald remained a layman. Yet throughout the *Vita brevior*—much more so than in the *Vita prolixior*—Gerald moved closer and closer to the monastic life: "as his age increased, he inched more fully into a life of contemplation" (6). Even as a young man, Gerald "carried with distress the sharp troubles and duties of his household, because in the hidden places of his heart he feared that he would be distracted and surrounded by earthly entanglements" (3). He not only refused to marry, but also "assumed such an obvious love for chastity that he avoided with women the embrace that is usual among friends as they kiss, even women who were related to him" (4). "Withdrawing himself gradually from the affairs of this world" as he grew older, he nonetheless remained outside the cloister, according to the advice of the bishop Gauzbert, "so that the malevolent and those who would think that he was a layman would be restrained by great fear." In Gerald's own mind, "he reckoned it preferable to remain as he was than to attempt the sublime proposition [of the monastic life] away from tested brothers," that is, monks who had some experience in the lifestyle (7). There is much less of the praise of lay holiness in the *Vita brevior* than in the *Vita prolixior*, and much more of the superiority of the monastic life. This sentiment is much more in keeping with Odo's other writings (and more on that subject in the next chapter). It also fits more neatly within the broader context of the early Cluniac tradition, within which a hagiographical tradition did not develop until around the year 1000, and, when it happened, it was fixed firmly on the superiority of the monastic life to the lay life.[46]

Toward a Historical Context for the *Vita prolixior*

In noticeable contrast to the positioning of Gerald as almost a monk in the *Vita brevior*, Gerald is firmly placed among the laity in the *Vita prolixior*. Right from the start, the *Vita prolixior* offers Gerald "as an example to the powerful [*potentes*]" so that they might see how they might imitate a man who was "near to them and of their order [*ordo*]" (1.*praef.*). Later, it cautions monks against using Gerald's example of eating meat and drinking to excuse their own indulgences because "many things are permitted to a layman [*homo laïcus*] that are not permitted to a monk" (2.*praef.*). In this last instance, the *Vita prolixior* has reworded the much more ambiguous comment in the *Vita brevior* that "many things he did piously and reputably that are properly fitting to an active life [*activa vita*]" (6). So even if the *Vita prolixior* recognized that "it was against his will, therefore, that he was kept in the world" (2.9), Gerald remained clearly in the world. Indeed, describing Gerald's worldly entanglements explains most of the episodes added in the *Vita prolixior*, and nothing is sketched out in more detail or more plainly confirms Gerald's position among the laity than his relationship to its violence. "No one should be disturbed at all that a just man ever made use of fighting, which seems to be incompatible with religion," the *Vita prolixior* asserts; "it was permitted, therefore, to a layman placed in the order of fighters [*laïcus homo in ordine pugnatorum*] to carry the sword, so that he might defend the unarmed common people [*inerme vulgus*]" (1.8). In turn, this emphasis on violence in the *Vita prolixior* helps us move toward establishing a more probable authorship for it. So while I will return later to other internal evidence, it is best to turn now to a historical context: one of not the early tenth century, when Odo wrote, but the early eleventh century.

The new millennium seems to have witnessed in what is now the south of France an invigorated religious enthusiasm, a "great awakening" that might have had something to do with apprehensions about the end of time.[47] Both versions of the *Vita Geraldi* allude to it. The *Vita brevior* says: "although now in the present time of the Antichrist the miracles of the saints ought already to cease, nonetheless the Lord . . . deemed this servant of His worthy to glorify" (9), linking the times to Gerald's healing abilities. The *Vita prolixior* moves a similar comment into the preface, emphasizing the whole of Gerald's life as an example for the times: "in this age of ours, when charity has almost entirely grown cold, and the time of the Antichrist is at hand, the miracles of the saints should not cease" (1.*praef.*). (Note that the opposite sentiment is being expressed in these two versions, yet another of the many indications that these are not texts written by the same author.) Perhaps churchmen exploited this apprehension as part of their efforts to pacify the men of the nobility.[48] The collapse of centralized government, especially in the tenth century, had made room for strong men to seize power, and they often wielded it ruthlessly. Through the assemblies of what we call the Peace of God movement that began in the late tenth century and continued into the early eleventh, noblemen were inspired to renounce violence against the unarmed and the clergy or face spiritual punishments that would have been all the more fearsome if they believed that the world was coming to an end.

Gerald's reluctance to engage in warfare is noted in the *Vita brevior*, but only briefly:

> Since a great need compelled him now and again to suppress with arms the violent who plundered his estates and peasants exceedingly,

he admonished his soldiers in a commanding voice that they should
fight against the enemy with their spears turned around [*aversis hastis*]. But the piety in the recesses of his heart that inspired this desire
in the waging of war soon made him irresistible to his enemies: and
yet it was not once heard that the good fortune of victory had disappointed anyone who fought out of loyalty to Gerald. But again, one
thing remained certain, that neither he himself ever wounded anyone whatsoever nor was he ever wounded by anyone. (3)

This same idea is repeated in the *Vita prolixior*, but with a substantial
enhancement of the tone:

> Therefore he exerted himself at that time for the sake of restraining
> the insolence of the violent, paying eager attention in particular to
> promise peace and the easiest reconciliation to his enemies. He made
> an effort to do it in order that he would either conquer evil with
> good or if they remained at variance, the justice of his side would
> then be more fully favored in God's eyes. And he soothed a few of
> them and led them back to peace. But when the insatiable malice of
> some mocked the peaceful man, then, exerting the sternness of his
> heart, "he broke the jaws of the wicked man," according to Job, "so
> that he dropped his prey from his teeth" [Job 29.17]. Yet he was not
> aroused by any lust or seduced by a love of vulgar praise, as is the
> custom with many, but inflamed by love of the poor, who were
> unable to defend themselves. . . . Whenever the unavoidable neces-
> sity of fighting settled on him, however, he ordered his men in an
> imperious voice that they should fight with the points of their
> swords held backwards and holding their spears in front of them
> [*mucronibus gladiorum retroactis, hastas inantea dirigentes*]. This
> would have been ridiculous to his enemies if Gerald had not been
> strengthened by divine power so that he was thereafter irresistible to
> those same enemies. Even that very much seemed to them to be
> absurd, if they had not tested by experiment that Gerald, whose
> piety won out in that same moment of fighting, was always invinci-
> ble. . . . But this much remains certain, that neither he himself ever
> wounded anyone nor was he wounded in any way by anyone. (1.8)

Not only is the unusual technique of war broadened—the "spears turned
around" in the *Vita brevior* has become a more complicated and much more

difficult to interpret maneuver in the *Vita prolixior*, and somehow involves the men's swords as well as their spears—but the justification for the fighting is also greatly extended. Indeed, the passage continues at length in the same vein.

The vocabulary of concern for the poor, protection of the defenseless, and ecclesiastical condemnation in the *Vita prolixior* repeats phrasing from Peace of God documents.[49] Scholars have already recognized the parallels, even while believing that the *Vita prolixior* dates from the early tenth century. Pierre Bonnassie and Jean-Pierre Poly claim that it "anticipates the first Peace of God."[50] Dominique Barthélemy says that it represents "a model for the promoters, a half-century later, of the 'Peace of God.'"[51] Yet it is far more plausible that these sentiments and the language chosen to express them reveal the date of the composition of the *Vita prolixior*, rather than the prescience of its ideas. After all, these ideas did not really begin to circulate until the 970s, and Cluniacs had little involvement in the early Peace movement.[52]

Even the notion of Gerald as belonging to "an order of fighters [*ordo pugnatorum*]" makes an eleventh-century context for the *Vita prolixior* likelier. This description echoes the tripartite functions of medieval society that Georges Duby dated to the early eleventh century. Indeed, Duby writes of the *Vita prolixior*: "With these words the abbot Odo not only anticipated Gerard [of Cambrai] and Adalbero [of Laon] by a century but went much further than they eventually would."[53] It is true that some have challenged Duby's conclusions, suggesting instead that it was King Alfred of Wessex or the monk Heric of Auxerre who first imagined these divisions already in the ninth century; yet even then it is admitted that the idea did not gain currency until the early eleventh century.[54] So the use of the term here—and this phrase might be compared with other references within the *Vita prolixior* to "those who profess religion [*professores religionis*]" (1.16 and 2.*praef.*), to "the powerful [*potentes*]" as an *ordo* (1.*praef.*), or to "the layman [*laicus homo*]" as an *ordo* (2.*praef.*)—is suggestive of a later date of composition. The alternative is to imagine Odo once again as ahead of his time. It is one more of the many ways in which the *Vita prolixior* seems to anticipate later historical developments solely because it has been misdated.

The *Transitus* and *Miracula*

Following both versions of the *Vita Geraldi* in many manuscripts are two accounts: the first, of Gerald's death (whenever named, called the *Transitus*), and the second, a series of posthumous miracles attributed to him (sometimes called the *Miracula* or variously *Miracula post transitum*, *Miracula post mortem*, or *Liber miraculorum*). The texts are first found in a manuscript of Limoges from the late tenth or early eleventh century, where they follow the *Vita brevior*.[55] (This manuscript also contains the earliest surviving image of Saint Gerald within the capital that begins his *vita* here; see figure 2.) The manuscript might seem to suggest a closer connection between these writings and the *Vita brevior*, but I believe that they were written by the author of the *Vita prolixior*, first as addenda to the *Vita brevior* (which had mentioned neither Gerald's death nor any posthumous miracles), and then reused in the author's own elaboration of the *Vita Geraldi*, probably with a few episodes added to each.[56] Whenever the *Transitus* and the *Miracula* follow the *Vita prolixior* in the manuscripts, they are included as part of the *vita* and listed simply as books 3 and 4, with only two exceptions; whenever they follow the *Vita brevior*, however, they are given titles, with only two exceptions, and are never numbered.[57] (For ease of reference, I will use the *PL* numbering when referring to them. See Appendix 2 for these and all other details about the manuscripts.[58]) Consider how implausible even this bit of information makes the traditional claim to Odo's authorship of the *Vita prolixior*: one must believe that the forger decided to abbreviate a lengthy *vita* that was divided into four books, beginning by rearranging the first two of these books into a *vita* and extensively revising their style, structure, and wording, but then turning the remaining two books into two separate texts, and giving them new titles but otherwise leaving them absolutely unchanged.

It is not difficult to prove that the *Vita prolixior*, the *Transitus*, and the *Miracula* were all authored by the same individual. The close relationship among the texts is evident, for example, from narrative elements in each. The *Transitus* begins with a description of the increasing bodily infirmity of Gerald's advancing age (3.*praef.*) that echoes the description of Gerald's appearance that the *Vita prolixior* had noted (1.12), but about which the *Vita brevior* had said nothing. The *Transitus* continues by noting that Gerald went blind again in his later years, and compared him to Tobias and Job in his sufferings (3.2); the *Vita brevior* had also compared Gerald to Job in its preface, but only the *Vita prolixior* had compared Gerald to both Job and Tobias (1.*praef.*). The *Transitus* then refers to the completion and consecration of the monastery church at Aurillac two years before Gerald's death (3.3), which fits neatly with the account, given in the *Vita prolixior* alone, of the collapse of the previous church and the necessity of rebuilding it (2.4). The author of the

Figure 2. Saint Gerald, illuminated capital, late tenth or early eleventh century, from a manuscript of the monastery of Saint-Martial, Limoges. Bibliothèque nationale de France, collection latine, ms 5301, fol. 221r, detail. Reprinted by permission of Bibliothèque nationale de France.

Transitus has Gerald "arm himself with the sign of the holy cross [*signo se sanctae crucis armavit*]" on his deathbed and repeat the words *Subvenite, sancti Dei* ("Help, you saints of God"), where the phrase is described as "the expression so long familiar to him" (3.7; cf. 3.5). The author of the *Vita brevior* had mentioned neither of these ritual actions, but the author of the *Vita prolixior* had already noted Gerald's use of the sign of the cross three times beforehand and the spiritual power of the action (2.23, 2.31, and 2.32); he had also described this same expression as Gerald's "usual words [*consuetum sibi verbum*]" (2.24).[59] The *Transitus* ends with a prayer for Gerald's intercession from heaven, described as "that eternal court of the Capitol [*illa sempiterna Capitolii curia*], where he already resides among the consuls of heaven [*consules coeli*]" (3.8). The same metaphor of the heavenly Rome also appears in the *Vita prolixior*, where the expression *superni Capitolii curia* is used and where the consuls are identified as Peter and Paul (2.22: *coeli consules, Petrum scilicet et Paulum*).

The miraculous episodes in the *Miracula* also parallel incidents found in the *Vita prolixior*. So, for example, the posthumous miracles assigned to Gerald demonstrate his power over animals almost as often as over human beings, much as did the miracles during Gerald's lifetime in the *Vita prolixior*. And just as Gerald had tried to turn violent men from their ways during his lifetime in the *Vita prolixior*, for example, appearing in a dream to the count of Toulouse, who held one of his nephews hostage, and warning him to desist from his wickedness (2.28), he appeared after his death in the *Transitus* to that same nephew to tell him to end his violent actions (4.11). It is worth adding that the *Vita brevior* does not even mention Gerald's nephews, while the *Vita prolixior* has already named them as Benedict and Rainald (2.28).[60]

Word usage in the *Transitus* and the *Miracula* bears out their ties to the *Vita prolixior*. Like the *Vita prolixior*, for example, both the *Transitus* and the *Miracula* refer repeatedly to Gerald as *beatus*, *sanctus*, and *confessor*. There are many other parallels, too, in the descriptions of Gerald,[61] and in the broader religious vocabulary used.[62] Even though the *Transitus* and the *Miracula* are much shorter texts, they still manage to mention a range of biblical figures and saints, as the *Vita prolixior* had done, including many of the same saints.[63] Secular vocabulary also shows the same rich diversity as in the *Vita prolixior* and lacking in the *Vita brevior*.[64] A profusion of Greek and late Latin words are included in the *Transitus* and the *Miracula*, as in the *Vita prolixior*, including some of the same words used there, as well as numerous superlatives, all of which are also features of the *Vita prolixior*.[65] On this point, the scholarly consensus is correct: the *Transitus* and the *Miracula* are from the author of the *Vita prolixior*.

The *Vita prolixior*, the *Transitus*, the *Miracula*, and Limoges

Taken together, the *Vita prolixior*, including the *Transitus* and the *Miracula* as its third and fourth books, offers hints as to where and when it was written. One of the posthumous miracles stands out because it is neither a cure nor a chastisement, but a vision that confirms Gerald's sanctity by describing how a priest saw Gerald in heaven in the company of four saints: Peter, Paul, Andrew, and Martial (4.5). Martial's presence among the apostles reminds us of the concerted effort at the monastery of Limoges in the late 1020s to elevate its patron saint, Martial, to apostolic status. Of particular importance is that there is no evidence apart from this vision in the *Vita prolixior* for any apostolic claim for Saint Martial before the turn of the eleventh century.[66] Indeed, it has been recently claimed that the expanded claims for Saint Martial happened only after 994.[67] Once again the scholarly consensus requires us to believe that Odo was precocious if not prescient in making these claims about Martial at least a half-century before the monks of Limoges themselves seem to have made them. It is far more plausible to interpret this incident as helping to identify the time and place of the forged version of the *Vita Geraldi*.[68]

Both Limoges and Saint Martial show up with a surprising regularity in the *Vita prolixior*, including in its third and fourth books, the *Transitus* and the *Miracula*. (Neither is mentioned at all in the *Vita brevior*.) It is said that Gerald regularly visited the shrine of Saint Martial at Limoges (2.22) and that he had collected a tooth belonging to the saint (3.3). Limoges even shows up in the description of Gerald's birthplace. As I noted above, the *Vita brevior* describes that place as near Cahors and Albi (1). The *Vita prolixior* repeats this, and adds "in the fort or town of Aurillac," but then also inserts "in the district of Limoges [*atque Limovicensi pago*]."[69] If Gerald was born somewhere near to Cahors and Albi, he could hardly be considered as having been born in Aurillac, let alone anywhere near Limoges, much farther to the north. Nonetheless, it was another opportunity for the forger to mention Limoges and possibly to make devotion to Saint Gerald seem local. Other mentions of Limoges are equally odd. A monk of the monastery of Saint-Martial at Limoges is mentioned by name in the *Vita prolixior* as a witness to the terrible death of one of Gerald's enemies; the same monk is said to have preached publicly at Limoges and also guarded the treasury of its monastery (1.39). It seems the sort of knowledge that a monk at Limoges might possess, and even if Odo knew it, it is difficult to imagine him as thinking it important enough to pass along. No other place apart from Aurillac itself receives anywhere near the same attention as Limoges in the four books of the *Vita prolixior*.

It would not have been difficult for a monk of Limoges to have known about Saint Gerald. It was to the brothers Aimon and Turpin that Odo's original work was dedicated, after all: the latter was already bishop of Limoges at the time and the former eventually became the abbot of its monastery of Saint-Martial. Two early sacramentaries from this same monastery inform us that Saint Gerald's feast day was celebrated there by the late tenth century, and monastic conventions in place from the same time encouraged the monks of Limoges and Aurillac to pray for each other's dead.[70] In 1021, some of Gerald's relics were translated from Aurillac to Limoges to be venerated there.[71] Even before then a church dedicated to Saint Gerald was built at Limoges.[72] Multiple threads, then, tied the cult of Saint Gerald to Limoges in the early eleventh century. The bishop of Limoges between 1014 and 1023 was even named Gerald and may have been a distant relative of the saint; he may have helped to spark interest in Saint Gerald there.[73]

Finally, the earliest extant copies of the *Transitus* and *Miracula* come from the monastery of Limoges. As mentioned above, they follow the *Vita brevior* in a manuscript copied there sometime between the 990s and the 1020s.[74] I believe that the *Transitus* and the *Miracula* were composed at Limoges in the early eleventh century, intended originally to follow the *Vita brevior* as separate texts, as they do here, before their author decided to write his own version of the *Vita Geraldi*, reuse them as numbered books within it, and forge it under Odo's name.

Ademar of Chabannes and the *Vita prolixior*

If the four books of the *Vita prolixior* were all written by the same author not before the last decade of the tenth century but probably in the 1020s, and if they were composed at Limoges, then the likeliest candidate for their authorship is Ademar of Chabannes. Admittedly, there were other monks at work at Limoges who could have composed these texts about Saint Gerald, but the reasons for this conclusion can be enumerated easily enough. First, Ademar was a master forger.[75] Second, Ademar was familiar with the *Vita Geraldi*, since his are the oldest external references to the work. Third, Ademar wrote hagiographical works and demonstrated his interest in several saints; indeed, he seems to have composed two other *vitae* also attributed to others.[76] Fourth, one of those was a more detailed *vita* for Saint Martial (also known as the *Vita prolixior*), created through a process of elaboration much like that done with the *Vita Geraldi*. Fifth, that *vita* for Saint Martial praised a lay leader much like Gerald—Stephen, an imagined duke in Roman Aquitaine—for his piety, support for the church, concern for the poor, even his pacifism and devotion to Rome.[77] Sixth, Ademar was deeply interested in the Peace of God movement.[78] Indeed, through his writings on it, Ademar outlined a theory of the sacrality of war in which God's favor might be shown through military victories, a notion that fits perfectly with the depiction of Gerald in the *Vita prolixior*.[79] Seventh, Ademar admired yet another virtuous layman, Duke William the Great of Aquitaine, who died in 1029. His account shares certain parallels with that of Gerald in the *Vita prolixior*, a similarity not quite so remarkable if they came from the same hand.[80] Eighth, it is even possible that Ademar was distantly related to Saint Gerald, which might have provided a powerful incentive for Ademar to want to reshape Gerald's legend in more compelling ways than Odo had left it.[81] At the very least, he was related to the brothers Aimon and Turpin to whom Odo's original *vita* had been dedicated.[82] Ninth, Saint Gerald shows up with surprising regularity in Ademar's other writings. In his *Chronicon*, the first version of which was written in about 1024 or 1025, Ademar described how William, the duke of Aquitaine, had tried unsuccessfully to arrange a marriage between Gerald and his own sister. Ademar quoted from the *Vita brevior* (4), which demonstrates his familiarity with that version of the *Vita Geraldi*. To the revised version of the *Chronicon* he made in about 1029, Ademar added a comment to this episode not in his original text about Odo of Cluny's authorship of the *Vita Geraldi* that I believe was intended to disguise his forged work.[83] In his *Commemoratio abbatum Lemovicensium*, written about the same time as this last version of his *Chronicon*, moreover, he included yet another mention of Odo's authorship of the *Vita Geraldi* as well as the dates of Gerald's birth and death. This last work was an enumeration of the good and bad qualities of the abbots of Limoges, and even if the first comment could be slipped in when listing Aimon, the abbot of Limoges to whom Odo had dedicated his version of the *vita*, Gerald's birth and death dates were hardly germane to the subject. Since no other saint is included in a similar manner, these repeated mentions seem to betray Ademar's abiding interest in Gerald.

Tenth and last in this list of reasons to suspect Ademar's authorship of the *Vita prolixior* is the interesting set of references to an individual named Ademar within it, in episodes not found in the *Vita brevior*. One of these episodes recounts Gerald's relations with a count named Ademar, who wanted Gerald to commend himself to him (*se commendare*, also described as his wanting "to put him under his authority [*eum suae ditioni subdidisset*]" and "to extort a pact [*pacto extorquere*]," 1.35, part of the rich secular vocabulary in the *Vita prolixior*), even through use of force, but without success. In one incident, this Ademar attempted to capture Gerald while the latter was in open encampment (1.35); in another, this Ademar went so far as to take Gerald's castle at Aurillac before he abandoned it and "returned to his own part of the country" (1.36). Two further incidents describe how Adelhelm, brother to this Ademar, also took Gerald's castle at Aurillac but was unable to keep it (1.38), and tried again to take it but failed (1.39). There is no further information within the *Vita prolixior* about this Count Ademar, but an episode in Ademar's *Chronicon* sheds light on his identity. There he mentioned a man named Ademar whom King Odo of France had named count of Poitiers after the death of the previous count, Ralph (Ranulphus) II, in 890. Ralph had an illegitimate son named Èbles (Eblus), nicknamed Manzer, who was described there as a young boy (*parvulum filium*), so he was probably not deemed capable of taking possession of his father's title and lands. Èbles did eventually succeed his father as count of Poitiers in 926 and died in 934 or 935. Ademar mentioned in his *Chronicon* that Saint Gerald had fostered the young Èbles until he reached adulthood, which seems to provide an adequate reason for the animosity between Gerald and this Count Ademar and his brother that is otherwise unexplained in the *Vita prolixior*. It also tells us that Ademar of Chabannes had some independent knowledge about Gerald not obtained from Odo's version of the *vita*. Since Duke William of Aquitaine in Ademar of Chabannes' own day was the great-grandson of Èbles, the episode also highlighted Saint Gerald's ties with the ducal house of Aquitaine even as it reinforced the unworthiness of its rivals.[84] Naming practices of the period suggest that there might be some family connection between Ademar of Chabannes and this Count Ademar, but it is impossible to do more than conjecture about a connection. Still, Ademar did characterize his relatives as "warlike in spirit [*animo bellicosos*]," which fits well with these brothers described in the *Vita prolixior*.[85]

These ten reasons, even taken together, may not satisfy the most skeptical of readers, although they surely make Ademar the most reasonable candidate for author of the *Vita prolixior* of any known historical individuals. At the very least, these ten reasons surely outweigh any that might be given to defend Odo's authorship of it.

Three Other Early Writings about Saint Gerald

Three additional writings about Saint Gerald need now to be brought into this discussion: the first is a hybrid version of the *Vita Geraldi* borrowing elements from both the *Vita brevior* and the *Vita prolixior*; the second, a sermon for Gerald's feast day, and the third, a series of additional posthumous miracles attributed to Gerald. They are all found in eleventh- or twelfth-century manuscripts, but their relationship to the other texts is a bit more complicated.

A Cluniac Variant of the Vita Geraldi

It was Bultot-Verleysen who first identified the variant *Vita Geraldi* that she called the *Vita prolixior secunda*.[86] Four manuscripts of it survive, all from the eleventh or twelfth centuries and all apparently from Cluny, but only one of them is long enough to study.[87] It differs from the *Vita prolixior* only in minor ways, omitting some episodes and rearranging others. For instance, both the *Transitus* and the *Miracula* follow the *Vita prolixior*, but the *Transitus* is included as part of the second book of the *Vita prolixior* and the *Miracula* is identified as book 3. There are also a few changes in language throughout; as Bultot-Verleysen notes, these are often improvements with more accurate use of tenses or the smoothing out of awkward expressions, which would indicate that the *Vita prolixior secunda* was written after the original, the *Vita prolixior* (which she calls the *Vita prolixior prima*). There are also a few factual changes: Gerald's birthplace is given as *valle Aureliana* in the *Vita prolixior secunda*, for example, instead of *villa Aureliaco* as given in the *Vita prolixior*. (If, as I suggested above, it was an error to consider Gerald as having been born at Aurillac, this may be yet another correction. *Valle Aureliana* is now Vailhourles in the modern French *département* of Aveyron, and belonged to the monastery of Aurillac already in the eleventh century. It is not an unreasonable location for Gerald's birth—and it is about halfway between Cahors and Albi.[88]) The *Vita prolixior secunda* is not simply a variant of the *Vita prolixior prima*: it also shares elements with the *Vita brevior*; in particular, its preface is that of the *Vita brevior* rather than that of the *Vita prolixior prima*, and there are a handful of other passages too similar to be coincidental.

Since Bultot-Verleysen considers Odo of Cluny as having authored the *Vita prolixior prima* and the *Vita brevior* as the later forgery, she argues that the *Vita prolixior secunda* was written before the *Vita brevior* and that the forger of the *Vita brevior* then borrowed the preface from the *Vita prolixior secunda* but took other elements from the *Vita prolixior prima*. Of course, since the *Vita brevior* exists in two very early manuscripts, she is obliged to argue that both the *Vita prolixior secunda* and the *Vita brevior* must have been written very quickly after the *Vita prolixior prima*. That is certainly possible, and it is also sensible enough for her to argue that the author of the *Vita prolixior secunda* began with the *Vita prolixior prima*, simplified its preface and corrected some of its language, omitting some episodes and rearranging others, and deciding to join the account of Gerald's death to the main text of Gerald's life, leaving only the posthumous miracles in a separate book. It is the next step that is much more difficult to accept. The author of the *Vita brevior*, she implies (though she never addresses this question directly), set out to craft a new version of the *Vita Geraldi*. He began it by copying the preface of one existing version, the *Vita prolixior secunda*, without any changes whatsoever. He ended it by copying books 3 and 4 from another existing version, the *Vita prolixior prima*, again without making any changes except giving these books separate titles. (It is clear that whenever the *Transitus* and the *Miracula* follow the *Vita brevior*, they follow the arrangement of the miracle stories as found in the *Vita prolixior prima* and not that of the *Vita prolixior secunda*.) Then he thoroughly altered everything in between, ruthlessly abbreviating but also rewriting and rearranging common elements, and even giving different details. It is far simpler to argue that the author of the *Vita prolixior secunda*, writing only in the late eleventh or early twelfth century when the first manuscripts appear, had both the *Vita brevior* and the *Vita prolixior prima* at hand and was attempting to reconcile what were two versions of the *Vita Geraldi*, both attributed to Odo of Cluny. This author relied most heavily on the *Vita prolixior prima*, making some corrections: mostly grammatical and stylistic, but including one about Gerald's birthplace, perhaps from some outside source of information. Yet he used the preface from the *Vita brevior*, perhaps because the preface to the *Vita prolixior prima* did not seem right to him either, if he knew that Odo had done more than visit Aurillac once. Its author had access to both the *Vita brevior* and the *Vita prolixior prima*, knowledge of Odo's abbacy of Aurillac either from within the monastic library at Cluny itself or through one of its daughter houses, which included by the end of the eleventh century both Aurillac and Limoges, and the desire to resolve the difficulties posed by the attribution of two very different *vitae* to one author.

A Sermon for Gerald's Feast Day

A sermon, written for Saint Gerald's feast day, is contained in four manuscripts, including two eleventh- or twelfth-century manuscripts, and was clearly composed at an early date.[89] Paolo Facciotto, who established a critical edition of it, argued that the author of the *Vita prolixior* (whom he accepted as Odo of Cluny) was also the author of the sermon, based on both thematic and stylistic similarities.[90] I concur that they were written both by the same man, although, of course, that man was Ademar of Chabannes. The sermon is brief: beyond the basic outline of Gerald's life it is mostly a *pastiche* of biblical quotations and allusions. Still, it contains an unusual passage that invites Gerald to clothe us with his forgiveness so as to cover up our wicked nakedness (9), which is entirely reminiscent of a similar passage found in the *Transitus* (3.8).[91] Its vocabulary also reinforces the connection to the *Vita prolixior*, including its books 3 and 4.[92] Why this sermon should be included only in some early manuscripts is unclear, but it may have something to do with the nature of the manuscripts in which it was omitted. Conspicuously, the sermon always follows the *Vita prolixior* and is never found with the *Vita brevior*. If Ademar began by writing the *Transitus* and the *Miracula* to follow Odo's *vita* and only later reused them as books 3 and 4 of his own *Vita Geraldi*, then he may have written the sermon at this later moment, too; and then one would not expect to see it in the manuscripts where the *Transitus* and the *Miracula* follow the *Vita brevior*.[93] Likewise, the sermon is absent from the Cluniac group that includes the *Vita prolixior secunda*, at least, from the only manuscript of that group that is complete.[94] Of the remaining complete manuscripts of the *Vita prolixior*, four include the sermon and one does not. (There are eight other manuscripts either too brief to be helpful or too mutilated to know if they once included it).[95] Accordingly, it is reasonable to conclude that it circulated for the most part alongside the *Vita prolixior*, lending support to its original connection to the whole.

Additional Miracle Stories

Two manuscripts, finally, contain additional miracles stories. The older of the two is now in northern Italy but was copied in southern France in the late eleventh or early twelfth century.[96] The second is now at Montpellier, copied sometime after 1227. Otherwise, not much is known about this second manuscript, although Bultot-Verleysen states that it was produced at the monastery in Aurillac.[97] In both manuscripts these stories follow the *Vita prolixior* and are given the rather lengthy title *Incipiunt miracula et de ecclesia qu[a]e primitus in honorem beati Geraldi constructa fuit, vel qualiter Stephanus episcopus ad dedicandum eam venerit, vel quale miraculum in die consecrationis ibi patratum sit* ("Here begin the miracles and [an account] of the church first built in honor of Saint Gerald, and also how Bishop Stephen came in order to dedicate it, and what sort of miracle was brought about there on the day of the consecration"; hereafter *Miracula addita* or additional miracle stories).[98] The consecration of the church to which the title refers happened in 972, which would indicate that at all or most of the text came together after this date.[99] The miracle that occurred to this Bishop Stephen was a vision of Saint Gerald in the company of Sainte Foy (whose shrine at Conques is not that far south of Aurillac, and whose popularity began in about 983, which also helps to date these stories); he was bishop of Clermont between 943 and 984, and also titular abbot of Conques.[100] Not all of the same stories are included in both manuscripts, but Bultot-Verleysen concludes that they should be considered as part of the same original text, and my own work with these manuscripts confirms that this conclusion is correct.[101]

The *Miracula addita* form a complicated annex to the writings about Gerald of Aurillac. Their preface begins by contrasting its author's limited talents with the "more learned style [*docciori stilo*]" of the author of Gerald's deeds but insisting that the abundance of miracles requires him to take up the task of writing. This is a fairly common disclaimer in medieval hagiography; still, that author is clearly someone else. By the fourth episode, however, the same author describes his work by saying, "I will now attempt to acquit myself of a debt tied to a promise that I formerly made at the end of [*in finem*] the book of the life of that blessed man" (4).[102] From these words, Bultot-Verleysen posits two earlier works for which there is otherwise no evidence, which she calls the *Liber vitae* and the *Liber miraculorum*, woven together into the *Miracula addita* by an anonymous monk at Aurillac.[103] Yet the words can be understood in a much less convoluted way. If it were Ademar who penned these additional miracle stories, after he had added the *Transitus* and the *Miracula* to Odo's version of the *Vita Geraldi* but before he had written his own version, he might easily have said both that a better writer had written about Gerald's deeds and also that he had added something of his own at the end of that *vita*. Indeed, the author of these additional miracle stories specifies that the promise he had given was to provide more examples in fuller detail of the miracles that Gerald had worked, which fits neatly with what was probably the original ending to the *Miracula* (4.7): that its author had been obliged to omit things about Gerald's miracle working for fear of being too long-winded, despite being concerned that he might seem to be ignoring them.[104]

What I am suggesting is that Ademar is also the author of the additional miracle stories. Bultot-Verleysen admits that their author is very familiar with the *Vita prolixior*.[105] Since she considers Odo of Cluny to have authored the *Vita prolixior*, though, and since these additional stories were written after 972 (and thus long after Odo's death in 942), it may not have occurred to her even to consider whether it might have been the same author. In the episodes contained in these additional miracle stories, the issues that appealed to Ademar return plainly enough. Gerald's power over the natural world is reiterated: a horse bolting during a snowstorm (1), a boat bringing pilgrims across a torrential river safely (8), even three fish allowing themselves to be caught (9, 11, and 12, much like episodes in the *Vita prolixior* 2.29 and 2.30). Gerald's opposition to violence is repeated: he punishes violent nobleman for their attacks (4 and 5, the former includes the putting out of an eye, a violent act already noted in several stories of the *Vita prolixior* as particularly commonplace; 1.18 and 1.19). Gerald's posthumous concern for peasants mimics that which he felt during his lifetime (6 and 7). Healing blindness, something of a *forte* for Gerald in the *Vita prolixior*, is also included as two of these additional miracles (17 and 20). And in the concluding remarks to the *Miracula addita*, Gerald's corporeal beauty and opposition to violence are again mentioned, both highlighted in the *Vita prolixior* (21).

Bultot-Verleysen notes that there are unusual word choices in the *Miracula addita*. The terms used to describe Gerald in the prologue (*praepotens*, *tutor providissimus, sollers procurator, non imperius moderator, terribilis*), and elsewhere in the text (*clarissimus*, 6; and *magnificus*, 14) are used in none of the other writings about him. Nonetheless, most other word choices follow the pattern already found in the *Vita prolixior*. So, for example, Gerald's *virtus* is repeatedly mentioned (used twenty-six times in the singular for his "strength" or "power," and twice in the plural for his "virtues"). One might contrast that to the complete absence of the term in the *Vita brevior*, either in the singular or the plural, but compare its use to that of the *Vita prolixior*, where it is used both in the plural and in the singular to describe Gerald (fifteen times in the singular, seven times in the plural). Other vocabulary in the additional miracle stories ties them much more closely to the *Vita prolixior* than to the *Vita brevior*, although there are also unique features.[106]

Is this a different author at work here, or the same author using a varied terminology? I'm not sure that this question can be answered from word usage alone.[107] Perhaps we need to turn to other clues. There is again recurring mention of Limoges. The author of the additional miracle stories specifically mentioned Gerald's many miracles performed in the Limousin, beginning with a miracle performed in Limoges, described as "a city of great renown [*opinatissima urbe*]" (8). The link to Limoges is confirmed with a miracle involving pilgrims from Limoges on their way home after paying a visit to Gerald's shrine at Aurillac. The passage describes how because of their prayers to Gerald a boat tied to the opposite bank of a river launched itself over to their side and permitted them to cross. "As soon as they arrived in our presence," the tale concludes, "overcome by the entreaties of others they described the succession of events to us" (9), clearly with the author there at Limoges at their return. Twice the same author mentioned "our community," presumably, a monastic community (*nostro sectande*, 8, and *nostri ordinis*, 10), yet three times the monastery at Aurillac is mentioned as such (*monachi Aureliacen[s]i cenobii*, 11, *cenobium beati Geraldi Aureliacen[s]e*, 13, and *loco beati Geraldi*, 17), and three times also the "guardians [*excubitores*]" of Gerald's shrine are mentioned as such (2, 14, 17), without the "our," implying that they are not the same thing. (Indeed, this usage recalls the reference in the *Vita prolixior* to "one of our brothers" [*quidam de nostris fratribus*, 2.24], regarding a canon traveling with Gerald on pilgrimage to Rome, which should be probably be understood as meaning that he was a monk from Limoges).

It is true that there are peculiarities remaining in the *Miracula addita*. There are, for example, figures represented there, like Sainte Foy, and places, like the church dedicated to Saint Gerald at Limoges, that do not appear in any of the other writings about Saint Gerald. Nonetheless, these remarks seem not wholly out of place. Placing Saint Gerald both in the presence of Saint Martial in the *Miracula* and of Sainte Foy in the additional miracle stories linked him with two of the most rapidly expanding cults in neighboring regions. And the existence of a church dedicated to Saint Gerald at Limoges not only reinforces the connection between Saint Gerald and Limoges that is evident elsewhere, but also returns us to Ademar of Chabannes, since the only other early mention of that church was in his chronicle.[108]

Why, then, do these additional miracle stories appear only in two manuscripts? First, there is no reason to expect that these additional miracle stories should have been included in any of the manuscripts where the *Transitus* and the *Miracula* follow the *Vita brevior*: as I have been arguing, they represent Ademar's initial effort to add to Odo's writings, before the *Vita prolixior*, the sermon, or these additional miracle stories were written. Of the remaining manuscripts, a few are mutilated, and it is no longer possible to determine precisely what they contained. A few more are greatly abbreviated, using only a handful of episodes mostly from Gerald's life, part of larger collections of saints' lives and without any posthumous miracles; we should not expect that they would have included these additional miracle stories. That still leaves several that might have included them but did not. Perhaps the best explanation has to do with Ademar's cognizance of his role as a forger. Even if he first added the *Transitus* and the *Miracula* to Odo's version of the *Vita Geraldi* without intention to deceive, by the time he had composed the *Vita prolixior* he was clearly trying to pass off his own words as Odo's, and these additional miracle stories—that were so obviously written after Odo's death—could not be so regarded. It seems likeliest that the additional miracle stories mark a kind of middle stage between the two, something written as a sign of Ademar's growing devotion to Saint Gerald, but which had to be abandoned as his devotion inspired him to reshape Odo's words. It is always possible that another monk, also writing at Limoges, added the additional miracle stories sometime between the 1020s when Ademar composed his version of the *Vita Geraldi* and the end of the eleventh century when the Mantua manuscript was produced. If so, one would have to invent a second work by this individual to which he referred when he said that he had already added something to the end of another *vita*, and for which there is no other evidence, and that is a conjecture equally difficult to accept. This is perhaps not the most satisfying of conclusions. Still, the evidence obliges us to conclude that its author was a monk writing at Limoges sometime in the century following 972. That and the similarities in theme and word choice make Ademar still seem to me the likeliest candidate. Yet if it is not Ademar's, it was the work of a second monk remarkably close in place and time to Ademar, and one who shared much of Ademar's vision about Gerald.

Yet Another Forgery by Ademar of Chabannes?

Given the differences in vocabulary between the writings about Saint Gerald, it would seem that one way to substantiate authorship would be to compare these texts to others that have survived by Odo of Cluny and Ademar of Chabannes. Unfortunately, no meaningful conclusions can be drawn from such comparisons. Elsewhere I explain the obstacles in much greater detail, but they can be summarized here as follows.[109] First and foremost, there are ongoing doubts about which writings can be confidently assigned to each. Texts once ascribed to Odo with certainty are now disputed.[110] Works also once attributed to someone else are now believed to have been written by either Odo or Ademar. Odo of Cluny may have composed a *Vita sancti Gregorii*, for example, and Ademar may have written a *Vita sancti Amantii*.[111] There are interesting parallels between both of these hagiographical works and the *Vita Geraldi*, but it makes no sense to use one uncertain attribution to confirm or deny another. Even relying solely on the works most confidently ascribed to each provides uneven results, since the bulk of Odo's reliable writings are theological while those of Ademar are historical. Since one of the significant differences between the *Vita brevior* and the *Vita prolixior* was the richer secular vocabulary in the latter, this imbalance risks skewing the results of any comparison. Add to that the fact that about twice as much text can be attributed to Odo with some certainty as to Ademar, and *any* words are likelier to show up in the writings of Odo than in Ademar's.[112]

One finds only a few provocative clues when examining Odo's and Ademar's other writings. Nowhere else did Odo of Cluny mention Saint Gerald, for example. In contrast, as already mentioned above, Ademar mentioned Saint Gerald several times, in different writings, and with a number of details. That alone may indicate Ademar's greater interest, of a sort that might have generated several writings, including a detailed *vita* rather than a briefer one. Likewise, nowhere else did Odo of Cluny make the same sort of defense of religious violence that is found at length in the *Vita prolixior*, indeed, in his other writings Odo consistently either metaphorized violence or discussed it only as an opportunity to exercise Christian patience, as he did, for example, in his *Collationes*, where the violent are always wicked.[113] In contrast, Ademar of Chabannes showed real attention to violence and the Christian life, as will be discussed below. The fact that Ademar had copied a Latin version of Aesop's fables early in his monastic career (and kept the manuscript with him until the end of his life) may have encouraged him to think about the sorts of moral comparisons between human and animal behavior that find frequent mention in the *Vita prolixior* and the additional miracle stories, but are found only once in the *Vita brevior*.[114] Ademar used the concept of the compulsion of necessity "as a veritable leitmotif" in his (as yet unpublished) sermons, Pascale Bourgain has noted; we might compare the same usage more than twenty times in the *Vita prolixior* in explaining Gerald's actions, as in "necessity compelled him" to do one thing or another, and contrast that with its use but once in the *Vita brevior* (3).[115] So we are left with this range of tantalizing but ultimately inconclusive hints.

Ademar of Chabannes died in 1034, which would establish a new *terminus ante quem* for the *Vita prolixior* as well as the sermon and the additional miracle stories.[116] Yet I think that he composed his texts in the 1020s. Ademar did much of his writing in stages, revising and adding new material. He seems to have done the same with his writings about Saint Gerald. He likely began simply enough by adding the *Transitus* and the *Miracula* to Odo's version of the *Vita Geraldi* in order to give a proper ending to a too-brief *vita*, maybe about the time of the arrival of Saint Gerald's relics in Limoges in 1021. A few years later, perhaps, he wrote additional miracle stories, after hearing pilgrims returning to Limoges tell stories about Gerald's miraculous deeds, as one of these stories itself suggests, including the vision of Bishop Stephen at the dedication of the new church at Aurillac, and within which Ademar was then able to refer to the "more learned style" of Odo's writing as well as to his own previous work added to it. Then, some time after that, he decided to rewrite the *Vita Geraldi* entirely—and to claim it as the work of Odo. Probably at the same time, he added a few more stories onto both the *Transitus* and the *Miracula* and joined them to his more detailed *vita*. Perhaps he composed his sermon to accompany this more elaborated *corpus* of texts. He did not try to incorporate the additional miracle stories into the revised *Vita Geraldi*, however, because it was so obviously not the work of Odo. This reconstruction is still speculative, to be sure, but is more sure-footed than the missteps that have tripped up other scholars.

In defending Odo's authorship of the *Vita prolixior*, Poncelet argued more than a century ago that "if this is a forger, one must admit that he worked to the utmost and with singular skill and impudence."[117] This is perhaps as good a description of Ademar of Chabannes as one might hope for, yet as Ademar himself put it, "truth is always truth and one should never spurn the truth . . . nor does it matter who speaks, but what is said."[118] Ademar seems to have decided to rewrite a *vita* that he judged incomplete or even indifferent and give Gerald his proper due. His "singular skill" has meant that his vital contribution to the cult of Saint Gerald has not previously been recognized. The challenge now is to abandon a scholarly consensus that has misled scholars and to rethink what these writings tell us both about Odo and Ademar as well as about the saint they crafted.

CHAPTER 2

The First Saint Gerald

The earliest remembrances of Gerald come from one of the most prominent monastic reformers of the central Middle Ages, Odo of Cluny. This is, once again, the *Vita brevior* (an English translation of which appears in Appendix 1 from my own critical edition) and not the better-known *Vita prolixior*. Why a man so devoted to the monastic ideal should have been willing to praise the saintliness of a layman is a difficult question. If we read with a modern (or, perhaps, a postmodern) sense of skepticism, however, we see revealed a hagiographer who did not so much craft a new model for noble holiness through his portrayal of Gerald as he wrestled with his own regrets and then resolved them by casting doubts on Gerald's sanctity.

Odo and Aurillac

It seems likeliest that Odo wrote his version of the *Vita Geraldi* while or shortly after he was abbot of the monastery of Aurillac. Although it is not mentioned in Odo's biography, he lived there probably in late 928 and/or early 929.[1] Odo was in his early fifties then.[2] He was already abbot of Cluny and remained so throughout his time at Aurillac; as he was also reforming other monasteries, he may not have spent more than a few months there.

How long after Gerald's death Odo arrived is impossible to know: we don't know either the years of Gerald's birth or of his death. The earliest mention comes from Ademar of Chabannes, who said that Gerald was born in 855 and died on October 13 in 906.[3] Bernard Itier, who also noted Gerald's birth and death dates in his late twelfth-century chronicle also written at Limoges, gave them as 836 and 887, respectively, though this is probably too early.[4] The earliest manuscripts to record the year of Gerald's death, both thirteenth-century ones, give it as 918.[5] Since Gerald's more detailed biography said that he died on a Friday, and since October 13 did not fall on a Friday in any of these three years, most scholars move that date to the nearest year in which it did (Gerald's nineteenth-century biographer, for example, thought it should be 909, and Bultot-Verleysen prefers 920) yet it is easy to imagine why a hagiographer should want to place Gerald's death on a Friday, that is, to recall Jesus' death, so there is no need to make this change.[6] Depending upon which, if any, of these dates is accurate—887, 906, or 918—it means that Gerald had been dead for perhaps as few as ten or as many as forty years when Odo wrote about him, but likelier between ten and twenty-three years.

What brought Odo to Aurillac is difficult to say. Cluny was over three hundred kilometers distant from Aurillac. And even while Cluny would eventually become the heart of a monastic empire encompassing Aurillac as well as most other monasteries in this region, that day was still far off, so when Odo finished with his reform of Aurillac, he left it to its own fate. Insofar as we can tell, once Odo left he never visited Aurillac again.[7]

There was not much to Aurillac in Odo's day. There is some material evidence of settlement in the district from the beginnings of the Common Era, and the name may be derived from Aurelius, perhaps a Roman nobleman who owned land there.[8] It would not take long for a town to form around the monastery that Gerald founded along the Jordanne River, but it was not there yet. A castle on a nearby hill may have overlooked the monastery; more likely, though, it did not yet exist. Odo mentioned no castle at Aurillac in his version of the *Vita Geraldi*, so it is one of the elements that Ademar added, and given that there were few castles at all in the mid-ninth century when Gerald was born, especially in Auvergne, Ademar may well have been mistaken.[9]

There were no natural geographical connections between Cluny and Aurillac. The upper Auvergne region where Aurillac lies is now extraordinarily picturesque, but in the central Middle Ages it probably seemed more foreboding than idyllic. The Jordanne still meanders through Aurillac before joining first the Cère and then the Dordogne, and has carved a broad flat valley around the town that creates a real contrast to the generally mountainous Auvergnat terrain. On almost all sides, it must have been extremely difficult to approach Aurillac. To the south, the direction of Figeac, Conques, and Rodez, a series of steep hills make that the most difficult route. To the

northeast, and the road to Clermont (now Clermont-Ferrand) and the lower
Auvergne as well as to Cluny far beyond, the banks of the Cère soon give way
to sharp slopes. Only to the northwest, the direction of Tulle and Limoges, is
the journey an easy one. To be sure, Aurillac's historical connections and the
memories of Saint Gerald were deeply shaped by these geographical features.
It was the abbot of Tulle and the bishop of Limoges, after all, who had
prompted Odo to write his *vita*.[10]

Aurillac's political connections were also northwestward ones. In Odo's
day, the chief local magnate was the count of Poitiers, Èbles Manzer, the
same whom Ademar of Chabannes said had been fostered by Gerald.[11] Perhaps Èbles played some unacknowledged role in Odo's decision to write a
vita of Gerald. Èbles had managed to extend his authority not only over
Poitou but also in Auvergne, and so styled himself duke of Aquitaine. Yet
only a dozen years earlier, the political power in the region and the title of
duke had belonged to the count of Auvergne, William the Pious. This William played some role in Gerald's life—Odo said that William had wanted
Gerald to marry his sister (4), so they were likely allied in some way. It was
same William who had founded the monastery of Cluny. (Indeed, Saint
Gerald may have been one of the signatories for its foundation charter, if he
was still alive in 910: there is a Gerald, otherwise unidentified, among the
witnesses to the transaction.[12]) These political connections may have helped
to shape Odo's decision to write the *Vita Geraldi*.[13]

Cluny's origins are well known, but worth briefly repeating. Unlike most
monasteries across western Europe in this period, which often had lay abbots
chosen from the powerful families of the district, Cluny's founder and first
abbot Berno had persuaded William the Pious that laymen should have no
control over that monastery. Instead, the monks of Cluny would elect an
abbot from among their own number, and any disputes over leadership or
any other matters would be adjudicated by the pope in Rome rather than the
local lay patron. Presumably, Berno worried that William's heirs might
attempt to seize future control of the monastery. Odo was only the second
abbot of Cluny, and so the first elected. Upon taking up that office, he began
seeking to reform neighboring monasteries along Cluniac lines, simultane-
ously extending Cluny's influence.[14]

It was in such a reformist capacity, presumably, that Odo came to Aurillac. Indeed, reform may provide the best explanation for Odo's presence
there. Isabelle Cochelin's analysis of other early texts associated with the
foundation of the monastery at Aurillac—a charter of Charles the Simple

from 899 and an undated testament by Gerald himself—is of real interest here. Scholars have traditionally judged both to be of doubtful authenticity because they conflict with the *Vita prolixior*, but Cochelin believes them to be genuine—and, as I suggested in the last chapter, the *Vita prolixior* is not reliable in its details. The royal charter refers to Gerald as *rector* as well as *fundator* of Aurillac; Cochelin describes him as a lay co-abbot.[15] Gerald left some of his lands in his relatives' hands and had them administer the monastery after his death, she believes, since Gerald's testament left his monastery to the control of his nephew Rainald, together with "the power to elevate or dismiss abbots, to investigate the causes of the monks before kings, counts, or their deputies, and to hold in his protection the various lands of the monks and their households."[16] Such lay control over monasteries was the opposite of the Cluniac spirit, of course, but not at all unusual for the times.[17] When, a decade or two later, this situation proved unworkable or undesirable, Odo was invited to reform Aurillac along Cluniac lines and to remove Gerald's relatives from influence over the monastery. Then, as Odo wrote his version of the *Vita Geraldi*, he reimagined the donation in such a way that Gerald appeared to have donated the whole of his property to his monastery and, like Cluny, gave it into the possession of the Pope. It is worth noting, as Cochelin does, that the first abbot of Aurillac after Gerald's death, John, was described as Gerald's kinsman, implying some sort of family authority over the monastery.[18]

The invitation to reform Aurillac was presumably extended to Odo by the brothers Turpin and Aimon. Turpin and Odo already knew each other, since it was Turpin who had ordained Odo a priest. How keen Turpin was about monastic reform is difficult to say. Odo did not have a high opinion of Turpin at all, according to his own biographer: and he "used to say of this bishop that no dog would dare to eat food that had been blessed by him, and if by chance one happened to do so it immediately died, as though it had taken poison."[19] Earlier in Odo's career and apparently at the command of his abbot and despite his unwillingness, he had written a treatise called the *Collationes* and dedicated it to Turpin. Perhaps Odo had grown fonder of Turpin, then, or perhaps he regarded Turpin's insistence that he write about Gerald as equally odious. Odo also spent some time at Tulle reforming that monastery after Aimon's tenure as abbot there, and that may say something of Aimon's zeal for the monastic life, too.[20] Not long after Odo finished his *Vita Geraldi*, Aimon left Tulle for the monastery of Saint-Martial at Limoges, likely through his brother's influence as bishop.

A more compelling reason may have prompted Turpin's and Aimon's interest in Aurillac. Léon Levillain first suggested that both brothers were related to Saint Gerald through Gerald's nephew Rainald.[21] There is no real way to be sure, given the obstacles to reconstructing most family trees for the central Middle Ages. Yet if true, it would easily explain both men's motivation in wanting to publicize Gerald's sanctity. The brothers may have impressed upon Odo the need for a biography celebrating Aurillac's holy founder, even suggesting that elevating Gerald to the rank of the saints might help the cause of reform. Perhaps they were thinking at the same time that a saint in their own family, duly advertised, could only add to its spiritual prestige. The short length and undemanding structure of Odo's *Vita Geraldi* (when contrasted with his *Collationes*, for example) may indicate how he viewed its relative importance.

Odo offered his own reasons for writing the *Vita Geraldi* in its prologue, even if they owe much to the literary conceits of hagiography. He said that it was not only Aimon and Turpin but also "not a small number of other noble men [*aliis non paucis nobilibus viris*]" who had requested it of him. Then he offered a much more encompassing—and more formulaic—reason, but one that perhaps helps us to understand how Odo justified his efforts: "Since nowadays we do not care about the examples of the Fathers and iniquity is growing," God "offered this servant of His to us so as to inspire imitation, or else as a witness." Gerald provided a particularly useful example, "for even if he was powerful in the things of this life, it is no obstacle to a layman who has managed well the things he has justly received: for there is no power that does not come from God" (prol.). These are all themes that would be repeated throughout Odo's version of the *Vita Geraldi*: above all, the peculiarity of holiness found in a layman.

Odo may well have intended his writing of the *Vita Geraldi* as an opportunity to bring the monks of Aurillac together by giving them a shared vision of their founder. As a saint, Gerald could serve as the symbolic and living heart of the monastery, giving it both integrity and legitimacy.[22] If crafted properly, Gerald himself could also provide an example of piety and discipline to its monks. Moreover, the public declaration of Gerald's sanctity gave the monks of Aurillac a new rationale for their existence: to venerate their saintly founder and to preserve his memory.[23] It may have been during Odo's stay that the monastery of Aurillac was rededicated to Saint Gerald himself, either through a formal event now forgotten or perhaps simply because the monastery became increasingly identified as the shrine of Saint Gerald.[24]

The crafting of a saint for Aurillac had a crucial practical as well as spiritual purpose. Unlike modern Catholic monasticism, where financial and human resources belonging to a religious order are shared equally among monastic houses, medieval monasteries were more or less autonomous. That autonomy sometimes meant unsupervised or unregulated activity—and thus the need for reform; it also meant that each monastery needed to attract donations and recruits on its own. If a monastery could not find either in sufficient number, it would close. The inspiration provided by a saint—to whom some might want to give from their possessions and some to dedicate their lives—was the best way of ensuring the continued flow of money and personnel into the monastery, and its ongoing viability. In making Gerald into a saint, then, Odo did the monks of Aurillac a great service.

Whatever Odo's reasons for or reluctance in writing the *Vita Geraldi*, he obviously meant it to be subsumed within the larger project of his lifelong efforts toward monastic reform. Odo added a detailed episode in the *vita* that described the difficult task of reform; it is one of only two places in his text in which he put words directly in Gerald's mouth. He began by saying that Gerald was "sickened [*nausiabat*]" by monks who lived without a proper rule and regretted his inability to find suitable monks. Yet the passage ends on a hopeful note, by predicting that one day his monastery would be successful and full: "It is often the case that this same house enjoys crowds of those assembled there" (8). Indeed, within a decade of Odo's time there, monks from Aurillac were sent to other monasteries, encouraging reform at Saint-Chaffre and helping to found Saint-Pons-de-Thomières, so Odo's efforts do seem to have been well rewarded.[25]

For Odo, of course, the monastic life represented the highest human aspirations. It offered individuals the opportunity to live more virtuous and prayerful lives and also to escape the distractions and evils of the world. But it was much more than that: Kassius Hallinger offered the intriguing suggestion that the Cluniac ideal made possible the very transcending of time. The life of the monk served to return not only to the original spirit of Christianity, when Jesus' followers lived and shared their possessions in common, but also to the original innocence of humanity at its origins. The life of the monk also pointed to the future, and his perpetual prayer and quiet seclusion were a foretaste of the angelic life and the eternal peace of paradise. These were not really new ideas about monasticism, but the early Cluniac reformers strove to implement them anew. Living the monastic ideal was an interior attitude nourished communally through prayer, including the elaborate daily liturgies that became so much a part of the Cluniac reform.[26] Barbara Rosenwein also understands the Cluniac ideal as offering predictability and calm in the midst of the world's disordered chaos.[27] Odo played a vital role in implanting this ideal.

Odo's Gerald

With these thoughts in mind, let us turn to Odo's biography of Gerald. "His ancestors were as illustrious in nobility [*nobilitas*] as they were rich in possessions," he began, then shifted to what really mattered: "and what is more excellent, most of them were distinguished by the reputation of their piety" (1). He named two sixth-century holy forbears of Gerald: Caesarius, bishop of Arles, and the abbot Aredius. What was most distinguished about Gerald's ancestry was its saints. (Was this even a nod—or a prod—of sorts at Turpin and Aimon—another bishop and abbot?) Odo noted that both of Gerald's parents were also holy in their own way: his father, who was also named Gerald, received a vision before Gerald was born: both parents heard a baby's voice miraculously cry out from his mother's womb three times, and "several miracles" were later performed at the tomb of his mother, Adeltrude (1). Oddly, Odo gave no further details about whether these miracles meant that Adeltrude should also be considered a saint. It is possible that some sort of devotion to Adeltrude existed in Odo's day, although any evidence for it is slight.[28] It is perhaps better understood as an example of what Jane Tibbetts Schulenberg describes as a "special fascination" in the Carolingian era with motherhood and sanctity and the signaling of sanctity through miraculous incidents even during pregnancy.[29] Still, the fact that Odo said nothing more on the subject is also part of the Carolingian disregard for female saints, especially within what became the south of France.[30] (And the *Vita prolixior* omitted even that brief statement about Adeltrude's miracles.)

Apart from listing these saintly relatives, Odo said no more about Gerald's ancestry. His claims are certainly not out of the question, and Gerald may have been descended from old landowning Roman families. Other facts hint that Gerald was of Frankish origins. Gerald's name is a Germanic one (it means "rule of the spear") as were those of both of his parents. Since Franks intermarried with Gallo-Roman families, though, there is nothing to preclude Gerald's descent from both.[31] How Gerald came into possession of the lands he held is also unknown: a count of Auvergne named Gerard died in 841, and a count of Bourges by the same name died in 867; it is possible that either or both of these men were related to Saint Gerald.[32]

Odo continued by describing Gerald's childhood. Unlike other boys, who tended to be "violent and contrary and vengeful," Gerald had "a certain sweetness of manners." A childhood illness meant that Gerald was "more fully instructed in literary disciplines, so that if he should not be suited for the secular army he would be made suitable for ecclesiastical office." Odo specified these literary pursuits as "the psalter," "chant," "a bit of grammar," and "recollection of the scriptures." Gerald later recovered from his illness so that he could take up his secular role, but his education had already had its effect and it "made him inclined toward spiritual matters and quite reluctant toward military matters" (2). Here is the first of numerous sets of contrasts between Gerald and other military men, since throughout his biography Odo construed Gerald as their opposite.[33]

Gerald's distinctiveness continued into young adulthood. "He did not, as so many young men do, take an immature sort of pride in his authority." Indeed, "he carried with distress the sharp troubles and duties of the household," fearing "that he would be distracted and surrounded by earthly entanglements" (3). This special nature could also be seen in Gerald's sex life. The devil "hurled love—as they call it—for a certain young woman at Gerald's breast, and from the moment the unguarded Gerald beheld her, suddenly his mind began to weaken into desire." Gerald did not succumb but took advantage of a cold spell, and "allowed himself to be frostbitten throughout the night, no doubt in order that the vast cold of winter might extinguish the flame of deformed desire." Thereafter, he resisted lust so much that "he avoided with women the embrace that is usual among friends as they kiss, even women who were related to him." He never married, was never seen naked, and washed himself whenever nocturnal dreams resulted in seminal emissions (4). In marking chastity as an especial sign of Gerald's purity, in seeing the eyes as the body's greatest occasion for sin, and even in warning of the moral dangers of nocturnal emissions, Odo followed closely behind a long line of monastic writers.[34]

Gerald's uniqueness could also be seen in his attitude toward violence. Here Odo provided the oddest of details: "Since a great need compelled him now and again to suppress with arms the violent men who plundered his estates and peasants excessively, he admonished his soldiers in a commanding voice that they should fight against the enemy with their spears turned around [*aversis hastis*]." The meaning is not entirely clear, but seems to imply that they butted the enemy with shafts of their spears rather than trying to pierce them; it seems to borrow a biblical phrase.[35] Perhaps they were supposed to harry rather than wound their opponents. Odo must have recognized that this comment risked seeming ludicrous; nonetheless, he defended the practice: "It was not once heard that the good fortune of victory had disappointed anyone who fought out of loyalty to Gerald." Odo even repeated the sentiment: "But again, one thing remained certain, that neither he himself ever wounded anyone whatsoever nor was he ever wounded by anyone" (3). The point is unmistakable: in a violent age Gerald refused to be violent.

Gerald's unrivaled qualities are further compounded as Odo detailed his adult life and responsibilities. Gerald surrounded himself with "respectable men" as his associates and retainers, considered himself the equal even of those beneath him, and "prosecuted those who were bold in assaulting peasants." Odo's description is not without some contradiction, since he also said that "frequently those who were under his authority reproached him, saying that he was soft and timid, since he allowed himself to be injured by the basest sort of persons as if he were powerless" (5).[36] Still, throughout Gerald's public life, his exemplary character could be seen: "He was not influenced in his support by the amount of reward but by the greater extent of the need." In his everyday life, Gerald gave away bread and coins to the poor, was read to at meals rather than engaging in idle conversation, and fasted (6).

It is easy to see what Odo was trying to do, in contrasting Gerald with his peers, whom we imagine as associating themselves with disreputable men, lording their authority over others, taking bribes, carousing at table, and meting out harsh vengeance for any supposed slight. It is obvious that Odo hoped to encourage his contemporaries to act like Gerald did, using him to mirror their faults. At times the pedantic tone is taxing: Gerald "was not unmindful of what was commanded to every single one of us, that he eat his bread with silence. He was so concerned with sobriety that he kept not only himself but also his companions at table from drunkenness, and certainly he did not at any time encourage his guests to drink," (6) disregarding the more boisterous conventions of hospitality. It is not much of a realistic portrait— there is an almost complete absence of any really personalized details about Gerald's life, and the same extolling of chastity, nonviolence, uprightness, and charity can be found in many other Christian writers—so we are probably more prudent to understand the *vita* more as an idealized and generalized model for male behavior than as the recollection of any specific biographical particulars about Gerald.[37] In fact, it fits a pattern of Carolingian didactic literature.[38] Odo's sense of Gerald, then, was clearly an abstract one, the symbol of a peaceful, chaste, and charitable warrior.

The precise nature of much of Gerald's life, including his social and political status, is left vague—all the better to signify Gerald as everyman—or, rather, as no man.[39] Even the nature of Gerald's connection with the king is absent. Odo's silence here may have been prompted as much by discretion as by disinterest: two rival dynasties were struggling for the kingdom of France at the end of the ninth and throughout the tenth century, the Carolingians and the Capetians, and it was still unclear in Odo's day which would win out. Thus, it may have been better to omit mention of any royal support for Gerald from either side or risk alienating the other.[40] It seems likeliest that Gerald's family was connected in some way with the Carolingians. The *Breve chronicon* of the abbots of Aurillac, for example, referred to Gerald as "a dear friend" of Charles the Simple. Since it was written in the early twelfth century, though, it may not have accurately recalled the political ties in Gerald's day. Nonetheless, both William the Pious, duke of Aquitaine, and Ralph II, whose son Èbles Manzer Gerald had fostered, were loyal to the Carolingians. Since Odo wrote his *Vita Geraldi* while Ralph, duke of Burgundy, was king of France, a man linked to the Capetians, it might not have been wise to recall Gerald's ties to the Carolingians.[41] Odo left Gerald's relationship with William vague, barely intimated except to say that Gerald refused to marry William's sister, and did not mention at all Gerald's fostering of Èbles. Likewise, Odo did not mention any title for Gerald, despite Ademar's erroneous insistence upon his having been a count, saying only that Gerald "had come into his authority and his possessions by hereditary right" (3). The royal charter of Charles the Simple from 899, if authentic, did refer to Gerald as a count, but in the phrase "illustrious man and beloved count [*illustris vir ac dilectus comes*]," which is probably better understood in its older Latin meaning as "friend."[42]

In his recollection of Gerald, then, Odo was clearly much less interested in situating Gerald concretely in history and more interested in providing a succinct role model for laymen: pious, slow to anger, and fair-minded. It is possible that Odo saw in the *Vita Geraldi* an opportunity to publicize an alternative model of manhood. It has been suggested that Odo's depiction of Gerald was intended to begin the project of reform outside of the cloister and thus to serve as a parallel to his work of monastic reform.[43] Yet it is not clear at all that men such as Odo described would have stayed around long enough to listen to Gerald's example.[44] (It is not even certain that they would have understood the Latin in which the *Vita Geraldi* was written.[45])

Odo probably had better luck in getting monks to listen to his lessons about Saint Gerald, and he must have known that it would be so. One cannot help but imagine that the monks would have felt more empathy for the kind of man that Odo was creating in Gerald, who had rejected the lustfulness and brutality of their contemporaries and had sought instead the safe haven of the monastic life. Guy Philippart asks: "Was not the success of hagiography in the West, especially in the monastic world turned entirely toward God, due first and foremost to the possibility of the identification in the mind that it afforded?" He calls all saints' *vitae* "mirrors" of the monastic life.[46] Odo seems not to have been able to resist putting reminders about monastic discipline into the *Vita Geraldi*: "He was not easily angered or humiliated, nor sharp tongued to injuries brought against him, nor stubborn in holding onto them" (5). Such admonitions, many of which were taken from the Rule of Saint Benedict or found in monastic handbooks, remind us again of the core of Odo's purpose at Aurillac: to reform its monks.[47]

Odo's Regrets

Even while Odo was constructing the memory of Saint Gerald as a portrait of what noble manhood could be, and what monastic manhood should be, it serves as a uncanny reflection of Odo's own life. Now we can have no greater certainty about the details of Odo's life from the hagiographical version of his life than about Gerald's. What we do know is that Odo was also later remembered as a saint remarkable in some ways in his likeness to Gerald.[48] We also know that Odo's first biographer, John of Salerno, insisted that it was Odo himself who had dictated the story of his life to him about a decade after having written the *Vita Geraldi*, in what might have been a medieval variation on life imitating art:

> It was at that time, while we were on our way [from Rome to Cluny] and conversing with each other, that putting aside my shyness, and contrary to the usual practice of monastic life, I boldly broke out and did not hesitate to inquire diligently from him his origin and way of life, at the same time begging him to expound them to me in detail. But he, as was always his manner, was silent for a little

time; then going somewhat pale, and sighing from the depths of his heart, he began to tell me his history; but nevertheless his words were full of tears and groans.[49]

What follows continues as a first-person narration, reinforcing the sense that the biographical details were a direct transmission from the subject to the reader.

We learn from the *Vita Odonis* that Odo had been raised in the household of William the Pious, the same count of Auvergne and duke of Aquitaine who appeared in Odo's *Vita Geraldi*.[50] John said in his *vita* that Odo was sixty years of age in 939, which meant that his childhood and youth would have taken place in the last two decades of the ninth century, and thus put him in the household of the duke at the time Gerald lived.[51] It is hard to see how Odo could not have met Gerald, who would have been perhaps twenty-five years his elder, if Gerald and William had been allies in any meaningful way, but it is even more difficult to understand why, if he had known him or even once met him, he would not have mentioned it himself.

John claimed not to have had any knowledge of Odo's ancestors, but clearly Odo was born into much the same environment as Gerald. His status was high enough that he could be fostered with the duke of Aquitaine; his father Abbo was educated enough to have known "the ancient histories and the *Novella* [laws] of Justinian," and the family lived perhaps in or near Tours.[52] Like Gerald, Odo had been given both training in military skills and formal education in letters. John described that upbringing, still in Odo's words:

> But it happened that as I grew to be a youth . . . [I] was proclaimed a vigorous and good-looking young man, and as time went on my father began to withdraw me from the ecclesiastical life and to set me to military exercises, and with this purpose he sent me to serve as a page in the household of Count William. Gradually I gave up my literary studies and began to be occupied more and more in hunting and fowling. But Almighty God . . . began to terrify me in dreams, and to show how prone my life was to evil. He turned all my pleasure in hunting into fatigue, and the more I threw myself into sports of this kind, the more I returned dispirited, unsuccessful, and exhausted.[53]

At the age of sixteen, Odo was taken ill with a sickness that lasted for three years—"torn by this pain as the earth by a ploughshare"—and he returned to his parents' home before deciding to become a monk at the monastery of Saint Martin in Tours, although he later left Tours for the more regimented life of Cluny.[54]

As it turned out, Odo's father had dedicated his son in his infancy to the saint, after a miraculous intervention much like the one remembered for Gerald. Odo had described Gerald's birth in these words: "His father, nonetheless, in order to purify himself within his marriage, frequently lay apart from his wife. It happened, though, that he once saw in a dream that a rod had sprouted as if from the big toe on his right foot, and grew gradually into a large tree. When he awoke, he marveled at the time about this vision, but another time while sleeping he saw again in another dream someone who told him that a son would be born to him" (1). Odo is then supposed to have described his own birth in these words: "He [Odo's father] was accustomed to celebrate the vigils of the saints throughout the night. . . . While, therefore, he was diligently celebrating these watches, it came into his mind that he should ask God, in the name of the Virgin birth, to give him a son, and by the insistency of his prayers he merited that his wife should bear him one, though past the age when that might be expected."[55] There are distinct biblical echoes in both.

We cannot untangle the varied threads of interconnection here. Had what Odo heard of his own birth and remembered of his childhood colored his depiction of Saint Gerald, or had the opposite happened? Had the elderly Odo who recounted his early life to John confused his own story with what he had written earlier about Gerald? Had John invented the episodes, either with a knowledge of the *Vita Geraldi*, or simply by borrowing from stock elements of saints' lives? We can only conclude that the recollections of elements of the early life of Gerald bear uncanny resemblances to those of Odo's early life.

Odo had every reason to identify with Gerald. He, too, had grown up in a warrior household even if he had renounced that life for the life of a monk. The portrait of Saint Gerald that Odo had painted takes on new hues since the faults for which Odo had denounced Gerald's contemporaries were, without a doubt, those he remembered of the men with whom he had been raised. Odo had also rejected the wanton violence of men of his class, their promiscuous sexuality, and their power-hungry ambitions; as John recounted it, it was only at the moment of his renunciation of a secular lifestyle that Odo's tormented dreams and his lingering illness ceased. One wonders how this choice helped to determine the likeness of Gerald that Odo had created.[56] We cannot help but ask about the thoughts that passed through Odo's mind as he wrote the *Vita Geraldi*, if its model of lay Christian manhood reverberated so eerily against his own decision to abandon the world.

One point must surely have been driven home as Odo contemplated his own life in comparison to that of Gerald: he had forfeited his secular identity for the ascetic life, first at Tours, then abandoned it for even greater discipline at Cluny, but if one could lead a saintly existence outside of the cloister, why bother with it? What advantage did the sacrifices of the monastic life provide that could not be obtained in any household? Like Gerald, Odo's *vita* also remembered him as having given alms regularly to the poor, as having avoided physical contact so as to steer clear of lust, and even as having freed robbers out of Christian forgiveness.[57] Perhaps these good deeds were sufficient to sainthood.

Odo must have felt that more was needed. His adolescent terror at not doing enough toward his own salvation must have stayed with him. He was remembered as having counseled several individuals to take up the monastic life as a necessary step in a wholehearted faith. According to John, Odo tried to persuade even Count Fulk of Anjou, one of the most powerful magnates of his day, to become a monk. "Odo began to admonish him that he should leave the world and act only so as to please God," John said. Instead, Fulk substituted one of his men, a man named Adhegrin, who "received the tonsure and having laid aside his military dress became forthwith a soldier of Christ." This Adhegrin became a hermit, and when the loneliness of the life drove him to desperation, he received a vision of Saint Martin that confirmed the wisdom of his choice.[58] Odo was also said to have been "much concerned about saving the souls of his parents, wondering how he might withdraw them from the bonds of this world," that is, questioning whether their secular lives would be sufficient to earn them salvation, and he eventually persuaded both to enter the cloister.[59] Likewise, when a group of wicked monks left the monastery of Cluny to return to their former lives, their fate is depicted straightforwardly enough: "having put off the religious habit they returned to the world, and later came to a terrible end."[60] The implied equation of perfect faith, monasticism, and salvation that these stories represent does not seem compatible with Odo's authorship of the *Vita Geraldi*—the praise of the saintliness of a man who did not renounce it all.

Writing the *Vita Geraldi* must at some point have led Odo to a difficult conundrum. Given his dedication to the monastic life, he had either to resolve it or risk undermining his own principles. Scholars have struggled to make sense of this contradiction. Isabelle Rosé believes that Odo was willing to write the life of a lay saint because he depicted Gerald as exhibiting monastic virtues.[61] Paul Rousset suggests that writing about Gerald allowed Odo to show how a man living amid violence and ambition could still live a life of piety.[62] Andrew Romig thinks that Gerald's particular holiness prompted Odo to make of him an exception to the general rule of his principles.[63] Still, Gerald's uncloistered life remained inextricably problematic, all the more so if we compare the *Vita Geraldi* to another of Odo's great treatises, the *Occupatio*. The *Occupatio* demonstrates both Odo's belief in the approaching end of the world and his conviction that only monasticism provided "a refuge against the coming Apocalypse."[64] Monks represented humanity's highest aspiration, Odo asserted in the *Occupatio*, set like the angels and saints midway between heaven and earth, and, like them, intended for the constant adoration of God.[65] How could the author of such sentiments have welcomed the glorification of a layman as a saint? Unless Odo could resolve this dilemma, moreover, he risked passing along misgivings about the necessity of the monastic sacrifice to the monks at Aurillac and to whoever else read the *Vita Geraldi*.

Odo had to depict Saint Gerald as a layman, of course, since anyone who had known him was well aware of it. Nonetheless, Odo tried to represent Gerald as leading a semimonastic existence even within his secular lifestyle. Odo maintained that, especially as Gerald grew older, "he inched more fully into a life of contemplation" (6). "He no longer wanted to be entangled in earthly activities, nor to journey to the royal court anymore and take part in the assemblies of princes" (7). That much may have been accurately remembered: royal courts of the late ninth century were dominated mostly by young men seeking advancement.[66] Yet Odo was able to depict a common retreat from public life also as a turn to a more cloistered life. This is the point at which Gerald decided to establish a monastery on his lands and "to bequeath his estates to the blessed Peter, prince of the Apostles" (7; if Gerald had done so, Aurillac would have preceded Cluny in being given over to Rome's jurisdiction, so it is possible that Odo added this detail to reinforce Aurillac's freedom from lay control.[67]) Gerald eventually found the necessary monks to staff his monastery, but did not himself take that final step toward perfection.

Here is the crux of Odo's dilemma: he had either to criticize Gerald's failure to act or admit that the monastic life was not the only or even the surest way to heaven. Odo demurred. Gerald deeply longed to become a monk, he suggested, but a bishop persuaded him to remain outwardly in his old life, "so that the malevolent and those who would think that he was a layman would be constrained by greater fear" and their violence would be kept in check.[68] Instead, Gerald took up the life of a monk in secret, tonsuring himself and shaving off his beard to signify his change of life: "He cut off his beard as if it were bothersome to him, and since his hair had fallen out from the top of his head he concealed the fact that he was pulling a blade over it in a circular shape [corona]." In a second ritual gesture associated with entrance to the monastic life, he had his sword and sword belt melted down and refashioned as a cross.[69] This half-step, one would think, would have compromised Odo's portrait of the saintly Gerald, were it not done at the command of a bishop. "Reluctantly," Odo concluded, "he abided with laymen" (7).

What Odo accomplished by turning the lay saint Gerald into a secret monk has for so long been accepted as fact that it is no longer questioned. There is no evidence for Odo's claim: only to God, "who is the observer of the heart," was Gerald's true life revealed. It is always possible that Gerald did secretly become a monk of sorts, and that his actions remained hidden until Odo publicized them: "He bound those who were there with an oath that they should disclose this thing to no one during his lifetime" (7). Gerald was not the only nobleman of the central Middle Ages for whom the cloister seemed attractive, especially toward the end of a life lived in the corruption of the world, although these other men actually entered monasteries.[70] But I think it more plausible that this suggestion allowed Odo to praise the layman Gerald while maintaining that sanctity was still best found in the monastic life. Who could, after all, contradict him? If any of Gerald's contemporaries still living denied it, they might have believed that they had fallen victim to the deception. Apart from Gerald's clean-shaven face and balding head, little other evidence would have been left behind. (And even if that description was accurately recalled, it might have signaled something else entirely, since within a century of Gerald's death Ralph Glaber criticized the men of Auvergne and Aquitaine for shaving off their beards and cutting their hair halfway up the sides of their heads—looking as effeminate "as actors," he grumbled—but probably not secretly living as monks.[71]) Especially if Gerald had led the community he founded, as its co-abbot, it was all the more urgent for Odo to make it seem as though he had been a monk, even a secret one.[72]

Derek Baker calls the story "curiously unsatisfactory" in making of Gerald a sort of "monk manqué."[73] Odo was himself perhaps not wholly satisfied with the portrayal, and, as if unable to help himself, he continued to justify Gerald's unique arrangement: "For himself, though, he reckoned it preferable to remain as he was than to attempt the sublime proposition" of the monastic life. Gerald always arrived in the church for the liturgies of the monks before anyone else and remained there longer afterward than anyone else in order that "both more freely and much more secretly he might cling to the things of divinity." He even slept "next to" the church (7). Odo's discomfort with the can of worms he has opened up perhaps reveals itself in the proliferation of such details. It also means that Gerald becomes not only an impossible ideal of noble lay piety, but also an implausible model as a monk who did not need the discipline of the rule and cloister.

Odo might really have heard about Gerald's semimonastic life, or he might have invented it to resolve the problems that Gerald's sanctity presented. It is even possible that Odo borrowed this model of lay piety from a man named Vectius depicted by Sidonius Apollinaris almost five hundred years earlier. Martin Heinzelmann first noticed the similarities between the two: like Gerald, Vectius was said to have been hospitable to strangers, humble even with his social inferiors, moderate in food and drink, and pious in chanting the psalms and reading the scriptures. He was, Sidonius wrote, a man "with a new manner of life, a complete monk, not under the monk's cowl but under the soldier's cloak [*novoque genere vivendi, monachum complet, non sub palliolo sed sub paludamento*]."[74] Yet Sidonius Apollinaris was hardly claiming that Vectius was a saint, for all his praiseworthy lifestyle.

Whether remembered or invented, Odo's presentation of Gerald provided him with an opportunity to imagine, even momentarily, what he had not become himself: a just layman, remaining in the world, acting piously and nobly in the life into which he had been born. Are there regrets in Odo's *Vita Geraldi*? The notion might seem anachronistic, but surely dissatisfaction with one's choices in life is a perennial feature of human life, and it is likely that regrets drove some men in Odo's day into the cloister after a life spent in the battlefields.[75] If God could turn a military man into a saint, an idea Odo was forced to confront as he composed his *vita*, it should not be unexpected if he wondered about the direction his life might have taken had he not in his adolescence interpreted his troubled dreams and his unexplained illness as God's anger at his choice of a military career.

It is especially tempting to speculate about Odo's regrets since in writing about Gerald he mentioned the same duke of Aquitaine in whose household he himself had been raised. How could he not have paused to reflect on what his own life might have been? According to Odo, Gerald never married, even though Duke William offered him his own sister.[76] Odo noted the pressure placed on Gerald to marry—and this is entirely believable, since William might well have seen a marriage as binding Gerald more closely to him—and proposed that the duke had said to Gerald "that he should consent to it for the love of sons." According to Odo, however, Gerald "replied that it was better to die without sons than to leave wicked heirs" (4). The faint echo of the Book of Wisdom (3:13–19) in Gerald's reply may disguise Odo's own relinquished "love of sons." We know nothing about Odo's prospects for marriage or about any women he might have declined to marry. Having come to adulthood at the court of the same duke of Aquitaine, he might well have recalled from his adolescence the woman he pictured as having been intended for Gerald. We must imagine that the renunciation of marriage brought regrets, perhaps not only for the sexual pleasures surrendered but also for the joys of fatherhood abandoned. As the founder of a monastery, Gerald became a kind of spiritual father, as did Odo in his role as abbot.[77] Still, Odo's comment, having Gerald attempt to convince the duke that renouncing physical fatherhood was the better choice, may provide some insight into Odo's own thoughts.

Understanding Odo as implicated with his biographical subject and perhaps even seeing Gerald as the model for the life he had renounced permits us to read his hagiographical account in a different light and, more generally, to imagine the hagiographical genre in a new way. We see how Odo tried to pull himself back from the threat of such regrets by having Gerald express regret at his own life. Again, it is one of only two passages in which Odo had Gerald speak directly, a choice that betrays its importance within the text: "For one day, while observing the construction of the [monastic] house, he shed copious tears. Then one of his associates inquired from him why he wept. 'Because,' he replied, 'I gaze upon that place which in no way whatsoever has come to its intended result, and I am overcome with sadness, like one who is alone and bereft, because the monks are missing'" (8).

Gerald's despair stemmed from his inability to advance the monastic life, he admitted, but also from his inability to advance *to* the monastic life, a despair that left him feeling "alone and bereft" and "overcome with sadness." It is the only place in Odo's *Vita Geraldi* that registers such strong emotion. Odo turned quickly from Gerald's despair—and perhaps his own regrets—and reminded his readers that everything worked out, that the monks were found and the monastery flourished. The discipline of monastic life provided an effective antidote even for one's regrets. At least, Odo had to persuade himself to believe that.

One final thought in this same passage is given over to the despondency that follows regret, remarkably different from the dispassionate listing of Gerald's virtuous actions that constitutes the rest of the text. "Indeed, quite often keeping silent for a long while, he would then draw a deep breath, in such a way that his chest would be shaken from its depths, and dissolving into tears, he would say: 'Oh Lord, keep us safe!' and other things of this sort, from which it is evident that his mind was heavy with something else. Of such a kind, then, was his speech, and of such a kind, his silence" (8). That is the last we hear of Gerald's life story in Odo's account. Even here there are echoes of Odo's own life, since Odo's own biographer began by recounting how he had begged Odo to tell his story: "But he, as was always his manner, was silent for a little while; then going somewhat pale, and sighing from the depths of his heart, he began to tell me his history; but nevertheless his words were full of tears and groans" (4). These are the silences and sighs, the "tears and groans" of telling the regrets of a lifetime, even the regrets of a saint.

Odo's Doubts

There is a final section in Odo's *Vita Geraldi*, all the more prosaic for following such poignancy. These are the eight miracles briefly recounted. Odo began the section surprisingly matter-of-factly: God rewarded Gerald for his holiness with "a certain grace of healing." There is an obvious reason for the inclusion of these miracles: they provide proof of Gerald's saintliness.[78] In fact, up to this point, Odo's *vita* has shown Gerald to be a good person, but apart from the spectacular occurrences before his birth nothing as yet has shown him to be *more* than a good person. So the miracles confirm both God's election and Odo's confidence in Gerald's holiness. And yet, I think that there is more to it. Odo seemed almost reluctant to begin his discussion of Gerald's miracle-working abilities: "Although now in the present time of the Antichrist the miracles of the saints ought already to cease, nonetheless, the Lord . . . deemed this servant of His worthy to glorify" (9). Gerald is a saint, Odo almost seemed to say, despite God's better judgment.

Gerald himself resisted the implications of his saintliness. "However much he might out of humility have avoided placing his hand on those who were sick," Odo wrote, "nonetheless, he often cured them both when he was not even there and although he was unwilling." This was made possible because "sick persons used to steal the water in which he washed his hands" (9). The examples that follow elaborate on this theme. When a lame boy of Aurillac was healed by being sprinkled with this wash water, Gerald "strenuously lamented, saying that it was the faith of the sick boy that had merited it," and implying that nothing of his own had contributed to the cure (10). Gerald began to take extreme measures, having his wash water poured out into the ground to avoid its distribution (11), but the healings continued, since one of his servants continued to distribute it clandestinely. When he discovered that a certain Radbald had given his water away and helped thereby to cure a blind girl of Argentat, "he threw him out at once from his presence." Odo continued, oddly enough, with these words:

> The nobleman Ebbo pleaded with the lord Gerald that the man
> who had been thrown out should be received back, addressing him
> plainly with reasoning and saying that perhaps he was sinning more
> through too much humility when he denied the grace that had been
> given to him for the sake of the sick he denied to those same sick
> persons. . . . When this man of the Lord, Gerald, heard these things,
> however, he cried and said that perhaps it was rather a deception
> from the devil, and that the devil would want to deceive him, so
> that even if Gerald were to do something good, he would perish at
> the same time. (11)

Now the topos of humility is nothing new for saints—nor, in fact, was restoring sight to the blind all that unusual for the saints of the central Middle Ages—but Odo's detailed description here, when compared to his far more concise reports of the healings themselves and his brevity overall, compels us to consider his words more carefully.[79] What did Odo have in mind by drawing such attention to Gerald's own doubts about his sanctity?

Whose doubts were these, exactly? If we return to Odo's prologue to the *Vita Geraldi*, we find other doubts, Odo's doubts, expressed to the two men to whom the work was dedicated:

> You have asked . . . that I should write something concerning the
> life or rather the miracles of the lord Gerald. I postponed it at first,
> however, in part because the matter seemed unclear to me on
> account of its newness and, I confess, in part because I was worried

and still am worried that this account might not be easy for me to relate. Indeed, uncertainty in this matter rises up particularly since this same man was powerful in this world; it was for this very reason that in certain places a group of peasants recently used to gather, and as it was a useless thing they gradually stopped. To be sure, when some noble laymen and pious clerics whom the same lord Gerald had raised from childhood had described to me his way of life as being of such a kind that through the will of God it was not unworthy of miracles, I put aside my doubts, considering with confidence that, according to the voice of the Apostle, God leaves no time without a proof of His goodness. (prol.)

It was here that Odo mentioned Gerald's earthly power and his wealth, attributes seemingly incongruous in a saint, but defended Gerald's possession of both by comparing him to Job and David. He then continued by offering the opinion that if God wished to manifest his glory through a layman in Odo's own day, that decision should not be questioned. He concluded with a wish that the account not be unworthy of the man, and that there be no "failure or sin in it" (prol.)

Nonetheless, the sin has already been confessed: Odo was not convinced that Gerald was truly a saint. It is a hagiographical commonplace to mention one's reluctance to write a saint's *vita*, but this declaration seems to me much more than that.[80] Even in the last part of the *vita*, Odo could not prevent himself from alluding to his doubts one more time before turning to Gerald's miracles: "Evidently, so that it would be thought more believable, it seems right to remember some persons who were cured" (9). Not even a story in which Gerald feeds a hungry cleric and his attendants to satiety with a single small fish—a story with clear biblical parallels, signaled even by the repetition of the name of one of Gerald's attendants, Samuel—could rescue Odo from his doubts, and he ended it as if distancing himself from the easy beliefs of others: "Some assert that fish were often obtained from God for the lord Gerald to eat" (15). After noting the use of Gerald's wash water, Odo concluded that "most were healed" (9)—most, but not all.

It is worth reiterating in this context that Odo never really referred to Gerald as a saint in the *vita*. Other saints are referred to as *sanctus* or *beatus*, the usual and mostly interchangeable titles, but Gerald is only referred to once as *beatus vir* (which might also simply mean "a holy man") in the prologue. Otherwise, Odo chose much less pointed terms, like *famulus Dei* ("the servant of God," used four times) and *vir Domini* ("the man of God," used three times), and most often simply as *domnus Geraldus* ("the lord Gerald"). Likewise, he never once referred to Gerald as a *confessor*, although in later centuries that title would be frequently applied to Gerald. Odo had no similar hesitation in describing in elaborate language the glories of other saints. Barbara Rosenwein describes Odo's enduring devotion to Saint Martin, for whom Odo wrote several sermons and antiphonal prayers. To be sure, Martin's life formed a sharp contrast with that of Gerald's. Both Martin and Gerald began life as soldiers, but Martin rejected utterly the violence of war, and his offer to fight unarmed and without armor in battle makes Gerald's order to his men to turn their spears around seem halfhearted at best. More importantly, Martin abandoned his military career for the ascetic life of a hermit, then a monk, and eventually a bishop. Martin reflected the same ideal that inspired Odo, which is perhaps why Odo remained so devoted to him. Gerald's life story was not the same at all; Rosenwein calls it "a radical transformation of the Sulpician ideal." It is probably why Odo could never bring himself to support unreservedly Gerald's claim to sanctity.[81]

Perhaps to make sense of this we need to think again about hagiography in broader terms. Before any papal procedure for canonization, to write the *vita* of a saint was one of the most important steps in the recognition and promotion of a saint; it was in many ways as formal and final a process as existed. It was certainly not a step to be taken lightly, and we see some of the weight of that judgment in Odo's doubts and in the care he took to describe Gerald, ending his prologue with the hope "that this very selfsame account not be unworthy of the blessed man in any way" (prol.). A combination of personal, spiritual, and practical reasons prompted Odo to write the *Vita Geraldi*, as I have outlined. Having agreed to put the life of Gerald into writing, though, it was up to him to mold the image of Gerald as he saw fit. That was part of Odo's responsibility and the responsibility of all hagiographers. As I have argued, Odo's used his opportunity to create a mirror image of the warriors of his day, possibly adding reminiscences from his own personal history and all the while trying to remain true to the monastic ideal.

There is more to Odo's hesitation than carefulness, however. Saints represented more than models for human behavior. They embodied human perfection, which meant that they were impossible to emulate: their perfection had come through God's grace, which was given indiscriminately to some but never to all. So while some individuals might be able to imitate the saints, those to whom God's grace was also granted, few others could hope to accomplish what they had done. As Odo himself stated in his prologue: God "offered this servant of His to us either so as to inspire imitation or else as a witness, just as He brought the queen of the south to the Jews" (prol.). That biblical queen who was so impressed by King Solomon's reputation for holiness that she traveled to meet him could never hope to become him; she remained simply a guest in his realm. Nor could most who heard about the glowing example of the saints hope to be saints themselves; they could only revere them with awe.

Would it be too much to wonder if some hagiographers, knowing full well that the saints lay beyond the reach of all but a few, felt jealous as they took up their quills to write? Was jealously the "sin" for which Odo asked forgiveness? Perhaps the articulation of his doubts served as a means to communicate that jealousy, and the voicing of his misgivings about Gerald's holiness, an occasion to reaffirm the importance of the monastic life and with it the choice he had made for himself. "If therefore God, the arranger of the ages," he wrote, "deigns to repeat in our days these deeds in His holiness, we should praise them and be eager to give thanks" (prol.). He quoted the Gospel of John (13:32): "since He is mindful of his promise that He himself made: 'Who glorifies me,' He says, 'I will glorify him.'" Odo had read his Augustine and knew perfectly well that God's grace of sanctity was given freely, but also without regard for personal merit. With this statement, nonetheless, Odo made of Gerald's holiness the reward for his good deeds. Perhaps he took comfort in this hope, that all good deeds would be rewarded with the grace of sanctity, and that he might also be rewarded for his own good deeds, including his writing about Gerald despite doubts and regrets.

Odo need not have worried. After he left Aurillac he traveled to Rome, where he reformed yet more monasteries. There he met John of Salerno, who would write the story of Odo's own saintly life. John provided something for Odo that Odo never did for Gerald: a holy death. It is curious that Odo never bothered to say when or how Gerald died. It cannot reasonably be thought that Odo learned nothing about Gerald's death, since it became part of the later legends told about him, legends that probably originated at his monastery in Aurillac. Moreover, Gerald's death must already have been the focus of his cult there where he was buried, and his feast day, as with other saints, celebrated on the day of his death. Why did Odo omit these details? One might speculate in a number of ways. First, Odo's focus on Gerald as a model for men would not have been substantially improved with a narrative of Gerald's death: it was Gerald's life, after all, that Odo wanted others to imitate. Second, if Odo was intrigued by the autobiographical opportunities in his telling of Gerald's story, a description of Gerald's death would have held little meaning. Third, and perhaps most significantly, Odo's doubts about Gerald as a saint may have prompted him to downplay this most important aspect of a saint's life. Saints' *vitae* were recited in monasteries especially on the saint's feast day, the day of their entrance into heaven. In Odo's telling of Gerald's life story, what would have been celebrated annually at his feast day was marked by its absence.[82]

In the end, Gerald seems not to have made much of an impression on Odo, despite the possibilities for self-reflection that Gerald presented. Far more important, in Odo's other writings, was his attachment to Saint Martin—a saint with whom Odo presumably felt much more comfortable identifying himself. Saint Martin appears again and again in the handful of sermons extant from Odo. John of Salerno said in his *vita* that Odo "imbibed a warm and lasting love [for Saint Martin] with his mother's milk."[83] Divine mercy even delayed Odo's death, according to John, so that he might visit the shrine of Saint Martin one last time and expire there.[84] Odo's later biographer Nalgod exclaimed more floridly: "What devotion Saint Odo had and how much love burned [within him] toward Martin it is scarcely possible or difficult to say."[85] But Odo seems never to have mentioned Saint Gerald again. It would fall to another monk to breathe new life into Gerald's memory, to remake him as a saint in a more lasting way.

CHAPTER 3

The Second Saint Gerald

Almost a century after Odo composed his *Vita brevior*, Ademar of Chabannes, writing from Limoges in the 1020s, extended the textual tradition on
Gerald in a number of ways. He began by adding a brief account of Gerald's
death and a half-dozen stories of Gerald's posthumous miracles to the existing
vita. Perhaps he hoped to dispel the doubts that Odo had raised about Gerald's sanctity. Later, he added further miracle stories, showcasing a series of
miraculous events that happened at the time of the dedication of the new
church in Aurillac in 972. Possibly at the same time, he composed a sermon
for Gerald's feast day, one that also asserted Gerald's saintliness. Finally,
Ademar rewrote Odo's brief *vita* altogether, rearranging and expanding it
into two books of a new *Vita Geraldi*, the *Vita prolixior*, that vigorously
defended Gerald's sanctity in contrast to Odo's lukewarm appraisal. To this
new *vita* he joined his earlier accounts of Gerald's death and posthumous
miracles as its third and fourth books. And he put forth the whole of the new
work under Odo's name.

Ademar and Gerald

Ademar of Chabannes, born in 988 or 989, was sent to the monastery of
Angoulême as a boy, one of the many child oblates given over to the church
by the noble families of the central Middle Ages. Later, he spent several long
periods at the monastery of Saint-Martial in Limoges, where his uncle was
an important monk. He wrote extensively throughout his life, from sermons

and saints' lives to a historical chronicle that is unique for the region. He was also a forger.[1]

Ademar is best known to scholars for his devotion to Saint Martial, the patron saint of the monastery at Limoges. Martial was a missionary said to have converted the Roman inhabitants of Limoges to Christianity before becoming its first bishop, but by Ademar's day some also believed that he had been among the close companions of Jesus and so was deserving of the title of apostle.[2] As part of his efforts on Saint Martial's behalf, Ademar took a brief *vita* of the saint and expanded it with details presumably of his own invention.[3] Eventually—in what Louis Saltet calls "a case of pathological lying" and Richard Landes a "megalomanic fantasy"—Ademar began to forge documents to support the cause of Martial's apostolicity. So skilled was he in these deceptions that it is still difficult to say with any certainty from what he wrote what really happened and what was only imagined.[4]

Scholarly interest in Ademar's promotion of the cult of Saint Martial has perhaps obscured his genuine interest in other saints, including Eparche (Eparchius), the patron saint of the monastery at Angoulême, Amant (Amantius) of Boixe to the north of Angoulême, and also Valerie (Valeria) and Austreclinien (Austreclinianus), two individuals associated with the legend of Saint Martial.[5] What these saints shared was a connection to Aquitaine, like Gerald's, and in an age keener on biblical and Roman saints, this localism set Ademar's devotion apart. The *vita* Ademar wrote for Saint Martial was ascribed to Aurelian, successor to Martial as bishop of Limoges, and the *vita* for Saint Amant was long attributed to Hugh, a tenth-century bishop of Angoulême. Perhaps Ademar encouraged these misattributions.

A number of factors seem to have prompted Ademar's turn to Saint Gerald. He may have meant to honor the Gerald who was bishop of Limoges between 1014 and 1023. Given the practices of the era, this bishop may well have been related to Saint Gerald. In the late tenth and early eleventh centuries, many of the bishops of Limoges and abbots of its monastery were drawn from the family of the viscounts of Limoges—a connection so close that Reinhold Kaiser has referred to the monastery of Saint-Martial as their personal or "home monastery."[6] Guy, the father of this bishop Gerald, was viscount until his death in 1025, after which this Gerald's brother, also named Ademar, became viscount, but the name Gerald repeats regularly in the family. So there may have been a sycophantic purpose to Ademar's interest in Saint Gerald if he hoped to gain the notice of this powerful family by drawing attention to the bishop's saintly relative or namesake. Nonetheless, connections existed between Aurillac and Limoges even before Ademar, and these may also have been established or encouraged by the men of this same noble family.[7]

Ademar may have had another, even more deeply personal reason for his interest in Saint Gerald. He claimed that he was related to the two brothers, bishop Turpin and the abbot Aimon, to whom Odo had dedicated his *vita*.[8] If Turpin and Aimon were related to Gerald, then Ademar was too.[9] Both the names Ademar and Gerald circulated within the same families, and their use by the viscounts of Limoges may also point to some connection there. If Ademar knew or believed himself to be from the same family as Saint Gerald, his lineage would have provided a compelling motivation for revisiting the *vita* as Odo had left it, especially given Odo's doubts about Gerald's sanctity. Such a conjecture is supported by the fact that Ademar showed a real and sustained interest in Saint Gerald throughout his career, mentioning him in most of his writings, even when the reference was not all that relevant to the subject at hand.[10] His continued interest provides a sharp contrast with Odo's apparent disregard for the man.

Gerald's Holy Death

As noted above, Ademar seems to have begun his writings about Gerald by appending two short texts to Odo's *vita*, one about the saint's death and the other recounting his posthumous miracles. Given the importance both of a holy death and of the miracles that followed it to saints' *vitae* generally, the usefulness of such texts for the cult of Saint Gerald is obvious. The first, called the *Transitus* ("Passing") in the earliest manuscripts, repeats many of the typical hagiographical features found elsewhere: the failing health in old age and the final illness of the saint serve as reminders of the frailty of human existence, the precognition of death confirms the saint's holiness, and the public lamentation after his death permits a recapitulation of the saint's virtues.[11]

Did Ademar invent what he wrote about the end of Gerald's life as generically appropriate, or did he learn about it from the monks of Aurillac, perhaps ones serving in the church of Saint Gerald at Limoges, or did he hear it from pilgrims? From this distance it is impossible for us to decide. Ademar depicted Gerald as having offered freedom to his serfs at the end of his life, for example—a hundred at his death, as restricted by law, and countless others before it—then added that "many of them, however, bound closely by their love for him and refusing their freedom, preferred to remain in servitude to him" (3.4). This might simply be pious tribute to a saint, but there might also be echoes of monastic complaints in the story, since peasants were forever claiming their freedom and monasteries forever denying the same. Were descendants of these serfs claiming that in his goodness Gerald had freed them all?

In the *Transitus*, Ademar downplayed Odo's doubts about Gerald. Odo said that Gerald had gone blind for a year as chastisement from God for his adolescent lust. Ademar added a second blindness toward the end of the saint's life, but did not suggest, as Odo had, that the illness had been a punishment for sin. Rather, "it was for him as befell blessed Job, and Tobias, since it was given to him to be tested," because "inasmuch as he was unable to gaze upon the beauty of the world, he turned a more plainly fitting contemplation of his heart to the true light" (3.2).[12]

Ademar sent Gerald out in proper saintly style in the *Transitus*, describing in poignant detail Gerald's final days: his failing body, the call to a bishop to lend him final succor, the wailing of bystanders, the crowds massing to bid him farewell. In maudlin tones, Ademar had the crowd call out to Gerald: "Oh, Gerald, you who were rightfully called 'the Good,' who will be a sustainer of the needy, as you were? Who will be a nourisher of children, a defender of widows? Who will be a consoler of those in distress? Who will lean down from the summit of power in the same way toward the poor? Who will consider the needs of each one of us, as you did, or set them aright? Most indulgent father, how charming, how sweet you always were!" (3.5). As Gerald sank into his final sleep, Ademar declared that only the joy of the angels in heaven counterbalanced the sorrow of the inhabitants of the earth (3.7).

In concluding, Ademar returned to the theme of Gerald's unmistakable sanctity in words spoken directly to him:

> Scripture says: Praise the Lord in His saints. For that reason, oh,
> blessed Gerald, in whatever ways we can we make account to Him
> for you. We praise Him in that He chose you and He justified you.
> He made wondrous His mercy in you. He led you down the right
> paths. He made known the fruit of your deeds. Lastly, even into
> your old age and decline He did not abandon you. What is more,
> He counted you among the sons of God. Furthermore, He glorified
> you in the eyes of all. Indeed, because praise befits the saints, when

we praise Him we also praise you, since—in the words of Jeremiah—you have worn the yoke of Christ from your adolescence,
since you did not draw back from the grace of His calling, since you
did not give up anything in exchange for your soul, since you did
not accept His salvation in vain, since you did not throw away what
was deepest within you and what you had conceived out of love for
Christ, since you did not relapse in a time of temptation, since you
did not indulge in the external glory of this present life, and since
you did not fail to do good. (3.8)

There are no reservations about Gerald's saintliness here. The praise is even
a bit exaggerated, as Ademar himself admitted: "Oh Lord, ignore my presumption about him, for I fear the excess in this account, since I have tried
to do what I was in no way capable of doing. Even if he is worthy of the
praise by which You are praised, I, on the other hand, oh Lord, am unworthy
of recounting it, for praise in the mouth of a sinner is not appealing" (3.8).

This passage marks the first of several shifts in Ademar's writings from a
discussion of Gerald to one of himself. Ademar elaborated further on this
contrast between Gerald's saintliness and his own sinfulness: "Your eyes see
this imperfect one of the Church [Ademar himself], and the stones of the
earth will have pity on him, I pray that they who are called stones because of
the solidness of their conduct [that is, the saints], condescend to assist me,
who am dirt [*terra*] on account of my wickedness, so that I, who do not have
the clothing of righteousness [*indumentum iustitiae*], might cling to the
stones, so that I might hide my nakedness behind their merits" (3.8). It was
a strange set of metaphors, to be sure, but through them Ademar completely
altered the skeptical tone of Odo's *vita*. The contrast between the saintly and
the sinful also gave Ademar the opportunity to insert himself into this praise
of Gerald's saintliness, the first indication that he would use Gerald to reflect
on his own salvation. It should also be noted that the dialectical style of the
Transitus, in which Ademar shifted back and forth from addressing the
reader, Gerald, and God, is not at all like that of Odo's *vita*: Ademar was
already more interested in improving Odo's style than in emulating it.

Gerald's Posthumous Miracles

Ademar's recounting of Gerald's posthumous miracles was probably written
about the same time, but was clearly meant to be separate from it. (The

Transitus ends with the comment: "But let me now finish this little book [*libellus*] lest it should displease perhaps with its rusticity as much as by its dragging on," 3.11.) The miracles included in this text—called *Miracula post transitum* ("Miracles after the Passing") in the earliest manuscript written at Limoges in Ademar's day—seem to have originated at Aurillac, since most of them happen in and around Gerald's tomb: one man is punished for dreaming of trying to lift the lid off of it—perhaps to steal from within (4.2), and a woman is told in a dream that she can be cured if she presents herself before it (4.3). Other stories included there were also apparently connected to local memory: a ring of grass miraculously grew before Gerald's first tomb when all else around was bare earth (4.4), and the tomb rose up out of the ground, signaling Gerald's wish to be translated into the interior of the church (4.6), where more healings occurred (4.7).[13]

These miracles provide much better proof that Gerald was a saint than the evidence Odo had mustered. Ademar commented specifically on this subject:

> Since a dead man quickly disappears from our hearts, and we give
> him over immediately to oblivion, and since we do not remember
> the reward that remains to the saints through their deeds, we
> become wickedly apathetic about those things that should be imi-
> tated. For that reason perhaps at this time God deigns to work mira-
> cles, so that we might thus understand the glory that Gerald has
> within, and also so that we might turn the sharpness of our minds
> to the recently performed deeds by which that same glory is attained,
> and so that we might learn to grow strong in those things that
> should be imitated (3.12)

(The *PL* has this as the last section of the *Transitus*, but all of the early manuscripts have it as the prologue to the *Miracula*, and Bultot-Verleysen's critical edition restores it to its proper place.) The criticism that Gerald's sanctity has been shamefully forgotten also fits well with observations made throughout these miracles. In one story, for instance, a nobleman refused to let his serf visit Gerald's tomb to be healed because he thought the reverence paid to him ridiculous (4.3).

The improper neglect of Gerald's sanctity is the thread that holds these miracle stories together, in fact. The people of Aurillac are mostly treated as rubes too stupid to appreciate Gerald's holiness or fear his power. They did not notice that Gerald's tomb was lifting out of the ground until "a certain cleric from the district of Limoges" pointed it out to them (4.6; one of the many references to Limoges found throughout Ademar's writings about Gerald, and the disparaging references to the inhabitants of Aurillac provide further proof that the author was not one of them). Such miraculous occurrences should have been immediately recognized as stemming from Gerald's sanctity: "Whoever accepts this cannot ignore that there is some divine power at work" (4.6). He even repeated it in the passage that followed: "If perhaps someone doubts these things, . . . he can test it with his sight and by it might affirm his faith in what has occurred" (4.7).

Throughout, the worthiness of devotion to Saint Gerald figures prominently. The growing ring of grass around Gerald's tomb, for example, seems far from miraculous: the greater numbers of pilgrims who visited it trampled the lawn and killed it. Yet Ademar cast aside so mundane an interpretation. Instead, the expanding zone of barren earth pushing the edge of the green grass outward is a metaphor for Gerald's growing reputation and a symbol of the "verdancy of virtue [*viriditas virtutis*]" that moves across a people "who through the aridity of good works are sterile" and makes them fertile. Maybe so forced an interpretation was too much even for Ademar, and he concluded the passage with a disclaimer of sorts: "Whether it truly signified this only the Arranger of things knew but it is certain that nothing on this earth is done without cause" (4.4). The episode hints at the lengths to which Ademar was willing to go to defend Gerald's sanctity.

In a few places, Ademar stated outright the doubts of some still unconvinced that Gerald was truly a saint. Most of these are found in the last sections of the *Miracula*, which Ademar probably added when it became the fourth book in his *vita*.[14] If so, it suggests that Ademar remained concerned about those who refused to take Gerald seriously. He acknowledged that Gerald was fond of collecting relics, and that some of these relics had extraordinary powers: a fragment of the True Cross if carried on horseback caused the deaths of those horses and made epileptics of those who perjured themselves while holding it (4.8). Nonetheless, he derided those who suggested that Gerald's miracles resulted solely from the power of these relics and not from his own abilities: "Doubtless, some claim, disputing rashly the glory of blessed Gerald, that this grace of healing was conferred not through his merits but through the virtues of these relics" (4.9). He did admit that Gerald's virtue and the relics might both have cooperated in the healings.[15] He then added the example of a viscount's son who was healed of a withered hand through Gerald's intercession. He paused to say that this cure was remembered because it involved the nobility, but that numerous cures had happened to lesser persons and been forgotten: "As the great number of them grew, attention to keeping count of them was neglected" (4.9). So few miracles had been attributed to Saint Gerald, in other words, because he had worked so many. It is a logic that permitted Ademar to dismiss any and all skeptics.[16]

Ademar also included several stories in this last part of the *Miracula* that revealed Gerald's anger against those who ignored his holiness. When a table on which Gerald used to dine was not treated as a proper relic, for example, a man who fell asleep on it "was suddenly made blind and deranged" and a dog that jumped up on it was paralyzed. That Ademar intended such stories to serve as warnings to any who continued to doubt Gerald's sanctity seems clear. Of the locals who observed this last event, Ademar wrote that "when they were chattering away at their meals and taking part in inane conversation, as usual, suddenly a powerful fear struck them all" (4.10). In contrast, when so negligible a relic as the block from which Gerald used to mount his horse was venerated and kissed by the sick, they regained their health (4.10). Gerald's righteous anger extended over the natural world. When cattle grazed on the spot on which Gerald's bier had rested on his return to Aurillac (presumably because the place had not been properly remembered), "immediately they began to be tormented and not a few of them died," after which an oratory was built on the spot, and many people were healed (4.10). A spring even began to flow there (and there is still a spring named after Saint Gerald with a small chapel not far from Aurillac at a place called Bourniou, which seems to indicate that Ademar's stories were not invented out of whole cloth).[17] Now there is nothing out of the ordinary in having the personal effects of a saint be revered as relics, but it is odd that these stories should all be saved up until the very end of this text. They make the case that it was dangerous to ignore Gerald's sanctity. They also gave the lie to anyone who claimed that it was only the relics Gerald had carried that had healed. A new Ademar was beginning to show through these stories of holy vengeance, one who reveled in Saint Gerald's power to hurt as well as to heal.[18]

One of last of these miracle stories involves Gerald's nephew Rainald, admonished by his uncle in a dream to leave the monks of Aurillac and their properties in peace. It seems to hint at ongoing tensions between the monastery of Aurillac and the individual who would otherwise have inherited the lands that Gerald bequeathed to it: perhaps Rainald felt unacceptably deprived. Of this nephew, Ademar said that "he was prone to evil, however much he was closely related by blood to the saintly man." Indeed, when one visit was insufficient to mollify Rainald's ways, Gerald appeared a second time, "and striking him on the head he threatened him with imminent death" (4.11).

A few manuscripts of the *Miracula* contain two more violent posthumous miracles. The earliest of these manuscripts dates from the eleventh century, so the stories are old, and although they were excluded from the *PL*, Bultot-Verleysen's recent edition restores them as original to the text. Yet none of the manuscripts from Limoges contains them, which may indicate that they are later additions. The two stories, which follow at the very end of the treatise in the manuscripts in which they do appear, certainly echo Ademar's criticisms that Gerald's sanctity was being ignored. In the first, a woman from Limoges (and so the town shows up yet again) went on pilgrimage to Gerald's tomb. Returning home, she was raped by a warrior, despite her protest to him that she was "a woman of Saint Gerald" so he should not dare to act so cruelly toward her. "When he had risen from lying with her," the story continues, "the man was struck through divine vengeance in the groin or testicles or, as I should say, in his manly parts [*virilia*], which putrefied and fell off from him. Not even then did he make amends for his crime," and he died a few days later, drowning in the Dordogne River. The second miracle story involved a man, who had already had a foot amputated for theft, arrested for spying. His captors gouged out one of his eyes, but when they attempted to remove his other eye and thus blind him, he begged them for Saint Gerald's sake to spare him at least the one eye. They ignored his plea but found that they could not continue, "whence they were given plainly to understand that the power of the man was so great." The words that end this episode are, of course, the general lesson we are supposed to take from these posthumous miracles.

Gerald's Feast Day

At some point Ademar wrote a sermon for Gerald's feast day. It exists in several early manuscripts, including two from the eleventh century, and Paolo Facciotto has published a critical edition of it.[19] Two sacramentaries in use at the monastery of Saint-Martial in Limoges confirm the commemoration of Saint Gerald's feast day there in Ademar's lifetime.[20] Perhaps the monks of Limoges, having decided to celebrate the occasion, invited Ademar to compose the sermon, knowing of his interest in the saint. It seems to have been written apart from and after his initial efforts, since it is not found in any manuscript where the *Transitus* and the *Miracula* follow the *Vita brevior*. The sermon is short on details from Gerald's life, although its elements can all be found in Odo's *vita*. It seems likely, then, that Ademar took these basic elements from the existing *vita*, before elaborating it himself.

The sermon also insists on Gerald's holiness, and right from the start listeners are reminded that even if his feast had not been observed "back through time and to the ends of the earth," it was "not unequal in renown" to the cults of longstanding and universal saints (1). That seems entirely in keeping both with Ademar's defense of Gerald's holiness and also with his more general admiration for Aquitanian saints. Much is made of the merits of Saint Gerald, who was the equal of any ancient confessor, and was perhaps even worthier since he lived in a time "when almost all the world is inclined to evil" (7; this is apparently the first reference to Gerald as a confessor that would become an integral part of his cult.) The metaphors in the sermon are a bit strained: since Gerald did not hide his light under a bushel, he is now a heavenly body shining brightly from above and illuminating the world through the radiance of his virtues (8), and since he followed the lamb of God, he is now among the flock of the just (9). But the pious sentiment is clear enough. There are none of Odo's doubts here. In contrast to Odo's assertion in the preface to the *Vita brevior* that peasants used to gather at Gerald's tomb but then stopped, the sermon rejoices in the growing devotion to Gerald: "For not only from neighboring parts but truly also from remote regions crowds of people often gather, wanting to visit the tomb of his body." Ademar briefly listed a very biblical set of miracles performed at Gerald's tomb: "sickness finds health, blindness receives sight, weakness obtains vigor, and the ears of the deaf are made capable of hearing," before adding what seems to reiterate his comments in the *Transitus* about his own sinfulness: "and what is more wonderful, here the souls of sinners, injured by their wounds and almost already dead through long inattention, are raised back to life" (9).

Despite its brevity, the sermon shows us that Ademar was still defending Gerald's saintly reputation, an issue that would remain foremost in his mind as he added further to his writings about Gerald.

The Vision of Bishop Stephen

Ademar found it hard to be done with Saint Gerald. He penned additional miracle stories to add to the growing pile of proofs of Gerald's true sanctity after he composed the *Transitus* and the *Miracula*, since he mentioned in one of these stories that he had already added something at the end of someone else's *vita* (4). The new miracles repeat many of the same themes found in Ademar's other writings. Since they are found only in two manuscripts, as described above, they might have been something of an afterthought, though it might simply be that most medieval copyists stopped before they reached them, because many of the manuscripts end at idiosyncratic places. Or, given that these miracle stories could not have been written by Odo of Cluny, Ademar may have tried to suppress them as he recrafted his writings as Odo's work.[21]

These additional miracle stories begin with what was becoming a refrain in Ademar's writings: Gerald's obvious sanctity and the need to record his miracles for posterity, despite the author's unworthiness. The first set of miracles took place at the time of the consecration of a new church at Aurillac in 972 by Stephen, the bishop of Clermont.[22] One of the first seems a bit forced: as the bishop began the consecration, the sun appeared in an otherwise rainy day (1). Ademar reminded his readers that the biblical Elijah as well as Saints Medard and Scholastica had also controlled the weather and that Gerald was thus proven inferior to none of them. It is a bit reminiscent of the remark Ademar made about the growing ring of barren grass around Gerald's tomb in the first part of the *Miracula*, that what seems sometimes to be no miracle at all might still be one. Of perhaps greater substance is the story said to have happened when the same bishop fell ill as he visited the monastery at Figeac. Fearing death, Stephen prayed to Saint Gerald, despite the criticisms of one of his priests, who suggested that there were far more powerful and influential saints to ask for healing, and he received a vision of Gerald together with Sainte Foy. Foy did not speak, but Gerald told him that it was because of Gerald's own merits that God had deigned to heal Stephen, and then offered to lie down beside the bishop in his bed until he was well again (2).[23]

The stories that follow return to the theme of violence and to the protection from it that Gerald offered. Several of them involved noblemen who threatened monks or peasants of the estates belonging to the monastery of Aurillac. They are named: Isarn Tatil, who menaced the monks of Varen, a priory of Aurillac (4), Bernard de Najac, who stole from the monks of the priory at Vailhourles (5), and Deusdedit, a vassal of the previous man, who also attacked the monks of Vailhourles (6).[24] All met violent ends. Even soldiers of the bishop of Agen had to make amends when they confiscated animals from an unnamed estate belonging to the monastery (7). Like the warning given to Gerald's nephew Rainald in the *Miracula*, these incidents reminded evildoers that Gerald's vengeance should not be underestimated.

The other miracles also repeat the patterns found elsewhere. Gerald's control over the natural world is shown, especially over animals. A packhorse bolted in a snowstorm, but led the same Bishop Stephen through the mountains to Aurillac (1). With Gerald's help pilgrims safely crossed a torrential river (9).[25] In four separate episodes, fish allowed themselves miraculously to be caught (10, 11, 12, and 15). Gerald twice healed the blind (17 and 20). Even the importance of physical proximity to Gerald's relics is reiterated in several stories in which the infirm must touch Gerald's shrine or otherwise come into direct contact with it or his remains (13, 14, 15, 17, and 18). These are all features of the *Miracula*. As before, Gerald's power might harm as readily as heal. When a father refused to provide his son-in-law with a promised dowry, and even dared to swear a false oath in church that he had not promised him any dowry whatsoever, he was thrown to the ground in an insane fit (8; the incident took place in the church of Saint Gerald in Limoges, another mention of the town).[26]

At the very end of these additional miracle stories, otherwise all posthumous, is one that happened during Gerald's lifetime. Why it should have been included here and not incorporated into Gerald's *vita* is difficult to say; there is nothing to suggest that it was added by a later hand. It tells of a man named Autrade (Autradus) who journeyed with Gerald and his men as they returned from a pilgrimage to Rome. When they reached Autrade's own property, the man refused to permit Gerald to camp on his field. Gerald left, but God struck Autrade with blindness. Two years later, as Gerald made another pilgrimage to Rome,[27] the same Autrade threw himself at Gerald's feet, begging for the restoration of his sight. Gerald agreed only if Autrade renounced forever his customary right that his peasants harvest for free the field from which Gerald had been excluded, but henceforth pay them to do it. The man refused, and remained blind until the end of his life (20).

This last episode introduces an additional facet to Ademar's fascination with Gerald: the saint's beneficence toward the lowest classes. Already Ademar had noted in the *Transitus* how Gerald had freed countless serfs (3.4), and how throngs of the poor joined with clerics, monks, and noblemen to lament Gerald's death and to escort his body to its resting place (3.5 and 3.9). In the *Miracula*, likewise, Ademar included examples of Gerald's healings of individuals from all social classes from a viscount's son (4.9) to a serving woman (*ancilla*, 4.3). With these additional miracle stories, Ademar showed how Gerald protected even the lowliest of those who revered him: a peasant woman on pilgrimage to Aurillac with a cruel husband was shielded from feeling the pain of his blows (3), for example, and the hand of a "very poor man" was healed after having been shattered by the monks of Aurillac who slammed it in a door when trying to limit access to Gerald's tomb (13; the disapproving tone toward the monks of Aurillac in this incident once again belies the fact that the author was one of them).

Ademar would also reflect on Gerald's gentle treatment of peasants in his version of the *Vita Geraldi*, adding several stories involving peasants, none of which came from Odo. There is a deeper lesson here: if Gerald were to succeed as a saint, he would have to be shown as more than either a model nobleman or a scourge to the wicked. He would have to seem a friend to the poor and powerless. Odo had scorned the piety of peasants as "a useless thing" (*res vana*, in the prologue to the *Vita brevior*), but Ademar seems to have understood that these humbler folk might be crucial in guaranteeing the survival of Gerald's cult.

Ademar finished the *Miracula addita* with a summation of Gerald's life and accomplishments, much like those in the *Transitus* and in the *Miracula*. "Thus rightly ends this series of stories," he said, "telling of the victories of this man of God" (21).[28] Perhaps he thought it would be his last contribution, but he clearly continued to reflect on what might be done with the image of Gerald and his opportunity to rewrite the past.[29]

Ademar, Martial, and Gerald

If we take a step back from a pious reading of Ademar's writings and refuse to see them simply as formulaic tributes to a saint—even to a saintly cousin—we find a strange sort of self-identification beginning to happen. Whether or not Ademar was related to Gerald, even simply imagining the saint's life and virtues as he wrote about them might have been enough to have brought about such an identification. This feeling becomes increasingly palpable as Ademar reshaped the memory of Saint Gerald.

The summation of Gerald's virtues in the sermon, for example, might have been intended to inspire those listening to it, and doubtless it did, but it also seems more than that. "Rightly, indeed, is he added today to the fellowship of the saints," Ademar wrote, "since with vigilant study he strove to learn through the example of the saints how he might follow their deeds and be pleasing to them" (4). The Gerald depicted in the sermon devoted himself especially to learning: "he had fixed his soul on the discipline of sacred scriptures, so that he seemed more capable of solving the questions of sacred scriptures than even some bishops" (4; a much greater claim than that made in the *Vita brevior*, which said only that Gerald "surpassed many clerics in his recollection of the scriptures," 2).

This last comment probably reveals a monastic sense of intellectual superiority within the church; in various forms, it was a commonplace of hagiographical writing. Nonetheless, the praise of the saintliness inherent to scholarliness betrays Ademar's own view of himself, a self-identification despite his feeling of sinfulness noted above. If devout study of the saints were sufficient for one's own holiness, in other words, then the attention that Ademar gave to Saint Gerald was already paying off. As the sermon concludes, the devout remembrance of Gerald's virtues emboldens even the worst of sinners to approach "the tribunal of the fearsome judge" with supreme confidence (9). In a sense, Ademar got to eat his cake and have it, too: he was both the sinner, hoping for heaven through another's merit, and the saint, setting an example through the writing down of Gerald's good deeds so as to lead others to salvation.

One sees in Ademar's description of Gerald a man tried by the same difficulties and perhaps expecting the same ultimate rewards. Seemingly random generalizing statements scattered here and there may also have been intended to offer hope to Ademar and all like him who had sacrificed their lives to the monastic principle. "As scripture says, he who is holy will yet still be sanctified, so it was fitting that this man of God be refined before his death through the scourge [of suffering]" (3.2). "However much, therefore, because of its mortal condition the flesh might perhaps be afraid, nonetheless the spirit, fixed intently on the face of glory, exults, inasmuch as it is confident that in fact it has already identified the hope it had long desired" (3.6). "Truly blessed is he whose days have passed in grief and whose years in lamentation: because he has now experienced how great is the abundance of goodness that the Lord keeps hidden for those who fear him" (3.7).

It is not difficult to imagine how Ademar felt as he composed such words. Monasticism as it had developed by the eleventh century was intended to assure salvation for those who participated in it. The dedication of the sons and daughters of noble families to the monastic life, including individuals like Ademar, in addition to practical benefits was meant to work toward the spiritual advantage of those who had placed them in the monasteries. It also promised particular recompense to the individuals themselves. Men like Ademar must have struggled to believe that their sacrifice—of marriage and family life, of social status and wealth, often, as in Ademar's own life, a sacrifice not of their own choice—was truly worthwhile. This spirit of self-surrender was part and parcel of the many monastic reform movements that gained such popularity in the tenth and eleventh centuries. By dedicating oneself to this ideal, the monastic life could be more than an empty gesture, an institutionalized means of pruning the family tree of its surplus members. Instead, the life of the cloister could be an individual's enduring prayer to God.

For those who wholeheartedly believed that the monastic sacrifice was worthwhile, or who wanted to believe it, the challenges posed by contemporary life may have seemed daunting. Noble families, like Ademar's own, whose tenure to lands was becoming more secure and whose income was growing, were scrambling for even more power and wealth and for better lands and titles, embroiled in endemic brutal violence against each other as well as against less well-defended properties. The various episodes of noblemen's threats against the church that Ademar included in his miracle stories recurred in infinite local varieties. The monasteries drew much of their membership from these same noble families caught up in the scramble, including Ademar himself, and it may well be that beneath these fantasies of a saint who wrought vengeance on the wicked lay the hidden frustrations of one who wondered whether his sacrifice was sufficiently appreciated. A saint who might exact a holy punishment against disbelievers was to be revered, indeed.

Ademar's most frantic efforts were those directed at securing the recognition of Saint Martial's apostolicity. Yet there is evidence for the same furious attention here in Ademar's writings about Saint Gerald, in the doggedness with which Ademar proclaimed Gerald's saintliness. The two were not entirely divorced. Comments already in these earliest writings about Gerald bear the marks of Ademar's growing preoccupation with Saint Martial. The vision that the cleric of Rodez experienced of Saints Gerald and Martial in the company of the apostles in the *Miracula* confirmed the special holiness of both (4.5). It was to Gerald's credit, Ademar also hinted, that he revered Saint Martial. When in his *Transitus* he described the consecration of the church at Aurillac, Ademar noted the many relics of saints honored there. Yet he singled out for particular mention the relics of Saints Martin of Tours, Hilary of Poitiers, and Martial of Limoges, preferring local saints once again to universal ones. The information comes as part of the following slightly gruesome description:

For in fact, along with the relics of Saint Martin as well as those of Saint Hilary, he placed the tooth of Saint Martial to the right of the altar—which none of the benefactors was able to pull out from the jawbone of his holy body, long though they tried. He, after sending forth a prayer, immediately plucked it out. At that same new altar something wondrous happened to take place that very same day of the dedication. A certain small boy, because the crowds were pressing in on him, grabbed the altar cloth from it, so as to hand it to a servant, even though some who were standing around him said that he should not presume to do that. But since he did not refrain from removing it, suddenly he was seized with a violent distress. At first his hands were stripped of their skin, then gradually the whole of his body, so that he was barely able to recover even after six weeks. (3.3)

Even in the midst of this episode that was supposed to be about Gerald's sanctity, then, Ademar's fixation on Saint Martial was allowed to intrude. It is never made clear whether it was Martial's or Gerald's power that was responsible for the terrible deed. Perhaps they are one and the same. The fearsome might wielded by these relics that might harm even a pilgrim betrays Ademar's mounting fascination with saintly vengeance for sinful disbelief.

The New Life of Saint Gerald

While Ademar was rewriting the past in order to buttress Martial's legend, he was also at work reshaping Saint Gerald's memory. His decision to rewrite the *vita* of Gerald may have come first, and it might have been his success there that persuaded him to do the same with Martial. It doesn't seem that Ademar had intended to disguise his earlier works as Odo's, but at some point he decided to rewrite and extend Odo's *vita* and yet still to claim Odo as its author. Possibly the forgery served in Ademar's mind as a kind of vicarious atonement for Odo's doubts about Gerald's holiness. It is worth noting that in his earliest version of his *Chronicon*, written in the mid-1020s, Ademar quoted from Odo's *vita*, but did not name him, yet by the late 1020s he had added a comment about Odo's authorship, and did the same in his *Commemoratio abbatum*, written also in the late 1020s. I consider both mentions as attempts to mask Ademar's own efforts, a smokescreen of sorts, reinforcing Odo's connection to the *vita* after he had composed his own version of it. In that later revision of the *Chronicon*, Ademar even referred to Odo as "most reverent" or "most respectful" (*reverentissimus*), as if making amends for Odo's doubts by writing the *vita* that Odo *should* have written.[30]

Ademar's new preface, supposed to be the words of Odo, reads easily as his own justification for the forgery. "Although I fear presumption by doing it [writing about Saint Gerald], as if exceeding my powers, I fear more stubbornness by not doing it, as if being disobedient. With obedience, truly, and confident in the goodness of Christ, I undertake it, and ask that you might implore the clemency of that same Christ, as much out of love for His servant Gerald, that He might deign so to appraise this account that it not be entirely unworthy of the man who it is supposed to glorify nor be a cause of sin for me" (*Auctoris epistola nuncupatoria*). It is difficult to understand how writing hagiography might be a cause of sin, so one might read in the last remark a tacit admission of the false authorship. I do not believe that this autograph manuscript still exists, but it may have been listed among the monastic library's possessions still in the thirteenth century.[31]

The work was a forgery *tour de force*. Boldly, he even rewrote the preface in which Odo had dedicated the work to Aimon and Turpin. But where Odo had expressed his doubts about Gerald's sanctity, Ademar invented a trajectory for Odo that moved from doubt to an unqualified conviction:

> Many are accustomed to doubt whether the things that are reported about blessed Gerald are true. Some among them believe wholeheartedly that he is not real but imaginary. Others, too, perhaps seeking excuses for their sins, extol him without thinking, saying outright that Gerald was powerful and rich, and lived with pleasures, and is certainly a saint; they doubtless depend on his example to excuse their luxurious life. To them I can and ought to respond even by what little I have seen. For even I, not long ago, having heard the fame of his miracles, nonetheless doubted them, mostly because in those kinds of places you can't imagine what rumors the common folk [*vulgares conventus*] are used to making, only to be ended eventually as worthless things. But when due cause presented itself that I should visit the brotherhood of the monastery at Tulle, it seemed agreeable to make a detour to Gerald's tomb. Then, having summoned four of the men he had raised himself, namely, Hugh, a monk, Hildebert, a priest, Witard, also a priest, and another Hildebert, a noble layman, with a great many others, I inquired about his

morals and the quality of his life, sometimes together, sometimes separately, to see what they would say when alone, or if they would agree with each other in what they said. I investigated zealously, silently measuring whether his life were such that perhaps miracles might be fitting to it. But having ascertained how religiously he had lived, and how God had shown him to be in His grace through many signs, I was now unable to doubt his sanctity. (1.*praef.*)

Here is much more "convincing" evidence about Gerald's true sanctity. Since Ademar was writing over a century after Gerald's death we must consider not only these individuals but also the whole process of investigation as fictitious, let alone the impromptu visit to Aurillac. The passage markedly ends by renouncing any doubts about Gerald's sanctity.

Ademar included the basic narrative that Odo had written about Gerald in his own version of the *vita*. He did separate it into two books, the first focused on Gerald's upbringing and secular life, and the second on Gerald's mounting desire to abandon the world for the monastic life, as well as the miracles that confirmed his saintliness even within his lifetime. Almost never did Ademar quote directly from Odo: in all but the most basic of phrases, Ademar consistently found ways to change Odo's words, even when telling the same tale. Likewise, he frequently shifted passages around, reordering the information given about Gerald's life. Perhaps this virtually complete rewriting was a subtle and hidden admission to his readers that these were not Odo's words in any sense.

Ademar also included an abundance of details not found in Odo's *Vita Geraldi*, not unexpectedly, since he expanded it more than fivefold. He included a detailed description of Gerald's physical appearance (1.12) and of his clothing (1.15), for example, neither of which Odo had really discussed. These additions were clearly intended as lessons for readers or listeners: Gerald was very good looking, according to Ademar, but not puffed up with pride, and he dressed modestly and without ostentation, but not shabbily. Just as Odo had formed his image of Gerald by mirroring the less-than-desirable traits of the noblemen of his day, so Ademar did the same, and his lessons often ended with the obvious contrasts between Gerald's actions and those of other men. Yet there are oddly inexplicable comments found there, too. Gerald was not merely handsome but "had a neck that was so white and one almost presented as the standard for living [or "the model for all necks": *ad normam vivendi decusatum*] that you would with difficulty think you had ever seen another so becoming. . . . His men [*sui*] happily kissed his neck" (1.12). What did that gleaming neck represent? It seems a sign merely of Ademar's idiosyncratic approach to Gerald's legend.[32]

Ademar played with many of the details of Gerald's life throughout the new biography, albeit mostly in minor ways. I mentioned above the small changes to the story of Gerald calling out from his mother's womb. The same takes place in Ademar's description of Gerald's childhood illness. Odo said that Gerald "frequently fell ill" as a child, adding that "when he was already growing into manly toughness, his illness ceased," but left it at that (2). Ademar suggested instead that Gerald was "sick for a very long time—with such feebleness of illness, indeed, that he should be pulled out of secular training but that would not impede his study of learning. For indeed he was suddenly so covered in pimples that for a very long time they did not think that he could ever be healed" (1.4). Note that frequent illness has become lengthy illness: Odo seemed to depict Gerald as having a weakly disposition, whereas Ademar seemed to be describing a bout with some specific ailment (perhaps imagining him as having suffered from smallpox, which was present in Europe throughout the Middle Ages).[33] It shows again how Ademar felt at liberty to rework even minor details in his version of the *Vita Geraldi* and to adapt the memory of Gerald to his own sometimes enigmatic purposes. It is at least conceivable that Ademar was borrowing elements from his own life. Most of the changes were slight, in fact, but they are noteworthy all the same. I also mentioned above Ademar's twists to Odo's tale of Gerald's having been tempted by lust for an unidentified woman during his adolescence. Ademar painted the scenario so much more vividly, and one can easily imagine the distortion of the woman's features as she stood warming herself before the fire in her family's home, Gerald's surprise at the change, and then his shame (1.9). Perhaps here is another incident drawn from Ademar's own life, or perhaps it merely reflects his skill as a storyteller.

Ademar added in many details, but it is impossible to know how accurate they were. He claimed that Aurillac's first monks had been trained at Vabres, for example, although they soon forgot the discipline they had learned there. It is yet another of the disparaging comments made about the monks at Aurillac in the *Vita prolixior*. Vabres had been founded in 862 by the count of Toulouse, only a generation before Aurillac, but there may well have been an early connection between them: two of the signatories on its charter of foundation were named Gerald (here, Garaldus), and it is possible that one of them might have been Gerald of Aurillac. If true, it is easy to see why Odo had not mentioned Vabres, since its monastery was led by a lay abbot, a tradition that Odo tried to undo at Aurillac.[34]

Other details Ademar added in may have been borrowed from contemporary events. The story of Gerald's capture by bandits, told only in Ademar's version (2.17), where these bandits are oddly called Marruci, the name of an ancient Alpine people, seems suspiciously like the stories told of Odo himself, and also of a later abbot of Cluny, Mayeul (Maiolus), both of whom were captured by marauders in the Alps. In the *Vita Odonis* they are called Marrones, and the episode ends with their repentance, as happened with Gerald.[35] It seems that Ademar interpolated an event that had happened instead to Odo in retelling Gerald's life. If the term Marruci was intended to mean Moors, some of whom did become bandits in the Alps, it is unclear whether they were there early enough to have harassed Gerald. The first mention of them is in 921, so the episode may be another anachronism on Ademar's part.[36]

Some of the trivial details Ademar added to the *Vita Geraldi* allowed him to reintroduce the mention of Limoges. He named a certain Madalbert, who had guarded the treasury of the monastery of Saint-Martial that had been sent to Turenne for protection from Viking raiders, and who later became a preacher at Limoges (1.39). Madalbert is described as an informant to the author, which might have been a slip of the tongue, since it implies that the author was at Limoges. No other source provides any more details about this man or helps us to date the transfer of this treasury to Turenne, but Ademar repeated the same information elsewhere.[37]

Throughout his version of the *Vita Geraldi*, Ademar changed not only the wording and arrangement of Odo's version but also even minor facts to suit his ends; he made it clear thereby that he intended to mold Saint Gerald to his own design. Nothing confirms that statement better or brings into brighter light Ademar's broader purposes than his reappraisal of Gerald's violence.

Gerald and Holy Violence

Odo's *Vita brevior* presented Gerald as a role model for laymen of his day, even if he gave Gerald that odd semimonastic lifestyle. Ademar's *Vita prolixior* worked more or less the same trick, albeit in a much more complicated way. As noted above, Gerald's participation in the routine activities of other noblemen provided the bulk of the information by which Ademar extended Odo's account of Gerald's life. Accordingly, in Ademar's retelling Gerald lived much more fully engaged in the violence of the warrior culture in his day—forcing Ademar to a much starker assessment of the relationship between violence and sanctity.

While Gerald was held up as an ideal to laymen in both versions of the *vita*, there is a palpable shift in tone between the two. For Odo, Gerald was a pious individual living the same honorable life to which any other men might aspire. Ademar was convinced, instead, that Gerald's example would never actually be imitated. True, Ademar implied in his preface that Gerald could be a model to others. "This man of God was given to the powerful as an example to them, so that they might see someone like themselves, from their own neighborhood, as it were, and that they might imitate him who is set before them from their own class [*ordo*]" (1.*praef*.). But where Odo was content to point out Gerald's good deeds, Ademar frequently added a comment about the unlikelihood that anyone else would ever act the same way.

Here, we must read Ademar's *Vita Geraldi* through his own ties to what he was writing. Ademar had been born into a military household, but had been dedicated to the monastic life at a young age, probably while still a young child.[38] By the time Ademar reached adulthood, he was leading a much less cloistered life, shuttling back and forth between the monasteries of Angoulême and Limoges. He also acted for a time as a scribe to William the Great, duke of Aquitaine (not to be confused with William the Pious, duke of Aquitaine in Gerald's day), and that brought him into direct contact with the military culture of his day. Ademar's efforts to make sense of secular society are plain enough from his historical chronicle, since much of it recalled the military campaigns and political alliances of the recent past. At the same time, Ademar always remained an outsider. Unlike the regrets that might be said to lie beneath Odo's *vita*, a disdain for military men and martial culture seems to filter through Ademar's.[39]

A few examples will suffice to make audible this hostile tone. Ademar's statements about Gerald's clothing, for instance, provide a clear sense of how Gerald's actions would only be ignored by a wicked world:

> His custom was for clothes of wool or linen, according to ancient
> practice—and not in the style created and adopted now by the sons
> of Belial [that is, sinful men], who are completely without
> restraint—so that his clothes simply covered him, and were neither

redolent of affected pomp nor marked by plebeian rusticity. He took pains not to adorn himself too much in silk or other precious fabrics, not even when observing any sort of feast or in the presence of any sort of marquis. That small belt [*reminiculum*] that often holds a sword he kept fastened around his waist, for twenty years if it was able to last that long, and he was not concerned with either changing or replacing it. What shall I say of the belt or buckle, the entwining girdles, the breastplates for horses [that others sport], seeing that not only did he not wear gold but in fact would also not allow himself to have it? (1.16)

Ademar likely had absolutely no idea what sort of clothes Gerald wore, and he was therefore obliged both to fudge the description—clothing neither too elaborate nor too plain—and also to depict Gerald mostly in contrast to what others wore in the fashions that Ademar thought immoral.

Of greater import were the duties required of Gerald's station. If he had actually been a count, as Ademar wished him to have been, he would have been called upon to hear local judicial cases of the sorts Ademar imagined for him, including capital cases, and to render judgment. Ademar was quite insistent on Gerald's impartial sense of justice:

Access was always free to him for the poor and those who had suffered a wrong, and they were not obliged to bring any small gift [as a bribe] to him for supporting their cause. . . . Nor did he allow it that any lord should take away benefices from his vassal for any sort of conflict [*commotio animi*]. . . . You would think the vigor of his uprightness quite steep in this one thing: he demanded, whenever a poor person should be held liable to a more powerful one, that he should therefore support the weaker of the two, insofar as he might overcome the stronger one without injury. (1.17)

The unspoken contrast with "real" judges is patent: they require gifts to hear cases and mostly ignore unjust seizures by powerful men, perpetuating enmities rather than resolving them. Ademar then provided a series of specific cases to bring his point home. In the first, Gerald repaid from his own money a man unjustly blinded by his soldiers (1.18). In the second, he rewarded a priest blinded by a neighbor's soldiers equally unjustly with a church and income, then also freed one of the offending soldiers when he was captured

(1.19). In the third, he allowed two men condemned to death to go out into the woods by themselves, ostensibly to select the trees from which they would be hanged, but really so that they might escape (1.20). (As Ademar composed these stories he might have had in mind the reputation of Saint Leonard of Noblat, a fifth-century hermit who lived near Limoges and who was remembered especially for freeing prisoners in a very popular *vita* also written at the beginning of the eleventh century. It would have been another way of making Gerald seem the equal of any saint.[40])

Ademar's conclusions about Gerald's judicial decisions are crucial. "Because he was able to judge from the basic qualities of individuals," he wrote, "those persons in cases who had decided to be evil he either restrained with fines or, taking their character into account, he branded them. Those persons, however, who had committed some kind of evil not through habitual malice, so to speak, he sent away untroubled." Ademar tried to picture Gerald as the best possible judge, distinguishing, like God, between the truly good and the truly wicked. Ademar's attempt, though, has forced him to reconcile Gerald's saintliness with the brutality that was inherent in the judicial system of his day. He tried to back away: "Never was it heard, nonetheless, that anyone was punished with death or with the amputation of limbs while he was present" (1.20). Let us think about what Ademar has said: Gerald did order brandings, and his own soldiers sometimes unjustly maimed or killed innocent persons, but Gerald himself did not witness or participate in any mutilations or executions, even if he might have ordered them for habitual criminals, and he tried to make amends whenever his men's aggression got out of hand. Ademar's Gerald was a man deeply implicated in the violence of his times, then, even if he attempted to stay somewhat aloof from it.[41] The ideal of the peaceable warrior was apparently too hard even for Gerald to attain.

Yet it was Gerald's attitude toward violence, more than any other characteristic, that made him a saint in Ademar's eyes. Ademar returned repeatedly and at length to violence in the *Vita prolixior*, especially to blood shed in war, but also to judicial punishments and domestic assault. It reveals an uneasiness that almost certainly arose from Ademar's strained relationship to the military culture around him. It was also a topic he had been mulling over for some time: more than a decade earlier he had copied out and illustrated Prudentius' *Psychomachia*, a lengthy poem that describes the personified virtues in graphic and singlehanded combat with the vices. Maybe it was this ancient poem that had first raised in his mind the possibility of violence in the service of good. He kept this manuscript with him until the end of his life.[42]

Ademar first introduced the topic of violence by modifying Odo's comments about Gerald's commanding his retainers to fight without using the points of their spears or lances. Odo had written "with their spears turned around [*aversis hastis*]" and thus implied that these weapons should be turned backwards so as to prod rather than to pierce the enemy (3). Odo had said nothing about swords, though, so presumably Gerald's men might still have used them. Yet Ademar seems either to have misunderstood or to have purposely altered these words, having Gerald order his men to put away their swords and fight only with their lances, and these apparently were to be used in the conventional ways: "with the points of their swords held back, they should fight holding their spears in front of them [*mucronibus gladiorum retro actis, hastas inantea dirigentes pugnarent*]" (1.8). Perhaps even Ademar thought it peculiar, because he hastened to add that "this would have been ridiculous to his enemies if Gerald had not been strengthened by divine power so that he was thereafter irresistible to those same enemies" (1.8; Odo had also mentioned the invulnerability but not the ridiculousness). The overall result was to provide yet another aspect of the impractical ideal that Gerald represented.[43]

Unlike Odo, however, Ademar was not content to leave Gerald's attitude toward bloodshed articulated in such brief and unsophisticated terms. He described at length how warring against the wicked might be warranted and how Gerald had managed to maintain his "piety even in the midst of fighting [*pietas in ipso praeliandi articulo*]." He began by saying that Gerald always offered "peace and the easiest reconciliation to his enemies," and that sometimes such diplomatic concessions were effective. Then he suggested that if Gerald felt obliged to take up arms against the obstinately wicked, he was not "as is the custom with many, aroused by any lust or seduced by a love of vulgar praise" for his military exploits, but rather "inflamed by love of the poor, who were unable to defend themselves." "No one should be disturbed at all that a just man ever made use of fighting," Ademar continued, "which seems to be incompatible with religion. No one whatsoever who will have considered the case with a fair set of scales will esteem the glory of Gerald to be obscured in this point at all." Ademar named some of the many biblical holy men who had fought in wars, including Abraham and David, and added that Gerald only fought to defend his own or another's property from unjust seizure rather than to invade others' property, and that he never used deceit or ambushes when fighting but always fought openly. Even then, Ademar felt that he had not said enough: "It does not therefore obscure his glory that he fought for the cause of God," since—and this point seems to have been Ademar's trump card—"he never stained his sword, as I said above, with human blood" (1.8).[44]

So detailed was this rationalization of violence in a just cause and so strained were some of the biblical references that they provoke the suspicion that Ademar was wrestling mightily with these notions himself. Later, Ademar noted an incident when Gerald's soldiers, fighting with Duke William's forces, were prevented from plundering the district in which they fought by Gerald's command, although William's forces did pillage, so much so that the local inhabitants fled (1.33). Obviously, Gerald had no authority to command William's troops, and the despoiling of peasants either to supply one's own forces or to weaken those of one's enemies was a tried and true stratagem in war. Still, Gerald's presence alongside these men in their theft reflects an acquiescence of sorts to the realities of unjust aggression. Even a saint could not avoid the brutality of his day, Ademar seemed to confess by including episodes such as this one.

There is more going on behind the scenes here than a commentary on Gerald's sanctity. Ademar was deeply moved by efforts going on in his day to limit the endemic violence caused by fighting men. Amid the collapsing state structures in the post-Carolingian era, local landowners and warlords competed with each other for greater wealth and status, and peasant populations and churchmen often fell victim to their predations. What modern scholars call the Peace of God assemblies began in the late tenth century as public demonstrations against such aggression, and leaders of the local churches issued decrees forbidding certain types of outrageous violence, especially when committed against the unarmed. Ralph Glaber, writing in the early eleventh century, described it thus: "It was then that the bishops and abbots and other devout men of Aquitaine first summoned great councils of the whole people, to which were borne the bodies of many saints and innumerable caskets of holy relics. The movement spread to Arles and Lyon, then across all Burgundy into the furthest corners of the French realm. Throughout the dioceses it was decreed that in fixed places the bishops and magnates of the entire country should convene councils for reestablishing peace."[45]

This description notwithstanding, the precise role of laymen in the Peace of God is disputed. The records of the assemblies reveal an obvious concern for ecclesiastical rights and respect for churchmen and church property, including the peasants who farmed that property, the most at risk and least capable of self-defense.[46] Accordingly, scholars have traditionally seen noblemen more as targets of the assemblies and as the violent predators against whom the movement was orchestrated. Churchmen may have also exploited laymen's fears about the approaching end of the world at the millennium so as to bind them to the decrees.[47] Or it is possible that the threat of excommunication itself played a sufficient role in coercing noblemen into accepting the Peace decrees without needing to hold to any widespread belief in the end of the world, if laymen were pious enough to be concerned about that threat.[48] More recently, scholars have proposed a more instrumental role for laymen in the assemblies even while they differ in explaining that role. The Peace of God might have been just another facet to the continually shifting political alliances and negotiations for power between the territorial magnates and local lords, including the church officials who were often from the same families.[49] For example, one of the earliest leaders of the Peace movement, Guy II, bishop of Le Puy, might have been inspired by secular attempts to preserve the peace, including those made by his family, who were counts of Anjou.[50] The assemblies that took place under Duke William the Great in Ademar's day might well have been intended to counter the abuses that his viscounts and castellans had committed, since it was as much in his interest as that of the churchmen to preserve the general peace.[51] Indeed, great magnates like William might simply have seen themselves as following the Carolingian political tradition of supporting the church even while maintaining control over it.[52] The assemblies, then, might well be linked to the declining royal presence in the southernmost regions of the realm.[53] Or perhaps the Peace movement functioned more as an alliance between church officials and local lords against the great magnates.[54]

Whatever the complex motivations for these assemblies, devotion to the saints formed a chief ingredient in the mix: peasants and monks asked for the protection of God and the saints, and noblemen willing to agree to the principles of the Peace of God swore oaths on the relics of saints brought to the meetings to lend gravity and divine favor to their decrees.[55] Richard Landes has referred colorfully to the Peace assemblies as "relic jamboree[s]."[56] The early assemblies in Auvergne showed the same pious uses of the cult of saints. Saint Gerald's relics were brought out of his shrine, for example, for an assembly near Aurillac in 972, one of the earliest recorded, and a meeting presided over by the same Bishop Stephen of Clermont who was there for the consecration of the new church at Aurillac. It both strengthened devotion to Saint Gerald even as it confirmed the monastery's position within the local community.[57]

Ademar of Chabannes was undeniably fascinated by the Peace of God. He is also a vital source for reconstructing its history, since he provided detailed descriptions of the assemblies that took place in Aquitaine in his day. Unfortunately, his reliability has been called into question. Ademar might have altered the record of the Peace council held in Limoges in 1031 in his desire to show widespread ecclesiastical support for the apostolicity of Saint Martial.[58] He might even have invented a Peace assembly held in 1021 out of nothing, placing various notable participants on the scene as well as forging decrees that had supposedly been issued from the assembly.[59] His trustworthiness aside, Ademar's enthusiasm for the Peace of God cannot be disputed. And for Ademar, at least, worries about the approaching end of time seem to have prompted his zeal. The Peace offered hope to the people of the world that they might abandon their wickedness as the year 1033 approached: the millennial anniversary of Jesus' death, but also the year in which Ademar left on a pilgrimage to Jerusalem and disappeared from the historical record.[60]

As noted above, the language and ideas contained in Ademar's *Vita prolixior* bear striking similarities to those of these Peace of God assemblies. Ademar, it would seem, wanted to make of Gerald an adherent to the principles of the Peace of God *avant la lettre*.[61] Perhaps Gerald's participation in some forms of violence while avoiding others, then, reflected Ademar's sense that the Peace of God did not so much attempt to eliminate violence as to limit it to more legitimate arenas like warfare or the administration of justice. If so, then Ademar's repeated disparaging of other noblemen who would never act like Gerald may have been a reluctant admission that peace could not really happen in the cruel times in which he lived.

Still, Ademar's commitment to the principles of the Peace of God can be seen in the stories he added to Odo's *vita* about Gerald's concern for peasants. Odo had rarely mentioned the lower classes. He did say that Gerald gave alms to the poor, and that he set up benches for them in his dining hall where he might see for himself that they were given something to eat (6). Twice Odo referred to assaults against peasants, but only in a phrase, and in the first instance together with attacks on property (3 and 5). That was all. In addition to extending Odo's remarks about Gerald's love for the poor to a much greater length, though (1.14, 1.15, and 1.17), Ademar also included several pointed episodes that demonstrated the extent of Gerald's beneficence toward peasants. In one, Gerald gave money to a countrywoman whose husband was too ill to plow so that she could hire a laborer (1.21).[62] In another, he made sure that the chickpeas his soldiers had taken from a peasant had been given freely (1.22). In yet another, he compensated a peasant for damage done to a cherry tree by his men (1.23). It is worth noting that the second and third of these stories depict the abuses of power made possible by the inequalities in medieval society and reveal a sensitivity to a violence that goes beyond physical brutality.

Ademar's fantasies about a peaceful society only made more obvious his distaste for the violent behavior that was so commonplace among the martial classes. I mentioned above his inclusion of a number of stories involving a Count Ademar and his brother Adelhelm. If we supplement what the *Vita prolixior* says with what Ademar wrote in his *Chronicon*, we can see a power struggle happening between William the Pious, count of Auvergne and duke of Aquitaine, and Ademar, count of Poitiers, intended to force Gerald's subordination to one man or the other. According to the *Vita Geraldi*, William accepted Gerald's refusal, but Ademar did not. None of these details are in Odo's version of the *vita*; again, Ademar of Chabannes seems to have had some independent knowledge about Gerald. Since several of the stories about these brothers happen in and around a castle of Aurillac that probably did not exist in Gerald's day, they were likely more of Ademar's inventions. It is also intriguing that while Count Ademar entered and left the *Vita prolixior* confirmed in his wickedness, his brother Adelhelm both times repented his evil deeds. Was Ademar making a subtle point about the greater goodness of second sons? (We don't know if Ademar had an elder brother who inherited the family title and lands; if he did, he didn't mention him.[63])

One further episode within Gerald's own household describes a different sort of violence to which noblemen were tempted. It is Ademar's elaboration of the comment that Odo had made when he had described Gerald's reluctance to use his wash water to heal the sick. Odo had said there that Gerald "threatened menacingly [*minaciter*] that no one should presume to give it to anyone at all," adding immediately: "But this threat was not able to be kept" (10). In Ademar's telling, the threat is made much more ominous. After a blacksmith was healed by Gerald's wash water given in secret,

> Gerald, upset at the unaccustomed thing, said that it had not happened by his merit but by the faith of those who had given that water to the blacksmith. And since he was not able to find out who

had given it to him, because it had been zealously hidden from him, he was aroused to a vehement threat, lest anyone should presume ever thereafter to do such a thing, maintaining that if it were a slave who were to do it, he would have a member [*membrum*, probably a hand] cut off; if he were free, though, afterward he would not be. (2.11)

There is nothing in Ademar's text to suggest that Gerald ever carried out these threats, but in some ways the damage had already been done, and the violence that Gerald tried to keep at bay in his public life resurfaced in his private life. In the very next episode, Ademar returned to the theme, telling of a blind woman who was given sight through Gerald's wash water: "For his men were not able to treat lightly the mutilation that he had threatened about this sort of thing only a short while earlier, knowing that he would not give way without punishing if he were to catch the one who gave it away" (2.12).

If Ademar seemed caught up in this vision of a violent saint, he backed away from it in the episode immediately following. A servant once again used Gerald's wash water to heal a blind woman: "When it became evident to him who had given the water, a man by the name of Radbald, he inquired vigorously, and as soon as Gerald found out the truth . . ."—did the reader or listener hold his breath at this point to see what would happen?—"he immediately cast him out." It was not the promised punishment, but one harsh enough. Later, after a dressing down by a friend, he took the man back into his service (2.13). Gerald's bark, it turned out, was much worse than his bite. The secret use of Gerald's wash water continued, mentioned in four more episodes, but without these threats (2.20, 2.23, 2.24, and 2.33). It seems odd for Ademar to have added such dreadful detail to Odo's simple threat, and to have returned to it twice again only to ignore it.

How much did Ademar compromise his image of Saint Gerald, though, when he had him threaten violence against his servants, who were, after all, acting against Gerald's wishes only for the good of others and in the service of God? Gerald's threats, a man in power intimidating his underlings, are not all that different from the plundering of peasants by armies or the individual bullying by fighting men. It is at these moments of internal contradiction that Ademar is most revealing. And if the Gerald of this first book of his new *vita* offered an impractical saint more likely to be ignored than emulated, the Gerald of his second book provides an even more unsuitable model for behavior.

The Proof of Sanctity

At first glance, the second part of Ademar's *vita* seems familiar enough. Like Odo, Ademar suggested that Gerald had confessed his desire to become a monk. A bishop had recommended instead that Gerald remain in the world, but to tonsure himself secretly and to follow a monastic discipline privately, and also to bequeath his lands to Saint Peter and to the monastery he intended to found (2.2–3). In this recounting, Ademar was simply following Odo's lead. As in the first book, though, Ademar added details not found in Odo's account: for example, that Satan, furious at Gerald's plan, caused the first monastery church to collapse, requiring rebuilding from the ground up (2.4–5).[64]

Odo suppressed some of his doubts about Gerald's sanctity by creating a semimonastic lifestyle for him. This was a much thornier matter for Ademar. Appearing in increasing numbers at the turn of the eleventh century were groups of Christians who rejected the monastic life even while they lived as monks, renouncing sex, violence, and wealth. Ademar himself wrote about these individuals, condemning them as heretics.[65] Gerald's lifestyle might have appeared in a much different light to those living in Ademar's day, even as part of a broader challenge to the Christian accommodation to medieval society by groups who renounced any sort of engagement with the life of this world. Ademar had to walk a fine line between encouraging devotion to Saint Gerald and promoting theological error. To put it more bluntly: if in some ways Saint Gerald *would* not be imitated by men, in other ways he *should* not be imitated.

Ademar found himself in an uncomfortable place. He wanted to praise Gerald's choice of celibacy as a layman, for instance, without making it seem obligatory for laymen. So it is interesting to note that Gerald's avoidance of *illicit* sex—his refusal to go through with his adolescent desire to have sex with a serf—is described in memorable detail, while Gerald's refusal to engage in *licit* sex—his rejection of marriage to Duke William's sister—is barely noted, attributed only to a "love of chastity [*castitatis amor*]" (1.34). And even while Ademar presented Gerald as willing to give all of his money away and spend the rest of his life begging, if he could only find suitable monks (2.8), he also reminded his readers that Gerald remained wealthy, even while he discounted that wealth as unimportant because Gerald was "poor in spirit" (2.*praef.*). The need to distance Gerald from the possibility of heresy also helps to explain Ademar's detailed justifications for the saint's

attitude toward warfare and judicial punishment. At one point Ademar
attempted to dismiss the danger: a layman who kept to monastic discipline
was much better than a monk who lived a worldly life (2.16). Yet its peril
remained. These heretical possibilities may have prompted Ademar to
emphasize Gerald's miracle-working abilities much more than Odo had.

Ademar ended the second book of his *vita* by returning at length to the
doubts about Gerald's sanctity that Odo had raised. "Let this suffice for his
miracles," Ademar wrote, "which should satisfy those who measure the glory
of any saint not from the quantity of good works but from the abundance of
miracles." He criticized those who required such miracles to believe, insisting
that "to those who are held piously in his love and who venerate him with a
discerning devotion, the works of justice that he engaged in will be more
pleasing" (2.34). Still, Ademar could not help but poke at the sore, repeating
Odo's doubts even if only to dismiss them. After telling the story of a fish
that allowed itself to be caught to feed Gerald and his men, he concluded
that "perhaps someone might suggest that something like that might happen
by chance. I believe, however, that any such person could not recall having
seen a fish in so wide a river as is the Aveyron ever suddenly jump out on top
of people in such a way" (2.29). Likewise, he condemned those who did not
believe in Gerald's sanctity only because he had not predicted the future: "if
by chance he had had the spirit of prophecy, I think no one would have
denied that he was a saint" (2.34).

Precisely the same type of remark about disbelief in Gerald's sainthood
began this second book of the *Vita prolixior*. "Those who thoughtlessly dispute Gerald's merits might be satisfied if they consider and inspect the quality
of his life. For, almost as if sitting in some sort of tribunal, they pass judgment
about whether he should be a saint or not, when it should fall under divine
judgment, according to which even by the reprobate miracles are commonly
done that are useful to good persons. Therefore let the testimony of the miracles suffice to them, which Christ deigned to be worked by him while he lived
and after his death" (2 *praef.*). It was not much of a recommendation of
Gerald's sanctity to say that "even by the reprobate miracles are commonly
done." Yet Ademar tried repeatedly to undo the damage that Odo had done.
So even as Ademar reiterated Odo's opinion that Gerald was a good person,
adding that many called him "Gerald the Good [*Geraldus ille bonus*]" (1.33),
Ademar demanded again and again that Gerald be regarded as much more
than that. I think we are seeing here the Ademar who has become familiar
through the controversy over the apostolicity of Saint Martial: determined at

all costs to persuade others to accept what he himself so deeply believed. The aggressive rhetorical stance adopted by Ademar when belittling those who doubted Saint Martial's apostolic status is also visible here.[66]

Ademar's harsh dismissal of those who refused to believe in Gerald's saintliness may have been directed more broadly than at Odo alone. There may have been continued skepticism about the value of devotion to Saint Gerald in Aurillac, or Limoges, or elsewhere, and Ademar may have felt it necessary to respond to contemporary as well as past disbelief. Maybe that continued disbelief stemmed from Gerald's acquiescence to violence or from the suspicious resemblances between his lifestyle and those of heretics. The good deeds that Gerald performed during his life and virtues he exhibited should have been enough to satisfy any doubters, Ademar insisted, but it was clearly not, nor apparently were the numbers or types of miracles enough to convince these persons of Gerald's holiness.

Ongoing doubts about Gerald's sanctity may also help to explain the elements he seems to have added to his earlier writings when he turned them into books 3 and 4 of his expanded *vita*. To the *Transitus* he added Gerald's prediction, taken from the *Vita brevior*, about the future need to expand the church at Aurillac, which Ademar said specifically had come from divine foreknowledge (3.1), but which thus contradicted Ademar's statement at the end of book 2 that Gerald lacked the gift of prophecy (2.34). He also added a story of Gerald's corpse being prepared for burial, and covering itself rather than being seen naked even by those who were washing it (3.10; with echoes of Gerald's unwillingness to be seen naked even by his servants while alive, 1.34). And to the *Miracula*, as described above, he added the stories of those who were punished for ignoring Gerald's sanctity (4.10).[67]

Ademar's Gerald is a saint who is a bundle of contradictions. He is the model warrior without much practical value as an example to others. He should be revered for his everyday virtues and simple good works but performed the oddest of miracles. He was a reluctant participant in violence who threatened those who aided the cause of his saintliness in life as well as those who refused to accept it after death. These contradictions let slip how Ademar used Gerald, not only to enhance the reputation of a man about whom there seemed still to have been much disbelief but also to project onto the saint his worries about military violence and the dangers of heresy, and his hopes about monastic life and the pursuit of personal holiness. Ademar crafted a complicated personality for Gerald, and then left his creation to those who came after him.

CHAPTER 4

Saint Gerald and the Swell of History

Odo and Ademar both struggled to define Saint Gerald's memory in crucial if fundamentally contrary ways. Even if hagiographers initiated a saint's reputation, though, only the response of the devout could sustain it over time. What can be pieced together of the history of devotion to Saint Gerald demonstrates the varied means by which his saintly standing was enhanced. These efforts, almost lost to time, were neither random nor mechanical, but served real and practical goals and provide a unique glimpse into how a saint was kept alive. Within the first centuries that followed his death, that is, from the eleventh to the thirteenth centuries, these efforts had striking results, and Gerald was a thriving saint, well known and greatly revered across the south of France and beyond.

The Spread of Devotion

Odo noticed the affection of peasants for Saint Gerald just a few years after the man's death, although he seemed disdainful, suggesting that the sort of devotion they offered was "a useless thing" (*res vana, prol.*). He might have wished to discourage the more unusual forms of reverence—maybe even the sort of folk veneration of Gerald's dining table or his mounting block that Ademar later publicized. Yet his very act of writing about Saint Gerald inaugurated a more formalized commemoration. Copies of his short *vita* he likely sent to the men to whom he had dedicated his work, at Limoges and Tulle, probably leaving the original at Aurillac, but knowledge about Gerald may not have traveled much farther at first. Ademar's writings about Gerald provided a much firmer foundation for widespread devotion to Gerald in elaborating Gerald's kindnesses to peasants, criminals, and others in need of help of the very kind that might offer models for that devotion, in publicizing the posthumous miracles happening at Aurillac, Limoges, and elsewhere, and in offering the means by which to celebrate Gerald's sanctity through a sermon.

The monks at Aurillac, the guardians of Saint Gerald's shrine, championed his cult throughout the Middle Ages. He remained for them a most "sacred commodity," in Patrick Geary's words.[1] I mentioned above how vital the public recognition of the cult of a saint was for the viability of monasteries in the Middle Ages, so the monks of Aurillac had the most at stake in the growth of devotion to Saint Gerald. The monks at Aurillac were also Gerald's chief devotees—they were the ones who had dedicated their own lives to him or been offered to him—and they also experienced firsthand the veneration of pilgrims. They wrote down what was most memorable: one of Gerald's seventeenth-century biographers mentioned that he had heard about a "large, handwritten volume [*gros volume escrit à la main*]" full of posthumous miracles attributed to Gerald that the monks had compiled but that had been destroyed in 1567.[2]

Little is left now of the earliest history of the monastery of Aurillac. The brief chronicle of the abbots of Aurillac, composed in the early twelfth century, provides only a few indications of the appeal of its patron saint.[3] Nonetheless, the chronicle demonstrates that already in the tenth century knowledge and veneration of Saint Gerald was beginning to radiate outward. Nothing identifies the first abbot listed there, Adelgarius, but the second abbot, a man named John, is said to have been related to Gerald, suggesting not only family control of the monastery, as noted above, but also that devotion might have remained largely within Gerald's family in these first decades. The third abbot named there was Odo of Cluny. And even while the fifth, seventh, and eighth abbots came from castles or villages close to Aurillac, the fourth abbot had been a monk of Conques and was said to have been from a noble family of Rouergue; the sixth and tenth abbots were from Quercy; the ninth came from near Toulouse; and the eleventh came from near Le Puy.[4] The fact that four of these early abbots were named Gerald is itself suggestive of the blossoming reputation of the saint. Perhaps they were also individuals dedicated at birth to the saint and given over by their families to the monastery at Aurillac.

Other minor sources, albeit questionable in their reliability, hint at a similar increase. According to the foundational charter of the monastery of Saint-Pons-de-Thomières, monks from Aurillac were brought there in about 937 (within a decade of Odo of Cluny's reforms) by Raymond-Pons or Raymond III, count of Toulouse, in order to instruct the monks of the monastery he had just founded. Élizabeth Magnou-Nortier describes this foundation charter as being of doubtful authenticity because of its claims about papal privilege; still, she does not doubt that monks from Aurillac were correctly remembered as having participated in the founding of the monastery.[5] (Since Raymond-Pons was attempting to assert himself as count of Auvergne despite the competing claims of the Guillemite house of Poitou, linking Aurillac and Saint-Pons-de-Thomières may well have had a deeper political purpose.) If the recollection is true, not only had Odo's mission of reform achieved success, but the numbers of monks at Aurillac within a decade of Odo's time there were also sufficient to lend some to another house. The event also hints at what might have been the origin of devotion to Saint Gerald that continues to this day in this part of France.[6]

In the tenth and eleventh centuries, the fortunes of the monastery at Aurillac were unmistakably on the rise, and Saint Gerald along with it. Probably the most famous of the early monks was Gerbert, who was born somewhere in Aquitaine and given as a boy to the monastery perhaps around 960. He remained there only until 967, when he left to study in Barcelona (and perhaps elsewhere in the Iberian peninsula), after which he was appointed tutor to the future emperor Otto II, then elevated to become archbishop of Rheims, archbishop of Ravenna, and finally pope: he took the name Sylvester II, and died in 1003. He continued to correspond with the abbots of Aurillac throughout his career.[7] Individuals such as Gerbert helped to raise the profile of the monastery. Others did the same in lesser ways. The seventh abbot was said to have had "a very rich mother" who gave much gold and silver to the monastery; he also accepted the donation of a fine crystal chalice from the countess of Narbonne.[8] Donations likely came from the Malemort, Laron, and Lastours noble families, too, all of whom claimed kinship with Gerald.[9]

We see the effects of Gerald's flowering reputation in the expansion of the church at Aurillac. It was the fourth abbot, he who followed after Odo of Cluny, who began the enlargement of the monastery's church, but it was his successor who saw it completed.[10] As described above, in 972 it was consecrated by Stephen, the bishop of Clermont, amid a flurry of new miracles attributed to Saint Gerald. Nothing now remains of the original church that

Figure 3. Vestiges of the late tenth-century church in the south transept. Church of Saint-Géraud, Aurillac. Courtesy of Pierre Moulier.

Gerald had built, but part of one wall survives from this second church (see fig. 3).[11] While the enlargement of the church might not offer direct evidence of the growing popularity of Saint Gerald, it does indicate that the monastery enjoyed a considerable endowment already in the middle of the tenth century.

One even wonders whether the enlargement of the church formed the next logical step in the making of Gerald's saintly reputation. Rebuilding of churches went hand in hand with surging devotion as growing numbers of pilgrims might no longer be easily accommodated in older and smaller churches, or as churchmen encouraged pilgrimages with increasingly impressive churches.[12] The new enthusiasm for pilgrimage in tenth-century Auvergne is clear. In the middle of the century, the bishop of Le Puy (Gottschalk, who may have been a former monk of Aurillac) led the first recorded group of French pilgrims to Santiago de Compostela and back.[13] The pilgrimages to Compostela would prove to be one of the most enduring of medieval pilgrimages, and the routes that took shape through southern France allowed pilgrims to pay their respects to many saints along the way there and back. We have only a few clues about Aurillac's participation in these pilgrimages.

A pilgrims' song in the Occitan language of southern France, regrettably undatable, suggests some local appeal. It begins: "We are pilgrims from this town called Aurillac, close to the Jordanne. We have left our poor children and dear wives and our parents to go in a great throng to Saint James of Compostela . . . from our little street and house near to the monastery of Saint Gerald." The song continues with brief but colorful comments about each stop along the way. In one place they cry out: "The Auvergnats are for Gerald and for the abbot!"[14] None of the main routes of the *camino de Santiago* traversed Aurillac, although its monks doubtless tried to steer pilgrims to the shrine of Saint Gerald, but pilgrims sometimes snaked their way arduously through the mountainous interior of France. The shrine of Sainte Foy at Conques that lay along the *via Podiensis*, one of the main pilgrimage routes, welcomed throngs of pilgrims on their return home from Compostela for her feast day on October 6, and some of them might have been persuaded to make the difficult journey north from there to the shrine of Saint Gerald at Aurillac for his feast day on October 13, and then east to the shrine of Saint Theofrid at Saint-Chaffre, whose feast day was October 19, before joining up with the main pilgrimage route again at Le Puy. Pilgrims might also have visited Aurillac at other times of year, in conjunction with the Marian shrines at Clermont and Le Puy, and also at Orcival and Rocamadour, or the shrines of Saint Robert at La Chaise-Dieu and Saint Julian at Brioude.[15]

We have no real indications of the numbers of pilgrims that visited Aurillac; we hear only of the distinguished ones. Gerbert noted in one of his letters that the count of Barcelona had visited the shrine of Saint Gerald in 967 when he came to marry a daughter of the count of Rodez (and when he took Gerbert back with him).[16] The French king Robert II (the Pious, ruled 996–1031) visited Aurillac as well as a dozen other shrines across the south in the winter of 1019–1020.[17] The *Breve chronicon* claims that a Leo, who had been bishop of Gaeta (midway between Rome and Naples), retired to Aurillac and died there. If true, it happened after 1064 and hints at a more widespread devotion to the saint in the eleventh century.[18] Pope Urban II also stopped at Aurillac as he traveled through the south of France in 1095.[19] How many others came without attracting attention is unknowable. In the twelfth century, a hospice was built to accommodate pilgrims to Saint Gerald's shrine; it survives, though greatly altered over the centuries, and its medieval entrance is still visible (see fig. 4).[20] (It is the only building that survives of the medieval monastic complex.[21] In front of it is a sizeable fountain probably also from the twelfth century.[22] Otherwise only a few fragmentary bits of

Figure 4. The hospice for pilgrims and, in front of it, a fountain, opposite the church of Saint-Géraud, Aurillac. Both probably date from the twelfth century, although the building has undergone later changes. Courtesy of Brian Giguere.

medieval sculpture remain, so it is difficult to get a sense of the monastery's wealth or patronage from the material evidence.[23])

Saint Gerald and Sainte Foy

Given the paucity of evidence remaining from medieval Aurillac, perhaps the best opportunity for imagining the shape of local devotion comes instead from the eleventh-century cult of Sainte Foy at Conques.[24] The proximity of Foy's and Gerald's cults in time and space makes it useful to compare the two. Abundant among the miracles attributed to Sainte Foy are healings from a variety of illnesses, often blindness, as with Gerald. Time and again an individual wishing to be healed was required to present him- or herself at the shrine of the saint, as with Gerald. Like Gerald, Foy occasionally appeared before persons in visions intended either to command or chastise. The nobility of Foy's ancestry was emphasized, a nobility made more noble by the purity of her virginity, and the beauty of her person was noted, outdone only by the beauty of her mind—all characteristics she also shared with Gerald.

The writings about Sainte Foy may disclose aspects of the medieval cult of Saint Gerald otherwise forgotten. Foy's repeated demands for donations, especially for jewelry, form a recurring part of the pattern of her miracles not found in the writings about Gerald, but a practice that the monks of Aurillac may also have recommended to pilgrims (although Foy's demands were often explained as the whims of a woman).[25] Foy also frequently played what her biographer called "jokes [*joca*]" on her devotees. (In one of the oddest episodes, Foy appeared to a knight afflicted with a malady of the scrotum and instructed him to go to a blacksmith and "put the part of you that is suffering on his anvil and tell him to strike his most powerful blow."[26] At the last moment, the knight withdrew from the approaching blow, but was healed. One miracle attributed to Gerald might be considered a similar sort of "joke": the priest who had obtained a relic of Saint Gerald and wore it around his neck to keep it safe found that he was stricken with constipation until he removed the relic from his person (*Miracula addita*, 16). Amy Remensnyder believes that Foy's jokes provide evidence for an illiterate and lay religiosity that both complemented and challenged the elite, literate, clerical culture, and this doubtless also held true for Saint Gerald's cult.[27] In the central Middle Ages devotion to Saints Gerald and Foy might well have complemented each other: the same pairing implied in the vision of Stephen, the bishop of Clermont, who saw both together in his dream (*Miracula addita*, 2). Still today in Auvergnat churches, statues of the two saints can often be found side by side.

There exists another even more noteworthy connection between the two that was also mediated through this bishop. He is said to have arranged for the sculpting of a statue of the Virgin Mary holding the infant Jesus, seated on a throne in the form called *maiestas* ("majesty"), for the cathedral he consecrated at Clermont in 946. It no longer survives. It seems more than coincidental that this same Stephen was also abbot of Conques when its monks decided to craft a statue of their own saint—and depict her also as seated on a golden throne. We don't know exactly when the statue of Sainte Foy was put together, but it was likely around 983. This statue still survives in place at Conques, studded with the jewels given to her by centuries of pilgrims (see fig. 5).[28]

Either or both of these statues may have inspired the monks of Aurillac to fashion their own sculpted image of Saint Gerald. It no longer exists, but

Figure 5. Reliquary statue of Sainte Foy, probably from the late tenth century, Conques (*département* of Aveyron). Courtesy of the Office du Tourisme, Conques.

we can imagine it was much like the statue of Sainte Foy. We don't know at what date Saint Gerald's statue was built, but its fabrication would seem to fit well with the expansion of devotion to him at the time of the reconsecration of his church in 972. If so, it might have been made before the statue of Sainte Foy. The *Breve chronicon* tells us that it was the seventh abbot of Aurillac who ordered it to be made, of gold, but since that chronicle includes almost no dates, its construction might have happened closer to the end of the tenth century.[29] The principal clue as to the form of the statue of Saint Gerald comes from the miracles of Sainte Foy. Bernard of Angers, who wrote between 1013 and 1020, had visited Aurillac some years earlier and had seen the statue of Saint Gerald. He described it in evocative terms as "gloriously fashioned out of the purest gold and the most precious stones, . . . an image made with such precision to the face of the human form that it seemed to see with its attentive, observant gaze the great many peasants seeing it and to gently grant with its reflecting eyes the prayers of those praying before it."[30] But he provided no other details.

This statue was most likely also in the *maiestas* pose. Impressions from the seal of the abbot of Aurillac, found on the handful of documents that survive from the medieval monastery, the earliest from 1347, shows Gerald seated on a throne, holding a palm frond in his right hand and a sword in his left, and might approximate the appearance of his statue (see fig. 6). Gerald's attributes are difficult to understand: the sword probably depicts his noble status, but seems to ignore his reluctance to engage in warfare. The palm branch is usually shown only with martyrs, but may have been intended to reflect Gerald's status as confessor. Gerald is also depicted as bearded, despite the pointed testimony of his medieval biographers, and at his feet is a scallop shell that represents the pilgrimage to Santiago de Compostela, apparently only because Aurillac had become a stop for some along this route. The late date of the seal's earliest use and the possibility that Gerald's statue may have been destroyed in 1233 make it impossible to do more than conjecture about any resemblance between this seal and the sculpted image of the saint.[31]

Gerald's statue must have been in existence when Ademar wrote about Gerald in the 1020s, yet at no point did he mention it. The *Transitus* says that immediately following Gerald's death his body "was placed in a stone monument [*aristonem lapidem*] to the left of his church" (3.11). In the *Miracula*, pilgrims are said to visit what is variously described as his sepulcher (*sepulcrum*, 4.3 and 4.12), crypt (*crypta*, 4.4), sarcophagus (*sarcophagus*, 4.6),

Figure 6. Drawing of the imprint
of the seal of the abbot of Aurillac,
from a document of 1347. Courtesy of
Pascale Moulier.

and tomb (*tumulum*, 4.9). Nor was Gerald's statue mentioned in the additional miracle stories; there the remains of Gerald are noted as having been
ceremoniously placed "under an urn in the crypt [*sub urna mausoli*]" in the
new church, and elsewhere, his tomb is again named (*sepulcrum*, 16, and
tumulum, 17, and even called *glaeba*, "a mound of dirt").[32]

Perhaps Ademar's silence reflects his discomfort with the image rather
than his ignorance of it. Bernard of Angers recounted that when he first saw
the statue of Saint Gerald, he took great offense at the idea of a Christian
saint venerated by means of a statue, saying that it smacked of the pagan
worship of idols. He also recorded the even stronger objection of a layman
with whom he spoke about it, a soldier who regarded such a statue as "a

demon that should be ridiculed and spat upon."[33] Ademar may have felt the
same. It is also possible that Ademar's silence may simply mean that Gerald's
image was not also a reliquary, as was Sainte Foy's, and that Ademar's focus
remained on the relics where Gerald's saintly power really lay.[34] In two of the
additional miracle stories he did mention Gerald's relics as having been carried about the region on a litter (*feretrum*, 13 and 14), implying that they were
occasionally taken out of his sarcophagus. Sainte Foy's relics were exhibited
in similar processions, within her sculpted image, but again there is no mention of any representation of Gerald. The only possible allusion to this statue
in Ademar's writings happens when he described Bishop Stephen's vision of
Saint Gerald, who is said to have been "dressed in a resplendent outfit, raising
one hand and holding in the other a staff [*virga*]" (2). There is nothing to
suggest that this was the look of the statue of Gerald, but the staff as a symbol
of Gerald's earthly authority remained a common attribute in later depictions
of the saint. (In one of the miracles of Sainte Foy, by way of comparison, a
man saw her in a vision specifically as she appeared in her statue, legitimizing
the vision and the image.[35]) Of Gerald's sarcophagus perhaps nothing
remains.[36]

Statues of the saints became so ubiquitous in the later Middle Ages and
afterward that it is difficult to imagine them as controversial, yet they were
still novel and often suspiciously regarded around the year 1000. Ilene Forsyth and Barbara Drake Boehm have described these new artistic developments in considerable detail, and both have pointed to the precocity of
central France in this regard.[37] In addition to the statues of Saint Gerald,
Sainte Foy, and the Virgin Mary at Clermont, a statue of Saint Martial was
fashioned at Limoges in about 952 and remade into a reliquary in 973, and
one of Saint Vivien (Vivianus) of Figeac was made before the end of the
tenth century.[38] The image of Saint Gerald stood very much at the forefront
of these innovations in Christian worship. The church synod of Arras held
in 1025 decreed concerning images of the saints, "not that they should be
adored by men but rather that we should be inwardly moved by them to
contemplate the operation of divine grace. . . . Observing images of confessors
and virgins, we are reminded to reject worldly desires in imitation of them,
to trample upon the incitements of the flesh, to offer to God our very own
selves as a sinless oblation."[39] So men like Bernard of Angers reflected an
opinion that was falling out of fashion when they condemned the reverence
paid to statues of the saints. As he recalled the statue of Saint Gerald, moreover, Bernard remembered that he had not dared to criticize it too loudly,

for fear of angering the peasants who were devoted to it and who surrounded him in the church at Aurillac. His comment corroborates the appeal of Saint Gerald among peasants that both Odo and Ademar had noted. That appeal may have been intimately connected to his image, which made the saint real and present especially to those viewers who had no other means to feel his presence—a feeling such as the literate might obtain from reading a *vita*.[40]

Further comparison with Sainte Foy highlights other purposes that Gerald's statue may have served. The regular procession of her image not only strengthened devotion and raised funds but also marked monastic territories. As the miracles of Sainte Foy described it, "it was a custom of our senior monks that when a very welcome gift enriched the monastery with the benefices of churches or the outstanding addition of manors, the shrine of the relics was borne to that place to put it under her protection. In this way the virgin claims these things for herself and the presence of her body subjects them to her forever."[41] Her statue was also used to threaten violent and unruly noblemen:

> For it is a deeply rooted practice and firmly established custom that,
> if land given to Sainte Foy is unjustly appropriated by a usurper for
> any reason, the reliquary of the holy virgin is carried out to that land
> as a witness in regaining the right to her property. The monks
> announce that there will be a solemn procession of clergy and laity,
> who move forward with great formality carrying candles and lamps.
> A processional cross goes in front of the holy relics, embellished all
> around with enamels and gold and studded with a variety of gems
> flashing like stars. The novices serve by carrying a gospel book, holy
> water, clashing cymbals, and even trumpets made of ivory that were
> donated by noble pilgrims to adorn the monastery.[42]

One imagines similar events using Gerald's image, given the predations that the estates claimed by the monastery of Aurillac suffered.[43] We do have hints that the relics of Saint Gerald were brought to public assemblies, although his statue is not mentioned here either. One of the early Peace of God gatherings involved the monks of Aurillac in 972. The record of the event, a collection of miracles attributed to Saint Vivien of Figeac, depicts a mixed group of monks, laymen, clerics, and bishops assembled "to deliberate about the common good and the ways to reestablish a lasting peace. To add greater weight to their deliberations, they brought their holy relics, so that by the intercession of these God would confirm in the heavens what the authority of the church decreed, in their presence, on earth." And while the focus of the text is on the miracle-working ability of Saint Vivien, particular mention is also made of the monks of the monastery of Aurillac at the assembly, "with the remains of their own glorious confessor of Christ, Gerald."[44]

In varied ways, then, the cult of Saint Gerald participated in broader trends of sanctity in the central Middle Ages. More elaborate churches and newly crafted statues were both part of a general increased visibility for saints and saints' relics wherever they were venerated.[45] Even if little documentation of Saint Gerald's medieval cult has survived, it was by such means as these that the memory of Saint Gerald was preserved and extended.

Saint Gerald beyond Aurillac

The dearth of sources precludes tracing the depth of medieval devotion to Saint Gerald with any great precision. Some speculation is possible by means of the network of churches and priories that belonged to the monks of Aurillac in the eleventh, twelfth, and thirteenth centuries. At the apex of the monastery's fortunes there were perhaps about fifty of these properties, although I was able to verify only about thirty of them as having once belonged to Aurillac.[46]

Already in the additional miracle stories written by Ademar, mention is made of several properties belonging to the monastery of Aurillac. Among them was the church dedicated to Saint Gerald at Limoges, built perhaps in the late tenth century.[47] Also named were two rural properties, Varen and Vailhourles, about twenty kilometers apart and each over a hundred kilometers from Aurillac.[48] Both are depicted in the text as farms, with peasants and livestock, and both were managed as priories by monks; both may have been among the estates Gerald bequeathed to his monastery. It is not difficult to imagine how the modern villages evolved from these medieval estates, and both are still largely agricultural. Varen still has its eleventh-century church dedicated to Saint Peter, and the church at Vailhourles, though it dates from the nineteenth century, is dedicated to Saint Gerald.[49] (These dedications are typical of the priories once belonging to Aurillac, most of which were consecrated to one or the other of these two saints.) Gerald's benevolence was central to the stories told about these priories, so in addition to providing income for the monastery at Aurillac, these priories created communities loyal to Saint Gerald, inspiring donations and attracting new monks.

So little documentation survives, even in local archives, that only an impressionistic glimpse into the history of these priories is possible. A few examples will have to suffice. Apart from the church at Limoges, the only other known church dedicated to Saint Gerald in a medieval town of any size was at Toulouse, built in the ruins of what had once been an ancient pagan temple. In this case, there was already a church on the site, dedicated to Saint Peter, that the monks from Aurillac seem to have claimed for themselves; over time, the church also took Saint Gerald's name.[50] Most of the other properties were rural ones, and most were found south of Aurillac and within a radius of about a hundred kilometers, although a few are more distant: a few west of the mouths of the Rhone River between Avignon and Montpellier, others north of the Garonne River closer to the Atlantic coast, and even some east of the Rhone River in the foothills of the Alps. Most seem to date from the twelfth century or thereabout, which must represent the apogee of the fortunes of the monastery at Aurillac. Many lie in clusters of three or more churches in close proximity that we can presume were managed together. Some take the shape of strings of properties so that it is possible to imagine traveling from one priory to another to and from Aurillac.[51] Nonetheless, how closely the abbot of Aurillac supervised any of these priories or how they were managed at all is unknown.[52] Most are simple, small structures.[53] Three of the priories housed women: the oldest of these was the convent of Saint-Jean-du-Buis, directly across the Jordanne River from the monastery of Saint-Géraud of Aurillac, that was first mentioned in the thirteenth century and may have begun as a residence for female pilgrims visiting the shrine of Saint Gerald.[54]

There were no priories in the north of France. At the same time, the cult of Saint Gerald encompassed properties in what is now Spain. A group of churches dedicated to Saint Gerald still exists in the region of Catalonia, although once again little survives to explain the origins of these churches or their connection to Aurillac.[55] Devotion to Saint Gerald in Catalonia may have begun when a queen of Aragon received relics of the saint from Aurillac because she claimed some distant relationship with Gerald. In this instance, the medieval document confirming the bishop of Girona's receipt of the relics has been preserved.[56] Whether that event marks the start of devotion to Saint Gerald there or is one element among many, however, is uncertain. Numerous connections, political, economic, and religious, linked the south of France with Catalonia throughout the Middle Ages, and in this expansion southward, Aurillac was not unique among French monasteries.[57] Yet another cluster of holdings was established in Galicia in and around the modern village of O Cebreiro. Its location betrays its purpose, since it lies along the main pilgrimage route to Santiago de Compostela. (In fact, it is situated at the top of the last mountain pass through which virtually all pilgrims would have to travel as they approached Compostela, in a terrain not unlike that of Aurillac.) It seems clear that the site was intended to welcome pilgrims and there is evidence for a medieval hospice or hospital staffed by the monks of Aurillac from 1072. It also seems clear that the monks hoped to inspire devotion to Saint Gerald among the pilgrims: its church was at first dedicated to Saint Gerald, although later reconsecrated to the Virgin Mary; doubtless they also to encourage travelers to visit Aurillac on their return from Compostela.[58]

Because the sites of the priories belonging to Aurillac have been altered over time, it is sometimes difficult to know which architectural details date from the period when the cult of Saint Gerald was expanding and which are later additions fashioned in a similar style. Back in France at Souillac, the priory church that was built in the early twelfth century as a dependency of Aurillac still has several pieces of Romanesque sculpture, probably close to what once existed elsewhere. Carol Knicely has observed themes of violence and suffering in the art there, arguing that it represents a monastic counter-vision to prevailing notions of noble male heroism.[59] While she does not tie those depictions to the cult of Saint Gerald, it is tempting to see in such representations a sensibility shaped by his life and legend.

The dissemination of the manuscripts of the writings about Saint Gerald provides one further small piece of evidence as to the success of his cult. The manuscripts that survive have already been described above but can be briefly listed here. The earliest manuscripts with extant copies were made at Moissac and Limoges. By the twelfth century, additional copies could be found at Limoges and Cluny as well as at Clermont, Paris, and possibly also at Cîteaux (now preserved at Dijon) and elsewhere in France, including at Évreux in Normandy.[60] Clearly by the twelfth century, then, Gerald's sanctity was being promoted even in northern France. The thirteenth, fourteenth, and fifteenth centuries witnessed additional manuscripts produced in some of these same places and some farther afield, including Toulouse (copied locally), San Millan de la Cogolla (in medieval Aragon, also copied locally), and Turin (now destroyed).[61] Over the course of the Middle Ages, Gerald found his way into many of the great monastic libraries of France and beyond.

A related piece of manuscript evidence for the medieval cult of Saint Gerald comes from the sacramentaries that reveal where his feast day was celebrated. We have no way of knowing how many have been lost over the centuries, but the sacramentaries extant in modern French collections also indicate widespread devotion. The oldest was produced in the late ninth or early tenth century at Aurillac, not surprisingly, although it is now preserved at Albi.[62] A few eleventh-century examples survive, including from Limoges, Moissac, and Gellone.[63] More curious are two early sacramentaries—one from the tenth century, the other from the eleventh—originating in the town of Angers, where political connections between the dukes of Aquitaine and the counts of Anjou might have brought the first knowledge of Saint Gerald.[64] By the twelfth century, sacramentaries celebrating the feast of Saint Gerald could be found throughout France: at Limoges and Angers, also at Cahors, Albi, and Clermont, but also at Saint-Alyre in Auvergne, Sainte-Melaine and Barbechat in Brittany, Souvigny and Tournus in Burgundy, Arles in Provence, and somewhere in the Narbonnais, near Gellone.[65] There were also two twelfth-century sacramentaries in use in Catalonia, one at Girona and the other at Arles-sur-Tech, that corroborate the medieval devotion to Saint Gerald there.[66] Between the thirteenth and fifteenth centuries, only a few more examples survive of sacramentaries that include the feast of Saint Gerald: from Paris, from Carcassonne in the Languedoc, and from Gap as well as Arles, both in medieval Provence.[67]

A final bit of information about medieval devotion to Saint Gerald comes from some of the music used in liturgies. Three manuscripts that mention the saint survive from the eleventh century. Two were once located in the monastic library of Saint-Martial of Limoges but are now in Paris.[68] The third, called the Graduale of Gaillac, came from the monastery of Saint-Michel in that town and is also now in Paris.[69] Two additional manuscripts can be dated from the beginning of the twelfth century, and while they show influences of musical styles of southern France, both are now located in the Iberian peninsula: one at Toledo and the other at Braga.[70] Their music seems to be derived from one common liturgy, the antiphons borrowed from both versions of the *Vita Geraldi*.[71] It is perhaps also worth noting in this regard that Ademar of Chabannes composed liturgical music, and since the earliest of these manuscripts comes from eleventh-century Limoges, it is not unimaginable that he was its composer.[72]

Overall we get the sense that the cult of Saint Gerald was very much on the rise between the eleventh and thirteenth centuries and poised for success. The monks of Aurillac were clearly working hard to make Gerald's saintly reputation known. The clusters of priory churches across the south of France and even into medieval Aragon, León, and Savoy helped to establish a viable, even thriving, monastic network. The medieval manuscripts that survive also suggest that the renown of Saint Gerald extended well beyond the region where it first began. All things pointed not only to a broader knowledge of Saint Gerald but also to his greater appeal. Yet the same evidence also points to the contraction of his cult in the last centuries of the Middle Ages and noticeably less interest in him. Without much historical evidence we can only speculate as to what happened to bring about the downfall of Saint Gerald, when he seemed to hold such promise, and yet, in reflecting on the unmaking as well as the making of a saint, finding an answer to that question is essential.

CHAPTER 5

Saint Gerald and the Ebb of History

Despite the manifold efforts to advance the cult of Saint Gerald, he was slowly sinking into obscurity by the end of the Middle Ages. Insofar as we know, in the fifteenth century only one new manuscript included his *vita* and only one church was built in his name.[1] Nonetheless, even the disappearance of the cult of a saint such as Gerald—near disappearance, to be fair, since devotion to Saint Gerald still survives in a limited sense—can provide an opportunity for thinking about the historical memory of a saint. What has been forgotten in history is often as meaningful as what has been remembered.[2] It is not possible to reconstruct entirely the story of Gerald's waning, given the limited historical evidence, yet tracking the declining fortunes of the devotion to Saint Gerald provides sufficient clues to help explain how a saint, so carefully crafted, was undone.

The Crisis of Aurillac

A series of disruptions at the monastery at Aurillac certainly contributed to the demise of Gerald's fame. The first of these were noted already in the brief chronicle of the abbots of Aurillac. During the rule of the tenth abbot, maybe as early as the mid-eleventh century, the monastery was said to have been filled with "dissolute and undisciplined monks" despite the best efforts of its reformers. About the eleventh abbot, it was said only tersely that he was deemed "to have merited no praise" and that he "thought only of his pleasure," and he was criticized for spending much of the wealth that had been accumulated by the monastery. The abbot who succeeded him was the target of similar criticism.[3] The mismanagement seems to have been settled only through a formal affiliation with the monastery of Cluny in the late eleventh century, after which the abbot of Cluny supervised Aurillac directly.[4] Jean Leclercq has depicted the eleventh and twelfth centuries as a period of "monastic crisis," and concludes that it was above all a crisis of prosperity: that is, as wealth flowed into the monasteries, men of high birth and influence followed, making it increasingly difficult to maintain the monastic ideals.[5] Even the attachment to Cluny did not restore these virtues to the monastery: at some point the abbots of Aurillac moved into the castle overlooking the monastery, which they enlarged in the late thirteenth century for greater comfort.[6]

There are other hints that at least some of the monks at Aurillac may have been attracted to the monastic life for reasons other than devotion to its founder. An interesting case in point survives from the early thirteenth century in the life of Peire de Vic, known more broadly as "the monk of Montaudon" (*Lo monge de Montaudon*).[7] His brief and anonymous biography records that he composed poetry in the style of the troubadours, and as his fame grew, he was given permission by the abbot of Aurillac to leave monastic life and attach himself to the court of King Alfonso II of Aragon, who "ordered him to eat meat and court women [*domnejes*] and sing and create poetry [*trobes*]." He eventually returned to the life of the monastery as prior of Villafranca, said to be "in Spain [*en Espaingna*]" and also a dependency of Aurillac.[8] While only a few examples of his poetry survive, they depict the pursuit of earthly pleasure without apparent regard for his vows. In one poem he listed the things he enjoyed most in life, among them, "a fat salmon in mid-afternoon" and "to have my lady [*amigua*], in secret, come, and . . . make love with her [*fauc una vetz de briu*]."[9] In one of his poems he imagined a conversation in which God granted him permission to leave the cloister, saying that he could do more good in the world than withdrawn from it, in what is clearly an ironic twist on Saint Gerald's own legend.[10] Peire de Vic was hardly a typical monk, to be sure, yet his disregard for monastic discipline, if more than a literary conceit, and the freedom with which he moved in and out of the cloister, if accurately portrayed, may have been shared by others. It is also worth noting that while the Monk of Montaudon often named popular saints in his poems—including Sainte Foy and Saint Martial—and even while it must be admitted that some of these saints' names provided him with a helpful rhyme, Gerald was not among them.[11]

The late twelfth century also witnessed substantial tensions between the monastery at Aurillac and the local nobility. Several minor noble families—in the twelfth century these included the counts of Rodez and Saint-Flour, the *dauphin* d'Auvergne, and many more neighboring families of castellans—all hoped to preserve their autonomy as best they could against the encroachments of the counts of Toulouse.[12] Both the kings of France and of England were also increasingly involved in the region; the king of England after 1154 was also the duke of Aquitaine. It was impossible for the abbots of Aurillac to remain neutral.[13] In 1184, according to the chronicler Geoffrey de Vigeois, the son of the count of Toulouse, in revolt against his father, led an armed troop into the town of Aurillac together with the son of the king of England and set fire to several of its buildings, then threatened to put the monastery to the torch, too, unless they received a payment of twenty-five thousand *livres* from the monks of Saint Gerald. In 1190 the count of Toulouse forged a pact with the abbot of Aurillac that promised protection for the abbey, but it came at the cost of the loss of several properties to the count.[14] Even that safeguard doesn't seem to have been enough, because in 1203 the abbot of Aurillac appears to have been killed by men in the service of a local lord, who was later forced to do penance for his men's actions.[15]

At the same time that the fortunes of the monastery of Aurillac were in decline, those of the town that had grown up around it were on the rise, and throughout the twelfth and thirteenth centuries the town of Aurillac grew and prospered. The town of Aurillac was ideally situated to help in the transportation of goods between the rural and mountainous upper Auvergne and the more densely settled regions around it. The production of beef and dairy products that typify modern Auvergne may not yet have been as extensive; still, by the beginning of thirteenth century, Saint Gerald served as patron in Aurillac for the guild of tanners, leatherworkers, and glovemakers.[16] As residents in a monastic town, though, Aurillac's merchants were required to purchase privileges from the abbots of the monastery, even as their wealth and opportunities increased, and they chafed increasingly at the restrictions the monks imposed on them, as townsfolk did elsewhere. The town was described in one fourteenth-century charter as belonging "to Saint Gerald and to the lord abbot and the monastery and their successors [*a beato Geraldo et a domino abbate et monasterio et eorum successoribus*]," although it is doubtful that the townspeople saw it this way.[17]

The last straw came in 1233 when, for some unknown reason, the merchants of Aurillac rose up in armed conflict against the monks. Some of the monastic buildings were damaged, and the relics of Saint Gerald were desecrated—perhaps the statue of Gerald was destroyed, too, since we have no further references to it. It was not until 1280 that the monks and towns-people of Aurillac reached an agreement to share political authority over the town, an agreement renewed in 1298 and again in 1347.[18] This concession significantly lessened the monastery's clout, and if the statue of Saint Gerald had been destroyed, perhaps also its ability to attract pilgrims bringing donations.

Tensions were also felt between the monastery of Aurillac and the bish-ops with jurisdiction over the region of Aurillac—at first, the bishops of Clermont, but from 1317 on, the bishops of Saint-Flour. A royal charter of Philip IV surviving from 1299 awarded the bishop of Clermont financial compensation from both the townspeople and abbot of Aurillac for injuries and insults he suffered when he tried to visit the town, a visit the abbot saw as a violation of the monastery's immunity, as is made clear from another charter of the same year in which the abbot appealed to the *parlement* of Paris to remit the fine.[19] This uneasy relationship may have prompted Pope John XXII (formerly the bishop of Cahors and one of the popes residing at Avig-non, who were generally much more involved in French affairs) to appoint the bishop of Saint-Flour as abbot of Aurillac in 1320. During his first visit to Aurillac in 1323, however, that individual swore solemnly not to exercise any jurisdiction over the town in his role as bishop but only in his role as abbot.[20]

The multiplying difficulties of the monastery meant of course that much less attention could be given to encouraging ongoing devotion to Saint Ger-ald. We don't know what kind of treasures the monks of Aurillac had been given in the years that marked the height of Saint Gerald's cult, but some of these may have had to be sold off, if they hadn't already been destroyed or stolen in the 1233 sack.[21] It seems, too, that many of the monastery's priories were abandoned beginning in the thirteenth century, probably the most dis-tant or least profitable first, as income fell and declining numbers of monks made it more difficult to staff those sites. The priory and hospice at O Cebreiro in Galicia, for example, fell into decline, and by the time King Ferdinand and Queen Isabella passed through in 1496 on a pilgrimage to Santiago de Compostela, it had long been abandoned.[22] In other places, the priories survived—under new management. Already in 1180, the priory at Puycelsi was transferred from the monastery of Aurillac to the count of Tou-louse, although that change may have had to do with the tense political situation between the count, his son, and Aurillac noted above.[23] In 1217 the abbot of Aurillac entered into an agreement with the *dauphin* d'Auvergne to share jurisdiction over the church at Dauzat-sur-Vodable.[24] The late thirteenth century seems to have witnessed the greatest losses. Aspres-sur-Buëch was handed over to the count of Forcalquier in 1276 or 1279.[25] In 1282 the bishop of Rodez acquired the priory of Saint-Géraud at Salles-Curan.[26] Saillans was transferred to the bishop of Die in 1299.[27] By the fourteenth century, Aurillac's claims over the monastery of Saint-Amand-de-Boixe were allowed to lapse and it became autonomous.[28] Only in a few places is there evidence of a continuing presence of monks from Aurillac into the fourteenth and fifteenth centuries. At Toulouse, for example, the abbots of Aurillac chose to rebuild the priory church in 1471; indeed, they still maintained a residence near the church until the sixteenth century (and this building still stands).[29] The abbots of Aurillac were also still asserting their claims to Cayrac and to its handful of dependencies in documents surviving from 1455 and 1457.[30]

New problems surfaced in the mid-fourteenth century. During the Hundred Years' War, military forces of both the French and English pillaged throughout the south of France, including the area around Aurillac. In 1271 Auvergne had become part of the French royal domain, but in 1360 it was given as a duchy to John, a younger son of the French king John II (and it remained in the hands of his descendants until 1527, when it reverted again to the royal domain). Nonetheless, the English kings still held some claims to overlordship of the region as dukes of Aquitaine, and military skirmishes were frequent. Those properties still belonging to the monastery were likely plundered and churches pillaged, for example, by the English mercenaries who raided throughout the upper Auvergne between 1356 and 1361. Aurillac itself fell victim to attack in 1360, this time by allies of the French, who were said to have "assailed in a plunderous manner and attacked with hostility, committing sacrileges, murders, robberies, adulteries and sexual immoralities, and also fires and other detestable crimes." Louis of Navarre led his troops through Aurillac and Auvergne in 1362.[31] Even those priories that had remained in the monastery's possession before the start of the war may have been abandoned after such raids: the flight of the peasant population in the region of Aurillac fearful of approaching soldiers was noted in 1371, and it happened elsewhere.[32] In a few places priory buildings were even converted to makeshift castles, as happened, it seems, at Salles-Curan and at Bournac.[33] The mid-fourteenth century also witnessed the first outbreak of what we call the Black Death, that returned in successive generations for a century and further reduced the viability of the monastery and its properties. The abbot of Aurillac may have died of the plague in 1361, and doubtless other monks and peasants belonging to the monastery's lands did, too.[34] Peasant revolts, finally, like those of the Tuchins that reached Auvergne between 1384 and 1389, meant further unrest.

None of these problems were unique to Aurillac, to be sure, but were shared by countless other monasteries across France and beyond. The wars and epidemics of the later Middle Ages devastated the rural economy on which most monasteries depended.[35] One sign of the times was an end to the popular pilgrimage to Santiago de Compostela. Even great Cluny itself, that had also reached its apogee by the end of the twelfth century, began a slow decline for the rest of the Middle Ages.[36] Cluny's intellectual reputation helped it to survive and its library remained one of medieval Europe's largest, so scholars at least still visited there. Aurillac, in contrast, had little international reputation, and without pilgrims to Compostela it must have been all the more difficult to attract visitors to the Saint Gerald's shrine. As it slipped into obscurity, so did the memory of its saintly founder.

Saint Gerald, the Mendicants, and Holy Poverty

The waning of Saint Gerald's fortunes was not simply the result of the economic or political troubles of Aurillac. Also in the twelfth and thirteenth centuries came new saintly rivals to the monastic ideal that had inspired Aurillac's monks and that generated a different kind of challenge to Saint Gerald.

Granted, there had always been saintly rivals to Gerald. Sainte Foy of Conques was perhaps his earliest and greatest. The miracles that she performed were plentiful, and the written account of them was continually added to over the course of the eleventh century, making them known and attracting new pilgrims.[37] Saint Vivien of Figeac, also mentioned above, was an even closer rival. When some persons were healed by the relics of Saint Vivien near Aurillac in 972, according to the *Transitus et miracula sancti Viviani*, the monks of Aurillac became "aroused by jealousy" and "a Jewish hatred" until the obvious cure of a boy who was lame as well as deaf and mute made Saint Vivien's power manifest even to them: "The stupefied monks repented. Barefoot and with the remains of their own glorious confessor of Christ, Gerald, they arrived at the feet of the holy confessor Vivien and, begging forgiveness for their insults, gave him worthy praise."[38] Gerald's own posthumous miracle-working ability seems to have adequately responded to such rivals, at least in the early centuries of his cult.

New forms of spirituality, however, made that response increasingly insufficient. New orders challenged the monopoly of Benedictine monasticism on cloistered life. The Cistercians, founded at the turn of the twelfth century, had by the middle of the century established or reformed monasteries across southern France, including at Obazine, near Tulle and not too distant from Aurillac. (A miracle story attributed to Saint Gerald that takes place at Obazine was tacked onto one copy of his additional miracles, and might represent a subtle rebuttal to this rival monastery.)[39] Much has been written about the Cistercian antipathy to the Cluniac accumulation of wealth.[40] The Dominicans and Franciscans also made their appearance in southern France in the first decades of the thirteenth century, and by the middle of the century, there were mendicant houses in all of the main cities of southern France, including one for Franciscans at Aurillac.[41] Heretical groups also emerged in growing numbers in the twelfth and thirteenth centuries, especially the Albigensians in southern France, who also denounced the church's wealth.[42] Some elements of this critique existed already in the early eleventh century; still, a more widespread criticism of the church's lavish wealth seems to have been circulating by the twelfth and thirteenth centuries. Numerous sculpted images of the sin of usury that began to appear across Auvergne in the twelfth century might be linked to these denunciations of ecclesiastical wealth.[43]

Such a shift in spiritual ideals had serious consequences for the cult of Saint Gerald. The issue central to Gerald's legend, especially in its later version, had been violence. It would be naïve to think that violence was no longer a problem for medieval society, but its function as part of the Christian life was no longer so open to question. In contrast, the role of wealth in the Christian life was the more hotly burning issue. Indeed, the more that voluntary poverty became associated with the imitation of Christ, the more a reluctance to relinquish one's wealth seemed not only selfish but also irreverent and even ungodly—the very opposites of saintliness.[44]

What had Saint Gerald to offer on this question? Odo had suggested that Gerald had remained "a pauper in spirit" despite his countless possessions (*prol.*). If he gave away any money he received, out of his "love of poverty" (6), his wealth was still such that he was able still to dispense alms to the poor and to endow monasteries as he traveled to and from Rome every other year (8). Ademar was a bit more forthcoming about Gerald's wealth, and that may be because it was already more of a contentious issue in the early eleventh century than it had been in the early tenth. He said that Gerald was "rich, and lived well," that he owned "a great quantity of estates endowed with serfs," but also condemned those persons who tried "to excuse their luxurious lives by his example" (1.*prol.* and 1.1). Of Gerald's clothing, Ademar suggested that "he took care not to adorn himself more than usual with silken or precious garments" and claimed that Gerald "forbade himself to wear gold" (1.16). Ademar maintained that Gerald also regularly tithed a ninth part of his income and then set aside another portion for the poor. And while Odo had said that Gerald immediately gave away any cash he received, Ademar said instead that "he always carried money with him, of which he secretly gave as much as he could to poor people whom he met" (1.28). Nonetheless, Ademar described how Gerald never attempted to add to his possessions, suggesting some discomfort with Gerald's wealth: "He himself never bought land, except one small field that happened to be surrounded by one of his properties. Some rich men become very ardent over this, forgetting the terrible threat of the prophet: 'Woe to those who join house to house, who add field to field.' For Gerald, according to the precept of the Gospel, was contented with his wages. . . . Nor did the number of his properties make him proud" (1.28, with reference to Isaiah 5:8 and Matthew 20:1–16). In the summation of Gerald's virtues, Ademar concluded that he had "conquered avarice" in retaining his wealth without succumbing to it, and rather "laid up treasure for himself in heaven" and "remained poor in spirit," and that this should be accounted as part of what made him a saint (2.34). Still, for individuals who believed that only a complete abandonment of riches could achieve a true spiritual poverty, these sorts of disclaimers may not have been sufficient.

Instead, new saints rose to take Gerald's place. One was Robert of Turlande, who had been born near Aurillac, and who had also founded a monastery, in this case, La Chaise-Dieu. Robert died in 1067, and his *vita* was written by Marbod of Rennes before the end of the eleventh century, indicating that his saintly reputation had already traveled as far as Brittany in less than half a century. Saint Robert was a man much more fitted to the new model of sanctity, since he was remembered as having abandoned his noble life wholeheartedly to become in turn a priest, a canon, a hermit, and eventually the abbot of the monastery he founded. He was said specifically to have rejected the Cluniac model of monasticism as insufficient for spiritual perfection. That Saint Robert was soon said to have been related to Saint Gerald only highlighted the contrast between them.[45] Another rival, Saint Roch, provides an equal foil to Saint Gerald. There is little historical evidence for Roch's existence, in fact, yet the details of the life that was given to him are worth recalling.[46] He was said to have been born in Montpellier in 1295 and died in 1327. Like Gerald, Roch belonged to the nobility and was raised by devout parents, but unlike Gerald, Roch renounced his title and distributed all of his wealth to the poor. Like Gerald, Roch also went on pilgrimage to Rome, but unlike Gerald, he stopped to care for those stricken with the plague and eventually succumbed to the disease himself. Here was someone who could much more easily find a place in contemporary discussions about Christian ideals, and it was even later claimed that Roch, too, was a distant relative of Gerald, apparently an admission of sorts that the parallels between their lives were noticed by others. He is still one of the most popular saints in the south of France, and many of the churches dedicated to Saint Gerald also include a statue of Saint Roch.[47]

The cult of saints itself was itself changing in the later Middle Ages. Increased devotion to the Virgin Mary distracted from loyalty to other saints. Aurillac's second church, built in the thirteenth century (and now demolished), was dedicated to the Virgin, a larger edifice than the church dedicated to Saint Gerald.[48] Several prominent shrines to the Virgin Mary were located in southern France where attachment to Gerald was strongest, at Le Puy, Rocamadour, and Orcival, and even closer to Aurillac at Thiézac and La Font-Sainte, attracting pilgrims to these places rather than to his shrine.[49] At these churches and elsewhere, sculpted representations of the Virgin, including the well-known "Black Madonnas," became increasingly abundant and served as visible foci of devotion in ways of which the statue of Saint Gerald had once been a rare example.[50]

New forms of eucharistic piety also impacted the relative importance of devotion to the saints. Within the church at O Cebreiro in Galicia, for example, a eucharistic miracle still commemorated was said to have taken place in about 1300, when the bread and wine of the eucharist turned into meat and blood in the hands of a skeptical priest. (No precise year was ever recalled, and the whole of it is suspiciously like the miracle of Bolsena that is supposed to have happened in Italy in 1263, which is commemorated in the feast of Corpus Christi.) The miracle of O Cebreiro, confirmed by the pope in 1487 (in the first extant historical reference to the legend, which perhaps places its origin only in the fifteenth century), overshadowed the place of Saint Gerald at the site, and the so-called Chalice of the Miracle, which probably dates from the twelfth century, became the primary object of devotion for later pilgrims. A twelfth-century statue of the Virgin, called Santa Maria la Real, is also found in the church, and is said to have leaned forward to observe the miracle more closely.[51]

Some forms of late medieval piety called into question the cult of saints altogether. The Albigensians in particular denounced devotion to the physical remains of the saints as unseemly. In the 1230s, the south of France was still very much mired in the Albigensian Crusade, and it was only in 1233 that the Inquisition began the task of eliminating these heretics in the Languedoc. (It is possible that contempt for Gerald's relics may have played a role in the destruction of his statue, if it happened when the townspeople of Aurillac revolted against the monks in that same year.)

Devotion to Saint Gerald was not wholly absent from the later Middle Ages. Ademar's *Vita prolixior* was translated into French in its entirety in the fourteenth century, although where and for what reason are unknown.[52] Similarly, a Catalan translation of Gerald's legend was made in the late fifteenth or early sixteenth century.[53] Saint Gerald also appeared in two well-known medieval collections of lives of the saints. The first was Bernard Gui's *Speculum sanctorale*, written in the 1320s.[54] The second was the *Legenda aurea* of Jacob de Voragine, although Gerald's life can be found only in a single fourteenth-century manuscript version of it.[55] In one late fifteenth-century breviary commissioned by the abbot of Moissac, a greatly abbreviated version of the *Vita Geraldi* follows a beautifully illustrated image of the saint, wearing the habit of a monk but taking communion as a layman (see fig. 7). Despite these efforts, the memory of Saint Gerald was by the end of the Middle Ages at risk of fading away.

The Protestant Reformation and Catholic Counter-Reformation

The Protestant Reformation of the sixteenth century dealt new blows to the cult of Saint Gerald. The first mention of Protestants at Aurillac was in 1548, but already by 1561 there was a Protestant minister in the town, who wrote in that year to John Calvin recounting how much his congregation was growing. Violence between Protestants and Catholics began in 1562 with the arrival of royal troops, who immediately expelled the Protestants from the town. Yet in 1567 Protestant forces regained entry to the town by subterfuge and pillaged most Catholic sites there, including the monastery. (If the statue of

Figure 7. Gerald receiving communion dressed as a monk, from a late fifteenth-century breviary commissioned by the abbot of Moissac. Pierpont Morgan Library, New York, manuscript 463, fol. 547v detail. Reprinted by permission. Photographic credit: The Pierpont Morgan Library, New York.

Saint Gerald had not been destroyed in 1233, it was almost certainly destroyed on this occasion.)[56] Writing in 1635, Dominique de Jésus (more on him below) said of this ruination: "This sepulcher was long honored . . . but the accursed reform of Calvin that violated both divine and human rights, has reduced it all to ashes" (18.2). "They pillaged everything, and pulled the sacred bones of Saint Gerald from his reliquary [*chasse*], and burned some of them and scattered the rest around the church, but which were later secretly removed by some Catholics and thereafter were put in a reliquary of wood, where for the most part they are still today, revered by the faithful" (18.8).[57] He added that the cloister of the monastery, "with its marble columns," was demolished to its foundations at the same time (18.4). Exactly how much damage happened to the church of Saint Gerald is not entirely clear, but a visitor of the early eighteenth century claimed that "the church was entirely in ruins except for a few bays that are quite sturdy and the ancient bell tower that still survives."[58]

Already by the date of this destruction, though, the monastery of Aurillac was a much changed place, because in 1561 it had been secularized by papal order: that is, its monks were sent to other monasteries and canons replaced them. The directive came as the result of an inquest begun in 1555 that had uncovered numerous abuses, including monks who resided outside the monastery, or hunted, dined out, and gambled, living impious lives. A chapel within the monastery was said to have been converted into a wine cellar—and even more serious was an accusation of murder. That inquest had already described several of the buildings of the monastery as being in a ruined state, so perhaps not all of the destruction should be blamed on the Protestants.[59] How far back these abuses went was left unsaid, but as early as 1462 an abbot of Aurillac had died under mysterious circumstances.[60]

These abuses all stemmed at least in part from the monastery's absentee abbots, a practice that had become the norm in the last century of its existence. Among the first and most famous was Cesare Borgia, an illegitimate son of Pope Alexander VI, who was made titular abbot of Aurillac in 1493 or 1494, and served in that post for five years without ever setting foot in the town.[61] With the signing of the Concordat of Bologna in 1516, the kings of France acquired the right to appoint Aurillac's abbots along with most other high church officials within their realm, and its holders did little more than collect whatever income still remained to the monastery.[62]

Even after the secularization in 1561 and the sack in 1567, the monastery continued after a fashion. Absentee abbots continued to be appointed, while only a handful of secular canons—probably about a dozen, at least according to documents of the eighteenth century—oversaw the management of the monastery and its remaining properties.[63] The monastery's church served as a parish church for the local inhabitants in the period following secularization, yet it does not seem to have served many of them: in the eighteenth century, at any rate, only 3 percent of the town's weddings were held at the church of Saint-Géraud and only 7 percent of its funerals.[64] The monastery's hospice likewise continued to function, but sixteenth-century documents refer to it as the Hôtel-Dieu rather than linking it to Saint Gerald, and even then it became so dilapidated by the eighteenth century that a new hospital was built in 1754.[65] The education of boys that the monastery had also once directed seems to have been taken over by a Jesuit college that opened within the former monastery precinct in 1619.[66] The monastery's walls were also eventually demolished, but their outline can still be clearly seen even today on a map of Aurillac in the pattern of the streets encircling the church.

Whatever former priories that still existed suffered various fates. Sieurac, for example, was pillaged twice by Protestants in 1569 and again in 1625; its church was destroyed and not rebuilt until 1737.[67] The priory dedicated to Saint Gerald near the modern town of Montgardin was also ruined during the wars of religion and never rebuilt; its location became known only because a local homeowner wanted to expand the cellar of his house in 1954 and uncovered the foundations of the church.[68] This is to give but two examples.

It can only be assumed that devotion to Saint Gerald also suffered greatly as a result of these changes. Once again, little documentation has survived, but the few clues that remain point mostly to neglect of his cult. By the seventeenth century there were several other religious orders with houses at Aurillac, part of the larger attempt to revitalize Catholicism in the south of France where Protestants were most numerous, and these communities might have diverted enthusiasm for Saint Gerald to their own founders. For men there were houses of Franciscans, Carmelites, and Jesuits, and for women houses of Poor Clares and Visitandines; the last of these took over the Benedictine convent of Saint-Jean du Buis that was located across the Jordanne River from the former monastery of Saint Gerald and had formerly been dependent on it.[69]

A century after the secularization and sack of the monastery, some signs of recovery could be found. One of the seventeenth-century abbots of Aurillac, Charles de Noailles, spearheaded a restoration of the church of Saint

Gerald. As part of this project, new stained-glass windows were completed for the church in 1623, none of which survive, but which included one of Saint Gerald on horseback.[70] Perhaps it was intended to reinvigorate devotion to the saint. This repair work belies the report that the church was still in ruins in the early eighteenth century, although it seems that the plans to restore the church were not fully accomplished. Only one bay of the new nave was completed, after which a temporary wall closed off the front of the church and remained in place until the mid-nineteenth century, so the church may have looked still under repair.[71] Another abbot later in the seventeenth century, Ercole de Manzieri, commissioned a new reliquary for Saint Gerald, but that also no longer survives.[72] These efforts to keep Gerald's memory alive seem to have been only marginally felt.

Saint Gerald's New Biographers

Among the attempts to revive enthusiasm for Saint Gerald were new biographies that appeared in the seventeenth century. The earliest was written in French by a Carmelite monk and priest called Dominique de Jésus, born with the name Géraud or perhaps Gérard Vigier in 1596 and a resident of the Carmelite monastery in Aurillac until his death in 1638. He published his biography in 1635 as part of a collection of three lives of medieval Auvergnat saints.[73] Dominique noted in a preface how vital it was to take inspiration from the Catholic saints in a time of widespread heresy, by which he meant the Protestant Reformation. Later, he suggested that Saint Gerald's intervention had helped to preserve the region of Auvergne "from the contagion of heresy in recent times," since it alone remained Catholic while "all surrounding places are infected with it" (11.5).

Dominique's detailed account depended upon the medieval writings about Gerald. He repeated lengthy passages more or less directly from Ademar's *Vita prolixior*, although he attributed the work to Odo of Cluny, "because everyone knows and agrees that he was the author" (1.1). Nonetheless, he seemed to have some knowledge of both versions. He also incorporated material from Ademar's historical chronicle, like Gerald's fostering of Èbles Manzer (7.6 and 9.2), and when providing the date of Gerald's death, Dominique mentioned this work directly, although he himself dated Gerald's death to 918 (17.7). He also quoted occasionally from the brief chronicle of the abbots of Aurillac, so he knew that, too (18.3 and 18.6). He also referred to the sermon written for Gerald's feast day (17.7). He made no mention, however, of any of the additional miracle stories found in the Mantua or Montpellier manuscripts, and we must conclude that he did not know them.

Dominique also referred to writings about Gerald that are otherwise unknown and that have not survived, but that seem to have been available to him from the monastic library at Aurillac, indicating that at least part of it had survived both the monks' neglect and the Protestant destruction. One was an account of Gerald's life by a monk of Aurillac named Maffré (named at 9.5 and 11.6), from whom he derived a few of his stories: among them, that the pope had given Gerald a chalice that had belonged to Saint Peter and that had been venerated at Aurillac among its treasures until it was destroyed in the Protestant sack (11.6).[74] He also quoted small excerpts of a Latin poem written by another monk of Aurillac, unnamed, "who made the Life of Gerald into rhyming Latin according to the style of the day" (10.8).[75] He referred, finally, to another work that was lost during the sack of 1567: a "large, handwritten volume [gros volume escrit à la main]" full of posthumous miracles attributed to Saint Gerald (19.1). A few of these sources Dominique quoted in full. One was the Latin text of what he called Gerald's will, "as it is in the archives of Aurillac" (13.4–5). Another was the Latin text of what is supposed to have been the royal charter from the Carolingian Charles the Simple (13.9), that he dated to 899 and that he said came from the papers of Pierre Cambefort, a member of a local noble family, to whom he was grateful, "since in the archives of the chapter of Aurillac, there is only an excerpt, albeit quite old, of this piece" (13.10). A bit of yet another text, dating from 1536, he also quoted at some length, describing the translation of the relics of Saint Gerald from a wooden reliquary to a silver one (18.4). We cannot be certain that any of these documents were genuine, and Dominique himself raised some doubts about them, but they remain valuable at least as fragments from what the monks of Aurillac used in remembering their founder.

Dominique's own contributions to the legend of Saint Gerald are worth highlighting. To begin, he divided his text into chapters based on Gerald's virtues. So while he began, as both Odo and Ademar had, with the description of Gerald's birth, ancestry, childhood, and adolescence (chapters 1 through 6 of his new biography), he then rearranged the stories from Gerald's adult life to depict in turn Gerald's justice (7), clemency and mercy (8), leniency toward his enemies (9), prudence, temperance, and humility (10), and piety (11), before turning to Gerald's miracle-working ability (12), his desire for the monastic life (13), his establishment of the monastery at Aurillac

(14), his charity (15 and 16), and his holy death (17). He then continued with a brief history of Gerald's cult (18), his posthumous miracles (19), and even a bit about Aurillac borrowed mostly from the chronicle of the abbots of Aurillac (20). The details he himself added are sometimes quirky, although it is difficult to know which belong to Dominique and which had become part of more widespread legends about Gerald by his day. He misidentified Gerald's name, for example, as meaning either "swift man" or "one who loves hunting" in what he called "old Gallic [*vieux Gaulois*]" (1.3). He claimed that Gerald sometimes disguised himself as a pauper and received alms incognito from his own steward—as if to verify that it was being done (16.7). He repeated Ademar's criticism that some skeptics claimed that Gerald's miracle-working abilities came from the relics he wore rather than from his personal saintliness, but he attributed the sentiment to Gerald himself, as a feature of his humility, rather than to Gerald's detractors (10.7).

Other details included in the reworking of Gerald's life are more telling. For Dominique, a fundamental marker of Gerald's sanctity was the greatness of his lineage. So even while he admitted that Gerald's medieval biographers had said only that he was descended from the family of Caesarius of Arles and Aredius, he added that there were also indications that Gerald was descended from the Merovingian Frankish king Childebert (1.5), from the Carolingian Frankish emperor Charlemagne (1.6), and even from the Roman emperor Constantine (1.4bis), linking Gerald transparently to three key Christian dynasties. He also traced Gerald's family's descent through the counts of Poitiers (1.8) to the medieval nobility more broadly, including families still extant in his day. Finally, he provided the earliest claim that Gerald was related to Saint Robert of Turlande and Saint Roch, "heirs to both his blood and his eminent sanctity," at least, as "some fine authors also assure us" (1.4bis).

That these royal, noble, and saintly connections meant something substantial to Dominique betrays a fascination with pedigree typical in early modern France. Moreover, he plainly felt that Gerald might still provide a model to noblemen in his own day, who had a double obligation to behave well, first, as subjects of God, but also second, because others looked up to them (6.1). Not that he had all that high an opinion of them himself. When describing Gerald's piety, for example, Dominique exclaimed: "All the virtues of the most valiant of princes, the most politic or the most skilled in all the world, are nothing but light shadows and fleeting blooms that do not last if they are not founded on the fear of God and the service of the altars. What a shame it is in the age in which we live when a petty and perfumed courtier wishes impiety and libertinage to be the pillars of the state, against everything that the greatest statecraft of the world has ordained?" (11.1).[76] Much like Odo and Ademar before him, Dominique worried that Saint Gerald's example would be ignored by those who needed it most. When discussing Gerald's formal education, he could not resist another rebuke: "A prince lacking letters is a body without a soul, and the greatest reproach made against the nobility of our nation among foreigners is the great disdain for letters that are called useless Latin" (3.5). Ignorance of Latin may have been what prompted Dominique to rework Gerald's *vita* into French. In an age that esteemed high birth and abundant wealth so intensely, Gerald might be precisely the sort of saint who could best be emulated by the rich and powerful, and, following Gerald's example, they would have to renounce neither their wealth nor their social privileges nor enter the cloister to be virtuous. The reinvention of a regal and imperial Gerald reinforced this message that linked rank, ancestry, and power to God's favor.

In what was also clearly a conceit of the day, Dominique seemed particularly anxious to show Gerald as the equal of any great man, whether from Christian tradition or from classical antiquity. When describing Gerald's upbringing and training in both arms and letters, for example, he noted how Marcus Aurelius had also exemplified the importance of both (3.4). In his bodily mortification, Gerald could be easily compared to Saint Benedict or Saint Francis (5.5). Gerald's temperance was the sort praised by both Saint Augustine and Aristotle (10.4), and Gerald's generosity equaled that of Saint Louis or Alexander the Great (6.6 and 15.1). The number and diversity of such allusions showed off Dominique's erudition, of course, but it seems also a bit of an admission that Gerald's qualities were being overlooked and other cultural heroes preferred.

Accordingly, Dominique added touches intended to add to Saint Gerald's appeal, among them the emotionality so emblematic of the Catholic Counter-Reformation that sought to humanize the saints. When Gerald's parents died, for example, "this separation was greatly felt by him since as he loved him and honored them with the whole extent of his heart, as much for their Christian virtues that he always saw shining in them with brilliance and in an unparalleled example as for the singular affection that he had borne them since his birth" (4.4). Gerald was especially touched by prayer: "When he recited the psalms in his chapel, sighs and tears so often interrupted his words that he compelled others to do the same" (16.4). Dominique also frequently paused to describe Gerald's bodily beauty, derived from Ademar's description and intended as an outward sign of inward grace, but hinting at a sublimated eroticism of a sort that would not be entirely unexpected for the era.[77] Already at the age of fifteen Gerald had "a ravishing bodily beauty [*vne beauté de corps rauissante*]," he wrote, with "a beautiful complexion that surpassed roses and carnations" (4.1). "He had such a majestic and agreeable deportment that it seemed as though severity and grace, that so seldom go together, had within him a perfect alliance. He had golden blond hair, lively and sparkling eyes. He was in coloring as white as the lily, intermingled with roses" (18.1).

Dominique furnished those who came after him not only with an updated biography of Saint Gerald but also with a new likeness. The frontispiece to his book shows a woodcut of Saint Gerald, attributed to Gaspard Isaac (see fig. 8).[78] He is clean shaven, and wears a crown on his head and a sumptuous cloak over his shoulders, beneath which can be seen a suit of armor. He carries a church in his right hand, and supports himself with a cane in his left hand. The words *Subvenite, sancti Dei* ("Help, saints of God") come from his mouth as he glances up to heaven. Behind him is Aurillac. The woodcut clearly derives from a close reading of Dominique's text, and each of the attributes in the image can be traced to one element of the description of Saint Gerald or another. The staff that Gerald holds may be the most traditional element, since the vision of Saint Gerald by bishop Stephen had already in the early eleventh century described him as holding a staff or cane (*virga*). What is new is the church he holds in his other hand, a clear symbolic reference to his support of the Catholic church more generally as well as of the church at Aurillac: holding a church was a frequent attribute of founders or patrons of a specific church throughout early modern iconography of the saints.[79] The other new element is a crown. It might simply be a misreading of the medieval Latin term *corona* that Odo used in describing Gerald's tonsure.[80] Or it might be an attempted to portray the *tiara* that Ademar said Gerald used to cover over this tonsure, which probably meant a headcovering in a general sense but which someone in the seventeenth century might well have interpreted as meaning a crown. It is even possible that Gerald's crown represented his virginity, since in Christian art virginal saints were often represented as wearing crowns, a symbol of their elevated status in heaven.[81] It seems likeliest, though, that it was intended to show Gerald's royal and imperial descent. At the very least, most viewers would have understood Gerald's crown as signifying royal status. If Gerald could not win devotion as a saint, the crown seems to recommend that he at least merited deference as a royal personage.

Dominique de Jésus inspired a second cleric to include Gerald's legend in a new collection of local saints' lives, titled the *Vie des saincts et sainctes de l'Auvergne et du Velay*. Its author, Jacques Branche (1590–1662), abbot of the Auvergnat monastery of Pébrac, completed the work in 1652.[82] Branche's biography of Saint Gerald is much shorter than that of Dominique de Jésus, but clearly derived from it; indeed, Branche recommended it to his readers at several points. Branche divided his own collection into three books: the first described local shrines to the Virgin Mary, the second, local saints, and the third, other local holy men and women who, if not officially saints, should still be piously remembered. In his forward, Branche explained that although more popular in his day were the cruel vices of "profane antiquity" found in classical literature, how much worthier should be the recollection of virtue and "the holy and glorious actions of those who, by the integrity of their life, have rendered the Catholic Church throughout the world all glorious in victories"—a triumphalist tone commonplace in Counter-Reformation writings.[83]

Branche's description of Saint Gerald replicated much of Dominique de Jésus' biography, including many of its elaborations. So Gerald remained the descendant of Roman emperors and French kings as well as saints. Branche's own elaborations seem a bit random. When explaining Gerald's upbringing and instruction in letters, for example, Branche added that from adolescence onward Gerald woke himself during the night to say the liturgical office alongside the clerics at his court, a detail also not found anywhere else (578). When mentioning Gerald's concern for the poor, Branche included a story in which Gerald helped out a fellow traveler from Brioude in Auvergne who had broken his hip while on pilgrimage to Rome with some money so he could return home, but where this story might have come from is impossible to say (581–82).

Other embellishments were unmistakably more pointed. He noted Gerald's devotion to the eucharist, for example, and then added that Gerald took it from good and bad priests alike, so as to show his belief in the "real sacrifice" of the sacrament and in its efficacy quite apart from the moral state of the celebrant, points of bitter contention between Catholics and Protestants (579–80). In some places Branche toned down the comments of earlier biographers: when describing Gerald's reluctant participation in warfare, for example, he said that Gerald obtained the victory over his enemies "most often [*fort souuent*]" instead of "always" (583). In other places he intensified the tone: when referring to Gerald's chastity he called him "that holy eunuch of Jesus Christ [*ce sainct Eunuque de Iesus-Christ*]" (584). Branche was also not afraid to revise the details of Gerald's life, likely those he considered peculiar or distasteful. While he included the vision of the priest of Rodez who saw Gerald in heaven in the company of four apostles, for example, he replaced Martial's presence there with that of Saint John (596–97). When recalling the near breach of Gerald's chastity with a young woman, moreover, he made her the daughter of a nobleman instead of a serf, and had Gerald provide her with a farm for her dowry rather than her freedom (584–85).

It is worth noting that Branche included a brief account of the lives of Gerald's parents, Gerald and Adeltrude, in the third part of his collection. In this decision, he was apparently following Odo's comment that miracles happened at Adeltrude's tomb in considering her a near saint worthy of some reverence. Branche's own version repeated Odo's statement and retold the story of Gerald's miraculous cries in his mother's womb and Gerald's father's vision of the tree that grew out of his toe. Of course, he had nothing much more to add about Gerald's parents, apart from commending their decision to have sex only rarely and "doubtless taking this chaste retreat during the greatest solemnities of the year, when it was necessary to approach immaculate the Table of the Lamb" (599). Branche noted that their feast day was celebrated on November 14, but I have found no real evidence elsewhere for any devotion to them.[84] Branche also ended this part by saying that Gerald's father died in 819 (600); it was clearly an error, since he had said that Gerald was born in 856 (575); he also gave 919 as the year of Gerald's death (594).

Apart from Dominique de Jésus and Jacques Branche, there is some evidence for continued interest in Saint Gerald in the seventeenth century through printed versions of his Latin *vita*. The *Vita prolixior* was published twice in the seventeenth century: first, by Martin Marrier at Paris in 1614, as part of his collection of Cluniac saints called the *Biblioteca cluniacensis*, and second, by Laurent Surius at Cologne in 1618 as part of his collection, *De probatiis sanctorum vitiis*. These publications helped to assure that Gerald would be remembered by scholars, but they also cemented into place the error that Odo of Cluny had authored this version of the *Vita Geraldi*.

Another example of continued engagement with Gerald's legend can be seen in a brief biography written in Catalan by Josep de Monpalau in 1664.[85] He also gave as his reason for writing the need to encourage greater knowledge about Gerald, which might have been particularly limited so far from

Aurillac. He hoped "that the pilgrims who go to visit the saint in the holy house of the hermitage of Tossa [de Mar] might at least be able to read it and to fall in love with [*enamorarse*] the saint and to imitate his heroic virtues, and to have some connection to the saint they celebrate and to whom they are devoted" (27). Monpalau's version came from the *Vita prolixior*; he stated outright that he had read the Latin text in the *Biblioteca cluniacensis* (35). Yet Monpalau omitted many of the traditional elements of Gerald's life while adding new and seemingly irrelevant details: for example, that in his studies Gerald "excelled [*reisqué excelentíssim*]" at music, something no one else had said (28). Anachronisms are plentiful, such as his saying that Gerald "was most devoted [*devotíssim*] to the souls in Purgatory" or that every day he "recited the rosary together with everyone who was at his home" (31), since neither form of religious devotion existed in Gerald's day, but his pious purpose in encouraging these forms of devotion in his readers is clear enough. He was also not above rewriting the details of the legend to improve Gerald's image, for example, suggesting that Gerald freed "all of his slaves [*tots sos esclaus*]" in his final testament, and not merely a hundred of them (34). Monpalau was also uncertain of the details in other places, so he gave the date of Gerald's death as "Friday, October 13, in the year 907, or as others would have it, 917" (34).

In several places Monpalau attempted to move beyond the specifics of Gerald's biography to more general reflections. When mentioning Gerald's blindness after being tempted to have sex, for example, he paused to question whether all infirmities should be reckoned as the consequence of personal sin (32). Most peculiar was a detailed analogy between the parts of Gerald's body and his virtues that was probably intended more as a means to meditation than saying much of anything about Gerald himself: "His faith was his head, prudence his eyes, truth his tongue, religion his breast, friendship his heart, obedience his ears, bashfulness his face, mercy his entrails, charity his soul, hope his blood, generosity his hands, patience his muscles, strength his arms, temperance his appearance, modesty his gestures and manners, justice his good looks [*hermosura*], abstinence his bowels, chastity his penis [*sexo*], perseverance his feet, humility his height" (30).

Monpalau ended his account with the information that Gerald had once slept at Tossa de Mar "three or four years" before he died, that the stone on which he laid his head was on display there still, and that touching the reliquary of Saint Gerald there had brought about (unspecified) miracles (35). Like Dominique de Jésus and Jacques Branche, Monpalau obviously hoped to inspire new affection for the saint, in this instance, not only by translating the story of Gerald's life into the vernacular so that it could be read and emulated by the laity, but also by linking Gerald in novel ways to places and forms of piety that might still appeal to the devout—to update Gerald for a new generation, to show that he still had something to offer to those who revered him, that he was still worthy to be remembered.

The Early Modern Images of Saint Gerald

How successful were these efforts to encourage the revival of Saint Gerald's cult in the early modern era? For the most part the question is unanswerable. Yet there are hints that other attempts were being made to disseminate information about Saint Gerald to the faithful. A series of liturgical prayers to be recited on his feast day also survives from seventeenth-century Auvergne. These prayers offer useful clues as to what the unlearned devout might have known about Saint Gerald. One summarized his life in succinct refrains: "You who, called by God in the womb of your mother, responded in a clear voice three times, intercede for us. You who, while among the pleasures of the court, remained a lifelong virgin, intercede for us. You who, while living in the world, were an emulator of the life of monks, intercede for us. You who, while fighting with blunted sword [*retuso ferro*] lest you should harm the enemy, obtained victory, intercede for us. You who, through the water poured over your hands, restored sight to the blind, intercede for us. You who consecrated your principality to the prince of the apostles, intercede for us." Gerald was once again "the good count," and his charity to the poor, his fondness for prayer, and even the restrained conversation at his table were all repeated. His building of the church at Aurillac and his pilgrimages to Rome were also mentioned. At the same time, more recent elements of Gerald's legend contributed to this liturgical image: he was "born of royal stock, prince of Auvergne, glory of the Gallic realm."[86]

New visual representations of Saint Gerald also served to publicize him afresh, and several images from the seventeenth century have survived. Among them is a polychrome plaster sculpture now in the church of Saint-Géraud in Aurillac that seems clearly to replicate the features also present in the woodcut printed by Dominique de Jésus (see fig. 9).[87] Gerald holds the church in his left hand and the cane in his right; more significantly, Gerald sports a full beard, so its artist had clearly taken some liberties with Gerald's

SANCTVS GERALDVS COMES ET CONFESSOR

Ardescit iuuenis facibus cælestis Amoris,
Admouet & tædas, cæca libido, truces,
Pugnat vterque ignis, sed Christi flamma Geraldum
Arte noua, vincens, ignis ab igne perit.

Figure 8. Saint Gerald, woodcut by Gaspard Isaac, from *Histoire paraenetique des trois saincts protecteurs du Haut Auvergne* by Dominique de Jésus, published at Paris in 1635, p. 438. From a copy held at the Bibliothèque de l'Arsenal, Paris. Reprinted by permission of Bibliothèque nationale de France.

Figure 9. Saint Gerald, seventeenth century. Polychrome plaster. Church of Saint-Géraud, Aurillac. Courtesy of Pierre Moulier.

story, or had not known it, or simply guessed at how a medieval nobleman should look.

It is only one of several similar statues, whose similarities in appearance and proximity in location suggest a campaign of sorts to provide local churches with visual representations of Saint Gerald, however crude, as aids to worship.[88] Sadly, few of these can be dated with any certainty, but they include statues of Saint Gerald at Lempdes-sur-Allagnon (fig. 10) and at Saint-Saturnin (fig. 11).[89] In the second of these statues, Gerald's cane has been replaced by a sword, a change that reinforces his status as a lay defender of the church even if it obscures his reluctance to engage in violence that his medieval biographers had tried so hard to underscore. In only the first of

Figure 10. Saint Gerald, seventeenth century. Polychrome wood. Church of Saint-Géraud, Lempdes-sur-Allagnon (*département* of Haute-Loire). Courtesy of Pierre Moulier.

Figure 11. Saint Gerald, seventeenth century. Polychrome wood. Church of Saint-Saturnin, Saint-Saturnin (*département* of Cantal). Courtesy of Pierre Moulier.

these statues, one might add, does Gerald wear a distinctive crown. It is tempting to interpret its absence in the second as the artist's way of minimizing or ignoring the royal ancestry that his seventeenth-century biographers had invented so as to reinforce identification between the average follower and the saint, although in both of these statues Gerald wears garments more suited to a monk or a cleric than to a layman. In the first of these images, moreover, Gerald also holds a book, an attribute usually reserved for saints who produced significant writings. These varied attributes might imply that even as Gerald's cult was renewed, confusion about him remained.

Attempts to revitalize the veneration of Saint Gerald on a popular level had their drawbacks. Dominique de Jésus noted this exact problem at some length in his biography:

It is not also out of context to remark the complaint of some . . . regarding the images that are made of the saint and that can be seen ordinarily in the churches and chapels where he is honored, because he is painted as a young horseman, all covered in plumes, dressed and mounted smartly, and holding a bird on his hand or throwing a lance at a boar. I would not like to fault the devotion of our fathers on this point, which seems quite old, in various vestiges from this great monastery [of Aurillac]. In addition, the esteem for nobility was immense among our old Gauls, who did no other profession than that of arms, having a warlike and martial disposition. It was that which brought them to honor this saint in such a manner, to provide an example to the young, because as we have said Saint Gerald was the paragon of nobility in his day. . . . But as the holy Council of Trent commands, so that within the Catholic Church images should be as controlled and devout as can be done, it seems that the image of the saint, who did none of these actions even in his youth, and who was so moderate and restrained in military matters, should be represented in a style more favorable to piety and devotion, and which would have nonetheless a majesty to it. (18.5)

In his criticism of how others reimagined Saint Gerald, even while ignoring his own literary embellishments, Dominique seems unmistakably to have been pointing to a painting that once belonged to the monastery of Aurillac but is now housed in the Musée d'art et d'archéologie there (see fig. 12). It represents Gerald in the midst of a boar hunt, precisely at the moment of

Figure 12. Saint Gerald hunting a wild boar, seventeenth century. 103 x 95 cm, oil on canvas. © Musée d'art et d'archéologie, Aurillac. Courtesy of the Musée d'art et d'archéologie, Aurillac.

launching his lance at a boar. Behind the depiction lies an early modern legend about the origin of Aurillac that Dominique repeated even while he mocked it: that Gerald had been hunting and stabbed a wild boar through the ear, and promised to found a town on the spot (*aure acus* in Latin means something like "wounding in the ear" and provides a false etymology of the name Aurillac). Dominique wrote that "it was a silly and ridiculous legend, based on the image of the saint" (20.1).[90] Despite these complaints, Gerald has many of the same attributes shown elsewhere of the saint: he is clean shaven and wears a crown and a suit of armor. In the background can be seen a castle overlooking a collection of buildings, among which is a church spire that obviously represents the monastery that Gerald had founded at

Aurillac.[91] More to the point, Dominique seemed to hint that this sort of Gerald would have been better received in his day by most men. Other art surviving from the seventeenth century includes paintings that represent scenes more closely tied to the life of Gerald and more in keeping with Dominique's counsel. Among these is a large tableau now in the church of Saint-Géraud in Aurillac showing Gerald kneeling before the pope and reflecting the donation of his property to Rome, along with the church that he had founded and that he holds in this image (see fig. 13).[92]

However colorful or varied the attempts made to inspire new forms of veneration for Saint Gerald in the seventeenth century, though, they seem not to have any long-lasting effects. Jacques Branche's own collection of saints' stories bears out this fact. Among the shrines to the Virgin Mary he discussed in the first part of his book was one in a side chapel in the church of Saint-Géraud in Aurillac and called Notre-Dame-du-Coeur.[93] Of it, Branche wrote: "It is ancient by five or six hundred years, and always has been visited by people, honored with several miracles; it is said that formerly people came from Italy, Spain, and elsewhere in such a great crowd that one was reduced to barricading the streets out of fear that someone would be suffocated in the throng of pilgrims" (94). Curiously, he made no similar comments about the popularity of Gerald's own shrine there. He also noted the many recent miracles that took place in the church, but carefully attributed all of them to the intervention of the Virgin Mary and not to Saint Gerald. One was described as happening to a widow of Aurillac, who was healed of a fever in 1646 when she prayed at the Virgin's shrine in the church; another involved an unnamed deaf woman who came to Aurillac in 1644 and was cured. One even occurred in 1640 to a canon of Saint-Géraud, who had been "abandoned by his doctors to the mercy of a ongoing fever that would have taken him to the grave," but who prayed to the Virgin Mary in the church and was healed (95–97). It is telling that Gerald was given no role even in these miracles that happened in his church, nor did Branche mention any recent miracles in his portrayal of Gerald.

In other ways, Gerald's cult continued its decline. While a mass of celebration had been held in the church of Saint-Géraud in 1581 after the retaking of the town of Aurillac from the Protestants, and Saint Gerald lauded for his heavenly assistance in that task, by the eighteenth century new versions of the legend remembered the Virgin Mary as having restored the town to Catholic worship.[94] A pastoral visit by the bishop of Saint-Flour in 1698 noted that the church of Saint-Géraud was unkempt, its altars neglected, and its windows in several places lacking panes of glass.[95] Worse still, a scandal erupted in 1738

Figure 13. Saint Gerald kneeling before the pope, holding the church of the monastery he has founded, seventeenth century. Oil on canvas. Church of Saint-Géraud, Aurillac. Courtesy of Pierre Moulier.

when the town consuls went to celebrate the feast of Saint Gerald with the usual procession of the saint's relics, and were informed by the parish priest that there was no point to it since the reliquary contained only the bones of a dog! (The following year the procession resumed.)[96]

One incident is worth mentioning, though, to show that the memory of Saint Gerald had not completely withered away. Summer floods threatened to overwhelm the town of Aurillac as well as the surrounding district in 1703. In response, "the relics of Saint Gerald were exposed for a week on the large altar of the chapter-church where every day was said a high mass for the saint. The whole body of monks and priests [*réguliers et séculiers*] attended it every day. . . . With an exemplary devotion, everyone kneeled for an hour. On Sunday took place a general procession at which the relics of the saint were carried with so great a crowd of people from the town and from the country-side that you had never seen the like, after which was sung the 'Te Deum' in front of the relics."[97]

In general, though, the eighteenth century saw little sign of devotion to Saint Gerald. A general decline in religiosity in France in this century, with shrinking numbers of priests, monks, and nuns, and fewer testamentary donations to churches, means that Gerald's condition was not unique.[98] I found only one biography of Saint Gerald published in the eighteenth century, in Aurillac in 1715. Its author, who identified himself only as M. Compaing, parish priest of Savènes in the diocese of Toulouse, dedicated his work to the abbot of Aurillac, and explained in his preface that the canons of the monastery there had asked him to translate the Latin *vita* into French.[99] It was mostly a loose translation of the *Vita prolixior*, though Compaing inserted his own opinions into the lengthy preface. He complained especially that Protestants, if they were to read the *vita*, would see that many of the practices they condemned in Catholics as novelties dated back at least to the ninth century and to Gerald's lifetime, among them, the use of candles in worship and the veneration of relics. What is perhaps the most unique feature of the translation is the final section of meditations, a sort of examination of conscience for readers (who may have been only the canons of Aurillac):

> Can it be said of you as of Saint Gerald, that he could have trans-
> gressed the law of God but did not, he could have done evil but did
> not? See if you have ever given entrance within your heart to pride, if
> the nobility of your ancestry, the advantages of body and mind, or the
> good things of fortune have not given you occasion to raise yourself

up and to despite others. See if you have guarded the precious treasure of chastity and, if after having committed offenses contrary to this virtue, you have expiated them with a rigorous penitence.[100]

Only two devotional works of art with Gerald as their subject can be firmly dated to the eighteenth century, both paintings completed in 1774. The first, signed F. Mauperin (probably the artist François Mauperin of Paris), depicts Gerald before Bishop Gauzbert, offering to abandon his comital duties for the monastic life but being handed back his crown and sword (see fig. 14). The second, signed J.-B. Lesueur, portrays the death of Gerald as described in the *Transitus*, in the presence of a bishop and surrounded by friends and well-wishers—and with the laurel of victory awaiting him in heaven (see fig. 15). Unfortunately, nothing has been preserved to tell us anything about who commissioned these paintings or for what purpose; the likeliest explanation is that the canons or some prominent citizens of Aurillac did so, and probably to adorn Saint Gerald's church.[101]

The French Revolution spelled a near end to the cult of Saint Gerald. Restrictions on the churches and religious orders in France were extended bit by bit until Christianity was abolished and churches across France were closed, demolished, or converted to temples to abstract principles. The church of Saint-Géraud at Aurillac itself was converted into a Temple of Reason, according to a proclamation of 1794, and the square in front of the church renamed Union Square (Place de l'Union). The canons of Aurillac were dispersed, although two of them were held for a time in the convent-turned-prison of Le Buis, across the Jordanne River from the church of Saint-Géraud.[102] Most of the monastery's remaining buildings were demolished, among them the medieval bell tower of the church, and those that were not were sold into private hands.[103] Similar transformations happened at the other locations where Saint Gerald was still venerated. Even after the reestablishment of Catholicism in France through the Concordat signed in 1801, much of the historical memory of Gerald—at least the material memory of him—seemed irretrievably lost.

If one can generalize from Gerald's example, it might be only the observation that saints have life cycles like most other things, and legion are the ones like Gerald, forgotten entirely or revered only where their devotion began. Indeed, rare is a saint whose cult spread across a wide region for any length of time, save perhaps those few more immune to fleeting spiritual fame. All the more remarkable, then, are those saints who show no similar historical "bell curve" of popularity, especially the long-deceased medieval

Figure 14. Saint Gerald receiving the tonsure at the hands of Gauzbert, F. Mauperin, 1774. 77 x 66 cm, oil on canvas. © Musée d'art et d'archéologie, Aurillac. Courtesy of the Musée d'art et d'archéologie, Aurillac.

saints, a Saint Martin of Tours or a Saint Nicholas, whose cults began early in the Middle Ages, were repeatedly reinvented or rejuvenated, and continue full apace even today, more than a thousand years later. They are the exceptions to the rule that made itself felt so ruthlessly in the case of Saint Gerald of Aurillac. Nonetheless, Gerald was not finished quite yet.

Figure 15. The death of Saint Gerald, J.-B. Lesueur, 1774. Oil on canvas. Church of Saint-Géraud, Aurillac. Courtesy of Pierre Moulier.

CHAPTER 6

The Modern Cult of Saint Gerald

The French Revolution seemed to signal the end of the cult of Saint Gerald. Yet the churches dedicated to Saint Gerald were closed for less than a decade, and when the Catholic religion was restored in France in 1801 Saint Gerald returned to Aurillac and to thirty or so of his other churches across southern France. With the dispersion of the last canons of Aurillac, however, the official keepers of the memory of Saint Gerald were gone, and even where devotion was renewed, knowledge of Gerald faded. A proposal sent to the bishop of Saint-Flour in 1803 even requested that the church dedicated to Saint Gerald in Aurillac be rededicated to the Virgin Mary—a request that was denied.[1] The fairs held at Aurillac and elsewhere on Saint Gerald's feast day, October 13, continued until the middle of the twentieth century, but these were slim reminders of the former devotion to the saint.[2] In the nineteenth and twentieth centuries (the period that will be called "modern" in what follows), Saint Gerald's memory survived—but in surprisingly distorted forms.

The Modern Churches of Saint Gerald

The church of Saint Gerald in Aurillac can stand as an example, better documented than most, of the fates of the churches dedicated to the saint. The church had been renovated over many centuries. Its origins date back to Gerald himself, although the earliest parts remaining today survive only from its reconstruction in the years before 972 and only in a few details.[3] Most of the church is from the late eleventh century, Romanesque in style, though it was renovated in the fifteenth century, perhaps to repair damage done to it

during the burghers' revolt of 1233, and modernized in the Gothic style. The
church suffered greatly during the Protestant takeover of the town in the
sixteenth century, but was also partly restored in the mid-seventeenth century.[4] During the French Revolution its Romanesque bell tower was demolished. A description of the church given in 1803 is pitiful:

> The church is very deteriorated and cut short, it is squared off and
> ungraceful, the windows are open and the vaults pierced through,
> with currents of air that disturb the lighted candles and cause melted
> wax to fall suddenly and abundantly over the altar cloths, the orna-
> ments, the steps, the gilt, and depreciate all of these objects. These
> currents of air make problems for the faithful, too. . . . A channel of
> water flows continuously across the square of the wheat market [in
> front of the church]. It has allowed large amounts of water to filter
> through the ground and the paving of this square and it immediately
> fills the trenches and holes dug to discover the state of the founda-
> tions. This water also penetrates under the pavement of the church
> and through the miserable wall that serves as its facade. To this water
> is added the water from the ordinary rains that swell this stream
> from their start both above and below the floor of the church.[5]

There were other priorities for civic restoration, however, so money was set
aside only for the most urgent of repairs to the church.[6]

The whirlwind changes in French governments in the nineteenth century seem to have alternatively helped and hindered the cause of restoration.
In 1820 the restored Bourbon monarchy pledged money for it. Additional
emergency funds were given again in 1825, 1828, 1838, and 1845 for the most
urgent repairs, but it was not until 1849 that a plan was developed that called
not only for the renovation of the church in a neo-Gothic style, but also for
enlarging it and furnishing it with a new bell tower. The work took place
between 1856 and 1864, financed in part by the imperial government of Napoleon III and in part by a public appeal launched on what was believed to be
the millennial celebration of the birth of Saint Gerald. Even then, when the
first stone of the renovation was laid in a public ceremony in 1857, the depth
of devotion to Saint Gerald was questionable. The bishop of Saint-Flour
presiding at the dedication wondered aloud whether anyone would frequent
the church, even if it were rebuilt. "Will you leave these altars deserted,"
he asked the attending crowd, "will you leave God alone in his abandoned
tabernacles?"[7] It was not until 1898, after another change in government and

Figure 16. Reliquary for Saint Gerald, manufactured in Lyon in 1894. Church of Saint-Géraud, Aurillac. Courtesy of Pierre Moulier.

a fire had destroyed part of the church in 1892, that it was completed. (The mayor of Aurillac is said to have climbed to the top of the new bell tower at its dedication and shouted "Vive la République!"[8]) In the early twentieth century changes were still being made: in 1923 the square on the north side of the church was enlarged, and in 1939 the buildings that had been erected abutting the exterior of the apse were demolished.[9] Today, the church is the least "medieval" of all the old churches of Aurillac.[10] Bits of medieval decoration have been placed haphazardly around the church, such as the bas-relief of animals and plants that may have once formed part of Saint Gerald's sarcophagus, and a sculpted lion, one of a pair that may have flanked the entrance to the Romanesque church.[11]

Relics of Saint Gerald are still venerated in this church. When I first visited the church in 2000, the parish priest showed me the latest reliquary in one of the side chapels—an ornate gilded box manufactured in Lyon in 1894 (fig. 16).[12] When I returned to the church in 2006, there were also two new reliquaries on either side of the main altar: gilded wooden boxes, glass

Figure 17. Reliquary for Saint Gerald, eighteenth century. Perhaps from the abbey of
Cluny. Church of Saint-Géraud, Aurillac. Courtesy of Pierre Moulier.

paned, in which the top of a skull and other bones were visible and identified
as Gerald's (see fig. 17). These are listed in an inventory of historical objects
related to the monastery of Aurillac, which traces them to the monastery of
Cluny and dates them to the eighteenth century.[13]

The other churches and priories that once belonged to the monastery suffered varied fates. Some fell victim to urban renewal. The church dedicated to Saint Gerald at Limoges, for example, built before the year 1000 and mentioned by Ademar of Chabannes, had a priory residence and hospice later added to it. These structures were enlarged and replaced over the centuries, and by the end of the eighteenth century they were among the largest public buildings in the town. Because of their size, and since the monastery of Saint-Martial had been demolished during the French Revolution, they served as the city hall for Limoges in the early nineteenth century. In the 1830s, finally, the old buildings were demolished to make way for a new edifice and a public square. No visible memory of Gerald remains in Limoges.[14] In Toulouse, the church of Saint Gerald, built probably in the eleventh century and rebuilt in the fifteenth century, was sold and used as a granary during the French Revolution. It was only briefly restored to religious worship between 1801 and 1815. When the square beside the church was enlarged in 1846 so that the covered market that stood in front of the church could be expanded, it was demolished. Now, a short alley is the sole recollection of Saint Gerald's presence there.[15]

Some of the churches dedicated to Saint Gerald in smaller towns and villages were rebuilt following the French Revolution. Encompassing a considerable geographical extent that includes Aspres-sur-Buëch,[16] Concourès,[17] Lédat,[18] Sieurac,[19] and Vailhourles,[20] most, like Aurillac, were rebuilt only in the second half of the nineteenth century. Also like Aurillac, many have incorporated elements of medieval sculpture or reused bits and pieces from the medieval priories they replaced. The parish was vital for the organization of community identity in France after the Revolution, especially in the rural areas of the Massif Central, and the churches to Saint Gerald doubtless played a critical role.[21] Their rebuilding may speak more to the general needs of their communities than to the perpetuation of particular devotion to Saint Gerald. Still, these churches meant that Gerald's memory was not entirely lost.

None of these reconstructed churches are architecturally significant, yet they participated in the larger project of restoration after the turmoil of the Revolution and in the nostalgia for the Middle Ages that typifies the era, in church architecture and otherwise. The renewed appreciation for medieval architecture is perhaps best remembered in the efforts of novelist Victor Hugo (1802–85) and others to preserve Notre-Dame Cathedral in Paris, but campaigns across France aimed both at preserving medieval church buildings and at rebuilding those that had been demolished in neo-Romanesque or neo-Gothic styles.[22] Efforts were spearheaded by Prosper Mérimée (1803–70), inspector-general for historical monuments in France from 1834 to 1853, and by his protégé, the architect Eugène Viollet-le-Duc (1814–79).[23] Mérimée traveled across France, describing the most notable medieval buildings and encouraging their reclamation. He published his notes from a journey through Auvergne in 1837, and mentioned two of the churches dedicated to Saint Gerald. One was the church at Lempdes-sur-Allagnon, which was in the process of restoration, and which included obscene sculpted medallions on the exterior of the apse that he considered "jokes in very poor taste" (*de très-grossières plaisanteries*).[24] The other was the church of Saint-Géraud at Aurillac that, he complained, "offers all of the failings of the Gothic style during its decadence: columns without capitals pierced by the ribs of the vault, with ornamentation either flamboyant or of the meanest sort." Mérimée also noted the public fountain in front the church, as well as the former hospice (see above, fig. 4).[25] The enthusiasm of these men and others encouraged a new appreciation for medieval architecture imitated, however coarsely, in the nineteenth-century churches dedicated to Saint Gerald.

The Modern Images of Saint Gerald

Nostalgia for the Middle Ages infused not only the structures of these churches but also their interior décor, and new visual images of Saint Gerald proliferated—indeed, became an essential means for remembering him. As depicted in the nineteenth century, however, Gerald hinted at new realities unimagined or rejected by his earlier biographers and devotees. Much still needs to be done in the study of nineteenth-century French religious art, which has long been ridiculed as *bondieuserie* (banal religious kitsch) and is often pejoratively called *art de Saint-Sulpice* after the neighborhood in Paris where it was mass produced and sold. The debates over the worth of such art, curiously enough, replicate some of the same issues debated in the first sculpted representations of the saints, that is, whether it helps or hinders religious devotion, even while it highlights class-based differences in that devotion, some disdaining as crude or uncultured what others find uplifting.[26]

So little is known of how the modern images of Saint Gerald were commissioned, designed, or produced, that it is difficult to draw any conclusions about these aspects of their creation. We can presume that they were made in workshops of religious art and based either on generalized features of saints or with instructions from church personnel.[27] Where records survive they show the involvement of regional workshops rather than those of Paris: several of the stained-glass depictions of Saint Gerald were crafted in Clermont-Ferrand, for example, at the factory founded by Émile Thibaud in 1835 that continued to produce religious art into the twentieth century.[28]

Also unclear are the specific ritual uses of the images of Saint Gerald. To be sure, many were there simply to adorn the interiors of churches. Stained-glass images of Saint Gerald are often located behind the main altar of a church, for example, and might easily have prompted meditation during mass. Most sculpted images of Saint Gerald, in contrast, are found in side chapels at a distance from the main altar, occasionally with elaborate altars of their own and with prie-dieux for individual prayer, but standing apart from the main ritual activities of the church and requiring particular devotion. How often these chapels were visited in the nineteenth and twentieth centuries is, of course, impossible to gauge. I found virtually no examples of *ex-voto* plaques offered to Saint Gerald in any of these chapels; such plaques were a popular nineteenth-century means of publicizing a saint's beneficence, paid for by individuals or families in exchange for answers to prayers.[29] Nor was I able to find much evidence of other ritual uses of the images of Saint Gerald in the living memory of the inhabitants of the towns and villages I visited, although a few of the churches possessed processional banners with his image that affirmed that processions did take place. The examples from La Capelle-del-Vern (see fig. 18, mentioned in an inventory of 1894) and Monsempron-Libos (see fig. 19, from 2004) show the range of periods of manufacture and a sustained ritual devotion of sorts.[30] Whatever their use, these visual representations were potent symbols to those who viewed them. Judith Devlin has suggested that in nineteenth-century rural France "people unfamiliar with the vocabulary of contemporary political and social debate naturally tended to express their thoughts and feelings through legends and images consecrated by tradition," including religious art and stories.[31] The ubiquity of images of Saint Gerald clearly imply that he held real import— even if we cannot determine with absolute clarity the full range of those meanings.

Modern images of Saint Gerald almost invariably present him in the guise of an idealized medieval knight: it is crucial to how he was remembered in the nineteenth and twentieth centuries.[32] Let us begin in the village of

Figure 18. Banner depicting Saint Gerald, before 1894. Church of Saint-Géraud, La Capelle-del-Vern (*commune* of Escandolières, *département* of Aveyron). Courtesy of Pierre Moulier.

Figure 19. Banner depicting Saint Gerald, 2004. Church of Saint-Géraud, Monsempron-Libos (*département* of Lot-et-Garonne). Courtesy of Pierre Moulier.

Figure 20. Stained-glass window
depicting Saint Gerald, 1903.
Church of Saint-Sigismond,
Saint-Simon (*département* of
Cantal). Courtesy of Brian
Giguere.

Saint-Simon, just outside of Aurillac, and the image of Saint Gerald in
stained glass from his church there, from 1903 (fig. 20).[33] Gerald retains the
attributes he had adopted already in his early modern representations, wearing a suit of armor covered by elegant clothes and carrying a church in his
left hand. He wears a crown, but it has also become a helmet. He has a beard,
contrary to his medieval description, probably because that is how medieval
knights were remembered in the nineteenth century.[34] He is depicted as a
middle-aged man, with a stern expression and the dignity of age. Many of
the churches dedicated to Saint Gerald closest to Aurillac contain very similar
stained-glass images of Gerald. The church of Saint-Géraud in the village of
Montvert, for example, northeast of Aurillac, contains a similar stained-glass
image from 1869, although Gerald appears a bit younger.[35] In the image of
Saint Gerald in the church of Banhars from 1898, he is also very similarly

depicted, although perhaps older. In each of these images as in many others less easily dated, Gerald sports a beard, wears a crown, and carries a church in one hand.[36]

What is most striking in these and most other images of Saint Gerald is that the cane or staff shown in earlier representations has become a sword. The sword was likely intended to symbolize Gerald's earthly authority, as his staff had done, yet by the change that authority is reinterpreted as military might. The depiction of an armed Saint Gerald was not entirely new to the nineteenth century, but its proliferation certainly was. The sword often appeared in contemporary images of lay protectors of the church, and that doubtless helps to explain its choice by the artisans who crafted the images, but few saints were so ambivalently linked to the issue of violence as Gerald, so the sword carries an additional symbolic charge.[37] That meaning may not have been appreciated by most viewers of these images; instead, given the nineteenth-century revival in France of the art of fencing and the resurgence of dueling, both often described in medieval metaphors harking back to chivalry and masculine honor, other connotations might have sprung to mind in those who admired the sword-wielding Gerald.[38]

Most modern sculpted images of Saint Gerald also present him in similar costume, crowned, dressed in medieval armor, and wielding a sword. The sculpture at Sieurac (see fig. 21), for example, seems so similar that it is difficult not to imagine some communication between the artists who carved it and those who worked the stained glass. At Vailhourles, Gerald's sword remains in its scabbard, in contrast to most other depictions where it is bared, which might be interpreted as an artist's attempt to demonstrate Gerald's reluctance to participate in violence, although that is likely reading too much into the piece (see fig. 22). Some sculptures, as at Sieurac, seem to show Gerald wielding his sword more as a symbolic cross than as a weapon, which may also be purposeful.

It is tempting to interpret the abundance of martial images of Saint Gerald in the late nineteenth century and the linking of church and sword as reflecting the uncomfortable political position of Catholics in the France of the early Third Republic. Devout French Catholics—precisely the sort who would have consumed these images of Saint Gerald—were mostly excluded from republican politics in the decades following 1870 and were under substantial retreat in areas such as education and in the registrations of marriages and deaths that had long been ecclesiastical prerogatives.[39] At the same time, French political conservatives were bitterly divided among themselves.[40] Even

Figure 21. Saint Gerald, late nineteenth century. Polychrome plaster. Church of Saint-Géraud, Sieurac (*département* of Tarn). Courtesy of Pierre Moulier.

Figure 22. Saint Gerald, late nineteenth century.
Polychrome plaster. Church of Saint-Géraud,
Vailhourles (*département* of Aveyron). Courtesy of
Brian Giguere.

the promise of a popular conservative military figure and politician in
Georges Boulanger in the 1880s failed to revive Catholic political influence,
since, at the height of his power, Boulanger was exiled amid scandal and later
committed suicide.[41] Pope Leo XIII did issue an encyclical in 1892 that urged
French Catholics to reconcile themselves to the republican government,
beginning what is called the *Ralliement* that made a necessary distinction
between French Catholicism and support for the monarchy.[42] Still, devout
Catholics remained most often excluded from French politics, a fact that

continued into the early decades of the twentieth century, further reinforced by the official separation of church and state by law in 1905.[43] In a telling example of the mood among traditionalists, the parish priest of the church of Saint-Géraud in Aurillac gave a speech on the saint's feast day following the enactment of this law and vowed "on the blessed bones of the illustrious founder and patron of this ancient city" never to abandon "the holy rights of the Church."[44]

In the wake of such political disenfranchisement, conservative French Catholics seem to have returned wholeheartedly to old forms of devotion in ways that often harked back nostalgically to a medieval past. The popularity of pilgrimages, for example, that mostly died out in early modern Catholic Europe, was revived in the nineteenth century. The appeal of Lourdes, where the Virgin Mary is said to have first appeared in 1858, is probably the best-known example. Equal in stature to Lourdes in late nineteenth-century France was La Salette, where the Virgin appeared in 1846. Both cults quickly received official sanction, and huge basilicas were built to accommodate the thousands of pilgrims who visited annually.[45] Attempts to revive devotion to Saint Gerald may have borrowed from these more fashionable devotions. Most of the churches dedicated to Saint Gerald also contain images of the Our Lady of Lourdes or La Salette, for example, although it is difficult to know when they were placed there. The revival of Marian pilgrimages could be exploited in other ways: closer to Aurillac at Quézac, annual pilgrimage to a medieval sculpture of the Madonna and Child was begun in the late nineteenth century. A huge church was begun there in 1878 and consecrated in 1887, and it contained a stained-glass image of Saint Gerald that encouraged pilgrims to consider him, too, in the midst of their devotions.[46]

Saint Gerald's military image may have inspired those who venerated him in other, more practical ways. As Catholic men were squeezed from influence in the Third Republic, many retreated to military careers. Indeed, given their exclusion from politics, such careers became vital opportunities for Catholics interested in pursuing public life.[47] At the same time, it was not mostly in the present that Catholics must have looked for their martial reputation, given France's catastrophic military losses in the Franco-Prussian War (1870–71) and the national soul-searching that tried to make sense of that defeat, but in the past. Symbols of the ancient and medieval past began to reappear in military iconography, including the use of Roman *fasces* and Frankish helmets. French military heroes, such as the mythical figure of Roland from the medieval *Chanson de Roland*, said to have been a knight of

Charlemagne, were also memorialized in new ways in art and literature in the late nineteenth century.[48] The representations of Saint Gerald as a medieval warrior, some of which have him wearing a Frankish helmet, as at Salles-Curan and Monsempron-Libos, are part and parcel of this romanticized memory of the French military past.

For Catholic conservatives in France, that glorious medieval past was spiritual as much as military. Like the developing cult of Saint Joan of Arc—beatified in 1909, canonized in 1920, and celebrated again in a major way in 1931 on the five hundredth anniversary of her death—the cult of Saint Gerald appealed especially to those who thought that France's martial greatness would not be found again unless joined to religious piety, and Saint Gerald's church and sword plainly reflected that mixture.[49] Saint Joan's support for the French monarchy, so central to her legend, attracted those who wished to distance themselves from republicanism, and the same could be said about devotion to Saint Gerald.[50] Indeed, in a ceremony to mark the start of restoration work on Saint Gerald's church in Aurillac in 1857, the prefect of the *département* of Cantal compared Gerald explicitly to Joan of Arc in his patriotism and faith.[51] Nonetheless, Joan of Arc was a much more ambiguous symbol because of her challenge to the church authorities of her day.[52] In contrast, Gerald provided Catholics with a saint who was clearly devoted to Rome and the pope. Indeed, Gerald's attachment to Rome could be called upon to reinforce the ultramontanism that was very much in vogue among French Catholics of the early Third Republic. When the push for Italian unification began in earnest in the 1860s, for example, the pope, who stood to lose control of the Papal States, called for Catholic volunteers to defend his lands, and devout Frenchmen signed up in large numbers. They called themselves the Papal Zouaves and promised a "ninth crusade," itself a vibrant symbol of the mix of medievalism, militarism, and Catholic traditionalism.[53] The images of Saint Gerald were not immune to such potent ideological influences. So, for example, a stained-glass window at Banhars from 1898 shows Gerald in an audience with the pope, who sports the elaborate triple crown worn by popes (only from the fifteenth century on) to symbolize their universal authority.

Curiously, though, in choosing to represent Saint Gerald so forcefully as a medieval soldier of Christ, nineteenth-century artists and their patrons highlighted the violence that Gerald's medieval biographers had sought to downplay while at the same time they ignored what was central to those medieval biographers' veneration for Gerald: his refusal to marry. Ademar said of Gerald that "what looms largest among his incomparable deeds is that up until old age he persevered in chastity" (2.34). There may have been conscious reasons for this disregard. Unmarried men were regarded suspiciously and judged harshly in the public discourse of late nineteenth-century France, according to Judith Surkis, condemned for their "failure to assume socially productive and reproductive roles" and through whom were "expressed larger concerns about the socially unsettling effects of modernity."[54] Surkis views the establishment of universal male military conscription in France in 1889 as intended not only to avoid the military catastrophe of 1870–71 but also to train young men in martial discipline; she then notes that fears of unbridled venereal disease among French troops sparked further worries about single men's sexuality.[55] Concerns about young men's reluctance to marry were in part demographic, and many French government leaders viewed the low birth rates in France with increasing alarm in the late nineteenth century.[56] These demographic concerns may have been felt most acutely in the isolated rural regions of France, since young men increasingly preferred to delay their marriages and to migrate to the industrial cities to look for work, rather than remaining on rural farms, marrying young and raising large families, as their fathers and grandfathers had.[57] In those communities where the veneration of Saint Gerald survived, the subject of his bachelorhood may have been deliberately avoided. No representation of Gerald, insofar as I have found, ever depicted him with the lily that had become the usual sign of male chastity in Catholic art—although both Odo and Ademar had described Gerald as a "lily among thorns," which would have made it a particularly apt symbol for him.[58]

Attempts to revive popular devotion to Saint Gerald through soldierly representations of him may also have responded intentionally to nineteenth-century concerns about the gendering of religious piety as feminine. Scholars have found especially in British and American Protestantism attempts to counter the feminization of nineteenth-century religion with a "muscular Christianity," but the same trends existed in nineteenth-century France, with much higher rates of mass attendance for women than men and the greater control of Catholic religious orders over the education of girls than of boys. The sentimentalization of religious devotion and art also probably appealed more to the sensibilities of women of the age.[59] Accordingly, the martial representations of Saint Gerald might have been a means by which to reassure male churchgoers that their manliness was not compromised by their piety.[60] In this regard, Gerald was a more successful reflection of a "muscular"

Catholicism than Joan of Arc could ever have been. Representing Saint Gerald as bearded as well as armed, also in contrast to how his medieval biographers portrayed him, may have also figured in this gendered response.

As *art de Saint-Sulpice*, these depictions of Saint Gerald ignored or rejected the efforts of some contemporary French artists to harmonize modern artistic trends and piety in art.[61] Perhaps if the purpose of religious art was to serve as a theology for the masses, as celebrated French philosopher and devout Catholic Jacques Maritain suggested in 1919, it was preferable that it should be indeterminate enough to permit the pious sentiments of its viewers to be projected onto it rather than to be overly influenced by the artist's meaning.[62] The modern representations of Saint Gerald were likely successful in that goal—though they helped to perpetuate Gerald's memory only imprecisely.

Bouange's Biography of Gerald

If the proliferation of images of Saint Gerald in the late nineteenth and early twentieth centuries served as devotional aids to some of the faithful, renewed interest in his biography provided new inspiration to others. In 1837 a tiny booklet published in Aurillac reprinted a crude version of the frontispiece from Dominique de Jésus's biography with a four-page précis of Gerald's life.[63] In 1845 the baron Delzons of Aurillac penned a fairly straightforward forty-page summation of the work of Dominique de Jésus.[64] At the midpoint of the century, the *Vita prolixior* was published with other writings attributed to Odo of Cluny in the *Patrologiae cursus completus, series latina*, edited by Jacques-Paul Migne and made available at low cost to Catholic scholars and religious institutions across Europe.[65]

The broadest impact, though, may have been felt through a new detailed French biography of Saint Gerald by Guillaume-Marie-Frédéric Bouange, published at Aurillac in 1881. Bouange was born in Aurillac in 1814, ordained a priest in 1838 (after which he celebrated his first mass at the church of Saint-Géraud in Aurillac), and consecrated bishop of Langres in 1877 (also in the church of Saint-Géraud in Aurillac).[66] Bouange obviously held a lifelong fondness for Saint Gerald, and he may have known former canons of the monastery.[67] He drew on varied sources for his new biography, especially the *Vita prolixior*, but in combination with other texts, printing many in appendices. He included there the Latin text of the *Vita brevior* (370–82), the sermon written for Gerald's feast day (520–28), and the anonymous chronicle of the abbots of Aurillac (455–61), all published for the first time.[68] He began his biography of Saint Gerald in 1857, shortly after the supposed millennial anniversary of Gerald's birth.[69] He then began a history of the monastery of Aurillac, which remained unfinished at his death in 1884.

Bouange plainly intended to highlight Gerald's sanctity while also providing a more sophisticated historical approach to his subject. He began somewhat disingenuously with the declaration that his biography was intended only for its historical value and noting that Gerald was considered a saint only according to the "common opinion of the faithful" since "none of the miracles attributed to Gerald has been investigated by church authorities nor even has Gerald been officially recognized" (vii). Nonetheless, Bouange's historical sense was repeatedly deflected by his piety. For example, when considering whether Gerald was truly a count or not—and Bouange was well aware that there is no other historical documentation for such a claim—he concluded that the evidence was insufficient to draw any firm conclusion, but he noted that the more detailed medieval *vita* of Gerald insisted on it, and that Gerald acted with the noble dignity and gentle authority of the best and most capable of counts, so he concluded that the king must have rewarded so excellent a subject in some meaningful way, such as with a title (63–65; see also 434–42). Likewise, he showed how Gerald's decision to free only a hundred of his slaves at his death accorded with ancient Roman law, which, he added, must have been still known and followed in Auvergne in Gerald's day. Yet he concluded this discussion with the undocumented claim that within a few years of Gerald's death the monks of Aurillac had freed all of the slaves on their lands, in keeping with their founder's moral intentions, and perhaps to excuse the awkwardness of a monastery's owning slaves (155). Bouange also paused to reflect on the historical evidence for Gerald's ancestry (411–20; he accepted that Gerald was a descendant of Charlemagne but doubted that he was also a descendant of Constantine), Gerald's birth date (424–28; he concluded that it was probably in 856), the date of the foundation of the monastery at Aurillac (471–77; he suggested that it happened in 898 or early 899), and the date of Gerald's death (504–15; he concluded that it was 909). A host of other ancillary topics were similarly dissected.

It is interesting and worthwhile, then, to see how Bouange depicted Gerald. He began with Gerald's lineage, birth, and childhood and then presented the episodes of Gerald's adult life through discussions of Gerald's many virtues, much as Dominique de Jésus, whom he had clearly read, had done. The first virtue he described, incongruously enough, was Gerald's love of poverty—exhibited despite his wealth, and not one of the virtues Dominique de Jésus had mentioned (Bouange's chapter 4). Curiously, too, while Bouange reflected from time to time on Gerald's views on sexuality (he included Gerald's near sexual experience with his serf, for example, 19–20), he never discussed Gerald's disdain for violence, so central to the medieval portrayals of Saint Gerald but which he apparently wished to ignore. Otherwise, he repeated the episodes of Gerald's life more or less as found elsewhere.

Bouange also felt compelled to interrupt his narrative with the moral lessons that had driven all of Gerald's earlier biographers. He occasionally reprimanded his contemporaries for their unwillingness to imitate Gerald's example. "The frivolous world that tosses its glance at these pages," he wrote, "will perhaps laugh, or at least will be surprised at the simple and naive faith with which we have recounted these extraordinary things. But we reply to it that the marvels of the divine omnipotence, when they are attested by witnesses worthy of respect, merit the same credence as the glories of the natural world" (8). "Oh, sublime virtues from ancient times," he exclaimed elsewhere, "what has become of you? Where can you be found today among the children of the world? Money, money! How can it come? Pleasure, pleasure! As much as possible! Here is the need, here is the cry of our age. Ah, with what happiness is the soul that is tired of this dolorous spectacle carried back in the mind to that age of faith" (38–39).

Bouange's biography also reflected the times in which he lived and wrote. His preface described Gerald as "one of the brightest glories of the Church and of France" (xiv). In that spirit, Bouange did not hesitate to ascribe to Gerald the sentiments of both a good Catholic and a good Frenchman—as would have been recognized in the nineteenth century. He praised Gerald at length for his affection for the Virgin Mary (51), for example, about which his medieval biographers had said nothing. He devoted a whole chapter (his chapter 10) to Gerald's loyalty to the pope. Within this chapter, it should be noted, Bouange excerpted an address given by Pope Pius IX to the Papal Zouaves on the ancient bond between France's might and papal right (104–7), showing how much contemporary events were in his mind. At the same time, Bouange also included a chapter showing how carefully circumspect Gerald was in his political dealings, given the tumultuous political changes of the ninth century (his chapter 9), and it is not difficult to see in it advice for French Catholics of his own era.[70]

The Variant Iconography of Saint Gerald

Despite Bouange's work, through which knowledge of the details of Gerald's life were much more readily available by the late nineteenth century, little effort seems to have been made to present Gerald in any historically accurate way in most of the visual depictions of him. At Lempdes-sur-Allagnon, for example, a stained-glass window depicts scenes from the life of Saint Gerald: his supervising the construction of the church at Aurillac and his distributing alms to the poor. Yet the latter takes place in the streets of Lempdes-sur-Allagnon, and Gerald rides his horse by the modern church there. At Saint-Cirgues, Gerald kneels in prayer before a stone cross that is found in that village and clearly tries to link him to the locality. In this instance, however, the artist seems not to have known that tradition placed Gerald's death at Saint-Cirgues, though it might have provided a more suitable event for depiction there.[71]

The modern images of Saint Gerald I have described thus far differ only slightly one from another. Their similarity may reflect their reliance on the representations of Saint Gerald found in the church of Aurillac, especially for those churches in its vicinity, while others farther removed may have relied on printed depictions of Saint Gerald, such as that contained in the seventeenth-century biography by Dominique de Jésus (see fig. 8 above). The stained-glass image of Gerald from Aspres-sur-Buëch (see fig. 23), crafted in 1879, for example, repeats the elements of that woodcut in virtually the same way, even to the draping of Gerald's robes and his stance.

Even near Aurillac, nonetheless, some of the images of Saint Gerald reveal a surprising ignorance of the details of his life. The chapel of Bourniou was built near a spring of water said to have appeared when Gerald's bier was set down as he was carried to Aurillac after his death.[72] One would think that it would have been relatively easy to see how Gerald was depicted at Aurillac, less than thirty kilometers distant. Yet while its stained-glass image of Gerald wears a crown and holds a church and staff in his hands, as elsewhere, he does not wear medieval armor but the short, pleated skirt of a Roman soldier (see fig. 24). Now the difference may simply reflect the artist's ignorance of military garb appropriate to the ninth century (as, indeed, do the images depicting Gerald in suits of plate armor), but it also may reflect ignorance that Gerald lived in the ninth century. Since many of the military saints lived in late Roman antiquity, it may have seemed a safe bet for the artist to clothe Saint Gerald in this way. A similar sculpted depiction of Gerald appears at

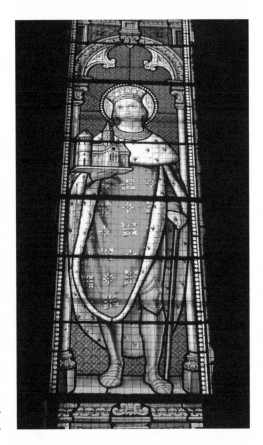

Figure 23. Stained-glass window depicting Saint Gerald, 1879. Church of Saint-Géraud, Aspres-sur-Buëch (*département* of Hautes-Alpes). Courtesy of Brian Giguere.

Saint-Cirgues. Other images of Saint Gerald show their own assorted peculiarities. A sculpted image of Saint Gerald at Drugeac (only about forty kilometers from Aurillac) from 1838 has him garbed in the long robe of a biblical figure; its early date may help to explain the error (see fig. 25).[73] In yet another stained-glass image at Saillans from 1862, Gerald carries the palm branch of martyrdom in his hand, though he was not a martyr.[74]

These differences pale in comparison to the unprecedented variations that one encounters in a few locations, especially ones far distant from Aurillac. A statue of Saint Gerald at Estézargues depicts him as a Roman soldier with a dark skin color, in what seems to be a confusion with one of the several North African soldier-martyrs of late antiquity (see fig. 26).[75] In another example of a confused pedigree, an image at Villetelle shows Saint Gerald carrying his staff and church, as elsewhere, but dressed as a bishop

Figure 24. Stained-glass window depicting Saint Gerald, date unknown. Chapel of Notre-Dame-des-Grâces, Bourniou (*commune* of Roumégoux, *département* of Cantal). Courtesy of Brian Giguere.

(see fig. 27).[76] Yet another statue within a chapel of Saint-Gérard at Mas-de-Londres shows Gerald as a bishop but without any of his usual attributes (see fig. 28).[77] What is most puzzling about these images is that they occasionally coexist with more conventional images in the same churches. At Estézargues, for example, a painting from 1859 depicts him as a light-skinned medieval nobleman.[78] And at Villetelle, a stained-glass image of Gerald opposite his statue presents him with his typical attributes.

This wide-ranging iconography seems to reveal how little was remembered in some places about the details of Gerald's life. Accordingly, the images of Saint Gerald were undoubtedly freer of artistic limitations than those of

Figure 25. Saint Gerald, 1838. Polychrome plaster. Church of Saint-Géraud, Drugeac (*département* of Cantal). Courtesy of Pierre Moulier.

Figure 26. Saint Gerald, identified as Saint Gérard, date unknown. Polychrome plaster. Church of Saint-Gérard, Estézargues (*département* of Gard). Courtesy of Brian Giguere.

better-known saints, and perhaps also freer to reflect a range of social or politi-cal concerns. Even the link between Saint Gerald and Aurillac seems to have been lost in the remotest of churches, so while it may seem logical to investigate how he looked there (where anyone would have found his church and its more typical images), that step may not have been so readily apparent. Still, these varied images of Saint Gerald also show us that in the wake of a fragmenting memory of Saint Gerald, alternative impressions were beginning to surface.

The Other Saint Geralds

In some of the communities where Saint Gerald was still revered in the nineteenth century, especially those far from Aurillac, his legend had been

Figure 27. Saint Gerald,
identified as Saint Gérauld, date
unknown. Polychrome plaster.
Church of Saint-Géraud, Villetelle
(*département* of Hérault).
Courtesy of Brian Giguere.

almost completely forgotten. That his name was common enough, even among saints, and that a variety of modern spellings were all derived from the same Latin name, meant that Gerald's life risked becoming entangled with the lives of other saints. What happened in some localities demonstrates astonishingly how devotion continued even in the absence of a genuine object of it, and how the local faithful generated a surprising array of new Saint Geralds to take the place of the one who was lost.

Some misidentifications are easy enough to comprehend. At Villetelle and Mas-de-Londres, for example, where Saint Gerald was depicted as a bishop, it seems that he was confused with a Guiraud who was bishop of Béziers and who died in 1123. Doubtless that is also how the nearby village of Saint-Guiraud took its modern name. Nonetheless, since the first mention of this village comes from 1101, before Guiraud had become bishop of Béziers,

Figure 28. Saint Gerald, date unknown. Polychrome plaster. Chapel of Saint-Gérard, Mas-de-Londres (*commune* of Saint-Martin-du-Londres, *département* of Hérault). Courtesy of Sylvie L'Hostis.

let alone before his death, it cannot have been named after him.[79] The earliest reference to the church at Villetelle is even older: it was already called *terra sancti Geraldi* in the eleventh century.[80] The church at Mas-de-Londres was first identified in 1135 as *capella sancti Geraldi de Rocafolio*, that is, as belonging to the noble Roquefeuil family, but there is an earlier mention of 1116 apparently to the same chapel, although without its name, and so that also seems too early for it to have been named after the bishop of Béziers.[81] This Guiraud seems to have been real enough, and was mentioned in the necrology of the bishops of Béziers, but otherwise virtually nothing is known about him. A biography was written in the late nineteenth century, to shed light on the man, but it is almost laughably devoid of facts. A typical passage reads: "But in whatever year the election [as bishop] of Saint Guiraud took place, it is at least certain that it happened against his wishes, given the profound humility that covered his virtues from his own eyes and thus made them shine all the more before the rest of the world, and that he fulfilled all of the functions of the episcopacy with great fervor."[82] The earliest evidence for devotion to this Guiraud comes only from the fifteenth century.[83] And the feast day of this Saint Guiraud is celebrated on October 13, the same day as Gerald of Aurillac, which betrays the origin of his cult.[84]

A different sort of confusion seems to have happened in Catalonia, where several churches dedicated to Saint Gerald existed since the Middle Ages.[85] The medieval church at Tossa de Mar fell into ruin but was rebuilt in the late nineteenth century as a private chapel and reconsecrated in 1882. A new statue of Saint Gerald was carved for it, correctly identified as Saint Gerald of Aurillac. Yet it depicts him as abbot of the monastery of Aurillac, dressed in Benedictine monastic garb, carrying a crosier in one hand and a miter and book in the other (see fig. 29).[86] The modern statues at other churches in Catalonia, at Sant Grau d'Entreperes (see fig. 30) and at Albons (see fig. 31), have taken this misidentification in different directions, the former imagining Gerald as a simple monk (but dressed in white, rather than black, that would seem to identify him as a Cistercian), and the latter as a bishop.[87] (A recently published dictionary of Catalan saints only adds to the confusion by identifying the saint venerated at Tossa de Mar and Albons as Saint Gerard Majella, an eighteenth-century Italian who was neither an abbot nor a bishop.[88]) All three churches still celebrate this Saint Gerald's feast day on October 13.

Other odd misidentifications happened elsewhere. In the seventeenth century Dominique de Jésus reported that relics of Saint Gerald had been given to the bishop of Sisteron in upper Provence in 1415, and were venerated

Figure 29. Saint Gerald, late nineteenth century. Polychrome plaster. Chapel of Sant Grau, Tossa de Mar (province of Girona, Catalonia, Spain). Courtesy of Brian Giguere.

Figure 30. Saint Gerald, date unknown. Polychrome plaster. Chapel of Sant Grau, Sant Grau d'Entreperes (municipality of Sales de Llierca, province of Girona, Catalonia, Spain). Courtesy of Miquel Palomeras i Anglada.

by the Knights Hospitaller at Castelmauresche.[89] Already by the time Dominique wrote, though, the origin of these relics had been forgotten where they were held, and were claimed instead to be those of Gérard Tenque, the founder of the Hospitallers, who died in 1120. In 1629 these remains were placed inside a silver likeness of Gérard Tenque by the commander of Manosque, then transferred to another in 1675.[90] Scholars unaware of their true origin have wondered how relics of the Knights' founder made their way to this location, since most of the other important relics in their possession were held at Rhodes and then Malta, where they remained until the end of the eighteenth century. Gérard Tenque's feast day is still celebrated annually on October 13 at Manosque, although elsewhere it is September 3.[91]

Other misrememberings of Saint Gerald are all the more curious in that they involve invented biographies for him. In the Cévennes region of modern France, Saint Gerald is still known as Saint Guiral, his name in the Occitan language of medieval southern France. Devotion remained strong to Saint

Figure 31. Saint Gerald, eighteenth century. Polychrome plaster. Formerly in the chapel of Sant Grau, now in the church of Sant Cugat, Albons (province of Girona, Catalonia, Spain). Courtesy of Josep Casas i Genover.

Gerald there, in part because it was a region of pastoralists, who drove their sheep high into the mountains each spring and descended again to the valleys on the same day in the fall: October 13, the feast of Saint Gerald. By the nineteenth century, however, the Saint Guiral revered here had a new life history: he was said to have been one of three noble brothers born at an unspecified date into the Roquefeuil family (the name of the noble family who built the medieval chapel to Saint Gerald at Mas-de-Londres, where—in an odd blurring of these misremembered legends—Guiraud of Béziers is now revered). All three brothers sought the love of the same woman, who instructed them to go on crusade and promised that she would marry the bravest of the three, but she died just as they returned. The three men renounced earthly love thereafter and became hermits, each making his home on a different mountain peak nearby and communicating only once a year by lighting bonfires visible each to the others from these peaks.[92]

This Guiral is a far cry from Gerald of Aurillac. The legend clearly derived from courtly romances in a nostalgic recollection of the medieval past, but at the same time it preserves the memory of annual bonfires lit in these mountains until recently.[93] Not surprisingly, the three brothers are identified with specific local mountains, and one of these peaks is called Saint Guiral, a name it had already in the twelfth century. There was once a chapel dedicated to Saint Gerald on its slope, now in ruins, that gives a likelier origin to its name. A hermit lived beside the chapel in the early eighteenth century, presumably to spend his life in prayer to Saint Gerald, but a century after his death he had become misidentified as the saint. An ancient dolmen on the side of the mountain is even said to be this hermit's—that is, Saint Guiral's—tomb. A painting made by a local artist in 1850 hangs in the church of the town of Arrigas at the foot of this mountain and depicts Saint Guiral as a hermit, dressed in a monk's habit, kneeling in prayer (see fig. 32). Annual pilgrimages from the church at Arrigas up the mountainside to the dolmen continue today, when devotional hymns honoring this imaginary Saint Guiral are still sung.[94]

Other alternative biographies for Saint Gerald happened elsewhere, even at places not far removed one from the other. At Estézargues Gerald was remembered by the nineteenth century as a thirteenth-century nobleman named Gerard of Lunel, who abandoned his life of privilege to become a hermit in a cave near the Pont du Gard. There is no historical evidence for any such individual in what is known of the Lunel family in the thirteenth century. The church at Estézargues, moreover, dates to the twelfth century,

Figure 32. Saint Gerald, identified as Saint Guiral, Camille Firmin, 1850. Oil on canvas. Church of Saint-Genest, Arrigas (*département* of Gard). Courtesy of Pierre Moulier.

that is, to the century before this Gerard is supposed to have lived.[95] This Saint Gerard was also identified with an Italian hermit of Montesanto in the Marche region named San Gerio or San Girio, through a claim that Gerard had abandoned his cave to go on pilgrimage to Rome and died en route. The canonization of San Gerio in the eighteenth century was then used as evidence for the historicity of this Saint Gerard, whose cult apparently began only in 1838.[96] The life of this Saint Gerard of Lunel repeats elements from the life of Saint Roch, oddly enough, already linked to Saint Gerald of Aurillac, in depicting a French nobleman who had renounced his wealth and title and who died while on pilgrimage in Italy.[97] There is another, even more striking parallel: just as a dog brought Saint Roch a loaf of bread each day in its mouth when he was too sick to rise from his sickbed, according to his legend, the story of Saint Gerard of Lunel includes an episode in which, after flooding temporarily sealed the mouth of the cave he inhabited, a snake swam in with a loaf of bread each day in its mouth to feed him.[98]

At Gannat in Auvergne an even more bizarre transformation of Saint Gerald took place through the cult of Sainte Procule. The earliest evidence for her legend comes from the seventeenth century: in 1652 Jacques Branche included her in his collection of Auvergnat saints.[99] According to his and to later retellings of the legend, Procule was a noblewoman from Rodez who lived in an unspecified century and who was betrothed to a nobleman from Aurillac named Gerald (Branche did not identify this suitor by name, but by the nineteenth century others did). She rejected him in favor of perpetual virginity, and when her parents insisted that she marry him, she fled north and became a hermit near Gannat. He pursued her and eventually caught up with her there, but she escaped him when by divine intervention a huge boulder split in half and then closed behind her. (A chapel was erected beside this boulder in the nineteenth century.)[100] Still, Gerald pursued Procule and met up with her again in front of the church of Gannat. In his anger he struck off her head with his sword, but she picked up her head and walked into the church as far as the high altar before collapsing. When he considered all that had happened, Gerald was overcome with remorse and returned to Aurillac where he became a monk. Procule's feast day was October 13.[101]

It is clear that here is a hodgepodge of elements taken from other saints. The virgin killed by her rejected suitor is a commonplace of Christian legend, and the decapitation miracle recalls the story of Saint Denis, first bishop of Paris. The legend most closely resembles that of Saint Valerie, whose cult was celebrated at Limoges and, ironically enough, had been promoted by Ademar of Chabannes. According to a *vita* that Ademar probably composed, Valerie's mother Susanna gave shelter to Saint Martial when he first arrived in Limoges, and the two women had been among his first converts. Valerie, having decided on a life of chastity, broke off her engagement to Stephen, the "duke of the Aquitanians," who, enraged, ordered her to be decapitated. She carried her own head and placed it at the feet of Martial, after which she died. Stephen, in his remorse, ordered a church to be erected over her tomb.[102] There is no serious historical evidence for Procule, and we cannot be as confident as was her nineteenth-century biographer that the collective memory of the Christian people can preserve the truth even when historical details are missing.[103] Bouange, who briefly discussed the legend of Procule in his biography of Gerald of Aurillac, called it "an absurd fable."[104] Still, her martyrdom is commemorated in a late eighteenth-century painting still on display in the cathedral of Rodez, her alleged hometown.[105] Behind the main altar of the church of Gannat, moreover, two mid-nineteenth-century stained-glass images honor both Procule and Gerald (see figs. 33 and 34).

One final and perhaps the weirdest twist to the memory of Saint Gerald is that of O Cebreiro in Galicia. The priory that the monks of Aurillac had once held was long abandoned by the end of the Middle Ages. Saint Gerald's connection to the place was forgotten until the late twentieth century; it was remembered instead for a eucharistic miracle said to have happened there.[106] Yet it is possible that some local memory of Gerald—called Sant Gral in the Gallego language of the region—remained. Pilgrims on their way to and from Santiago de Compostela who had never heard of Gerald of Aurillac were told of Sant Gral and shown the miraculous chalice, and seem eventually to have thought that they were seeing the Holy Grail (Sant Grial in the local language). By the start of the twentieth century, indeed, it was believed locally that the Holy Grail lay hidden at O Cebreiro. The tale was popularized by the poet Ramón Cabanillas, whose poem "O cabaleiro do Sant Grial," published in 1922, celebrated the virtues of the chaste Christian warrior, but in the guise of Lancelot rather than Gerald.[107]

What lessons should be taken from these strange metamorphoses? They are all manifest signs that the cult of Saint Gerald no longer retained much popular memory. Without official sponsors or formal limitations, his legend could be transformed in any number of ways. However fantastic these tales might be, they recapitulate in uncanny ways some of the central themes of Gerald's first biographies. Forms of lay piety, the holiness of sexual renunciation, and the use and misuse of violence find a place in them as they did in

Figure 33. Stained-glass window
depicting Sainte Procule, 1850.
Church of Sainte-Croix, Gannat
(*département* of Allier). Courtesy
of Brian Giguere.

the first telling of Gerald's story—perhaps most wondrously intermingled in
the story of Sainte Procule. At the same time, Gerald's transformation into
bishop, hermit, or crusader mark him as a saint in much more obvious and
straightforward—even mundane—a manner than in his first biographies. If
the original Gerald was not saint enough to last, these new Saints Gerald
might better survive the swells and ebbs of history. At the same time, the
random association of these new Geralds with the saintliness of martyrdom
or the holiness of the grail seems designed less to keep his memory from
dissolving entirely and more to fill a vacuum already created.[108]

It might more generously be said that the distortions in the images and
legends of Saint Gerald reflect the ultimate impossibility of materializing the
spiritual, and their ambiguity a necessary marker of the otherworldly. "As all
symbols," Louis Dupré writes, religious symbols "are so polyvalent that no

Figure 34. Stained-glass window depicting Saint Gerald, 1850. Church of Sainte-Croix, Gannat (*département* of Allier). Courtesy of Brian Giguere.

single rational interpretation can ever exhaust their meaning."[109] Or perhaps the variations in the cult of Saint Gerald functioned as markers of specificity and locality, something that differentiates *this* Saint Gerald from *that* one, an individuality that corrects for the predictability of ubiquitous devotion.[110] Maybe it does not matter which Saint Gerald is venerated by the faithful, so long as they are able to pull elements of meaning from his life, however it is imagined, and so long as he still points to a greater mystery beyond himself.

The modern eclipse of Saint Gerald provides a fascinating departure from the otherwise familiar banality of the cult of saints. The images and legends about Saint Gerald reflect an unmistakably modern nostalgia about the Middle Ages. Knight, pilgrim, hermit, virgin, martyr: beyond whatever Saint Gerald had come to represent in the remote locations where his memory still glimmered, even if faded almost into nothingness, can be seen these persistent stereotypes of the Middle Ages, and Gerald reflects what is remembered gladly about the Middle Ages as well as what should be forgotten.

Memory, Sanctity, Violence

Saint Gerald is virtually unknown today except to scholars of the Middle Ages. He no longer functions convincingly as a saint. Vestiges of Gerald's saintly memory still linger at Aurillac and also in the towns and villages where his churches still stand, although many of the residents with whom I spoke during my travels were hard pressed to come up with any details of his life. It is also true that in a few locations Gerald's holy reputation has been revived: the modern hostel for pilgrims in O Cebreiro, Galicia, is now named after Saint Gerald, thanks to a historically minded priest.[1] Still, it is a fractured memory at best.

Let us return to the pretty chapel at Auris-en-Oisans with which I began. It may have been built as early as the eleventh or twelfth century, in the greatest fullness of Gerald's fortunes. By 1454, when the bishop of Grenoble passed through his visit to the district, it lay half-ruined, an apt symbol of Gerald's own dimming renown.[2] Bouange briefly mentioned the tiny chapel in his nineteenth-century biography of Saint Gerald, a work that struggled mightily to hold onto the saint's fading memory; he claimed that this chapel's patron had preserved the local folk from the cholera epidemic of 1854.[3] But most of its history, like so much about Saint Gerald, is utterly lost. A grainy and undated photograph in the local archives shows a mass being conducted in front of the chapel in what seems, to judge from the clothing styles, to have been the 1940s or 1950s.[4] But nothing happens there anymore.

The memory of Saint Gerald has always been at risk of ruin, as I have argued throughout this book, placed too close to the edge of oblivion. Odo of Cluny first composed a *vita* for Saint Gerald in about 930 only a decade or two after Gerald's death. Perhaps Aimon and Turpin pressured him into doing it, hoping to glorify a relation, probably recommending the fashioning of a saintly founder as the best way to ensure the success of the monastery Odo was reforming. It was brief and straightforward, filled as much with reminders to the monks of Aurillac about the principles of the monastic life as with real incidents from Gerald's life. As he wrote the *vita*, he infused it with random thoughts drawn from his own life, having lived a childhood and adolescence much like those of Gerald before his own determined break with this life's path. Forced into imagining the life he himself might have led, Odo might have resisted any regrets by offering misgivings about the real holiness of a life led outside the cloister. Maybe he even went so far as to invent Gerald's semipacifism and semimonasticism as a means of excusing Gerald's refusal to abandon the world. Odo's Saint Gerald was but half-formed.

Almost a full century later in the 1020s, Ademar of Chabannes decided to bolster the cause of Gerald's sanctity: to finish the making of the saint, as it were. He might have done it to honor or flatter the powerful men of Limoges, who may have been related to Gerald, or perhaps he did it for his own aggrandizement or that of his family. He began simply enough, adding short accounts of Gerald's death and his posthumous miracles to Odo's *vita* so as to end it properly. But he couldn't quite stop thinking about Saint Gerald, adding a sermon and additional miracle stories before deciding to rewrite Odo's *vita* in his own words. Within this forgery he gave himself free rein, taking the episodes from the existing *vita* and mixing in new elements apparently borrowed from other saints or from contemporary discussions of violence and peace, and even granting Gerald the false title of count. Throughout it all he castigated and threatened with holy retribution those who doubted or ignored Gerald's worthiness.

For a few centuries, this recast Saint Gerald flourished. Popular devotion configured Saint Gerald in diverse ways: as patron and benefactor to the poor and the peasant, as model and mirror to the military man and the monk. An enlarged church and sculpted likeness further enhanced Gerald's saintly standing, together offering an appealing focal point for devotion to him. The shrine of Aurillac attracted increasing numbers of monks, pilgrims, and donors and soon oversaw a network of churches and properties that stretched across the Midi of France and beyond.

By the end of the Middle Ages, however, the recognition of Gerald's sanctity was fading. Corruption within the monastery and war and disease without diminished Aurillac's reputation—and Gerald's along with it. For some, rival saints bested Gerald in the new arenas of saintly competition; for others, the cult of saints itself was brought into question. The sacks of Aurillac in 1233 and again in 1567 despoiled not only Saint Gerald's relics, but also the books and buildings within which his memory was kept secure. It was perhaps the seventeenth century that provided the best chance for his continued success. His church at Aurillac was partially rebuilt, new statues and paintings of him commissioned, and he was enshrined once again in a magnificent reliquary. The first printings of the *Vita Geraldi* and its influence in new vernacular biographies also offered hope for the restoration of devotion to the saint. Through all of these efforts, Saint Gerald was remade in newly regal splendor. Yet even then, the memory of Saint Gerald was dimming, especially in places far distant from Aurillac, and the violent upheavals of the French Revolution merely hastened that decline.

Rather than discard a saint, though, even one stripped of memory, some chose to reclothe him in the diverse robes of a bishop, hermit, or crusader. Whether Saint Gerald remains tucked away within the folds of these garments or has disappeared completely inside them is not for a historian to answer. Even in Aurillac, the city that he founded and where he still serves as patron saint, Gerald has largely been overshadowed by a local rival. Gerbert of Aurillac was born not long after Gerald's death and became a monk at Saint Gerald's monastery before he made an exceptional exit from it. He achieved real renown, eventually becoming Pope Sylvester II. He wrote about applied mathematics as well as theology and ecclesiology; indeed, some feared that he had studied magic, and some believed even that he had made a pact with the devil. Such a colorful figure has been revered in modern times as a rare free spirit of the Middle Ages. So it was Gerbert of Aurillac whose statue was chosen to grace a new public square in Aurillac in 1851 to represent the greatness of the city's past.[5] Not so Saint Gerald. When remembered at all, he is regularly associated with the worst of the Middle Ages: its religious superstitions, its brutal violence, its repressive sexuality, its harsh class divisions, even its unstable political and economic structures.[6]

Whether Gerald should ever have been revered as a saint at all is a good question, though not one for a historian to answer. Gerald's participation in violence, even halfhearted, is perhaps the best example of how uncomfortably he wore his sanctity—as his medieval biographers were well aware—and, living in the midst of the horrific violence of the early twenty-first century, we still notice how ill fitting it is. Both Odo and Ademar presented Gerald as a man who was violent only reluctantly and moderately, yet both said that he made use of violence and could still be considered a saint. Both said it in such a way that implied that neither was too happy in saying it. And yet they said it, and thereby imagined occasions when violence in the course of even the best of Christian lives might be tolerated.

Their acquiescence to the possibility of a Christian violence carried woeful consequences. Another monk from Cluny named Odo, a man also born into a military family and one who had also rejected that upbringing for the peace of the cloister, became Pope Urban II in 1088. He lived at the time when devotion to Saint Gerald was at its peak. He may have reflected on the deeper meanings within the example of Gerald as he heard one version or the other of his *vita* recited each year on October 13, and he might also have pondered how violence could be put into the service of God and the church. His elevation as pope was hotly contested by the emperor, who chased him from Rome, and he fled back to Cluny, from which he visited the great churches in the south of France in late 1094 and early 1095, including Saint Gerald's in Aurillac. Not longer after, at Clermont, he proclaimed the need for Christians to take up arms against Muslims in what would be known as the First Crusade. Urban may not have had Saint Gerald in mind when he decreed that Christians could wage war without sinning.[7] Yet without the precedent of a violent Christian saint, such a proclamation might not have been so easily imagined.

What other saint might have provided so neat an excuse? Granted, among the earliest Christian martyrs were many soldiers, men like Saint Martin of Tours, revered throughout the Middle Ages. Yet Martin is supposed to have answered a Roman emperor with "I am a soldier of Christ. Combat is not permitted to me." Church authorities had consistently defended the permissibility of warfare for centuries, it is true, but had always insisted that it was less than ideal. Pope Leo I, for example, required all soldiers to do penance at the end of their careers, in atonement for the killing they had done.[8] Many other examples could be used in evidence, but the conclusion drawn from all of them is that no other Christian saint provides so early a precedent for linking violence and sanctity. True, other laymen were depicted as pious even while engaged in warfare.[9] William of Gellone was remembered as both a valiant soldier and a saint, and lived a century before Gerald's time, but he abandoned his military career for the life of a hermit and, moreover, his celebrity happened only in later centuries.[10]

After Saint Gerald, increasing numbers of the saints were called in to justify the holiness of warfare. One of the best known is Santiago Matamoros

("Saint James the Moorslayer"), the same apostle James who was also venerated at Santiago de Compostela. The image of Saint James' wearing the pilgrim's hat and cape while on horseback and trampling Muslims to death is
incongruous, perhaps, but potent, and became a forceful symbol of the Christian reconquest of the Iberian peninsula.[11] Eventually there were many martial saints, and scholars have wondered about the influence of the legend of
Saint Gerald on their *vitae*.[12] Through the gradual development of the chivalrous ideal of Christian knighthood, the spiritual benefits of violence were
broadly proclaimed.[13]

Saint Gerald's memory places the inherent contradiction in the notion
of Christian violence first and foremost. Whether reading Odo's or Ademar's
awkward circumlocutions on the subject or gazing up at modern images of
Saint Gerald with sword and suit of armor in the quiet churches of rural
France, the problem is inescapably raised. It is also this issue that most clearly
exposes his limitations as a saint. Perhaps the fabric of sanctity is not infinitely
flexible, and it may be that Gerald pulled it too far out of shape, so that what
had been made in Saint Gerald had to be unmade. Still, it is not for me to
blame him or his hagiographers for the tragic ubiquity of violence, either in
the Middle Ages or in the present. The purpose of history is not to blame.
Even if in the end hagiography may not satisfy our search for human ideals,
creating less than perfect heroes for less than perfect times, though regretta-
ble, is at least understandable.

Translation of the *Vita sancti Geraldi brevior*

Here begins the prologue to the life of the man of God, Gerald, [whose feast day is] 13 October, related by the Lord Abbot Odo.

To the Reverend Father and Lord Abbot Aimon, his fellow servant of the brothers and the most insignificant of abbots,[1] Odo sends perpetual greetings in the Lord. You have asked, Father, together with Lord Bishop Turpin and not a small number of other noble men, that I should write something concerning the life or rather the miracles of the lord Gerald. I postponed it at first, however, in part because the matter seemed unclear to me on account of its newness[2] and, I confess, in part because I was worried and still am worried that this account might not be easy for me to relate. Indeed, uncertainty in this matter arises particularly since this same man was powerful in this world. It was for this very reason that in certain places groups of peasants recently used to gather, and as it was a useless thing they gradually stopped. To be sure, when some noble laymen and pious clerics whom the same lord Gerald had raised from childhood had described to me his way of life as being of such a kind that through the will of God it was not unworthy of miracles, I put aside my doubts,[3] considering with confidence that, according to the saying of the Apostle, God leaves no time without a proof of His goodness. Maybe it is for this reason, since nowadays we do not care about the examples of the Fathers and iniquity is growing, that He offered this servant of His to us either so as to inspire imitation or else as a witness, just as He brought the queen of the south to the Jews.[4] For even if he was powerful in the things of this life, that is no obstacle to a layman who has managed well the things he has justly received: for there is no power that does not come from God.[5] It is all the more greatly laudable, though, since he had possessions of the sort that make men proud, and yet he remained a pauper in spirit, according to the example of Job or rather of David. For in fact no law constrains the grace of God, who gave different tongues to Peter when he spoke to the gentiles before their baptism,[6] and who furnished so many good things for the quarrelsome people of the Hebrews in the desert for the salvation of those to come. If therefore God, the arranger of the ages, deigns to repeat in our days these deeds in His holiness, we should praise them and be eager to give thanks, since He is mindful of his promise that He himself made: Who glorifies me, He says, I will glorify him.[7] And so now, finally, confident of the kindness of Christ, I undertake what you command. I ask you, however, Father, that you beg that same Christ that his faithfulness might grant this very selfsame account to be not unworthy of the blessed man in any way and that he remove from me any failure or sin in it.

Here ends the preface.

Here begins the life of Saint Gerald.

1. Gerald, then, had his origin in the province of Aquitaine, namely, in the territory that is the district of Auvergne and also of Cahors and bordering Albi besides,[8] begotten of his father Gerald and his mother Adeltrude. His ancestors were as illustrious in nobility as they were rich in possessions, and what is more excellent, most of them were distinguished by the reputation of their piety. For in fact Saint Caesarius, bishop of Arles, and the blessed abbot Aredius are said to have been from the same ancestry;[9] and concerning his mother Adeltrude it is said that several miracles have already been performed at her tomb. But the splendor of mind that Gerald received from his ancestors he poured out again in himself, greatly multiplied, and truly his forebears are the more glorious for that reason, in that they have merited to produce so fortunate an offspring. And because the Lord is in the offspring of the just, it follows clearly that his family be blessed through him.[10] His father, nonetheless, in order to purify himself within his marriage, frequently lay apart from his wife. It happened, though, that he once saw in a dream a rod that sprouted as if from the big toe on his right foot, and grew gradually into a large tree. When he awoke, he marveled at the time about this vision. Another time while sleeping he saw again in another dream someone who told him that a son would be born to him.[11] If faith should be employed with these dreams, however, which are not always devoid of meaning, it can be seen that this vision signified the future greatness of Gerald. After a time, then, the father begot the aforesaid boy, whom he called by his name, Gerald.

Indeed, even before he was born, as it happened, his father was lying awake with his mother, also awake, and although I don't know what they were talking about, the child gave a cry from the womb of his pregnant mother, which both of his parents heard. Both were shocked by it, and called a servant woman to bring a light so that they might discover where in the world a child had been crying. When she came with the light, she searched the place thoroughly. And when she declared that no child was present, the infant cried a second time. After a moment, he cried again a third time, precisely the way a newborn infant typically screams. At that point, they were unable to ignore the fact that the voice came from the mother's womb. It is a surprising thing, all in all, because as everyone knows it happened against the order of nature as determined by God, the cause of all things. Five days later, his mother brought forth her son.

2. And so he was born and weaned, and when he had come into that age in which boys are wont to be violent and contrary and vengeful, a certain sweetness of manners already appeared in Gerald, so that through those childish actions he hinted in some way at what kind of a man he was going to be. Even then he was inclined to literary studies, and such was the will of his father that after he had learned the psalter he was instructed in secular studies. But by the divine will—as I believe—it so happened that he frequently fell ill. When his father had considered this fact, he ordered him to be more fully instructed in literary disciplines, so that if he should not be suited for the secular army he would be made suitable for ecclesiastical office. It was on this occasion that he both became acquainted with church chant and picked up a bit of grammar in addition, which was a benefit to him later on, since his mind, as if polished, became more skilled at those things he intended and his memory more experienced at retaining them. For it so happened that he surpassed many clerics in his recollection of the scriptures. Having passed through childhood, when he was already growing into manly toughness, that illness of his ceased, but knowledge and love of the scriptures remained in his adolescent heart. And since he excelled other men amply in body and in speed, he joined the ranks of armed men, but the sweetness of the scriptures, from which his mind had already imbibed, made him inclined toward spiritual matters and quite reluctant toward military matters. I believe, in fact, that he had already decided that wisdom was better than strength and that nothing was richer than it.[12] As the Book of Wisdom itself says, then, it had already showed itself to him and was a sweet comfort to his way of thinking.

3. After his parents died, and when he had come into his authority and his possessions by hereditary right, he did not, as so many young men do, take an immature sort of pride in his authority, and he did not change the humility of his heart that had been earlier conceived. From then on, although unwilling, he was compelled to spend his time in managing and taking care of these same affairs, [but arranged it] so that he might have leisure and might devote himself to the advantage of others. Indeed, he carried with distress the sharp troubles and duties of the household, because in the hidden places of his heart he feared that he would be distracted and surrounded by earthly entanglements. In truth, since a great need compelled him now and again to suppress with arms the violent men who plundered his estates and peasants excessively, he admonished his soldiers in a commanding voice that they should fight against the enemy with their spears turned around. The piety in the recesses of his heart that inspired this desire in the waging of war soon made him irresistible to his enemies: and yet it was not once heard that the good fortune of victory had disappointed anyone who fought out of loyalty to Gerald. But again, one thing remained certain, that neither he himself ever wounded anyone whatsoever nor was he ever wounded by anyone.

4. The ancient enemy had investigated the morals of this young man, and reflected on what was some sort of divine quality within him, and flared up in envy against him. And longing to bury the desire for piety in Gerald's heart, the Devil[13] hastened back to that old point of deception that had first deceived Adam and then so often his descendants. As you might expect, he hurled love—as they call it—for a young woman at Gerald's breast, and from the moment the unguarded Gerald beheld her, suddenly his mind began to weaken into desire. He was tormented as a result, and behold, his mind was melted by fire. At length, returning to the sweetness of celestial love that he had tasted, he began to return to his senses, and pleading for the mercy of Christ, gradually he began to overcome that which had blazed up in the flame of lust by dwelling upon the fear of the Lord. Therefore the Lord turned it to good result and defended His servant who had taken refuge in Him. Just at that time, the exceeding inclemency of the weather had caused frost to appear, so they said, and Gerald the servant of God allowed himself to be frostbitten throughout the night, no doubt in order that the vast cold of winter might extinguish the flame of deformed desire. From then on, however, keeping himself prepared against a [further] dangerous test, he was careful enough lest something enter into his heart through his eyes that would

incite in him a battle of lust. And truly, not long afterward blindness crept in, which completely veiled his eyes for the extent of one year. I believe that the internal Judge, who does not want there to be anything that would offend His eyes in the ones He has chosen, introduced this scourge both so that the mind of the young man would be purged from what had happened and so that it would be preserved more spotlessly in the future. Thereafter he assumed such an obvious love for chastity that he avoided with women the embrace that is usual among friends as they kiss, even women who were related to him. So much was this the case that he shunned a marriage for himself, so that not even William, duke of Aquitaine, was able to get him to marry his sister. And when he said to him that he should consent to it for the love of sons, he replied that it was better to die without sons than to leave wicked heirs. Notwithstanding, having passed through an earlier well-known temptation, it was not heard that he was [ever again] wearied thereafter by such an assault. Whenever he incurred illusory images in his sleep,[14] he immediately washed his body, and changed by himself into clothes prepared for such an occasion. And, since modesty is the companion of religion, it seems proper not to omit that he never wanted to be seen naked.

5. Now, indeed, with his vices nearly dried up and his conscience polished up, he led a life full of piety and respectability; and not only did he withdraw himself from secular activity, as he had with good reason requested, but he also did not permit himself to be hindered from the activity of religion. He associated himself without fail with respectable men and with clerics of good reputation, knowing how it is written that the sort of followers one has reveals the kind of person one is. He accommodated himself to his followers and to others who were subjected to his authority in such a way as if he were the equal of the good ones [among them], mindful of that precept according to which it is commanded: Be among those set below you as if you are one of them.[15] Yet he was also sufficiently formidable to the malevolent, according to that which is likewise taught concerning the wicked: Do not show your joyful face to them;[16] the light of his face did not descend on the earth.[17] He prosecuted those who were bold in assaulting peasants and took note of the willful, but he often long acted otherwise when it came to the injustices done to him. For frequently those who were under his authority reproached him, saying that he was soft and timid, since he allowed himself to be injured by the basest sort of persons as if he were powerless. To be sure, his men remember many things from his public pronouncements and from the sayings that he used. For you see, he spoke of those things that are joyous;

he was pleasing and sweet; the words that he offered reproachfully, however, were feared almost more than the lash, so that they were, according to the Book of Wisdom, like a goad positioned on high.[18] He was not easily angered or humiliated, nor sharp tongued in inflicting insults, nor stubborn in holding on to them.

6. How, then, he lived soberly and justly and piously, in a manner according to apostolic precept, and how he conducted himself zealously both in these and in the other precepts of God, my ability does not fully suffice for the telling. To be sure, it was possible to him by the grace of God, but in our days it is so unusual for almost everyone that what he did seems scarcely believable. I point out certain things from his conversation and actions, through which it can be clearly understood at least in part what sort and how much of a man he was: to begin, by noting that he was so devoted to almsgiving, always thinking about the needy, so that what is said in the Book of Job would suit him: Pity grew up within me from my infancy.[19] Indeed, benches for the poor were always arranged facing him, so that he could see for himself what and how much was given to them; he always handed over the middle of his bread to them. No one cried whom he did not hear or who withdrew out the door without alms. Whenever he returned from his estates the poor assembled: he had taken out one-ninth [of what he had collected there] beforehand to give to them. For he desired to be made equal to those in want through love of poverty and of humility. He often accepted coins given to him as alms, which nonetheless he immediately gave away. Great respect for him was maintained at mealtimes.[20] For he took up the custom of being read to at his meals, not only when there was nothing else happening, which was more typical, but even when guests were present, so that there would be conversation only afterward. He was not unmindful of what was commanded to every single one of us, that he eat his bread with silence.[21] He was so concerned with sobriety that he kept not only himself but also his companions at table from drunkenness, and certainly he did not at any time encourage his guests to drink. And if it were necessary, he gave them something to eat early in the morning, yet in no way was he himself going to taste anything before mid-morning,[22] on account of that which is said: Blessed be the prince who feasts in his own time.[23] Days of fasting he observed in such a way that if a vigil for fasting fell on a Sunday, he fasted on the preceding Saturday. Seldom at any time, however, except for Easter and on special feast days, did he eat twice. There was always free access to him for the poor and for those who had suffered injury, and he did not require that anyone offer him any

little gift in order to receive his protection. He was not influenced in his support by the amount of reward but by the greater extent of the need. For he was afraid to accept any reward to such a degree that if someone happened to offer him the sort of candles that are made out of wax, to go in front of the relics that he always had with him, he had them melted; his attendants either made something similar out of wax or little torches out of bark or sticks with pitch for his own use. Freely, then, he brought aid to the poor, and he was never too proud to offer them whatever they needed, whether done himself or through his men. Indeed, if he heard of a settlement between those in discord, he had a mass celebrated for the sake of their reconciliation, acting similarly when anyone he had known died, even a poor man. Many things he did piously and reputably that are properly fitting to an active life.[24] Nonetheless, many things he suffered from his enemies, from whom divine grace alone wondrously freed him. For indeed, just as ecclesiastical custom demands, at first he conducted himself admirably in a practical life, and thereafter, as his age increased, he inched more fully into a life of contemplation. Now let us return to some of the things which relate to that same life.

7. Accordingly, when this man of God had assumed more and more a longing for heaven, he shone out among the wicked like a lily growing among the thorns.[25] And withdrawing himself gradually from the affairs of this world, he no longer wanted to be entangled in earthly activities, nor to journey to the royal court anymore, nor to take part in the assemblies of princes. Rather, having surrendered in all things to divine worship, he gave his very self to God and everything that he possessed in this world. For this reason, he summoned Gauzbert, a venerable bishop and one worthy of praise, and said to him that he wished to profess the religious habit, that he wanted to bequeath his estates to the blessed Peter, prince of the Apostles, and that if it were at all possible for him to obtain regular monks in some way or another, he wished to be converted [to the monastic life] with them. But since they were unable to obtain such monks, he was led to the following advice in order that he might receive the blessing of the clergy: that he hide it from men for the time being, so that the malevolent and those who would think that he was a layman would be restrained by greater fear. To God, on the other hand, who is the observer of the heart, it would have been revealed. He bound those who were there with an oath that they should disclose this thing to no one during his lifetime. He hit upon this excuse for hiding his tonsure: he cut off his beard as if it were bothersome to him, and since his hair had fallen out from the top of his head he concealed the fact that he was pulling

a blade over it in a circular shape. He wore a cloak atop his clothes, but he never owned two at the same time. From his sword belt and the finer bits of his sword he made a golden cross. Thereafter he set out for Rome, and made the final testament that he had conceived in his mind. Afterward, he built a monastery and collected together such monks as he was able to find; for himself, though, he reckoned it preferable to remain as he was than to attempt the sublime proposition [of monastic life] away from tested brothers. Reluctantly, he abided with laymen, although it seemed to him to be a good and joyful thing when brothers live as one.[26] Yet like Noah's dove when it did not find a place to rest outside, he was nourished happily with spiritual delights, returning to Christ and to the secret places of his heart as to the ark.[27] It was always arranged with great diligence, however, throughout the many years before him, that [whenever he visited the monastery] he should never stay anywhere except next to the church.[28] Indeed, an ample number of clerics and the supplies for all divine services were always at hand. At night he was accustomed to arrive before everyone else at the chapel, and when they left, he remained alone, when at least then both more freely and much more secretly he might cling to the things of divinity. How very reverently he remained in the church it is not possible to relate sufficiently, but you would have thought him to be as though observing some splendor.

8. He made it his custom to travel every second year to Rome; indeed, he brought there the tithe of the aforesaid monastery hanging from his neck like a servant to his master. But who can adequately explain how devotedly he traveled the length of that road? For he passed almost no pauper by, and what is more, he bestowed many things on the monasteries along the route. Often, indeed, it was as if he would make a kind of complaint, letting out a voice of lamentation and sighing that everyone seemed disposed to evil, that assuredly all men were perishing for love of this world, that piety was failing, that iniquity was rising to overflowing, and that already almost everyone in the world was letting innocence slip from his heart and truth from his mouth. He would repeat it over and over again: "Oh, how the holy man has disappeared! How truth has been shattered by the sons of men!"[29] Not being able to accomplish the gathering of monks that he wanted, he was sickened over those who dwelt in the place without a [monastic] rule. Indeed, he often conferred with his associates about it, saying: "The other things that are necessary to monks are not missing, through the dispensation of God. But, alas, monks alone are not obtained, they alone cannot be found." For one

day, while observing the construction of the [monastic] house, he shed copious tears. Then one of his associates inquired why he wept. "Because," he replied, "I gaze upon that place which in no way whatsoever has come to its intended result, and I am overcome with sadness, like one who is alone and bereft, because the monks are missing. Nonetheless, I hope that almighty God, when it should please Him, will deign to satisfy my desire. But I want you to know that this house will frequently be too small for those assembled within it." Yet by saying this, he revealed no small thing, because in fact it is often the case that this same house enjoys crowds of those assembled there;[30] those who recall that lord Gerald had predicted it reckon that he knew it through divine revelation. Indeed, already his mouth was filled from the fullness of his heart in such a way that the law of God always echoed fully within him. For certain sacred words that seemed to fit with his duties in the flesh he designated for himself, such as: "Place, oh Lord, a watch on my mouth,"[31] and others that he employed for his individual actions, so that, whether rising from his bed or putting on his boots and clothes or taking up his sword belt, and whether beginning a journey or anything else, according to the saying of the Apostle, he seemed to do all things in the name of the Lord.[32] Indeed, quite often keeping silent for a long while, he would then draw a deep breath, in such a way that his chest would be shaken from its depths, and dissolving into tears, he would say: "Oh Lord, keep us safe!"[33] and other things of this sort, from which it is evident that his mind was heavy with something else. Of such a kind, then, was his speech, and of such a kind, his silence.

9. As for the rest, although now in the present time of the Antichrist the miracles of the saints ought already to cease, nonetheless the Lord, mindful of his promise by which it is said: He who glorifies me, I will glorify him,[34] deemed this servant of His worthy to glorify by means of a certain grace of healing. For the kind of healing was such that, however much he might out of humility have avoided placing his hand on those who were sick, nonetheless, he often cured them both when he was not even there and although he was unwilling. Sick persons used to steal the water in which he washed his hands, of course, and most were healed. Evidently, so that it might be thought more believable, it seems right to remember some persons who were cured.

10. A lame little boy used to dwell near Aurillac. Admonished in a dream, he sprinkled himself with that same water and was immediately healed. He, taking up the builder's craft, offers himself as a witness in this

matter. This man of the Lord, hearing such things about himself, strenuously lamented, saying that it was the faith of the sick boy that had merited it. Gerald asked nonetheless who had given that water to the lame boy. And in fact, since it was carefully concealed from him, he threatened menacingly that no one should presume to give it to anyone at all. But this threat was not able to be kept.

11. A blind man, living not far from Solignac,[35] was likewise admonished in his sleep that he should take possession of water from Gerald without his knowing it; once his eyes were washed, he was soon able to see. There is a city in Tuscany called Lucca, and when Gerald was traveling to Rome, he arrived at the hostel there.[36] A woman, leading along her blind son, requested water from his hands. Summarily cursing her, he forced her to leave. Then, once he had set out, fearing in fact lest the woman should follow him on account of his water, he had the water poured into the ground whenever he washed. But the woman, who followed him from a distance, at last obtained water from him without his knowing it, from which her son received his sight. As the pilgrims returned from Rome she showed them her son, who could now see. Afterward, this same thing was often performed in others, such as happened to a servant girl of his who received her sight in his own church not far from Argentat.[37] But then, in fact, he caught the attendant of his named Radbald who had been giving the water away: he threw him out at once from his presence. The nobleman Ebbo pleaded with the lord Gerald that the man who had been thrown out should be received back, addressing him plainly with reasoning and saying that perhaps he was sinning more through too much humility when the grace that had been given to him for the sake of the sick he denied to those same sick persons, and also that it would be more fitting, when any wretched person gave testimony that he had been thus admonished, for him to hand over the situation into God's control, especially since it was already proven that through him divine grace had healed a good many persons without his knowledge. When this man of the Lord, Gerald, heard these things, however, he cried and said that perhaps it was rather a deception from the devil, and that the devil would want to deceive him, so that even if Gerald were to do something good, he would perish at the same time.

12. When he was attending the mass of Saint Lawrence in the aforesaid chapel, though, surrounded by others who had come together for the feast day, a woman possessed by a demon approached. Because she was obviously being cruelly harassed by the demon, the lords who were standing around

asked Gerald to bless her. Accordingly, when he had done so, the woman's demon was expelled, and she was cured at once.

13. He was once on his way to Rome. Coming to the town that is called Aosta, though, he spent time wandering throughout the church buildings there.[38] Meanwhile, a thief stole two of his pack animals. Coming to a stream, this thief was not able to force them by any possible means to cross over the stream, until he was apprehended by the lord Gerald's men. Since the pack animals had been returned, Gerald did not harm the thief at all.

14. A sick man had remained in his homeland, and Gerald heard the man's voice in the air telling him that he had died. When he recognized the voice, he ordered his men to find out how Ragabald was: for that was the sick man's name. But they replied: "When we began this journey, oh lord, he was already ill." Then the lord Gerald, having called his clerics, had the office of the dead said for him. When he returned, he learned in fact that the sick man had departed this life a little more than an hour before Gerald heard his voice.

15. There was with Gerald an abstemious monk. In fact, one day when the man had nothing to eat except for bread, Gerald, the man of the Lord, was saddened, saying: "If all of us have a full larder, how is it that a servant of God is not supplied from it?" His attendants responded that they had not been able to get anything to eat. So he entered the tent where the relics of the saints were kept, and prayed. Meanwhile, when Samuel, one of his attendants, ran to draw water for washing—they were next to the Rhone River—almost immediately a little fish measuring half a foot threw itself onto dry land, leaping out of the river. Samuel caught it and brought it to his lord. Gerald, giving thanks to God, ordered[39] the fish to be prepared, from which the monk ate his fill. And when half of it still remained, this man of God urged the monk to continue eating, saying that he did not have anything else for him to eat: but since the monk claimed to be full, Gerald marveled, and he as much as everyone else shared the holy gifts from what was left.[40] Indeed, some assert that fish were often obtained from God for the lord Gerald to eat.

16. A man by the name of Heldoard, having fallen from his horse, completely shattered one of his knees; the pain that it caused him meant that he spent the next six days without eating. And since he was not able to find anything for himself as a remedy, he was carried to Capdenac,[41] and had brought to him water from the hands of the lord Gerald. A wonderful thing happened: as soon as the aforesaid water was sprinkled over his knee, he rose up whole and freed from all pain.

Here ends the life of the blessed Gerald.

The Manuscripts of the *Vita Geraldi*

Manuscript	Date	Origin	Preface	Vita brevior	Vita prolixior (Books 1 and 2)	Transitus	Miracula	Sermo	Additional miracle stories
Paris, Bibliothèque nationale de France (BNF)									
BNF lat. 3783 t. II	Tenth or eleventh century	Southern France, possibly Moissac	fol. 341r: *Reverendo patri*	fols. 341v–344v: *Incipit vita sancti Geraldi confessoris*					
BNF lat. 3809A	Fifteenth century	Southern France	fol. 153r: *Reverendo patri*	fols. 153v–155v: *Incipit vita sancti Geraldi*		fols. 155v–156v: *Incipit transitus beatissimi confessoris sancti Geraldi*— missing PL 3.1	fols. 156v–158v: *Incipit miraculis post mortem*		

Manuscript	Date	Origin	Preface	Vita brevior	Vita prolixior (Books 1 and 2)	Transitus	Miracula	Sermo	Additional miracle stories
BNF lat. 3820	Fourteenth century	Arles	None		fols. 144r–144v: *In festo beati Geraldi et confessoris* (*PL* 1.1–1.4 only; Gerald's birth place includes *atque limovicensi pago*)				
BNF lat. 5298	Twelfth century	Moissac	None		fols. 87v–89r (*PL* 1.1–1.3, 1.5, 2.10–2.12 only)	fols. 89r–89v (*PL* 3.5, 3.7, 3.10–3.11 only)			
BNF lat. 5301	Late tenth or early eleventh century	St.-Martial, Limoges	fol. 221r: *Reverendi* [sic] *patri*	fols. 222r–227v: *Incipit vita sancti Geraldi*		fols. 227v–231r: *Incipit transitus domni Geraldi* (missing *PL* 3.1 and 3.10)	fols. 231r–233r: *Miracula post transitum domni Geraldi* (*PL* 3.12, 4.1–4.7)		

BNF lat. 5315	Twelfth century	Southern France, possibly Cluny	none	fols. 5v–10r: *Incipit vita sancti Geraldi confessoris* (PL 1.1–1.14 only; Gerald's birth place includes *atque limovicensi pago*)		
BNF lat. 5353	Fourteenth century	Bonport, Normandy	None	fols. 136–136v: *Incipit vita sancti Geraldi confessoris*; first part of text only: fols. 137–143 missing		
BNF lat. 5365	Twelfth century	St.-Martial, Limoges	fol. 99v: *Reverendo patri*	fols. 99v–101v: *Incipit vita sancti Geraldi confessoris*	fols. 101v–103r: abbreviated *Transitus* and *Miracula* together; *Incipiunt miraculi* [sic] *eiusdem*	fols. 101v–103r: abbreviated *Transitus* and *Miracula* together; ends *Explicit vita domni Geraldi*

Manuscript	Date	Origin	Preface	Vita brevior	Vita prolixior (Books 1 and 2)	Transitus	Miracula	Sermo	Additional miracle stories
BNF lat. 5399	Fourteenth century	unknown	fols. 232r–233r: *Plerique dubitare* (includes *PL* 1.2 after preface)		fols. 233r–236r: *Vita beati Geraldi confessoris* (abbreviated *PL* 1.1, 1.3–1.5)				
BNF lat. 11749	Eleventh or twelfth century	St.-Germain-des-Prés, Paris	fols. 120v–121v: *Affectu recolendo*; titled *Epistola Odonis in vita sancti Geraldi confessoris*, followed by *Plerique dubitare*; titled *Praefatio in vita eiusdem*		fols. 121v–137r: Titled *Liber primus de vita sancti Geraldi confessoris* and *Liber secundus* (no mention of Limoges in Gerald's birth place)	fols. 137v–140v: Titled *Liber III* (includes 3.1)	fols. 140v–142v: Titled *Liber quartus*		
BNF lat. 12601 (identified by Bultot-Verleysen as *Vita prolixior secunda*)	Eleventh or twelfth century	St.-Taurin, Evreux; possibly originally from Cluny	none		fols. 139r–140v: abbreviated version of *PL* 1.1–1.5				

BNF lat. 15149	Elements from the twelfth, thirteenth, and fourteenth centuries	St.-Victor, Paris	fols. 17r–17v: *Affectu recolendo* and *Plerique dubitare*	fols. 17v–38v: *Incipit liber primus de vita sancti Geraldi qui legitur iii idus octobris* and *Incipit liber secundus* (no mention of Limoges in Gerald's birth place)	fols. 38v–41(bis)r (two folios are numbered 41): *Incipit liber tertius* (includes *PL* 3.1)	fols. 41(bis)r–43v: *Incipit liber quartus* (*PL* 3.12 given as lesson 13 of *Liber tertius*, but ends *Explicit prologus*)	fols. 43v–44r: *Incipit sermo de eadem festivitate*
BNF lat. 15436	Elements from the eleventh through fourteenth centuries; relevant folios are eleventh century	St.-Marcel, Paris	none	fols. 46v–49v (*PL* 1.1–1.9, 1.12): the text breaks off because folios 50 and 51 have been replaced with an unrelated palimpset, and possibly other folios removed (no mention of Limoges in Gerald's birth place)	fols. 52r–52v: (*PL* 3.2, 3.7–3.8 only; the ms resumes after a break; see left)		

Manuscript	Date	Origin	Preface	Vita brevior	Vita prolixior (Books 1 and 2)	Transitus	Miracula	Sermo	Additional miracle stories
BNF lat. 16733	Twelfth century	St.-Martin-des-Champs, Paris	none	fols. 96r–98r: *Incipit vita sancti Geraldi confessoris*		fols. 98r–99r: *Incipit de transitu eius* (missing PL 3.1, 3.4, 3.6, 3.10)	fol. 99v: *Incipiunt miracula* (PL 3.12, 4.1–4.4 only)		
BNF lat. 17006	Twelfth century	St.-Bernard de la Pénitence (Feuillants), Paris	none	fols. 127v–130r: *Incipit vita sancti Geraldi confessoris*		fols. 130r–131r: *Incipit de transitu eius* (missing PL 3.1, 3.4, 3.6, 3.10)	fols. 131r–131v: *Incipiunt miracula* (PL 3.12, 4.1–4.4 only)		
BNF lat. nouvelles acquisitions 2246 (hereafter n.a.; identified by Bultot-Verleysen as *Vita prolixior secunda*)	Twelfth century	Cluny	none		fols. 155v–156v: *In natale sancti Geraldi confessoris* (PL 1.1–1.5 only; Gerald's birth place given as *villa quae vocatur aureliana vallis*)				

BNF lat. n.a. 2261 (identified by Bultot-Verleysen as *Vita prolixior secunda*)	Eleventh or twelfth century	Cluny	fols. 135r–135v: *Reverendo patri*; titled *Incipit prologus in vita vel transitu beati Geraldi confessoris* (includes a list of chapter titles, fol. 135r)	fols. 135v–143r: *Incipit libellus primus vitae beati Geraldi confessoris* (PL 1.1–1.3, 1.5–1.11, 1.13–1.19, 2.12–2.13, 2.23–2.28, 2.30–2.32, 2.34: Gerald's birth place given as *villa quae vocatur vallis aureliana*)	fols. 143r–145r: not titled but ends *Explicit liber secundus* (PL 3.2–3.9 only)	fols. 145r–147v: *Incipit liber tertius* (PL 3.12, 4.1–4.12; includes a list of chapter titles, fol. 145r)
BNF lat. n.a. 2663	Twelfth century	Southern France, Massif Central	fol. 209v: *Reverendo patri*	fols. 209v–213r: *Incipit vita sancti Geraldi*	fols. 213r–215r: *Incipit de transitu eiusdem beati Geraldi* (PL 3. prol., 3.2–3.3, 3.5–3.8, 3.11)	fols. 215r–217r: *Incipit prologus in mirabilibus eiusdem*, but no other title (PL 3.12, 4.1–4.10)
Other libraries						
Aurillac Archives départementales de Cantal 101 F 32	Thirteenth or fourteenth century	Probably from Aurillac	None			Two folios with fragments

Manuscript	Date	Origin	Preface	Vita brevior	Vita prolixior (Books 1 and 2)	Transitus	Miracula	Sermo	Additional miracle stories
Clermont-Ferrand Bibliothèque municipale 149	Eleventh or twelfth century	Unknown	None	fols. 139r–140v: *Incipit vita sancti Geraldi confessoris* (greatly abbreviated version)		fol. 140v: text continues without new title into *PL* 3 *prol.*, then ends)			
Dijon Bibliothèque municipale 660	Eleventh or twelfth century	Possibly Cîteaux	fols. 2r–4r: *Affectu recolendorum* followed by *Plerique dubitare*, both titled *Praefatio* (dedication is titled *Incipit Odonis praefatio patris Amandi in vita domni illustris virtute Geraldi*)		fols. 4r–49r: *Incipit eiusdem patroni vita beati* (complete text of *PL*; Gerald's birth place includes *atque lemovicensi pago*; second book titled *Incipit liber secundus*)	fols. 49r–57r: *Incipit liber tertius*	fols. 57r–64r: *Incipit liber miraculorum* (*PL* 3.12, 4.1–4.12, plus two additional miracles)	fols. 64r–67v: *Sermo de eadem festivitate*	

Manuscript	Date	Origin	Incipit	Contents
El Escorial Real Biblioteca H III 11	Twelfth century	unknown	none	fols. 216v–217v: *Incipit vita sancti Geraldi confessoris*; PL 1.1–1.3, 1.5, 2.10 (Gerald's birth place includes *atque lemovicensi pago*)
Évreux Bibliothèque municipale 101	Twelfth century	Évreux	fols. 10r–10v: *Reverendo patri*	fols. 10v–14r: *Incipit vita sancti Geraldi abbatis* (Ends *Explicit vita sancti Geraldi abbatis*)	fols. 14r–16r: *Incipit transitus eiusdem* (greatly abbreviated PL 3.prol., 3.2–3.3, 3.5–3.9; ends *Explicit transitus sancti Geraldi abbatis*)
Madrid Real Academia de la Historia 9	Twelfth or thirteenth century	San Millan de la Cogolla	none	fols. 188r–189r: Titled *Natale sancti Geraldi* (PL 1.1–1.5)

Manuscript	Date	Origin	Preface	Vita brevior	Vita prolixior (Books 1 and 2)	Transitus	Miracula	Sermo	Additional miracle stories
Mantova Biblioteca Teresiana 455	Eleventh or twelfth century	from San Benedetto di Polirone, but of southern French origin	fols. 1r–2v: *Affectu recolendo*, followed without title by *Plerique dubitare* (dedication is titled *Incipit Odonis praefatio patris Amandi in vita domni illustris virtute Geraldi*)		fols. 2v–36r: *PL* books 1 and 2; no title to first book, but second identified as *Liber II* (Gerald's birth place includes *atque limovicensi pago*)	fols. 36r–40v and 49r–50r (the ms was taken apart and reassembled incorrectly, so the folios here are out of sequence, and this text is mistitled *Lectio evangelii secundum Marcum*)	fols. 50r–54v: No title	fols. 55r–56v and 41r–41v : *Sermo de eadem festivitate* (the folios are also out of sequence here)	fols. 41v–48v: *Incipiunt miracula et de ecclesia que primitus in onorem sancti Geraldi constructa fuit vel qualiter Stephanus episcopus ad dedicandum ecclesiam venerit vel quale miraculum in die consecrationis ibi patratum sit*

| Montpellier Bibliothèque de la Faculté de Médecine 142 | Thirteenth century | Southern French origin, possibly Aurillac, but previously at Troyes | fols. 182r–183r: *Affectu recolendo*, followed by *Plerique dubitare*, ends *Explicit prologus* | fols. 183r–207r: *Incipit eiusdem patroni vita beati* in two books of PL text, second identified as *Incipit liber secundus* (Gerald's birth place includes *atque lemovicensi pago*) | fols. 207r–211r: *Incipit egregii meritis signisque Geraldi transitus ad superum Christus qui vexit olimphum* | fols. 211r–215r: *Incipit prologus in libro miraculorum beati Geraldi* (no title to book, but ends *Explicit liber miraculorum*; includes PL 3.1) | fols. 215r–217r: *Sermo de eadem festivitate* | fols. 217r–230v: *Incipiunt miracula et de ecclesia que primitus in honorem beati Geraldi constructa fuit, vel qualiter Stephanus episcopus ad dedicandam eam venerit, vel quale miraculum in die consecrationis miraculum patratum sit*; followed by a miracle involving a man named Bodetus, fols. 231r–232r |

Manuscript	Date	Origin	Preface	Vita brevior	Vita prolixior (Books 1 and 2)	Transitus	Miracula	Sermo	Additional miracle stories
Paris Bibliothèque de l'Arsenal 162 (identified by Bultot-Verleysen as *Vita prolixor secunda*)	Twelfth century	St.-Arnoul de Crépy-en-Valois	none		fols. 219r–220r: Titled *In natale sancti Geraldi* (continues with *PL* 1.1–1.2, 1.4–1.6)				
Rouen Bibliothèque municipale 1389	Eleventh or twelfth century	St.-Evroult, Normandy	none (but ms is mutilated here)	fols. 64v–66r (only the last part of the text is preserved)		fols. 66r–67v: continued without title from *Vita brevior* (missing *PL* 3.1 and 3.10, and greatly abbreviated)			
Toulouse Bibliothèque municipale 478	Fourteenth century	Toulouse	fol. 56v: *Reverendo patri*	fols. 57r–60v: titled *Vita sancti Geraldi confessoris* (before preface)		fols. 60v–62v: *De transitu ipsius* (missing *PL* 3.1 and 3.10)	fol. 62v–65r: No title (entire *PL* book 4, with two additional miracles)		

Tours Bibliothèque municipale 156	Thirteenth century	Tours	none	fols. 19r–20v: *Incipit legenda beati Geraldi* (only parts of *PL* 1.1–1.5, 2.17–2.21, 2.23, 2.25)	fol. 20v (continues without break or title; only brief parts of *PL* 3 prol., 3.2–3.3, 3.5–3.7)
Vaticano Biblioteca Vaticana Registra latina 517	Twelfth or thirteenth century	unknown	none	fols. 29r–30v: *Incipit vita beati Geraldi confessoris* (greatly abbreviated from *PL* 1.1, 1.4–1.8, 2.4–2.5, 2.10–2.11, 2.13, 2.20, 2.23–2.24)	fols. 30v–31r (continues without break or title; greatly abbreviated from *PL* 3.5 and 3.7)

Sources: This table is derived from my own investigations of these manuscripts, but similar investigations were conducted by Bultot-Verleysen; see her "Le dossier"; and her *Odon de Cluny*, 86–100, including her own table of some of these manuscripts, 110–12.

NOTES

INTRODUCTION

1. *Visitatio capell[a]e sancti Giraldi*, 4G257 (2MI270), fol. 76r/v, Archives départementales de l'Isère, Grenoble. See also Chevalier, *Visites pastorales*, xxi.

2. See Chapter 2, below, for a discussion of what is known about Gerald's birth and death dates. There is no surviving account from Aurillac that provides either date.

3. On this theme Poulin, *L'idéal de sainteté*; Lotter, "Das Idealbild"; and Baker, "*Vir Dei*."

4. Airlie, "The Anxiety of Sanctity," 373.

5. See Rosenwein, "Piety and Power"; and Rosenwein, *Rhinoceros Bound*; see also on this theme Rosé, *Construire une société*, 456–508.

6. See Nelson, "Monks, Secular Men," 124.

7. Charbonnel ("La ville de Gerbert," 58–59) describes some seventeenth- and eighteenth-century copies of the earliest documents related to the monastery of Aurillac, although it is impossible to know how accurately they preserved the original documents. Joubert (*Saint Géraud*, 53–54) lists what he considers to be the four medieval manuscripts that survive from the monastery's library, now scattered, but without precise information as to their location, and he may not be reliable in his attribution. Lemaître (*Mourir à Saint-Martial*, 203, 332) mentions three manuscripts that he says came from the monastery, now BNF. lat. 1085, 1084, and 944, liturgical texts from the tenth, eleventh, and twelfth centuries, respectively. These are all that survive of a library that had perhaps five hundred books at the height of its success—about the number of books that the monasteries of Cluny and Limoges had in the thirteenth century (de Lasteyrie, *L'Abbaye de Saint-Martial*, 338). On the damage done during the Wars of Religion, see also Bouange, "La divine libératrice," 107; on that done during the French Revolution, see Joubert, *Notre-Dame-aux-Neiges*, 28.

8. I am greatly impressed by Samantha Kahn Herrick's "Studying Apostolic Hagiography," in which she attempts to unravel the threads of connection in three versions of the *vita* of Fronto of Périgueux, and also to situate them within the context of the medieval history of Périgueux, a place where—like Aurillac—little documentation has survived. See also her *Imagining the Sacred Past*, where she attempts to reconstruct the early cults of three Norman saints.

9. See, for example, Duby, "The Origins of Knighthood," 167. Guy Philippart ("Le saint comme parure de Dieu") points out how the idea of a new and heroic male saint—daring athlete, valiant soldier, and generous patron—began to surface in the tenth century.

10. Poulin, *L'idéal de sainteté*, 157–58.

11. Noble, "Secular Sanctity," 10. See also Romig, "The Common Bond," which makes a similar point.

12. Jestice, "A New Fashion," 167.

13. Lotter ("Das Idealbild") was perhaps the first to recognize Gerald's curious demonstration of both ordinary and extraordinary holiness. Dominique Iogna-Prat ("La place idéale du laïc," 292) notes how Gerald particularly embodied the tension between an ascetic model of sanctity and a moral model that focuses instead on the goodness of the saint.

14. See Weinstein and Bell, *Saints and Society*, 8.

15. For example, Geary, *Living with the Dead*, 17. Head ("The Cult of Relics," 274) even wonders whether the increasing popularity of the cult of saints in the eleventh century (when the bulk of the writings about Saint Gerald were made) reflects simply an increase in literary production.

16. Landes, *Relics, Apocalypse*.

17. See Jay Winter ("Historians and Sites of Memory," 255), who prefers the term "historical remembrance" to "historical memory" so as to "avoid the pitfalls of referring to memory as some vague cloud that exists without agency." On the unnecessary distinctions between hagiography and other historical writings of the Middle Ages, see Felice Lifshitz, "Beyond Positivism."

18. Rubenstein, "Biography and Autobiography," 22–23.

19. Ibid., 25.

20. Fouracre and Gerberding, introduction to *Late Merovingian France*, 41–42.

21. Ibid., 44. Cf. Gail Ashton (*The Generation of Identity*, 12), who offers similar thoughts: "Each [hagiographical text] focuses upon an idealized . . . subject whose saintly worth is validated through a series of external, immediately recognizable holy symbols, forming part of a particular code of saintliness. . . . It is the imposition of that code, plus the hagiographer's intention to both venerate and offer the saint as exemplum, that tends to lead towards a text marked by control, suppression, and closure. Any potential transgressions . . . are glossed, and a potentially subversive subject is brought back into the safe confines of hagiographical genre and the Church."

22. Fouracre, "Merovingian History," 11.

23. Ibid., 28.

24. Ibid., 37.

25. Pohl, "History in Fragments," 349. See also Heinzelmann, "Manuscrits hagiographiques"; Philippart, "L'hagiographie comme littérature"; and Diesenberger, "How Collections Shape the Texts" for similar thoughts on the importance of new scholarly understandings of hagiography. I am grateful to Joseph-Claude Poulin for bringing to my attention two of his articles on new approaches to reading medieval manuscripts: "Les *libelli*" and "Un élément négligé."

26. Ashley and Sheingorn, *Writing Faith*, 124–26 and 134–35.

27. Remensnyder, "Legendary Treasure."

28. See Sinding-Larsen, *Iconography and Ritual*; or Miles, *Image as Insight*, 15–39. Miles refers to a "hermeneutics" of the "history of image users."

29. See Dupré, *Symbols of the Sacred*, 8.

30. See Hahn, "Picturing the Text," 7.

31. Paxton, "Forgetting Hathumoda."

32. See, for example, Blanton, *Signs of Devotion*, on Saint Aethelthryth; Gaposchkin, *The Making of Saint Louis*; Bitel, *Landscape with Two Saints*, on Saints Genovefa/Geneviève of Paris and Brigit of Kildare. Saint Geneviève can be traced through the early modern period, thanks to Sluhovsky, *Patroness of Paris*.

33. See, for example, Warner, *Joan of Arc*, or her *Alone of All Her Sex* (on the Virgin Mary). Bulles, "Saint Amadour," is the one example I know that follows the evolution of the cult of a relatively minor saint from its beginnings to the present day.

34. Sluhovsky, *Patroness of Paris*, 2, 214, 212.

35. See, for example, Geary, *Phantoms of Remembrance*; Remensnyder, *Remembering Kings Past*; or Booker, *Past Convictions*.

36. De la Roncière, "De la mémoire vécue."

37. See Lawrence Kritzman, introduction to Nora, *Realms of Memory*, 1: xii.

CHAPTER 1

1. It was first published in the *Biblioteca cluniacensis* of Dom Martin Marrier in 1614 and reprinted from there in J.-P. Migne, ed., *Patrologiae Cursus completus, Series Latina* (hereafter *PL*), 133:639–710. It is numbered 3411 in the *Bibliotheca hagiographica latina*. A critical edition of this version, edited by Anne-Marie Bultot-Verleysen (*Odon de Cluny*), has recently appeared. For ease of reference I will use the *PL* numbering for the *Vita prolixior*, which is also given throughout and generally followed by Bultot-Verleysen; hereafter cited in the text. All translations of all texts are my own unless otherwise indicated.

2. A partial critical edition of the *Vita brevior* was published in the *Catalogus codicum hagiographicorum*, 392–401; my fuller "A Critical Edition of the *Vita Geraldi brevior* by Odo of Cluny" is forthcoming. It is numbered 3412 in the *Bibliotheca hagiographica latina*, and is also hereafter cited in the text.

3. See, for example, Jean Dunbabin (*France in the Making*, 57) on Gerald's exercise of justice in ways reserved to counts. Anne-Marie Bultot-Verleysen admits that the naming of Gerald as a count in the *Vita prolixior* is an error: "il n'existait aucun comté d'Aurillac" (*Odon de Cluny*, 53). She also tries to figure out how he might have had the authority to exercise this sort of justice (ibid., 55, esp. n239).

4. On Aurillac's origins, see Charbonnel, "Aurillac, ville romane," 21–22; or Delzons, *Origine de la ville*. Olivier Bruand, who also accepts the scholarly consensus that Odo wrote the *Vita prolixior*, has tried to understand why Odo should have referred to Aurillac as *oppidum*, when the only settlement in the district in Gerald's day was at what is now Arpajon-sur-Cère ("Géraud d'Aurillac, 5–6). Whether there was even a castle there in Gerald's day is uncertain; see below, Chapter 3.

5. The charter of Charles the Simple, if authentic, refers to a double dedication of the original church to Saints Peter and Clement, rather than to two separate churches (that charter is printed in Bouange, *Saint Géraud d'Aurillac*, 487; see also below, Chapter 2). Durliat ("Saint-Géraud d'Aurillac," 336) suggests that the original church built by Saint Gerald's father was rededicated by Gerald, but that is not what the *Vita prolixior* says. Durliat notes that the thickness of the walls found in archeological digs precludes any vaulted roof's having existed (ibid., 332–33). Charbonnel ("La ville de Gerbert," 61–62), trying to overcome this seemingly insurmountable problem, offers the opinion that the enlarged church at Aurillac, completed in 972, obliterated the traces of the earlier church. Yet Beaufrère ("Découverte de peintures") describes traces of Romanesque frescoes that seem to depict Saint Clement in the church of Saint Géraud, which might imply that the church was once dedicated to that saint. Pierre Moulier (*Églises romanes*, 2: 27n2) notes the "more than thirty-year debate" to reconcile the archeological evidence about the origins of the church of Saint Gerald at Aurillac with the *Vita prolixior*, and Charbonnel ("À propos de Saint-Géraud d'Aurillac," 43n21) has recently repeated how unresolved most questions about the original church or churches remain.

6. The two scholars are Settipani, *La noblesse du Midi*, 182n3; and Bultot-Verleysen, *Odon de Cluny*, 59. On the origins of the county of Turenne, see also Aubel, "Les comtes de Quercy," who writes: "le texte de la *Vita Geraldi* est le seul à donner existence à un 'comté de Turenne'" (326).

7. For those who use the *Vita prolixior* as an example of tenth-century Cluniac ideals, see Fumagalli, "Note sulla 'Vita Geraldi' "; or Rosenwein, *Rhinoceros Bound*, chap. 3; or Rosé, *Construire une société*, 458–505.

8. For those who use the *Vita prolixior* as a tenth-century example of lay piety, see Barthélemy, *Chevaliers et miracles*, chap. 2; Jestice, "A New Fashion," 167; or Bull, *Knightly Piety*, 226–29. For those who use it as an example of tenth-century economic history, see Reynolds, *Fiefs and Vassals*, 179; or Duby, *The Early Growth*, 145 and 151; and Bonnassie, *Les sociétés de l'an mil*, 200–5. For those who use it as an example of tenth-century social relations, see Flori, *L'idéologie du glaive*, 108–12; Bonnassie, *From Slavery to Feudalism*, 54–59; Poly and Bournazel, *The Feudal Transformation*, 19, 52, 57, 64, 68, 146, and 239; and Poble, "Les structures territoriales."

9. For discussions of this debate, see Barthélemy, "La mutation de l'an mil"; and Poly and Bournazel, "Que faut-il préférer"; and see also the series of essays in *Past and Present* all titled "The Feudal Revolution" by Barthélemy, Bisson, Reuter, White, and Wickham.

10. Poncelet, "La plus ancienne vie."

11. See Hauréau, *Histoire littéraire du Maine*, 7: 273–78. One of Gerald's biographers (Bouange, *Saint Géraud d'Aurillac*, 355–69) in 1881 listed his reasons for disagreeing with Hauréau's assessment of the relationship between the *Vita prolixior* and the *Vita brevior*, including many of the same as those given in 1895 by Poncelet, and so it seems that Poncelet borrowed some of his points from Bouange. The nineteenth-century discussion of the authorship of the *Vita Geraldi* has also been summarized by Rosenwein in an appendix to her dissertation, "Piety and Power," 159–64.

12. Poncelet, "La plus ancienne vie," 91–92.

13. Anne-Marie Bultot-Verleysen has published a detailed description of all of the manuscripts containing texts related to Gerald of Aurillac: "Le dossier." She repeats some of this information in the introduction to her critical edition of the *Vita prolixior* (*Odon de Cluny*, 86–100, 120–23). Based on my own research of these manuscripts mostly accomplished before her article appeared but then comparing my findings to hers, I have also described them in Appendix 2, below.

14. Poncelet, "La plus ancienne vie," 93.

15. Ibid., 102.

16. Ibid., 97.

17. See below in this chapter on this version that Bultot-Verleysen calls the *Vita prolixior secunda*.

18. Poncelet, "La plus ancienne vie," 97–98.

19. Ibid., 99.

20. Ibid., 100.

21. Ibid., 101.

22. Ibid., 99.

23. Airlie, "The Anxiety of Sanctity."

24. Facciotto, "Moments et lieux," 223.

25. Rosé, *Construire une société*, 205–6.

26. Bultot-Verleysen, *Odon de Cluny*, 2. See also more detailed comments on authorship, including her résumé of the arguments made by other scholars, in her "Le dossier." Iogna-Prat ("La *vita Geraldi*") also notes the problems with the sources, but accepts Bultot-Verleysen's conclusions.

27. See Rosé, *Construire une société*, 219, for Aimon's tenure as abbot of Tulle (now in the *département* of Corrèze). Odo himself succeeded Aimon as abbot of Tulle, so he would have known precisely when Aimon ended his office. The preface to the *Vita brevior* (with the incipit *Reverendo patri*) is found in both of the earliest manuscripts of that version: Paris, Bibliothèque nationale de

France, collection latine (hereafter BNF lat.) 3783, tome II, fols. 341r–344v, and BNF lat. 5301, fols. 221r–233r (both from the late tenth or early eleventh century). The preface to the *Vita prolixior*, in two parts (with the incipits *Affectu recolendo* [identified as *Auctoris epistola nuncupatoria* in *PL* 133: 639–40] and *Plerique dubitare* [identified as *Praefatio* in *PL* 133: 639–42]), is found in three of the earliest manuscripts of the *Vita prolixior*: BNF lat. 11749, fols. 120v–142v, Dijon, Bibliothèque municipale (hereafter Dijon) 660, fols. 2r–67v, and Mantova, Biblioteca Teresiana (hereafter Mantua) 455, fols. 1r–56v; all are from the eleventh or twelfth century. See Appendix 2 for more details. Odo dedicated his *Collationes* also to the same Turpin (see *PL* 133: 517), without repeating any phrases from either dedication (although both versions of the prologue to the *Vita Geraldi* point in its dedication more to Aimon than to Turpin).

28. It was probably in 928, when he was already abbot at Cluny, that Odo was also made abbot of the monastery at Aurillac, and remained there at least a few months but probably not longer while he initiated its reform along Cluniac lines. The dating of Odo's abbacy at Aurillac is described in Rosé, *Construire une société*, 213–18. She relies especially on the early twelfth-century *Breve chronicon Auriliacensis abbatae* (published in Bouange, *Saint Géraud d'Aurillac*, 2:455–59; trans. Bouyssou, "La chronique"): "Oddo, venerabilis abbas, tertius Auriliacensis et Cluniacensis." This chronicle contains few dates; it does say that Odo was abbot at Aurillac while Ralph was king of France (thus between 923 and 936) and while Leo was pope (presumably Leo VI, who held office from mid-928 to the beginning of 929). See below, note 43, on the dating of this chronicle.

29. Odo's earliest *vita* was written by John of Salerno after Odo's death in 942. A second *vita* was composed by Nalgod in the twelfth century; neither mentions Odo's abbacy of Aurillac. Both *vitae* are included in *PL* 133: 43–104.

30. See Rosé, *Construire une société*, 218; Bultot-Verleysen, *Odon de Cluny*, 19–21.

31. The text of the *Vita prolixior* is well known to scholars (including having been translated into English by Sitwell, *St. Odo of Cluny*, 89–180, in 1958; reprinted Noble and Head, *Soldiers of Christ*, 295–362). In Appendix 1 I have translated for the first time the *Vita brevior* into English.

32. In the *PL* (133: 648) Gerald makes the arrangements with the girl's mother, but the manuscripts of the *Vita prolixior* all identify this person as her father. Bultot-Verleysen (*Odon de Cluny*, 148) has also corrected this error.

33. An excellent example of the more usual abbreviations in medieval manuscripts is found in one copy of the *Vita prolixior* (Vaticano, Biblioteca Vaticana, Registra latina [hereafter Vatican] 517, fols. 29r–31r, from the twelfth or thirteenth century) that takes the first sentence or two from sixteen separate sections of the text, running them together and adding a phrase or two from elsewhere in these sections, if needed for clarity. On the typical variations of medieval copyists, see Philippart, "Le manuscrit hagiographique," 33; and for more substantial variations, see Veyrard-Cosme, "Problèmes de réécriture."

34. I have used here the punctuation and wording of Bultot-Verleysen's edition (*Odon de Cluny*, 138) for the *Vita prolixior*, but not the spelling, rather than that of the *PL*; for the *Vita brevior* I have used my own forthcoming critical edition (see note 2 above).

35. There was considerable discussion of the relationship between the miraculous and the natural in the Middle Ages; see Ward, *Miracles and the Medieval Mind*, chaps. 1–2.

36. See Barone, "Une hagiographie sans miracles," who comments on the *Vita prolixior* but, believing it to be the work of Odo of Cluny, concludes that it was an exception to this rule. Odo's authentic work, however, clearly fits the larger pattern.

37. So, for example, the *Vita prolixior* tends to describe relics as *pignora* (used three times) rather than *reliquiae* (used only once), whereas the *Vita brevior* only refers to them by the latter term

(twice). Likewise, the *Vita prolixior* uses *signum* as a frequent equivalent for *miraculum* but the *Vita brevior* never uses the word *signum*. The *Vita brevior* uses only the word *clericus* to describe a priest (six times), but the *Vita prolixior* alternates that term with *presbyter* and *sacerdos* (used eighteen, three, and four times, respectively). Other differences are even more obvious. The *Vita brevior* mentions only five biblical names (Adam, David, Job, Noah, and Peter) and only three names of other saints (Aredius and Caesarius, named as Gerald's ancestors, as noted above, and Lawrence, only because his feast day is mentioned). The *Vita prolixior* adds liberally to this list, with multiple biblical names (Abel, Abraham, Achitophel, Balaam, Belial, Cain, Esau, Ezekiel, Jeremiah, John the Baptist, Josiah, Leah, Mordecai, Moses, Nabuzardan, Paul, Rachel, and Tobias), including, as should be evident, some rather odd choices, as well as names of saints (Ambrose of Milan, Clement, Gregory the Great, Hilary of Poitiers, Jerome, Martial, Martin of Tours, and Oswald), and even an obscure name from classical mythology (Molossos, 1.4; he was the grandson of Achilles).

38. Gerald's lands are referred to only as estates (*praedia*) or fields (*agri*) in the *Vita brevior*, while in the *Vita prolixior* there are also references to vineyards (*vineae*), large estates (*latifundia*), with mention of a certain freeholding (*alodus*, 1.41 and 2.12). Rural peasants are referred to simply as *pagenses* and *rustici* in the *Vita brevior*, a slave girl is called *ancilla* (11), and Gerald's household servants are his *ministri* (5, 6, 11, and 15). There is a much more specialized terminology in the *Vita prolixior*: peasants appear as *pagenses* (1.7 and 1.25) but also as *rusticani* (1.18, 1.22, 1.23, 2.10, and 2.26), *ruricolae* (1.24) *humiles* (1.8) and *agricolae* (1.21), or, more generally, as the "inhabitants [*incolae*]" of a region (1.33); when attached to Gerald's estates, they are also *mancipii* (1.1), *villici* (1.28), *coloni* (1.24), *servi* (1.25 and 2.11), and *ancillae* (2.13 and 2.23). When serving in Gerald's household, individuals are *ministri* (1.14, 1.23, 1.27, 1.30, and 1.34), *servitores* (2.10 and 2.12), *domestici* (1.6), and *cubicularii* (1.15 and 1.25). Gerald's fighting men are called simply *sui milites* in the *Vita brevior*, but in the *Vita prolixior* they are also referred to as *armati* (1.36) and *satellites* (2.1); other fighting forces in the *Vita prolixior*, including those of Gerald's enemies, are referred to in similar terms, but also described collectively as *exercitus* (1.33 and 1.36) as well as *armatorum cuneus* (1.35) and *militum agmen* (1.37). Only one word is used for a settlement or fortification of any size in the *Vita brevior*: it is *civitas*, used for the Italian towns of Lucca and Asta (11 and 13). In sharp contrast, the *Vita prolixior* describes various encampments, forts, villages, and towns with a rich vocabulary that includes *oppidum*, *castrum*, and *castellum* (1.1, 1.36, 1.38, 1.39, 2.5, all used for Gerald's castle above Aurillac), as well as *oppidulum* (1.40, for a place called Sanctus Serenus), *villa* (1.1, for Aurillac, and 2.13, for another village called Crucicula), *vicus* (1.31, for Brioude, 2.30, for a place near Figeac, and 2.32, for Argentat), *burgus* (1.23, for an Italian town on the road to Rome), *municipium* (1.30, an unnamed town), *civitas* (2.18, for "Aôsta," 2.20, for Lucca, and 2.21, for Turin), and *urbs* (1.27, 2.20, and 2.24, for Rome). It is tempting to imagine that some of the more unusual terms—*castellum*, for example, or *burgus*—could help to date the *Vita prolixior*, although both of these terms may be found in fourth-century texts. *Castellum* was used already by several ninth-century authors, and if *burgus* appears much less frequently, its use by Richard of Fleury (in his *Consuetudines et iura ecclesiae de regula*) in the late tenth century, the closest contemporary to either Odo of Cluny or Ademar of Chabannes, puts it precisely but unhelpfully midway between the two. In fact, much of the military vocabulary seems to be derived from patristic sources rather than from contemporary discussions, and most of the terms above are found in one or more of the church fathers or in the Vulgate.

39. The *Vita brevior* uses *eleemosyna* (6) and *eulogia* (15); the *Vita prolixior* uses *eleemosyna* (1.9, 1.14) and also *antidotum* (1.9), *apologetica* (1.praef.), *athleta* (2.1), *charitas* (1.praef., 1.6), *cithara* (1.15), *draco* (1.32, 1.41), *glaucomatus* (1.10), *gyrus* or *gyratus* (1.35, 2.9), *lyra* (1.15), *palaestra* (2.1), *phalerae* or *phaleratus* (1.16, 2.3), *schematus* (2.5), *thalamus* (1.11), *thesaurus* (1.39, 2.praef., 2.34), *tiara* (2.3), and *tyrannus* (1.39).

40. See Souter, *A Glossary*. The *Vita prolixior* uses *bucella* ("bread roll," 2.27), *capsella* ("reliquary," 2.21), *castrametari* ("to set up camp," 1.27 and 2.23), *deosculare* ("kiss," 1.12, 2.30), *discalceatus* ("barefoot," 1.19), *flasco* ("bottle," 1.29, 2.21), *iugiter* ("immediately," 1.4, 1.14, 1.16, 2.3, and 2.16), *laesio* ("injury," 1.17, 1.39, and 2.34), *parvipendere* ("to hang little by or give little consideration for" 2.12—and also *vilipendere*, "to consider as worthless," 2.14), *redargutio* ("refutation," 1.15), *sagmarii* ("pack animals," 1.33, 2.18, and 2.21), and *supellectilis* ("belongings," 1.24, 1.36, and 1.40); the *Vita brevior* uses only the terms *iugiter* (7) and *sagmarii* (13).

41. Ademar de Chabannes, *Chronicon* 3.25: "Odo reverentissimus, Turpione rogitante, vitam sancti Geraldi edidit."

42. Ademar of Chabannes, *Commemoratio abbatum*, ed. Duplès-Agier, 4.

43. *Breve chronicon*: "Oddo, venerabilis abbas, tertius Auriliacensis et Cluniacensis rogatus a Turpione, Lemovicensi episcopo, et ab Aimone Tutelensi abate, descripsit vitam beati Geraldi." On the dating of the *Breve chronicon*, see Charbonnel, "À propos de Saint-Géraud d'Aurillac," 41n5.

44. Peter the Venerable, *De miraculis* 2.25 (*PL* 189: 944): "Nam ut sanctus Pater noster Odo in Vita sancti viri Geraldi scripsit, somniorum visiones non semper sunt inanes." *Vita prolixior* 1.2: "Siquidem somniorum visiones non semper sunt inanes." Cf. *Vita brevior* 1: "Si autem somniis, quae non semper vana sunt."

45. See Facciotto, "Moments et lieux," 223.

46. Iogna-Prat, "Hagiographie, théologie et théocratie."

47. On the scholarly controversy about the nature and extent of millenarianism around the year 1000, see Peters, "Mutations, Adjustments, Terrors"; or Barthélemy, "La paix de Dieu."

48. Landes, *Relics, Apocalypse*, 31, 49. The precise meaning of a term like "nobility" cannot be easily defined for this period, but I use it as shorthand for the landowning and military classes, even though these two groups were not identical and a variety of gradations as well as regional differences existed within them. See Bouchard, "The Origins of the French Nobility." For some of the problems in defining nobility within a text closer in time and place to the *Vita prolixior*, see Caitucoli, "Nobles et chevaliers."

49. See Magnou-Nortier, "The Enemies of the Peace." There is similar language, for example, in the decrees of the Council of Elne-Toulonges in Roussillon in 1027 and an oath of fidelity from the canons of the church of Saint-Julien of Brioude in Auvergne from ca. 1000; both are reprinted in Magnou-Nortier, *La société laïque*, 613–16.

50. Poly and Bournazel, *The Feudal Transformation*, 146. See also Bonnaissie, *Les sociétés de l'an mil*, 318.

51. Barthélemy, *Chevaliers et miracles*, 47. These similarities in vocabulary have also been noted by Rosé, *Construire une société*, 484, who simply says that it is "tout à fait remarquable."

52. Goetz, "Protection of the Church," 273–74. Magnou-Nortier (*La société laïque*, 372), for example, sees the first "Peace of God" language in sources from the region of Narbonne only in the 990s.

53. Duby, *The Three Orders*, 98.

54. Powell, "The 'Three Orders' of Society"; Iogna-Prat, "Le 'baptême' du schéma." See also Brown, "Georges Duby"; Constable, "The Orders of Society"; and Van Meter, "The Peace of Amiens-Corbie" for other critiques. Duby himself admits that the Anglo-Saxon writers Aelfric and Wulfstan were writing in similar terms in the 990s (*The Three Orders*, 102–8).

55. That manuscript is BNF lat. 5301.

56. Only two of the manuscripts of the *Vita Geraldi* contain the *Transitus* but not the *Miracula* (and both of these also have greatly abbreviated *vitae*), which suggests that the *Transitus* and the

Miracula were written to accompany each other. The two exceptions are BNF lat., no. 5298, fols. 87v–89v (with a much abbreviated version of the *Vita prolixior*) and Rouen, Bibliothèque municipale (hereafter Rouen), no. 1389, fols. 64v–67v (with an abbreviated *Vita brevior*). See Appendix 2 for details. The earliest manuscript of the *Transitus* and the *Miracula* (BNF lat. 5301, where it follows the *Vita brevior*) is missing the *PL* equivalents 3.1 and 3.10 from the *Transitus* as well as the last sections of the *Miracula* (the equivalents of *PL* passages 4.8–4.12). Another early manuscript in which the *Transitus* follows the *Vita brevior* (Rouen 1389) is also missing the *PL* equivalents of passages 3.1 and 3.10 (the *Miracula* is not included at all in this manuscript). So it is likely that these episodes were later additions to these two texts, inserted when this author decided to take the *Transitus* and the *Miracula* and turn them into books 3 and 4 of the expanded *Vita Geraldi*. The episodes themselves support this point of view, since *Transitus* 3.1 interrupts the author's thoughts on Gerald's growing infirmity with age with Gerald's vision of the future growth of his monastery, 3.10 interrupts the public mourning for Gerald with a story about washing him for burial, and *Miracula* 4.7 seems to finish the discussion of Gerald's miracles. It should be said that these additional episodes are included in all of the earliest manuscript copies of the *Vita prolixior*: BNF lat. 11749, fols. 120v–142v, BNF lat. 15149, fols. 17r–44r, Dijon 660, and Mantua 455, so they are all still early additions. See Appendix 2 for more details.

57. The exceptions for the *Vita prolixior* are Dijon 660, where the *Transitus* is called *Liber tertius* but the *Miracula* is called *Liber miraculorum*, and Montpellier, Bibliothèque de la Faculté de Médecine (hereafter Montpellier) 142, fols. 182r–230v, where the *Transitus* is so titled and the *Miracula* is called *Liber miraculorum*. The exceptions for the *Vita brevior* are BNF lat. 5365, fols. 99v–103r, where greatly abbreviated versions of the *Transitus* and the *Miracula* are referred to together as *Miraculi* (*sic*), and Toulouse, Bibliothèque municipale (hereafter Toulouse) 478, fols. 56v–65r, where the *Transitus* is titled but the *Miracula* follows it without a title. See Appendix 2 for more details.

58. Bultot-Verleysen's critical edition has renumbered these texts somewhat, among other changes, restoring what the *PL* erroneously numbers 3.12 as the prologue to the *Miracula*/book 4. She also refers to them as the *Transitus* and the *Liber miraculorum* rather than as books 3 and 4 of the *Vita Geraldi*.

59. The expression is a liturgical one; it appears in the *Liber antiphonarius*, of uncertain date but attributed to Pope Gregory I, and is also found in the ninth century in Prudentius of Troyes' *Excerpta ex pontificali, sive antiqui ritus ecclesiae Trecensis*.

60. This count of Toulouse is identified as Raymond, son of Odo. See Bultot-Verleysen (*Odon de Cluny*, 50n127; cf. ibid., 303n120), who notes that this man did not become count until 918, perhaps years after Gerald's death. It may be another of the errors found in the *Vita prolixior*, although since we do not know the date of Gerald's death, we cannot be certain about it. Bultot-Verleysen concludes: "peut-être Odon commet-il un anachronisme."

61. Mention is made of Gerald's soul (*anima*, four times) and his spirit (*animus*, once), as the *Vita prolixior* often does but the *Vita brevior* never does. Gerald is described as "just" in three places in the *Transitus* (3.4, 3.6, and 3.7), recalling his description in the *Vita prolixior* but not emphasized in the *Vita brevior*. See above in this chapter.

62. For example, *pignora* is used as a synonym for relics of the saints in both the *Transitus* and the *Miracula* (3.1, 3.3, 4.9, and 4.12), and *signa* as a synonym for miracles (3.*praef.*, 3.7, and 4.5); likewise, both of these texts also use *sacerdos* and *presbyter* to refer to priests. These are all features of the *Vita prolixior* but not of the *Vita brevior*. See above note 37.

63. Named are Andrew (4.5), Daniel (3.*praef.*), David (3.1, 3.7; cf. 1.*praef.*, 1.6, 1.8, 1.18, 1.42, 2.6), Hilary of Poitiers (3.3), Jacob (3.*praef.*), Jeremiah (3.8; cf. 1.*praef.*, 1.35), Job (3.2, 3.6; cf. 1.*praef.*,

1.6, 1.8, 1.18, 1.28, 1.32, 1.41, 2.1, 2.14), Martial (3.3, 4.5; cf. 1.39, 2.22), Martin (3.3, 4.10; cf. 1.34, 2.22, 2.23), Nathaniel (3.6), Paul (4.5; cf. 2.17, 2.22, 2.26), Peter (3.4, 3.11, 4.5; cf. 2.2, 2.4, 2.17, 2.22, 2.24, 2.32), and Tobias (3.2; cf. 1.*praef.*).

64. The *Transitus* includes mention of Gerald's intentions regarding the disposition of his secular properties; mention is made there of "all those who belonged to him [*omnes ad se pertinentes*]" being remembered in his will, including his relatives (*propinqui*), his soldiers (*milites*), his servants (*servitores*), and even his slaves (*mancipia*, 3.4). Shortly before his death, Gerald is said to have addressed "his clients and most beloved associates [*clientuli et comites amabillimi*]" (3.*praef.*). Both *nobiles vires* as well as *pagensium plebes* mourned his death (3.5). Gerald's castle at Aurillac is referred to as an *oppidum* (3.1 and 4.10), as is another fort called Mulsedonum (4.10); other properties are a *villa* belonging to a man named Grimaldus (4.2), another *villa* called Vaxia (4.10), and an *alodus* given to the monks at Aurillac (4.9, by a viscount [*vicecomes*], a title also used by the author of the *Vita prolixior* [2.28] but not the *Vita brevior*). To compare to the *Vita prolixior*, see above, note 38.

65. Greek-borrowed words in the *Transitus* and the *Miracula* are: *charitas* (3.5, 3.6, 3.8; cf. 1.*praef.*, 1.6), *chorus* (4.1), *chymilia* (4.8), *cilicium* (3.7), *gyrus* (4.4, 4.6; cf. 1.35, 2.9), *harmonia* (3.5), and *sceptrum* (4.5). Late Latin words are: *antepodium* ("a raised platform," 4.5; cf. 2.9), *caragius* ("magician," 4.7), *deosculare* ("to kiss," 4.10; cf. 1.12 and 2.30), and *epistilium* ("mounting block," 4.10). Diminuitives are: *iuvenculus* (3.3), *corpusculus* (3.6, 3.10), *plateola* (4.4), and *fonticula* (4.10). Superlatives are: *beatissimi* (3.3), *indulgentissime* (3.5), *dulcissimo* (3.9), *splendidissimos* (4.5), and *studiosissimus* (4.8).

66. Landes, *Relics, Apocalypse*, passim and 475 for the reference to the *Transitus*. See also Landes, "Autour d'Adémar." Recently Samantha Kahn Herrick ("Studying Apostolic Hagiography," 245) has also argued that other apostolic legends in France began around the year 1000.

67. There is a reference to Saint Martial in Odo's *Sermo* 4, but only that the basilica in which the saint's remains were found had been destroyed by fire; no mention of the apostolicity of the saint is made by him there. See also below, note 110, on the uncertainty about Odo's authorship of this sermon. Both Alain Dierkens ("Martial, Sernin, Trophime," 31–32) and Edina Bozóky ("Les miracles de saint Martial," 59–69), confirm that apart from this reference, claims about Saint Martial's apostolic status seems to have begun only following an epidemic in Limoges in 994.

68. Jean Schneider ("Aspects de la société," 10) also suggests that this vision pointed to a Limousin origin for the *Miracula*, but only for that text, which he feels had been added to the *Vita prolixior* as a fourth book to the first three books written by Odo of Cluny. He is the only scholar insofar as I know who believes that the author of the *Miracula* was not the same as that of the *Vita prolixior* or the *Transitus*. Schneider was also the first to note that *PL* 3.11 was the proper preface to the *Miracula*.

69. This phrase *atque Limovicensi pago* is not included in *PL*, perhaps because it seems so obvious an error, but perhaps also because it is not found in all of the manuscripts of the *Vita prolixior*: see Appendix 2 for details.

70. On the sacramentaries, see Leroquais, *Les sacramentaires*; and Callahan, "The Peace of God," 181. On the monastic conventions, see Lemaître, *Mourir à Saint-Martial*, 327.

71. Landes, *Relics, Apocalypse*, 198–99, from BNF lat. 2469, fol. 91v. For more information on Limoges in this era, see Aubrun, *L'ancien diocèse de Limoges*. Oddly, this medieval devotion to Saint Gerald at Limoges is not mentioned by Becquet, "Les saints dans le culte."

72. We don't know when this church was built: Ademar of Chabannes mentioned it as having been in existence in 991 (*Chronicon* 3.35). What little is known about the early history of this church is summarized by de Lasteyrie, *L'Abbaye de Saint-Martial*, 215–16; and by Aubrun, *L'ancien diocèse de Limoges*, 159–68 and 194–217.

73. On this bishop Gerald, see Kaiser, *Bischofsherrschaft*, 218–20. On his possible relation to Saint Gerald, see Settipani, *La noblesse du midi*, 192, 237; or Landes, "Autour d'Adémar," 43 (both of whom have him descended from a sister of Saint Gerald). See also below, Chapter 3.

74. Again, the manuscript is BNF lat. 5301. A fire destroyed much of the monastery, including its library, sometime in the 980s. According to Besseyre and Gousset, "Le scriptorium de Saint-Martial," 338–39, only one manuscript survived. The manuscript refers to Saint Martial as a *confessor*, but that word has been rubbed out and replaced with the word *apostolus*, so the manuscript existed before the monks' efforts to elevate Martial in the late 1020s. In general on the *scriptorium* of St.-Martial, see Gaborit-Chopin, *La décoration des manuscrits*, including 14–15 (on the fire), and 67–68 (on BNF lat. no. 5301, including the *confessor/apostolus* palimpsest on fol. 331v of the ms).

75. On Ademar as forger, see Landes, *Relics, Apocalypse*, passim, esp. 265–66, where he quotes Ademar's lengthy self-justification for his forgeries; or Landes, "A *Libellus*." See also Frassetto, "The Art of Forgery," 11–26, for more on Ademar's actions.

76. See Landes and Paupert, *Naissance d'apôtre*, 18, 65, 77.

77. See Landes, *Relics, Apocalypse*, 53–65, 59.

78. See Head, "The Development of the Peace."

79. Martindale, "Peace and War."

80. Ademar (*Chronicon* 3.41) described William as "beloved by those around him, great in wisdom, conspicuous in prudence, most generous in giving, a defender of the poor, a father to monks, a builder and lover of churches, and above all a lover of the holy Roman church." On the comparison between William and Gerald, see Fletcher, *Saint James's Catapult*, 92–93. See also Bachrach, "*Potius rex*"; or Bachrach, "Toward a Reappraisal"; Brisset, "Guillaume le Grand"; and Callahan, "William the Great" on this duke's career.

81. See below, Chapter 3.

82. Ademar, *Chronicon* 3.45.

83. Ibid., 3.25 (added between A and C). On the dating of these versions, see Landes, "Autour d'Adémar," 41, who also dates the composition of the *Commemoratio abbatum* to mid-1029.

84. Bultot-Verleysen (*Odon de Cluny*, 57–59) suggests that not naming Ademar as Count of Poitiers in the *Vita prolixior* was intended to avoid offending Èbles Manzer, still Count of Poitiers when Odo wrote, who had been this Ademar's rival and had never recognized his title. Yet it might have been to avoid offending Duke William, Ademar's contemporary and a descendant of Èbles, for the same reason. For more on politics in the tenth- and eleventh-century Auvergne, see Lauranson-Rosaz, *L'Auvergne et ses marges*, with a genealogical table (60).

85. Ademar, *Chronicon* 3.45. On naming practices in the central Middle Ages, see Werner, "Liens de parenté," 13–18 and 25–34. See also Bouchard, "The Origins of the French Nobility," 505–8, who is sceptical of scholarly claims that individuals with the same names are necessarily or even likely from the same family, noting that individuals from one noble family might have been named to honor another noble family. Yet even Bouchard's argument supposes that names were linked to certain families.

86. Bultot-Verleysen, "Le dossier," 194–97; see also her more detailed discussion in *Odon de Cluny*, 67–81, where she credits Vito Fumagalli as the first to notice the significant differences in one manuscript of the *Vita prolixior*.

87. The detailed manuscript is BNF lat. nouvelles acquisitions (hereafter n.a.) 2261; fols. 135r–147v; the others are BNF lat. 12601, fols. 139r–140v, BNF lat. n.a. 2246, fols. 155v–156v, and Paris, Bibliothèque de l'Arsenal 162, fols. 219r–220r. See Appendix 2 for details.

88. *Valle Aurelianis* is mentioned as an estate belonging to the monastery of Aurillac in the additional miracle stories (5). There is still a modern church dedicated to Saint Gerald in modern Vailhourles.

89. The manuscripts containing the *Sermo* are Mantua 455, Dijon 660, Montpellier 142, and BNF lat. 15149. See Appendix 2 for details. Hereafter cited in the text.

90. Facciotto, "Il *Sermo.*"

91. The passage alludes both to 2 Corinthians 5:2–3 and Apocalypse 3:18.

92. Gerald is described at *beatus* nine times and *sanctus* (once, 2, but with several other mentions of him among the saints), his soul is mentioned twice (*anima*, 4 and 8), and the miracles at his tomb are "signs" (*signa*, 8), all features of the *Vita prolixior* but not of the *Vita brevior*. There is little secular vocabulary in the sermon from which to compare it to the other texts, but in one place crowds of people are said to visit Gerald's tomb "not only from neighboring parts but also from far distant regions [*non solum enim ex vicinis partibus verum etiam ex longuinquis regionibus*]" (9), a phrase that echoes the wording of the *Vita prolixior*, in which Gerald's kindness is said to have echoed "not only in nearby areas but also in far distant regions [*non solum vicinis sed etiam longuinquis regionibus*]" (1.17). The *Vita prolixior* is also distinguished from the *Vita brevior* in its much more frequent use of Greek borrowed words, late Latin words, and superlatives. The sermon does not use any Greek vocabulary except *eleemosyna* (5), but it does include several late Latin words: *fulgida* ("light, brightness" 8), *fiducialiter* ("confidently," 9), *imbribus* ("as in a heavy rain," 4), *supervestire* ("to don an outer garment," 9), and *veniabilis* ("pardonable," 9). It also uses many superlatives (*dilectissimi, sacratissima,* and *dignissima* in the first lesson alone).

93. Again, the oldest of these *Vita brevior* + *Transitus* + *Miracula* manuscripts is BNF lat. 5301 (from Limoges, and described above). Clearly derived from it are a group of seven twelfth-century manuscripts: BNF lat. 16733, fols. 96r–99v, BNF lat. 17006, fols. 127v–131v, BNF lat. 5365, BNF lat. n.a. 2663, fols. 209v–217r; Clermont-Ferrand, Bibliothèque municipale (hereafter Clermont) 149, Évreux, Bibliothèque municipale (hereafter Évreux), 101, fols. 10r–16r, and Rouen 1389. There is also one fourteenth-century and one fifteenth-century manuscript of this version: Toulouse 478, and BNF lat. 3809A, fols. 153r–158v. See Appendix 2 for more details.

94. Again, that ms is BNF lat. n.a. 2261. See Appendix 2 for more details.

95. The four that include it are: BNF lat. 15149, Dijon 660, Mantua 455, and Montpellier 142; the one that does not is BNF lat. 11749; and the eight that are either very brief or mutilated are: BNF lat. 5315, BNF lat. 3820, BNF lat. 5399, BNF lat. 15436, Real Biblioteca de El Escorial, H III 11 (hereafter Escorial), fols. 216v–217v; Madrid, Real Academia de la Historia, 9 (hereafter Madrid), fols. 188r–189r, Tours, Bibliothèque municipale, 156 (hereafter Tours), fols. 19r–20v, and Vatican. See Appendix 2 for more details.

96. It is now preserved at the Biblioteca Teresiana in Mantua (ms. 455), where it was transferred at the dissolution of the monastery of San Benedetto di Polirone, to which it had been sent sometime after that monastery's affiliation with Cluny in 1077. Italian scholars concluded that it was produced near the end of the eleventh century at Moissac—which itself became affiliated with Cluny in 1048. See Piva, "Il monastero di S. Benedetto"; Piva, *Da Cluny a Polirone*, esp. chap. 1; Zanichelli, "La produzione libraria"; and Schwarzmaier, "The Monastery of St. Benedict." Yet French scholars have shown the similarities between the *scriptoria* of Moissac and Limoges in this period. See, for example, Fraïsse, "Un traité des vertus," 242, where she speaks of "l'existence de relations étroites entre les *scriptoria* de Moissac et de Limoges, que plusieurs auteurs ont déjà défendue"; this point was confirmed in conversation with Fraïsse, director of the Centre Art Roman de Moissac, in June of 2003.

Accordingly, Anne-Marie Bultot-Verleysen, who published a critical edition of these additional miracle stories, describes the manuscript only as originating somewhere in southern France; see her "Des *Miracula* inédits"; cf. Bultot-Verleysen, "Le dossier," 178; and Bultot-Verleysen, *Odon de Cluny*, 88–91.

97. The ms. is Montpellier 142. It once belonged to the Collège de l'Oratoire de Troyes, as an inscription indicates (fol. 1r), but that institution was founded only in 1630, so it must have been copied somewhere else. Bultot-Verleysen ("Le dossier," 179–80; cf. *Odon de Cluny*, 95–97) does not explain why she believes it was copied at Aurillac. Possibly its mention of the 1227 translation of Saint Gerald's relics may seem to her to refer to an event commemorated only in Aurillac. Alternatively, it may be because the manuscript provides the date of Gerald's death immediately following the sermon (fol. 217r; the date given is 918), and the same combination also appears in a brief fragment of a manuscript from the monastery of Saint-Géraud at Aurillac (now Aurillac, Archives départementales du Cantal, ms. 101 F 32).

98. In the Mantua manuscript, both the *Transitus* and the *Miracula* follow the *Vita prolixior* without titles. In the Montpellier manuscript, the *Transitus* begins "Incipit egregii meritis signisque Geraldi." The *Miracula* has no title but its sections are separately numbered. See Appendix 2 for more details.

99. The date listed for the dedication of the new church in the *Breve chronicon* (see Bouyssou, "La chronique," 325) is 932 and said to have happened during the papacy of John (who would have been John XI), but since Stephen was not bishop of Clermont then, it is usually corrected to 972 (that is, correcting DCCCCXXXII to DCCCCLXXII), during the papacy of John XIII. For more on archeological evidence for the church at Aurillac, see Beaufrère, "L'Église Saint-Géraud d'Aurillac et ses bâtisseurs"; and Durliat, "Saint-Géraud d'Aurillac."

100. Stephen may have had other reasons for wanting to make his presence felt in Aurillac; he was the younger brother of Viscount Robert II of Auvergne, who was attempting to rival the authority of Count William III of Poitou in the upper Auvergne. This same Stephen held peace assemblies in Aurillac that might also have tried to tie the monastery more closely to Clermont and thus to his family's authority; see Kaiser, *Bischofsherrschaft*, 185. For Stephen's dates, see Bultot-Verleysen, "Des *Miracula* inédits," 138n2. On the cult of Sainte Foy, see Sheingorn, introduction to *The Book of Sainte Foy*; and Ashley and Sheingorn, *Writing Faith*. On Sainte Foy's popularity from about 983, see Sheingorn, *The Book of Sainte Foy*, 10.

101. The Mantua manuscript begins with a prologue and continues with the first five chapters of the text. The Montpellier manuscript omits the prologue but includes those five chapters and fifteen additional ones. There are a number of similarities in the word usage between the earlier and later chapters that suggests the same authorship throughout. To give but a few examples: the expression *moderno tempore* appears in earlier and later parts of the text (3, 10, and 15), as does the expression *pro votis* (1, 4, 7, and 20), and also *tantus patronus* referring to Gerald (*prol.*, 2, 3, 7, 13, 15, and 16). One passage early on in the text begins: "Aliud quoque beati viri miraculum relatione" (3), while a passage later in the text begins: "Aliud quoque eiusdem beati viri narratur miraculum" (11). The Mantua ms was at some point taken apart and then reassembled incorrectly, so it is probable that these later chapters were lost from it at that point. The Montpellier ms also adds an additional miracle story that Bultot-Verleysen concludes was not part of the original text but a later addition. That last miracle story refers to a Cistercian monastery at Obazine founded only in the mid-twelfth century, so it could not have been written early enough to have ever been included in the Mantua manuscript; that story appears in the text, moreover, after the summation of Gerald's virtues in the previous chapter, which also suggests it was added later to the text. See Constance Berman (*The Cistercian Evolution*, 146), who dates the affiliation of Obazine with the Cistercians to between 1146 and 1165.

102. "Iam nunc igitur euoluere debitum premisse pollicitationis satagimus, qualiter in finem libri uite beati uiri iam olim spopondimus." Hereafter cited in the text.

103. Bultot-Verleysen, "Des *Miracula* inédits," 48–55; Bultot-Verleysen, "Le dossier," 179, 205.

104. See above, note 56, on the later addition to the *Miracula*.

105. Bultot-Verleysen, "Des *Miracula* inédits," 57: "L'auteur connaît bien la *Vita prolixior.*"

106. Gerald is described as *beatus, confessor,* and *sanctus* in the additional miracle stories, as in the *Vita prolixior.* Religious vocabulary shows parallels: *pignora* and *reliquiae* are both used, and *signum* and *miraculum,* as in the *Vita prolixior,* as well as *clericus* and *presbyter,* although not *sacerdos. Animus* is used multiple times but not *anima.* Secular vocabulary: the additional miracle stories use both *pagenses* and *plebs* for the peasant population, as in the *Vita prolixior,* and, more specifically, *servi, famuli,* and *ministri* for serfs and servants, and *milites* and *pugnantes* for military men, as well as *vassus* and *satellites,* all as in the *Vita prolixior,* but also *apparitores* (7) and *excubitores* (2, 9, 14, 17). *Possessiones* is also the sole term used for landholdings in the additional miracle stories, unlike the varied terms in the *Vita prolixior,* but also unlike the *praedia* in the *Vita brevior.* And while there are various terms in the additional miracle stories used for settlements and fortifications, including *villa* (2, 5, 7, 10) and *vicus* (20), or *castrum* (1, 7, 10) and *oppidum* (7, 13), and comparable to uses in the *Vita prolixior,* new terms are also found (such as *suburbana,* 7, for the areas around towns). Sometimes the usage of the same terms in the additional miracle stories does not correspond to that of the *Vita prolixior: civitas* is the term used for towns generally, but whenever a town is mentioned by name, it is called *urbs:* Clermont (called *Aruernensium urbs,* 1), Agen (*urbs Agennensium,* 7), Limoges (*urbs que Lemouicas vocatur,* 8), and Tours (*urbs Turonica,* 16). In contrast, both the *Vita brevior* and the *Vita prolixior* use *urbs* only for Rome. Other examples, however, suggest closer ties between the additional miracle stories and the *Vita prolixior.* Biblical names are found throughout the additional miracle stories, as in the *Vita prolixior,* and their usage is sometimes parallel: Elias is mentioned in one of the stories from the additional miracle stories (1), as in the *Vita prolixior* (1.15), and an allusion is made to the story of Balaam's ass (1), although his name is not mentioned as it is in the *Vita prolixior* (2.34). A range of saints' names are likewise found in the additional miracle stories, as in the *Vita prolixior:* Medard of Noyons (1), Scholastica (1), the apostles Simon and Jude (9), and the first martyr Stephen (14). Two of the borrowed Greek words used in the *Vita prolixior* are found in the additional miracle stories: *schema* (3) and *tyrannus* (4). Late Latin words are found, too, in abundance. Some are found in both the *Vita brevior* and the *Vita prolixior,* such as *iugiter* (4) and *sagmarii* (10); others are found only in the *Vita prolixior,* such as *capsella* (17; here spelled *capsula* but clearly meaning a reliquary as it does in the *Vita prolixior* 2.21), *castrametari* (10 and 20), and *parvipendere* (2, 4, 6, and 21); some found in none of the other texts, such as *ligumines* ("vegetables," 15), *molendinus* ("mill," 19), *porcarius* ("swineherd," 4), and *vasculum* ("cup," 11). Other eccentric uses include the term *solidi* for coins in the additional miracle stories (7) as in the *Vita prolixior,* although the *Vita prolixior* also uses *nummi.* Many superlatives are found in the additional miracle stories, as in the *Vita prolixior;* the *Vita brevior* had no superlatives.

107. See Dolbeau, "Les hagiographes au travail," 64, who suggests that stylistic differences alone cannot be used to distinguish hagiographical authors, since the same author might have used varied styles for different writings.

108. Ademar of Chabannes, *Chronicon* 3.35. On the early history of this church, see above, note 72.

109. See my "Dating and Authorship," 84–89.

110. So, for example, scholars have recently mostly rejected the *Epitome moralium in Job* and two of the sermons included as Odo's in the *PL* (*PL* 133: 105–512) as authentically his. See Braga,

"Problemi di autenticità"; Rosé, *Construire une société*, 108; Bultot-Verleysen, *Odon de Cluny*, 6–7. Two sermons ascribed to Odo in the *PL*, numbered as 2 and 4, are also disputed; see Iogna-Prat, "La Madeleine du *Sermo*"; Farmer, *Communities of Saint Martin*, 313. *De reversione beati Martini a Burgundia tractatus*, also included in the *PL* among Odo's writings (*PL* 133: 815–38), is also rejected as authentic by Farmer, *Communities of Saint Martin*, 305–6.

111. *Vita sancti Gregorii episcopi Turonensis* (*PL* 71: 115–28). See Rosé, "La *Vita Gregorii*," who argues for Odo of Cluny as author. On Ademar of Chabannes' authorship of the *Vita sancti Amantii* ("Vita s. Amantii"), see Pon, "La culture d'Adémar," who credits the idea to Léopold Delisle, *Les manuscrits de Saint-Martial*, 322.

112. I searched about five hundred words and phrases using the *PL* electronic database and compared my results by hand to works of both Ademar and Odo not included there, and I summarize my results in my "Dating and Authorship," 84–89, but there is little of real significance in the results. Some of the most unusual words and phrases used in the writings about Gerald were used by both men; some were used by neither. Even a comparison of such words and phrases to those of other writers in the *PL* provided unhelpful results: many of the terms were used by patristic or Carolingian era writers, so they were not useful even in helping to date the texts, irrespective of authorship. An unusual word like *Romei*, used to mean "pilgrims to Rome," appeared in the *PL* database as first used by Bernard of Angers in the early eleventh century; *tortella*, used for a rolled wax candle, as first used by Peter Abelard in the twelfth century. These results would seem to indicate that both are late additions to Latin usage, but since both of these terms appear in both the *Vita brevior* and the *Vita prolixior*, nothing useful is learned.

113. See, for example, Odo of Cluny, *Collationes* 1.35, where Odo repeated the Augustinian division of the world into cities of the wicked and the good, referred to here as the sons of Cain and the sons of Abel, and where the wicked are equated with the violent, a differentiation that would seem to me to make difficult a more subtle justification of violence in the cause of good. Cf. Odo of Cluny, *Collationes* 3.27 for the contrast between the vice of violence and the eternal damnation of the violent and the virtue of patience.

114. The manuscript (University of Leiden, ms. Voss. lat. 8) is described by Gaborit-Chopin, "Les dessins d'Adémar." The *Vita brevior* rarely mentions animals at all, and makes only one comparison between animal and human behavior, in comparing Gerald to Noah's dove in not finding anything worthwhile in the world (7; a reference to Genesis 49:27). The *Vita prolixior*, in contrast, frequently compares human to animal behavior always in biblical allusions and always disparagingly: the violent man is a wolf in the night (1.8 and 1.40, referring to Genesis 49:27 and/or Jeremiah 5:6), and the powerful man is a rhinoceros (1.8, probably a reference to Job 39:9–10). Gerald is not only Noah's dove but also pointedly not the raven from the same biblical story that remained content in the world (2.16, cf. Genesis 8:7–8). In his dealings with these violent and powerful men, Gerald is "a brother to dragons and a companion to ostriches" (1.32 and 1.41, quoting Job 30:29). Likewise, in one of the miracles from the *Miracula* not included in the *PL* but found in the early manuscripts and published by Bultot-Verleysen, a man who rapes a woman is "like a horse and a mule" in lacking understanding (quoting Psalm 32:9; Bultot-Verleysen, *Odon de Cluny*, 278). Similarly, the additional miracle stories note that Gerald destroyed "the roaring lion" (21, quoting Proverbs 28:15, defined there as "an impious prince over a poor people"). These analogies between animal and human behavior, of course, reveal yet another point of similarity in literary style between the *Vita prolixior*, the *Miracula*, and the additional miracle stories that points again to the same author for all, since these are the sorts of allusions likely to have been included in a less than conscious manner. On the moral use of animals in monastic writings, see Boglioni, "Les animaux dans l'hagiographie."

115. See Bourgain, "La culture et les procédés littéraires," 419.

116. Bernard Itier, *Chronicon*, ed. Duplès-Agier, 47; Landes, *Relics, Apocalypse*, 10.

117. Poncelet, "La plus ancienne vie," 97.

118. Ademar de Chabannes, *Epistula de apostolatu sancti Martialis*: "cum ueritas semper ueritas est, et nunquam ueritas respui . . . nec aduerti oportet quis dicat sed quid dicat." Quoted and translated in Landes, *Relics*, 265, from a marginal notation in an autograph manuscript by Ademar, BN lat., 5288 (*PL* 141:96). See also Jones ("Discovering the Aquitainian Church," 98) for further thoughts on Ademar as forger.

CHAPTER 2

1. See above, Chapter 1.

2. According to John of Salerno, when he met Odo in 938, Odo was sixty years of age, which means that he would have been born in about 878.

3. Ademar of Chabannes, *Commemoratio abbatum* 2 (for Gerald's birth, said to have happened in the fifth year of the rule of abbot Abbo of Saint-Martial in Limoges, when Charles the Bald was consecrated as king in Aquitaine) and 3 (for Gerald's death, in the sixth year of abbot Fulbert's rule).

4. Bernard Itier, *Chronicon* 38, 40. If the 899 royal charter granted for the monastery that Gerald founded is authentic, Gerald's death in 887 is impossible; see below in this chapter on this charter. Such an early date for Gerald's death is also unlikely since Gerald was said in both versions of the *Vita Geraldi* to have been an associate of Duke William the Pious of Aquitaine, who did not become duke until 893. See Dunbabin, *France in the Making*, 58–60.

5. They are Montpellier 142 and a brief fragment of a manuscript now Aurillac, Archives départementales du Cantal, ms. 101 F 32.

6. Bouange, *Saint Géraud d'Aurillac*, 504–15; Bultot-Verleysen, *Odon de Cluny*, 64–65. The other possible date is 915.

7. Odo's earliest biographer said simply that Odo reformed several monasteries (John of Salerno, *Vita sancti Odonis* 2.23). Rosenwein (*To Be the Neighbor*, 153–61) describes a variety of ways in which monasteries were linked to Cluny in the tenth century using three examples of monasteries reformed by Cluny in this period, where good evidence has survived: Romainmôtier, Paray-le-Monial, and Sauxillanges. Iogna-Prat (*Études clunisiennes*, 151–60) also discusses the relationship between Cluny and Romainmôtier. None of them seems to have been tightly bound to Cluny but remained mostly independent, as did Aurillac. Gradually Cluny built up a network of dependent monasteries, but how to describe this complex has been debated: see Iogna-Prat, "Cluny comme 'système ecclésial' "; and Poeck, "Abbild oder Verband." See also Rosenwein (*Rhinoceros Bound*, 44–50), for discussions of what is known about Odo's reform of other monasteries, including that of Aurillac (47). The best comparison might be made with the monastery of Baume that, like Aurillac, predated the foundation of Cluny but was gradually linked to it; see Constable, "Baume and Cluny."

8. See Charbonnel, "Aurillac, ville romane," 21–22. A pagan temple, abandoned in the fourth or fifth century C.E., has also been located three kilometers from the site of the former monastery; see Degoul, "Découverte d'un temple." See also Delzons, *Origine de la ville d'Aurillac*; and Bouange, *Saint Géraud d'Aurillac*, 401–11.

9. See Degoul, "Les châteaux seigneuriaux," 52–54, who dates the oldest part of the current structure to the end of the twelfth century or the beginning of the thirteenth. Even that has been heavily restored, since a major fire in 1868 destroyed much of it (Moulier, *Églises romanes*, 2: 31). It was restored in 1881 to what Durand (*Aurillac*, 216) calls "a ponderous copy of the Palace of the

Popes in Avignon." Generally on the early castles of southern France, see Bonnassie, *From Slavery to Feudalism*, chap. 4; and Magnou-Nortier, *La société laïque*, 247−52. On the earliest castles in Auvergne, see Lauranson-Rosaz, *L'Auvergne et ses marges*, chap. 4; and Poly and Bournazel, *The Feudal Transformation*, 26−27 (who note that the number of castles in Auvergne more than doubled at the beginning of the eleventh century as evidenced from the archeological record and from the use of the term *castrum* in charters).

10. For more on medieval routes to and from Aurillac, see Durand, *Aurillac*, 88−96.

11. See Ademar of Chabannes, *Chronicon* 3.21.

12. BNF lat. nouv. acq. 1497, fol. 9r, where Gerald is the second-to-last in a long list of names. The manuscript is from about 1030; the original charter was copied there and is no longer extant. See Geary, *Phantoms of Remembrance*, 103−5.

13. For a survey, see Lauranson-Rosaz, *L'Auvergne et ses marges*. To compare negotiations of marriage and alliance for contemporaries of Gerald in the Po valley in northern Italy, see Rosenwein, "The Family Politics of Berengar I."

14. An overview of the early Cluniac movement can be found in Rosenwein, *Rhinoceros Bound*, chap. 1; or Constable, "Cluny in the Monastic World." Life at Cluny in Odo's day is also described by Rosé, *Construire une société*, 223−54, who also details (in her chap. 3) the expansion of Cluny's influence under Odo, and (in chap. 6) monastic reform in Odo's day. More details may be found in L. M. Smith's two volumes, *The Early History of the Monastery of Cluny* and *Cluny in the Eleventh and Twelfth Centuries*. More biographical details about Odo of Cluny may also be found in Duckett, *Death and Life in the Tenth Century*, chap. 7. On the need for monastic reform, see the description provided by Lauranson-Rosaz, "L'Auvergne au Xe siècle," 13−15. And on the importance of the transference of monasteries from royal to papal protection, see Lemarignier, "Structures monastiques."

15. Cochelin, "Quête de liberté," 197. The text is reproduced in full in Bouange, *Saint Géraud d'Aurillac*, 487−89; and in Grand, *Les "paix" d'Aurillac*, 137−38.

16. Quoted in Cochelin, "Quête de liberté," 198. The Latin text is given in her note 70, but the text is also reproduced in full in Bouange, *Saint Géraud d'Aurillac*, 500−502.

17. Despite the concern by Cluniacs and others over lay control, laymen were very much involved in many of the attempts at church reform in the eleventh century; see Howe, "The Nobility's Reform."

18. Cochelin, "Quête de liberté," 198. See also Rosé, *Construire une société*, 217; and Fray, "Le véritable fondateur," both of whom accept Cochelin's conclusions. For John as abbot of Aurillac, see Bouyssou, "La chronique," 324.

19. John of Salerno, *Vita sancti Odonis* 1.37, trans. Sitwell, 39. Neither of the later versions of Odo's *vita* repeated this comment. Aubrun (*L'ancien diocèse de Limoges*, 159−66) also questions Turpin's commitment to the type of reforms that Cluny's early abbots initiated, especially the removal of lay influence from ecclesiastical appointments. Still, Anna Trumbore Jones (*Noble Lord, Good Shepherd*, 145−46) mentions this same Turpin's foundation of a monastery in Limoges apparently for the sake of church reform.

20. See Rosé, *Construire une société*, 218−22, on the evidence for Odo at Tulle.

21. Levillain, "Adémar de Chabannes," 259; the same relationship has been reconstructed more recently by Settipani, *La noblesse du midi*, 250−59. See also Becquet ("Les évêques de Limoges, 75−82), who notes that we do not know much else about them except that they were of the family of the viscounts of Aubusson.

22. See Farmer (*Communities of Saint Martin*, 8) for an interesting comparison with the medieval cult of Martin of Tours.

23. See Remensnyder (*Remembering Kings Past*, 89–90) on how often monasteries in southern France in the central Middle Ages attempted to remember their founders as saints, including a number of lay founders (ibid., 25).

24. See above, Chapter 1, on the debate about the dedication of the original church.

25. The shifting of monks from one monastery to another to promote the cause of reform became commonplace. See Remensnyder (*Remembering Kings Past*, 27) on the monks from Aurillac sent to the monasteries of Saint-Chaffre (now Le Monastier-sur-Gazeille in the *département* of Haute-Loire) and Saint-Pons de Thomières (*département* of Hérault) in 937; Saint-Chaffre in turn sent monks to Sainte-Enimie (*département* of Lozère) in 951. On Saint-Pons de Thomières see also Rosé, *Construire une société*, 292–96.

26. Hallinger, "The Spiritual Life of Cluny."

27. Rosenwein, *Rhinoceros Bound*, chap. 4.

28. Bouange ("La divine libératrice," 106) claimed that the tomb of Adeltrude was venerated until it was destroyed by Huguenots in 1569. Since Bouange also mentioned the destruction of the tombs of Saint Gerald's father and his sister Avigerne, if the tomb existed there or elsewhere, it may have been part of a family burial site rather than a saint's shrine. Branche (*La vie des saincts*), writing in 1652, mentioned a feast day of Adeltrude, mother of Gerald, as well as of Gerald's father, both commemorated on 14 November, but I have found no other evidence for her cult; on Branche, see below, Chapter 5.

29. Schulenberg, *Forgetful of Their Sex*, esp. chap. 5 (on motherhood and sanctity), 221–28 (on what she calls *coitus sacer*, "sacred sex" that produces a saint), 211 (quotation). Valerie Garver (*Women and Aristocratic Culture*, 144–59) has also described the central role given over to mothers as teachers of morality to their sons.

30. See Julia M. H. Smith, "The Problem of Female Sanctity"; Julia M. H. Smith, "Gender and Ideology"; and Magnou-Nortier, "Ombres féminines."

31. There has been much scholarship on this question: for the ninth-century nobility in particular, see Martindale, "The French Aristocracy"; and Poly and Bournazel, *The Feudal Transformation*, chap. 3, who note the preference for Germanic names over Roman ones among the nobility by the ninth century, 220. Yet, as Georges Duby notes ("The Structure of Kinship," 146), it is virtually impossible to trace most noble families earlier than the tenth century except by conjecture. See also Lauranson-Rosaz, ("L'Auvergne au Xe siècle," 10–13), who emphasizes the predominately Roman ancestry of the Auvergnat nobility.

32. See Settipani (*La noblesse du midi*, 192–225) for further speculations on Gerald's ancestry and on his relationship to these men, which he rejects as implausible.

33. As has been pointed out (see the various essays in Wormald and Nelson, *Lay Intellectuals*), Gerald was not entirely unique in combining a noble lineage, military lifestyle, and intellectual pursuits in the Carolingian or post-Carolingian era.

34. Phyllis Jestice ("Why Celibacy?") describes Odo's attempts to reinvigorate the love of celibacy as part of his monastic reforms. Although she mentions the *Vita prolixior* in her analysis, thinking it to be Odo's, she relies more heavily on Odo's authentic *Collationes*, which she believes was directed mostly at the secular clergy. The reference to the eyes as the occasion for sin can be found in many patristic and early medieval writings, including the Rule of Saint Benedict (7); see also Diem (*Das monastische Experiment*, 107, 224, 254), who finds it also in Augustine, Jerome, John Cassian, the sixth-century Rule of Tarn, and the seventh-century Rule of Donatus. See also Murray, "Masculinizing Religious Life." The mention of nocturnal emissions depends on a monastic tradition seen in the fifth century in John Cassian and in the sixth in Gregory the Great but seldom after that;

see Leyser, "Masculinity in Flux"; Brakke, "The Problematization"; and Diem, *Das monastische Experiment*, 109–10, 225, 230, 236, 245, 291. Diem claims that it was treated in early medieval texts less as a moral problem and more as a practical one.

35. 2 Samuel 2:23; *aversa hasta* in the Vulgate.

36. Martínez Pizarro ("On *Nið*") shows how longstanding and widespread this accusation of unmanliness was in the central Middle Ages, and wielded especially against men who refused to participate in violence and in sexual activity.

37. See Rosé, *Construire une société*, 456–508, on Gerald as a model of lay noble manhood. Rosé accepts Odo's authorship of *Vita prolixior*, but her analysis on this point might be as easily applied to the *Vita brevior*.

38. See Dubreucq, "La littérature des *specula*"; Savigni, "Les laïcs dans l'ecclésiologie carolingienne;" and Vauchez, *The Laity in the Middle Ages*.

39. On the absence of Gerald's secular duties in the *Vita brevior*, see above, Chapter 1.

40. The Carolingian Charles the Simple might have inherited the French throne in 887. Instead, since he was only ten years old, the nobles of France elected Odo or Eudes of the Capetian line in the following year. By 893 Charles was crowned king, and civil war began. When Odo died in 898, the rivalry quieted for a while, as most seemed to accept Charles as king, but was revived when Odo's brother Robert was crowned king in 922, and then, after Robert had been killed in battle in 923, when Robert's son-in-law, Ralph of Burgundy, claimed the throne. See Dunbabin, *France in the Making*, 27–31; Guillot, "Formes, fondements et limites"; or Fournier, "Saint Géraud et son temps."

41. Charles the Simple might still have been alive when Odo of Cluny wrote the *Vita Geraldi* (he died in late 929), but Ralph was definitely still alive (he died in 936). Ralph prevented Èbles Manzer from taking up his father's title as count of Auvergne, giving it instead to Raymond Pons, count of Toulouse, who also briefly claimed the title of duke of Aquitaine (and whose father was remembered as having held hostage one of Gerald's nephews in the *Vita prolixior*, 2.28, which may reflect accurate political antagonisms). See Dunbabin, *France in the Making*, 84–87. See also Rosé, *Construire une société*, 447–56, for Odo's thoughts generally on royalty; she notes (ibid., 442) that Odo did not mention the role of kings in his *Collationes*.

42. See Charbonnel, "La ville de Gerbert," 60; or Cochelin, "Quête de liberté, 197n66. Since this charter survives only in an eighteenth-century copy, it is always possible that the word *comes* was introduced then and not found in the original (Charbonnel, "La ville de Gerbert," 58).

43. Rosenwein, *Rhinoceros Bound*; Lotter, "Das Idealbild," 94.

44. Airlie ("The Anxiety of Sanctity," 379) wonders about this, too. See Noble ("Secular Sanctity," 26–30) for interesting speculations on the extent to which the Carolingian nobility heard the moral exhortations of churchmen.

45. Most laymen were illiterate in Odo's day, of course; on their ability to understand Latin if recited, see Van Uytfenghe, "The Consciousness"; and McKitterick, "Latin and Romance," both of whom examine a range of ninth-century sources without reaching clear conclusions. Heene (*"Audire, legere, vulgo"*), speculates more specifically about the comprehensibility of Latin *vitae* of the saints to lay listeners in the ninth century, although she also concludes that the evidence is ambiguous. Leclercq ("Recherches"), discussing tenth- and eleventh-century Latin sermons, believes that the language was still comprehensible enough to all that they might be directed at both monastic and lay audiences.

46. Philippart, "Le saint comme parure de Dieu," 137–38.

47. Facciotto ("Moments et lieux," 223) describes the *Vita brevior* as much more reflective of the monastic rule than the *Vita prolixior*.

48. See Rosé (*Construire une société*, 27–32); or Iogna-Prat (*Études clunisiennes*, 38–44) for a discussion of the sources for Odo. Rosé (*Construire une société*, chaps. 1–3) attempts to reconstruct Odo's life with as much precision as possible. Iogna-Prat also notes that a cult of Saint Odo was not officially celebrated at Cluny until the late eleventh century (*Études clunisiennes*, 185–87). Already in 1959 Joachim Wollasch ("Königtum, Adel und Klöster," 132, 138) noticed the similarities between elements of the biographies of Odo by John of Salerno and of Gerald by Odo, and it has been mentioned in passing by many others since: Fumagalli, "Note sulla *Vita Geraldi*," 217–22; Poulin, *L'idéal de sainteté*, 89; Nelson, "Monks, Secular Men," 130; Cochelin, "Quête de liberté," 194.

49. John of Salerno, *Vita sancti Odonis* 1.4, trans. Sitwell, 7. John's text was revised in the middle of the eleventh century by a monk named or who called himself Humillimus and again in the early twelfth century by a Cluniac monk named Nalgod. These versions are not all that different from John's text, except in mostly minor details, and do not seem to have relied on other sources for their information, so I will focus my analysis on John's text. On these other versions see Fini, "L'*Editio minor*"; and Fini, "Studio sulla *Vita Odonis*"; Iogna-Prat ("Panorama de l'hagiographie," 81–87; on John of Salerno, see also Cochelin, "Quête de liberté," 184–87.

50. John of Salerno, *Vita sancti Odonis* 1.3.

51. Ibid., 1.4.

52. Ibid., 1.5, trans. Sitwell, 7–8. Rosé (*Construire une société*, chap. 1) concludes that it is impossible fully to reconstruct Odo's early life. Wollasch ("Königtum, Adel und Klöster, 120–42); and Lauranson-Rosaz ("Les origines d'Odon") provide the most detailed discussions of what is known of Odo's ancestry.

53. John of Salerno, *Vita sancti Odonis* 1.8, trans. Sitwell, 9–10.

54. Ibid., 1.9, trans. Sitwell, 10. Nelson ("Monks, Secular Men," 130) describes this adolescent crisis in Odo's life as a failure to cope with the demands of lay noble masculine adulthood; see also Rosé, *Construire une société*, 69.

55. John of Salerno, *Vita sancti Odonis* 1.5, trans. Sitwell, 8.

56. McNeill ("Asceticism versus Militarism") sees the rejection of the military lifestyle as a major incentive for the adoption of the monastic life in the Middle Ages, and uses Odo as an example in support of his argument. Bouchard (*Sword, Miter, and Cloister*, 46–64) describes a broader range of motivations for noble conversions to clerical or monastic life from eleventh- and twelfth-century sources that may also have held true for the tenth century.

57. See John of Salerno, *Vita sancti Odonis* 1.18 and 2.4 (on Odo's almsgiving), 1.30 and 1.33 (on Odo's refusal to talk with the boys of the monastery alone and begging forgiveness from his fellow monks for a breach of that rule), 2.10 (on Odo's freeing of a horse thief).

58. Ibid., 1.21 (on Odo's conversation with Fulk, trans. Sitwell, 24), 1.22 (on Adhegrin's conversion to the monastic life, trans. Sitwell, 24), 1.25 (on Adhegrin's conversion), and 1.26 (on Adhegrin's vision of Saint Martin).

59. Ibid., 1.35, trans. Sitwell, 36.

60. Ibid., 1.34, trans. Sitwell, 36.

61. Rosé, *Construire une société*, 456–75. She and these other scholars are, of course, reflecting on what they consider to be Odo's authorship of the *Vita prolixior*.

62. Rousset, "L'idéal chevaleresque," 625–27.

63. Romig, "The Common Bond," 49.

64. Ziolkowski, "The *Occupatio*," 567. See also Christopher A. Jones, "Monastic Identity," 10–11, on the impossibility of dating the *Occupatio* precisely, to between about 909 and 927 and thus between two and twenty years before his *Vita Geraldi*.

65. See also Rosé, *Construire une société*, 540–43.

66. Matthew Innes ("A Place of Discipline"); see also Dunbabin (*France in the Making*, 240–45) on court life in this period.

67. Patrick Geary (*Aristocracy in Provence*, 144) describes a similar bequest from the late eighth century at Novalesa, and suggests that bequeathing one's lands to Saint Peter rather than to a local saint might be understood as an assertion of Carolingian centralism over regional autonomy. Rosé (*Construire une société*, 146–47) notes that the monasteries at Vézelay and at Pothières were also said to have been dedicated to Rome in the ninth century, and thus also before Cluny, but adds that there are problems with the historical sources. On the centrality of Rome to the early Cluniac movement, see Constable, "Cluny and Rome."

68. Odo gave the name of this bishop as Gauzbert. It was long thought that he was a bishop of Rodez but there is no other evidence for a man by this name holding that office (see Dufour, "Essai de simplification," 169). Instead, Odo was likely referring to the bishop of Cahors of that name who held office from 892 to 907.

69. Both the tonsure and the shaving of the beard, it should be noted, had long been associated generally with Christian asceticism; see Trichet, *La tonsure*, esp. chaps. 1 and 3; and Mills, "The Signification of the Tonsure." At Cluny in the tenth century, both the act of tonsuring and the ritual removal of the sword belt may together have marked the ritual of entrance into the monastic life for a retired warrior, so it is interesting that Odo placed the two actions together here; see Katherine Allen Smith, *War and the Making*, 183–84.

70. See Wollasch, "Parenté noble"; Frassetto, "Violence, Knightly Piety," 19–20; Blanc, "Les pratiques de piété, 145; and especially Katherine Allen Smith, *War and the Making*, 52–63, and Katherine Allen Smith, "Saints in Shining Armor," all of whom provide examples of noblemen who "retired" into monasteries.

71. Ralph Glaber, *Historiae*, quoted by Platelle, "Le problème du scandale." See also Geary, *Phantoms of Remembrance*, 3–7, for an interesting comment on this passage. Compare the early twelfth-century comments of Orderic Vitalis, who complained that young men shaved the front part of their heads but grew their hair long in the back, a style he compared to penitents, prisoners, and pilgrims (*Historia ecclesiastica* 8.10). See also Dutton, "Charlemagne's Mustache," for a discussion of the rich signification of head and facial hair in the central Middle Ages. The Carolingian rulers, he notes, including Louis the Pious and Charles the Bald, used tonsuring to remove potential rivals from political power, and also obliged men to enter monasteries (32).

72. See above, in this chapter, for Cochelin's discussion of Gerald as *rector* of the monastery he founded.

73. Baker, "*Vir Dei*," 46.

74. Heinzelmann, "Sanctitas und 'Tugendadel,'" 750, including the original Latin.

75. See above, note 70.

76. Odo did not name her, but if the story is true she may have been Ava, who married the count of Nevers, or Adelinde, who married the count of Razès and Carcassonne; see Lauranson-Rosaz, *L'Auvergne et ses marges*, 60, for a family tree.

77. On this theme see McLaughlin, "Secular and Spiritual Fatherhood," albeit for eleventh-century texts.

78. Gajano ("Uso e abuso del miracolo") offers interesting reflections on the ambiguity of miracle stories in saints' *vitae* and their autonomy from the narrative form that otherwise dominates hagiography.

79. Ashley and Sheingorn (*Writing Faith*, 30) suggest that blindness occurs so regularly in saints' lives of the central Middle Ages because of its rhetorical use as an obvious symbol for lack of faith.

80. Ashley and Sheingorn (*Writing Faith*, 26), referring to this preface, see it merely as "the motif of the skeptical searcher converted to faith in the saint."

81. Rosenwein, "Saint Odo's Saint Martin," 325.

82. On the importance of a death scene in early medieval hagiography, see Boligioni, "La scène de la mort."

83. John of Salerno, *Vita sancti Odonis* 3.12; trans. Sitwell, 85.

84. Odo died in 942 in Tours; see Flodoard of Rheims, *Annals* 24.

85. Nalgod, *Vita sancti Odonis* (*PL* 133: 102), 46. See also Rosenwein, "Saint Odo's Saint Martin."

CHAPTER 3

1. On Ademar's life and writings, see esp. Landes, *Relics, Apocalypse* (including 77–80 on what is known of his ancestry). For the dating of the events in his life, see also Landes, "Autour d'Adémar." On the history of the monastery of Limoges see de Lasteyrie, *L'Abbaye de Saint-Martial*. Thomas Bisson ("Unheroed Pasts") notes that there was not really much of a historiographical tradition in the southern lands between the tenth and twelfth centuries, that is, for a century before or after Ademar, so much of what we know about his times comes from him.

2. See Landes, *Relics, Apocalypse*, passim.

3. On the two versions of this *vita*, and Ademar's authorship of the more detailed one, see Callahan, "The Sermons," 253–54, 258–63; Landes, "Autour d'Adémar," 27–32; and Landes and Paupert, *Naissance d'apôtre*, who include a French translation.

4. See Landes, *Relics, Apocalypse*; see also the series of articles by Louis Saltet, who first brought the forgeries to light: "Une discussion"; "Les faux d'Adémar"; "Une prétendue lettre"; and "Un cas de mythomanie." For more on Ademar's forgeries, see also Frassetto, "The Art of Forgery"; and Becquet, "Le concile de Limoges."

5. For Saint Amant, see Pon, "La culture d'Adémar," 391–410; for Saints Valerie and Austreclien, see Callahan, "The Sermons of Ademar"; and Emerson, "Two Newly Identified Offices." Boixe is now Saint-Amant-de-Boixe in the *département* of Charente.

6. See Kaiser, *Bischofsherrschaft*, 218–20, or Landes, *Relics, Apocalypse*, 338–39, on this bishop. See also Sohn (*Der Abbatiat Ademars*, 13–45), or Anna Trumbore Jones (*Noble Lord, Good Shepherd*, chap. 3) on the larger history of relations between the abbots, bishops, and viscounts of Limoges in the early eleventh century. See Settipani (*La noblesse du midi*, 192, 237); or Landes ("Autour d'Adémar," 43) both of whom have this bishop Gerald descended from a second sister of Saint Gerald, unnamed in either *vita*.

7. See above, Chapter 1.

8. Ademar, *Chronicon* 3.45.

9. See above, Chapter 2.

10. See above, Chapter 1.

11. See Boglioni, "La scène de la mort," who notes all of these stock features in early medieval hagiographical depictions of a saint's death; see also Dalarun, "La mort des saints fondateurs," who

notes that last instructions to disciples and precise information about the disposition of the saint's body, also elements found in the *Transitus*, were common in the accounts of the deaths of founders of monasteries.

12. Shahar ("The Old Body," 177) notes how often the aging body served in medieval saints' lives as a symbol of the fleeting nature of human existence and the need to prefer spiritual to earthly matters.

13. Beaufrère ("L'Église Saint-Géraud d'Aurillac: Découvertes," 375–77) believes that vestiges of this sarcophagus survive, now as bas-relief sculpture imbedded in the walls of a side chapel in the church of Saint-Géraud in Aurillac. He offers a possible reconstruction of the appearance of this sarcophagus. Durliat ("Saint-Géraud d'Aurillac," 334) notes the difficulties in reconciling the literary and archaeological record as to the placement of Gerald's tomb. On the translation of saints' relics generally see Sigal, "Le déroulement des translations."

14. See above, Chapter 1. (These last sections, equivalent to *PL* 4.8–4.12, are not found in the text in any manuscripts where it follows the *Vita brevior*. See Appendix 2 for details.)

15. It is entirely possible that Gerald collected relics; see Geary, "The Ninth-Century Relic Trade."

16. See Sigal, "Le travail des hagiographes," 155, who documents how common this theme was in hagiographical writings of the eleventh and twelfth centuries.

17. Bourniou is now part of the *commune* of Roumégoux in the *département* of Cantal.

18. Barthélemy (*Chevaliers et miracles*, 79) calls these "revenge miracles." See also Helvétius, "Le récit de vengeance."

19. Facciotto, "Il *sermo*." See Appendix 2 for a list of the manuscripts that include it.

20. Leroquais, *Les sacramentaires*; or Callahan, "The Peace of God," 181; both refer to the manuscript now BNF lat. 1118.

21. See above, Chapter 1, for the more detailed discussion.

22. See above, Chapter 1.

23. The episode also hints at the tensions between Figeac and Conques (where Sainte Foy's shrine was), since the monks of Conques claimed their independence but the monks of Figeac argued that Conques was subordinate to their authority. See Sheingorn (*The Book of Sainte Foy*, 8), who says that the dispute reached its "high point" in the eleventh century.

24. Varen is now in the *département* of Tarn-et-Garonne, Vailhourles in the *département* of Aveyron.

25. Bultot-Verleysen ("Les *miracula* inédits," 139n29) tentatively identifies this river as the Isle, but Chambon ("*Icitus*") says it is the Maronne; both are tributaries of the Dordogne.

26. Solignac is now in the *département* of Haute-Vienne.

27. Both the *Vita brevior* (8) and the *Vita prolixior* (2.17) mention Gerald's pilgrimages to Rome as taking place every other year; this story would seem to show a familiarity with that tradition, too.

28. There is an additional chapter to the Montpellier manuscript that describes how a man of Aurillac with a painful facial deformity visited Obazine (a monastery founded only in 1147) where he had a vision of Saint Gerald, dressed in white on a white horse, who touched and healed him. Clearly the story could not have existed in the eleventh-century Mantua manuscript, and is a later addition only to this manuscript. Bultot-Verleysen ("Les *miracula* inédits," 75) agrees on this point.

29. Landes, "The Dynamics of Heresy," 494.

30. Ademar of Chabannes, *Chronicon* 3.25 (ed. Bourgain et al., 147); cf. similar comments made in his *Commemoratio abbatum* 4, also composed about the time of this last version. On the dating of these texts see Landes, *Relics, Apocalypse*, 158–61, 217–23. See also above, Chapter 1.

31. Two listings survive, one of a *codex* called only "Oddo ad Turpionem" and the other one also called "Odo ad Turpionem." See Duples-Agier, *Chroniques de Saint-Martial*, 325, 335, 343. It is possible that these references were to any one of several manuscripts at Saint-Martial copied before the thirteenth century that contain the *Vita Geraldi*, although in all those that survive it is included among numerous other lives of the saints, so the *codex* should not have been identified solely by that inscription.

32. Stephen Jaeger has argued that the expression of moral virtue through physical beauty was typical of writings from the central Middle Ages, and often associated with public office, and he uses the example of Saint Gerald briefly as part of his argument (but he does not try to explain this depiction of Gerald's neck). See Jaeger, *The Envy of Angels*, chap. 4, esp. 92–111.

33. For a discussion of smallpox in medieval Europe, see Knapp, *Disease and Its Impact*, 79–81.

34. See *Cartulaire de l'Abbaye de Vabres*, 35. Fray ("Le véritable fondateur," 39), believing the *Vita prolixior* to be Odo's version, wonders why he should have mentioned the link between them. Vabres is now Vabres-l'Abbaye, in the *département* of Aveyron.

35. John of Salerno, *Vita sancti Odonis* 2.18; Odilo, *Life of Mayeul* 3.14. The second story is repeated by Ralph Glaber, *Historia* 1.4.9. See also Meckler, "Wolves and Saracens," for a discussion of this incident.

36. Flodoard of Rheims, *Annals* (in the year 921, when a group of English pilgrims on their way to Rome were killed). See Cruvellier, "Note sur l'expulsion," for more on the historical uncertainties, although raiders from North Africa appeared along the Mediterranean coast from 889 on. These accounts are also described by David Blanks in his "Islam and the West."

37. The *PL* refers to this man as Adalbert, but all but one of the manuscripts of the *Vita prolixior* names him Madalbert (the Dijon manuscript is the exception: it refers to him as Maldebert). The ms. within which Ademar mentioned the removal of the treasury of Limoges to Turenne is BNF lat. 2469, fol. 69v, quoted in Delisle, *Les manuscrits de Saint-Martial*, 287: "Gentilitas ab Aquilone Aquitaniam paulatim irrupit, adeoque increvit et viribus numeroque invaluit, ut illam propre modum desertam reddere videretur provintiam. Quocirca factum est ut pia christiana Lemovicensis timore repleretur de amissione corporis patroni fortasse futura, si ipsa fugiens tantum thesaurum nefandae genti patere desereret; ideoque cum tanto thesauro saepius tutiora montana expetiit, castella firmissima eligens, usque ad ipsum qui locus Torenna per omnia inexpugnabilis tunc videbatur." According to Jean-François Boyer ("Reliquaires et orfèvrerie," 57), the treasury of Limoges was transferred to Turenne in 885 and then returned in 895, but he does not say from where he derived these dates. See also Anna Trumbore Jones (*Noble Lord, Good Shepherd*, 147–62) and her "Pitying the Desolation" more generally on the Viking raids in Aquitaine and their effects on churches and monasteries. Turenne is now in the *département* of Corrèze.

38. Landes, *Relics, Apocalypse*, 79–80.

39. The hostile tone toward military leadership in the *Vita prolixior* has been noticed by Isabelle Cochelin ("Quête de liberté," 202–7), but since she regards it as Odo of Cluny's work, she mistakenly links it to the Cluniac ideal of removing monks from lay control. In contrast, Lauranson-Rosaz, "La vie de Géraud d'Aurillac," sees the *Vita prolixior* as a much more straightforward model for noblemen's behavior.

40. On Saint Leonard of Noblat, see Cheirézy, "Hagiographie et société"; and Bull, *Knightly Piety*, 237–42. Guy Philippart and Michel Trigalet ("L'hagiographie latine," 295–97) have determined that his legend was one of the most popular in the eleventh century, at least according to the numbers of manuscripts that have survived of it.

41. Barthélemy (*Chevaliers et miracles*, 52) has also concluded that Gerald as represented in the *Vita prolixior* was not all that less violent than his contemporaries.

42. This manuscript, now at the university library of Leyden, Netherlands (ms. Voss. lat. 8), is fully described by Gaborit-Chopin, "Les dessins d'Adémar." See also Landes, *Relics, Apocalypse*, 97–99.

43. Anne-Marie Bultot-Verleysen (*Odon de Cluny*, 291n16) tries to make sense of the passage as reflecting new military technologies, but the confusion is probably best understood as resulting from the fact that Ademar was not all that familiar with military tactics.

44. Rosé, *Construire une société*, 486–89, discusses these biblical models for Gerald's participation in violent activity—also concluding that it formed an awkward attempt to justify the behavior.

45. Ralph Glaber, *Historiae* 4.5.14; quoted and trans. Head, "The Development of the Peace of God," 657.

46. See Goetz, "Protection of the Church."

47. The most detailed exposition of the literary evidence for millennial expectations is Fried, "Endzeiterwartung." See also Landes, "Between Aristocracy and Heresy." Ralph Glaber, writing at Cluny in the late 1020s, also seems to link the Peace of God movement to popular millennial expectations (*Historiae* 4.14–16). The extent of belief in the approaching end of time is now much disputed. Dominique Barthélemy, for example ("La paix de Dieu"), rejects it. See also Peters, "Mutations, Adjustments." On the Peace of God, see Paxton, "History, Historians, and the Peace of God."

48. Frassetto, "Violence, Knightly Piety."

49. Head, "The Development of the Peace of God."

50. Bachrach, "The Northern Origins." Le Puy is now Le Puy-en-Velay in the *département* of Haute-Loire.

51. Martindale, "Peace and War."

52. Treffort, "Le comte de Poitiers."

53. Taylor, "Royal Protection in Aquitaine."

54. Lauranson-Rosaz, *L'Auvergne et ses marges*, chap. 5.

55. In general, see Töpfer, "The Cult of Relics"; for the Peace of God in Auvergne, see Lauranson-Rosaz, "Peace from the Mountains."

56. Landes, "The Dynamics of Heresy," 472. See also Callahan, "The Peace of God."

57. Lauranson-Rosaz, "Peace from the Mountains" (110–11 on the assembly at Aurillac in 972).

58. Becquet, "Le concile de Limoges de 1031."

59. Head, "The Development of the Peace of God." See also Callahan, "Adémar de Chabannes"; and Landes, *Relics, Apocalypse*, 28–37 on Ademar and the Peace of God in the Limousin.

60. On Ademar's beliefs see Fried, "Endzeiterwartung," 417019; Frassetto, "Heretics, Antichrists"; or Landes, *Relics, Apocalypse*, chap. 14.

61. See above, Chapter 1.

62. For an analysis of the medieval notion of "women's work," see Kuchenbuch, "*Opus feminile*."

63. See Landes, *Relics, Apocalypse*, 79.

64. These details are not *in se* implausible. Roger Stalley (*Early Medieval Architecture*) describes both how frequently collapse resulted from imprecise calculations or inferior materials (121–44).

65. On these heretical groups see Lambert, *Medieval Heresy*, chap. 2; for Ademar's comments on these groups see Frassetto, "Heresy, Celibacy"; or Frassetto, "Heretics, Antichrists." See also Van Meter, "Eschatological Order," who links the push for clerical celibacy and monastic chastity to fears of the approaching end of the world; or Duby, *The Three Orders*, 130–34, who sees it as a challenge to the social hierarchy.

66. Callahan, "The Sermons," 273–80.

67. See above in this chapter.

CHAPTER 4

1. Geary, "Sacred Commodities"; see also Geary, "The Saint and the Shrine: The Pilgrim's Goal in the Middle Ages," in *Living with the Dead*.

2. Dominique de Jésus, *Histoire parænetique*, 19.1; see also below, Chapter 5.

3. See Charbonnel, "À propos de Saint-Géraud d'Aurillac," 41n5, on the composition of this text. More historical evidence survives from the monastery of La Chaise-Dieu, founded in the mid-eleventh century also in Auvergne, that might therefore provide parallels to the early history of the monastery of Aurillac; see Gaussin, *Huit siècles d'histoire*.

4. Only three more abbots are named in the chronicle: the origin of the twelfth was not given; the origins of the thirteenth and fourteenth cannot be firmly identified, although the former had been a dean of the monastery of Souillac and died at Cahors, which suggests an origin in one region or the other, and the latter was said to have been born "one league" from Aurillac. See Bouyssou, "La chronique."

5. Magnou-Nortier, *La société laïque*, 403–4; see also Bouange, *Saint Géraud d'Aurillac*, 249–55.

6. See below, Chapter 6.

7. On Gerbert's years at Aurillac, see Labande, "La formation de Gerbert"; Darlington, "Gerbert, the Teacher"; and Joubert, *L'Abbaye bénédictine*, 81–95. See also the essays collected in Charbonnel and Iung, *Gerbert l'européen*; or Riché, *Gerbert d'Aurillac*, for more on Gerbert's biography.

8. Bouyssou, "La chronique," 325–26.

9. Bull (*Knightly Piety*, 228–29) shows that these families were benefactors of other monasteries, where records have survived.

10. Bouyssou, "La chronique," 326.

11. Ibid., 325. See Durliat, "Saint-Géraud d'Aurillac," 329–42; Beaufrère, "L'Église Saint-Géraud d'Aurillac et ses bâtisseurs," 170–72, 178–92; and Moulier, *Églises romanes*, 2: 33, 44; the arches may have been late eleventh-century changes to the church. Kubach (*Romanesque Architecture*, 81) and Stalley (*Early Medieval Architecture*, 196–97) refer to the blind arcades of arches set into the walls of churches as typical features of early Romanesque architecture.

12. The expansion of the church at Aurillac also formed part of a more general rebuilding program across western Europe, made possible by a rising standard of living. See Conant, *Carolingian and Romanesque Architecture*. On the role of relics and the cult of saints in the physical transformation of churches in this period, see Caillet, "Reliques et architecture religieuse"; Jacobsen, "Saints' Tombs"; Stalley, *Early Medieval Architecture*, 147–65; Lyman, "The Politics of Selective Eclecticism"; and Abou-El-Haj, "The Audiences."

13. See Fletcher, *Saint James's Catapult*, 97. Gottschalk's connection with Aurillac is claimed by Moulier (*Églises romanes*, 2: 44), but without supporting documentation. On the popularity of the pilgrimage to Santiago de Compostela in medieval France, see Jacomet, "Pèlerinage et culte de saint Jacques."

14. The song is quoted in full by Beaufrère, *Aurillac et la Haute-Auvergne*, 48–51.

15. Saint-Chaffre (now Le Monastier-sur-Gazeille), La Chaise-Dieu, and Brioude are all now in the *département* of Haute-Loire, Orcival is in Puy-de-Dôme, and Rocamadour is in Lot.

16. See Zimmermann ("La Catalogne de Gerbert") on the discrepancies in the historical record on this event.

17. Helgaud of Fleury, *Vie de Robert le Pieux*, 76; see Facciotto, "Moments et lieux," 225.

18. Bouyssou, "La chronique," 326. This is difficult to verify. There was a bishop of Gaeta named Leo in the mid-eleventh century, who was consecrated in or shortly after 1049 and whose last recorded act there happened in 1064. See Skinner, *Family Power*, 220, 283–84.

19. See Beaufrère, "L'Église Saint-Géraud d'Aurillac et ses bâtisseurs," 166; Crozet, "Le voyage d'Urbain II."

20. The precise dating of the structure is uncertain, since it has been greatly altered over the centuries. Grand ("La sculpture et l'architecture," 242–50) suggests that it dates from between the late eleventh and early thirteenth centuries. Charbonnel ("Aurillac, ville romane," 23) suggests that it was built after 1119, since there is no mention of it in the chronicle of the abbots of Aurillac. Moulier (*Églises romanes*, 2: 28–29) dates it to the end of the eleventh century or the beginning of the twelfth century based on its surviving medieval elements. See also Delmas, "Une découverte archéologique"; and Durliat, "Saint-Géraud d'Aurillac," 338. It seems to have been built before 1190, since a charter from that date included among its signatories the "hospitaler of Aurillac" (*Aureliacensi ospitalario*); see Grand, *Les "paix" d'Aurillac*, 1–2. The structure may have served originally as the residence of the abbot; if so, the building is mentioned in the chronicle as having been built under abbot Peter of La Roque, who died in 1119. On hospices in general, see Touati, "Un dossier," who describes the twelfth century as the "flowering" of hospice building across France (29); or de Mérindol, "Le soin des malades," who describes hospices attached to monasteries.

21. Beaufrère ("L'Église Saint-Géraud d'Aurillac et ses bâtisseurs," 172–77), Charbonnel ("Aurillac, ville romane," 23–24), Moulier (*Églises romanes*, 2: 30–31, 38–39), and Durliat ("Saint-Géraud d'Aurillac") all list the architectural vestiges from the medieval monastery buildings, including a few decorated elements from the cloister, a rounded archway, a well for water, a section of the wall enclosure, and perhaps a bit of a fortified tower.

22. Peter of La Roque (d. 1119), the fourteenth abbot of Aurillac, was said to have had two large fountains built, one in the middle of the cloister and the other in front of the abbot's residence, and this is presumably one of those. It is comparable to the one still present in the cloister at Conques, not only similar in appearance but also made of stone from the same quarry; see Charbonnel, "Aurillac, ville romane," 24; Charbonnel, "La ville de Gerbert," 72–73; and the photograph in Delmas and Fau, *Conques*, 49–50. The fountain in Aurillac may not have been in this location until the middle of the nineteenth century: a lithograph made in 1832 by Adrien Dauzats shows no fountain in the square; see Muzac ("Visages," 463), who describes it.

23. Inside the church of Saint-Géraud in Aurillac is a sculpted capital that includes a bust of Samson and that may have been paired with a similar capital depicting Hercules; I have not been able to determine the location of the latter, if it still exists. Delzons (*Origine de la ville*, 61), describes both as having been found buried in the former cemetery of the church in the mid-nineteenth century, and suggests that they had been capitals within the medieval cloister.

24. See Sheingorn, ed., *The Book of Sainte Foy*.

25. *Liber miraculorum sancte Fidis* 1.17, ed. and trans. Sheingorn, *The Book of Sainte Foy*.

26. *Liber miraculorum sancte Fidis* 4.23, ed. and trans. Sheingorn, *The Book of Sainte Foy*. See also Ward (*Miracles and the Medieval Mind*, 211–13), who describes similar "jokes" from other saints' *vitae* of this period.

27. Remensnyder, "Un problème de cultures," 372–78; on this general issue, see also Manselli, *Il soprannaturale*. See also Pierre Moulier ("Le 'jet de pierres' ") for folk traditions behind another of the stories contained in the additional miracles (3) in which pilgrims visiting Aurillac threw pebbles into the opening of a boulder.

28. See Forsyth, *The Throne of Wisdom*, 95, on Stephen and the sculpture at Clermont; Delmas and Fau, *Conques*, 72–78 on the statue of Sainte Foy. We know little about the artisans who created these sculptures, but Boehm ("Medieval Head Reliquaries," 127) reminds us that whenever we do know anything about them, they are invariably monks within the monastery.

29. Bouyssou, "La chronique." Boehm ("Medieval Head Reliquaries," 78), suggests that the chronicle may have mistaken the seventh abbot, named Adraldus, for the Adraldus who was the fourth abbot of Aurillac, who had been a monk at Conques, and who modeled the statue of Saint Gerald on that of Sainte Foy; but since he probably held office in the 940s, the date seems a bit early for either statue. Joubert (*Saint Géraud*, 100–3) and Moulier (*Églises romanes*, 2: 45–47) also speculate about the origin, appearance, and uses of the statue of Saint Gerald.

30. *Liber miraculorum sancte Fidis* 1.13, ed. and trans. Sheingorn, *The Book of Sainte Foy*. Bonnassie and de Gournay ("Sur la datation du *Livre des miracles*," 458–59) believe that Bernard composed his account in stages, so while he began writing in 1013, he completed this section only in 1020.

31. See below, Chapter 5, on the possible destruction of this statue in 1233. This seal is also described by Pascale Moulier, "Iconographie de saint Géraud," 60–61.

32. The *Transitus* implies that Gerald was buried within his church, even adding that he was placed near the altar to Saint Peter, but the *Miracula* seems to have him buried outside of it. The same problem appears in the *Miracula addita*, where Gerald's relics, while said to have been placed within the church, are not in the same interior position as implied by his being buried next to the altar to Saint Peter, which, given the first church's dedication, was probably the main altar, not to mention those relics described as being within a "mound of dirt." The confusion may stem from the fact that Ademar may have been writing after Gerald's remains had been brought inside the church, probably at the dedication of the new church in 973, and so was only imagining Gerald's previous burial place. Beaufrère ("Sur la sépulture") also attempts to sort out the contradictions without success.

33. *Liber miraculorum sancte Fidis* 1.11, ed. and trans. Sheingorn, *The Book of Sainte Foy*. The soldier was describing the statue of Sainte Foy.

34. In other sculptures from this period, the head of the saint was placed within a reliquary while the body remained within its sarcophagus, and it is possible that this is what happened at Aurillac with Gerald's remains, although there is nothing that specifically suggests it. See Solt, "Romanesque French Reliquaries."

35. *Liber miraculorum sancte Fidis* 1.25, ed. and trans. Sheingorn, *The Book of Sainte Foy*. See also Dahl, "Heavenly Images," who notes the importance of the brilliance attributed to Sainte Foy in accounts both of her sculpture and of visions of her, and concludes that it was a central element to these early sculptures.

36. Abel Beaufrère ("L'Église Saint-Géraud d'Aurillac") speculates that sculpted bas-reliefs now embedded into one of the chapel walls in the church of Saint-Géraud at Aurillac were from a second tomb built for him with the enlarging and rededication of the church in 972. See also Solt, "French Romanesque Reliquaries," 183–86 for a discussion of contemporary tombs. Dierkens ("Les funerailles royales," 48–49) notes that sarcophagi from late antiquity were often reused for the Carolingian nobility.

37. The first known sculpture was a bust of Saint Maurice, fashioned in the 880s (Forsyth, *The Throne of Wisdom*, 77).

38. Boehm, "Medieval Head Reliquaries," 47–50 and 59–60, who includes other examples. Forsyth (*The Throne of Wisdom*, 79) also mentions early statues of saints of Saint Martial at Limoges and Saint Peter at Cluny, and Mâle (*Religious Art*, 32) also mentions other early sculptures of Saint Mary (Marius) at Vabres in Rouergue and of Saint Armand at Rodez. Boehm includes detailed descriptions of all known statues in an appendix. See also Noble, *Images, Iconoclasm*, for eighth- and ninth-century Frankish writers' opinions on the propriety of religious images; Hubert and Hubert, "Piété chrétienne"; Schmitt, "Les reliques et les images," and Dierkens, "Du bon (et du mauvais)

usage"; and Camille, *The Gothic Idol*, on continuing Christian discomfort with such images into the later Middle Ages. See also the special issue of *Gesta* 36, no. 1 (1997) on such images

39. Quoted and translated in Forsyth, *The Throne of Wisdom*, 93–94 (Latin in note). The councillors of Arras noted the connections between visible with invisible realities in the eucharist. Guy Lobrichon ("Le culte des saints") links the decrees of Arras to the suppression of heretical notions about the divine within the material world by bishop Gérard of Cambrai-Arras.

40. See Schmitt, "Les reliques et les images."

41. *Liber miraculorum sancte Fidis* L.3, trans. Sheingorn, *The Book of Sainte Foy*. See also Head ("Letaldus of Micy and . . . Nouaillé," 258–60), Bozóky ("La politique des reliques"), and Hubert and Hubert ("Piété chrétienne") for other examples of relics taken on processions to inspire devotion, cement claims to land, or reinforce authority.

42. *Liber miraculorum sancte Fidis* 2.4, trans. Sheingorn, *The Book of Sainte Foy.* Cf. ibid., 3.17. See also Ashley and Sheingorn, "An Unsentimental View of Ritual."

43. A range of actions existed for monasteries to deal with the threats of rivals: see Barbara Rosenwein, Thomas Head, and Sharon Farmer, "Monks and Their Enemies," 767–68; Geary, *Living with the Dead*, 125–60.

44. *Translatio sancti Viviani* 13, quoted in Lauranson-Rosaz, "Peace from the Mountains," 123.

45. See Hahn, "Seeing and Believing." Barbara Abou-El-Haj, *The Medieval Cult of Saints*, describes the multiple means by which the cult of Saint Amand d'Elnone was encouraged between the ninth and twelfth centuries in a variety of ways that may be compared to the cult of Saint Gerald, including building projects, elaborate reliquaries, and reliquary-statues.

46. Bouange (*Saint Géraud d'Aurillac*) attempted to list all of the properties that had belonged to the monastery of Aurillac, as did Joubert (*L'Abbaye bénédictine*, 117–82), Moulier and Moulier, "Essai de géographie," and Gerbeau, "Dans la tourmente," 104–9. Since their number was constantly changing, with new properties being donated or bought, and others sold or otherwise alienated, since many of the dependencies of Aurillac had their own dependencies, and since the historical record is poor for most localities, it seems an impossible task. Better, perhaps, is the choice of Juillet ("Les domaines") or Boudet (*Aspres-sur-Buëch*, 12–22), who attempt to reconstruct the history of the priories and estates of Aurillac only for one region, Juillet for Quercy and Boudet for the Drôme River valley. See also Magnou-Nortier (*La société laïque*, 430–35) for a comparative attempt to track the patterns of rural churches of the region of Narbonne in the same period, or Maury ("Le rayonnement") for a discussion of the priories of another monastery, that of Saint-Victor in Marseille, in much the same regions of France as those belonging to Aurillac. On the difficulties even in understanding the terminology of priories and other monastic dependencies, see Bautier, "De 'prepositus' à 'prior.'"

47. On the early history of this church, see Becquet, "Les débuts de l'Hôpital"; de Lasteyrie, *L'Abbaye de Saint-Martial*, 215–16; or Aubrun, *L'ancien diocèse de Limoges*, esp. 159–68, 194–217.

48. On Varen, see Alibert, "Le maître de Varen," 499–501 (who dates the establishment of the priory to before 910). On Vailhourles, see Bedel and Gaffier, *Vailhourles*, 21 (who date the establishment of the priory to 890, without explanation), 27; or Cabanes and Cabanes, *Panorama*, 376. Alibert notes (ibid., 515) that the surviving medieval carved capitals at both priories were apparently made by the same unknown hand, and perhaps indicate similar dates of foundation for both.

49. See Constable, "Monasteries, Rural Churches," on the use of priories as parish churches.

50. On this church, see Arramond, "L'Église Saint-Pierre-Saint-Géraud"; Chalande, *Histoire des rues de Toulouse*, 7–16; and Joubert, *L'Abbaye bénédictine*, 162–64. Chalande notes that the church had been rebuilt in 1471 after collapsing through neglect of repairs, though a report of 1593 concluded

that it was again in danger of collapse. It was entirely demolished in the nineteenth century during the enlarging of Place Esquirol. There have been several newspaper articles about this church since its demolition: see Bremond, "Le Prieuré de Saint-Géraud"; de Lahondes, "L'Église Saint-Géraud"; Chalande, "Une vieille église"; Brousse, "Une découverte archéologique"; and Terelliac, "Églises et chapelles."

51. In general, the priories and other dependencies of Aurillac in the eleventh and twelfth centuries seem similar in number and type to those of other monasteries. See, for example, the list of the priories of Baume, a monastery also associated with Cluny (Constable, "Les listes de propriétés"); or the priories of Vabres listed in a document of 1116, from the *Cartulaire de l'Abbaye de Vabres*, 48–49. De Labriolle ("Insertion monastique") notes the many priories built by major houses, including Cluny and Marseilles, even in a distant region like the Durance valley, in the eleventh and twelfth centuries. (He does not mention the fact, but Aurillac's priories in this region also date from this period.)

52. Jean-Eric Iung ("Des prieurés lointains") has examined the writings that survive for two of the priories far distant from Aurillac, Saillans and Varen, and has concluded that they had only irregular contact with the abbot of Aurillac, although they did make payments to him and received occasional directives from him. Whether they were typical or not remains in question. Roger Grand, likewise, has published a study on the ties between the monastery of Saint-Amand-de-Boixe (in the modern *département* of Charente) and Aurillac. This monastery, donated to Aurillac sometime before 988, was confirmed in its subordination by a charter of 1197 that outlined the rights that Aurillac exercised over it. The monks of Saint-Amand were obliged to provide hospitality for the abbot of Aurillac and up to ten of his soldiers for up to three days no more than once every other year. Each abbot of Saint-Amand, after having been elected from among the monks of that monastery, had to travel to Aurillac and make his submission to the abbot there, only after which would his election be confirmed. See Grand, "Un épisode de la restitution," who also includes a transcription of the 1197 accord (270–72). Saint-Amand-de-Boixe may have been unusual in having its own population of monks; other priories were likely staffed by monks from Aurillac on a more temporary basis and their priors appointed directly by the abbot of Aurillac. A seventeenth-century copy of an early fourteenth-century set of regulations for Saillans and Aspres-sur-Buëch, both priories of Aurillac, has survived. Curiously, it mostly directed the monks on what they might or might not eat or drink. It did, however, require each of the priories to have at least four monks, one of whom was designated the prior, another, the sacristan, and another, the cook. It also required them to say liturgical offices together as frequently as when they were in the monastery at Aurillac. In addition, monks were forbidden from leaving the priory precinct without permission, and prohibited from fraternizing too closely with the local population: the regulations condemned specifically eating, drinking, and conversing with the peasants who lived near the priories. See Guillaume, "Règlement des prieurés," who reprints the document. For general information on the daily life of priories in general, see also Dubois, "La vie quotidienne," with information from twelfth-century customaries on prayer and meals. For more details of interactions between monks and the local population at the priory of Aspres-sur-Buëch, see also Boudet, *Aspres-sur-Buëch*.

53. The largest and grandest of all that survive is at Monsempron (now Monsempron-Libos in the *département* of Lot-et-Garonne). The church is Romanesque in style and dates from the twelfth century, although it was built over an older church that now forms its crypt. The priory residence dates from the eleventh century, although it was greatly altered in the late fifteenth or early sixteenth century. See Joubert, *L'Abbaye bénédictine*, 157; Marboutin, "Monsempron"; Quintard, *Monsempron-Libos*, 27–37; Dubourg-Noves, "Église de Monsempron"; *Répertoire des monuments*, 214–15; and

Zaballos, "Monsempron-Libos." The church was restored in the nineteenth century and the residence in the twentieth century, but the other monastic buildings and its cloister have not yet been restored.

54. In 1277 a charter mentioned a "hospital or hostel of Buis [*hospitalis de Buxo*]" but in 1284 a charter mentioned an "abbess of Buis [*abbatissa de Buxo*]" so it may have been between these dates that it was reorganized; see Grand (*Les "paix" d'Aurillac*, 19–20, 133). Joubert (*La colline inspirée*, 10) claims that the convent was moved from within the monastery precinct at Aurillac across the Jordanne River in 1289, where it remained until the French Revolution, when its nuns were expelled. The other female houses, dependencies of Buis, were at La Capelle del Vern (in the modern commune of Escandolières in the *département* of Aveyron, now a parish church still dedicated to Saint Gerald) and at Fontgaufier (also spelled Fontgauffier and Font-Gauffier, in the modern commune of *Belvès* in the *département* of Dordogne, now a private residence). On La Capelle del Vern, see Bedel, *Rignac*, 18; Cabanes and Cabanes, *Panorama*, 113; and Flohic, *Le patrimoine*, 1368–69, who says that the convent was united with that of Aurillac only in the early fifteenth century but that it existed from 1108. On Fontgaufier, see Vigié, *Histoire de Belvès*, 303–9; Verdon, "Recherches sur les monastères," 119 (who dates its foundation to 1095); and de Gourgues, *Dictionnaire topographique*, 127.

55. The oldest known of these churches is at Albons near Empúries and dates from the eleventh century, but whether it has always been dedicated to Saint Gerald is unknown. See Casas et al., *A l'entorn del Puig Segalar*, 74. A second church, called Sant Grau d'Entreperes, lies high in the mountains north of Olot and dates from the twelfth century (in Catalan Saint Gerald is known as Sant Grau). See Baraldés et al., *Una petjada*, 271–77; the authors add that it was originally dedicated to the Virgin Mary, and only later at an unknown date, reconsecrated to Saint Gerald. Two other medieval churches once existed, one outside of Tossa de Mar and the other near Sant Gregori outside of Girona, but the former is a nineteenth-century reconstruction and the latter is now in ruins; the origins of neither can be firmly dated. On the church of Sant Grau near Sant Gregori, see Calzada i Oliveras, *Sant Gregori*, 162–64, who says that the first reference to it is from 1548, but since it is of Romanesque construction and since a visit in 1563 referred to it as dilapidated, it was clearly older, and might have originally been the chapel to a nearby eleventh-century castle. For a mostly modern history of the church of Sant Grau near Tossa de Mar, see Girbal, *El santuario*; see also Zucchitello, *Tossa*, 101n198, who notes that the first mention of it dates from 1411.

56. See Beaufrère, "San Grau"; see also Esteben i Darder, "Tota una història"; and Moulier, "De saint Géraud à saint Guiral," 105–7. The document is now held in the Archives départementales de Cantal, Aurillac, 4 G 9, but Beaufrère, "San Grau," includes a facsimile and transcription of it. Beaufrère suggests that the queen of Aragon, named Maria in the document, was the sister to King John II of Aragon and was actually queen of Castile. Dominique de Jésus also noted the story (*Histoire paraenetique*, 18.7), but he believed the relics to have been given to Marie de Montpellier, who married King Peter II of Aragon in 1204 and whose family claimed descent from Saint Gerald's family, which seems likelier. Elsewhere ("Sur les pas quotidiens," 209), Beaufrère himself seems to have confused these two women.

57. See Ainaud de Lasarte, "Moissac et les monastères catalans"; or Dufour, *La bibliothèque*, 8–9, for the establishment of Catalan priories of the monastery of Moissac.

58. The modern village is called O Cebreiro in the local Gallego language (El Cebrero in Castilian Spanish), a corruption of the medieval Latin Februarius for the mountain on which it is located. King Alfonso VI of León granted the monks of Aurillac the property; it was not unusual for the Christian kings of Iberia to encourage French monks to settle in their territories. Perrel ("Le bas Limousin") has described how the bishops of Tulle were given priories on the pilgrimage road to

Santiago de Compostela, notably at Hornillos from 1181, where they also established a hospice, and which helped to promote the cult of the Virgin at Rocamadour; see also Mouzat, "Visite à une fondation." Many French monasteries opened hospices; see Vázques de Parga et al., *Las peregrinaciones a Santiago*, 1: 302; or Segl, "Die Cluniacenser in Spanien." For a more general discussion of the religious climate of Galicia from the tenth to the twelfth century, see Fletcher, *Saint James's Catapult*. On monasticism in medieval Galicia, see Andrade Cernadas, *Monxes e mosteiros*. On the medieval church and priory at O Cebreiro, see Frontón, *El arte románico*, 189; Alvilares, *El Cebrero*; Valiña Sampedro, *El camino de Santiago*, 133–75; Vázquez de Parga et al., *Las peregrinaciones a Santiago*, 2: 313–18; Huidobro y Serna, *Las peregrinaciones jacobeas*, 3: 18–35; and *A arquitectura do camiño*, 23–24. By the twelfth century, other nearby properties had also been given to the monks of Aurillac to supervise from this priory. In 1118 Queen Urraca gave the monks the hospice at Pereje; in 1186 King Fernando II gave them houses in Villafranca del Bierzo and Santa Maria de Bercianos; and at some point they also obtained rights over the village of Liñares. See Gitlitz and Davidson, *The Pilgrimage Road to Santiago*, 302, 305, 308; see also Beaufrère, *Aurillac et la Haute-Auvergne*, 13–16. On Pereje, see also Valiña Sampedro, *El camino de Santiago*, 103–12. The nearby village of Liñares is said to have taken its name from the linen made there to supply the hospice at O Cebreiro; see *A arquitectura do camiño*, 24; or Delgado Gómez, *El camino francés*, 33–36. Generally on the hospices of the road to Santiago de Compostela, see González Bueno, *El entorno sanitario* (who mentions O Cebreiro and its dependencies, 125); or Ruiz de la Peña Solar, *Foncebadón*. It may have been difficult for the monks of Aurillac to defend their rights in a region so far distant; in a dispute between the monks of O Cebreiro and those of Villafranca del Bierzo (a daughter-house of Cluny) over the church of Pereje in 1188, the monks of Aurillac were obliged to demolish a church they had just completed. See Valiña Sampedro, *El camino de Santiago*, 104–10. The dispute began when the monks of Aurillac built a church on their property of Pereje, which the monks of Villafranca said had violated their rights in the district; the dispute was resolved the following year when the prior of O Cebreiro agreed to demolish the new church. Saint Gerald may even have had a presence even at the cathedral of Santiago de Compostela: one of the ambulatory chapels in the cathedral is still dedicated to Sainte Foy, and other saints of the pilgrimage routes were doubtless also honored, if not with chapels, at least with statues or relics. A modern chapel of relics contains thousands of relics, most unidentified. See Barral Iglesias and Yzquerido Perrín, *Santiago Cathedral*, 74.

59. See Knicely, "Food for Thought." Souillac is in the modern *département* of Lot.

60. Évreux is now in the *département* of Eure.

61. See Appendix 2 for details. See also Philippart, "Le manuscrit hagiographique," who calls for what he describes as "hagiogeography": the study of the dissemination of hagiographical writings as part of the study of their influence.

62. Albi, Bibliothèque municipale, ms. 34. It is described by Lauranson-Rosaz, "Entre deux mondes," 42n47.

63. Gellone is modern Saint-Guillem-le-Désert in the *département* of Hérault.

64. There were, for example, a pair of weddings between the duke Guy Geoffrey of Aquitaine and Hildegarde of Anjou, and between the count Geoffrey Martel of Anjou and Agnes of Aquitaine in the middle of the eleventh century, and one or the other of the Aquitanians might have carried the cult of Saint Gerald northward. Anna Trumbore Jones ("Lay Magnates") describes several other connections, both secular and spiritual, between Anjou and Aquitaine in the early eleventh century. Augry ("Reliques et pouvoir," 264) notes that monastic ties were forged during the marriage between William III Tête d'Étoupe, duke of Aquitaine, and Adele of Normandy, daughter of Duke Rollo, that lasted from 935 to 962. If Anjou was a rare northern site of medieval devotion to Saint Gerald,

it might have served as a center for the dissemination of the cult of Saint Gerald into other parts of northern France.

65. Souvigny is now in the *département* of Allier, Saint-Alyre in Puy-de-Dôme, Sainte-Melaine in Ille-et-Villaine, Barbechat in Loire-Atlantique, Tournus in Saône-et-Loire, and Arles in Bouches-du-Rhône.

66. Arles-sur-Tech is now French, in the *département* of Pyrénées-Orientales, but was part of medieval Catalonia.

67. For the full list of these liturgical books, see Leroquais, *Les sacramentaires*. See also Bultot-Verleysen, "Saint Géraud d'Aurillac," 83–88, on the diffusion of Saint Gerald's cult as traced through liturgical books. Carcassonne in now in the *département* of Aude, and Gap, in Hautes-Alpes.

68. BNF lat. 944 and 2826.

69. BNF lat. 776. Gaillac is in the modern *département* of Tarn.

70. Toledo, Biblioteca capitular, ms. 44.2, and Braga, Arquivo municipal, fragment 12.

71. Ferreira, "Two Offices." Ferreira places the point of origin for this liturgy at Aurillac, at least probably, but given the location of the early manuscripts for the music, it may well have come from Limoges. He also discusses the influence of this music on that composed for Saint Gerald of Braga.

72. On Ademar as musician, see Grier, *The Musical World*; see also Hooreman, "Saint-Martial de Limoges"; and Emerson, "Two Newly Identified Offices."

CHAPTER 5

1. The manuscript is BNF lat. 3809A. The church is that of Salles-Curan (in the modern *département* of Aveyron); on this church see Bedel, *Salles-Curan*, 16–17, 30; or Chaigne, *Le Rouergue*, 183–84 (who says that the church dates from the thirteenth or fourteenth century); or "Textes et documents," 38, 40 (where it is more reliably stated that the church was begun in 1452, after the church had been sold by the monks of Aurillac to the bishop of Rodez).

2. See Geary, *Phantoms of Remembrance*, 25–26 and passim.

3. Bouyssou, "La chronique," 326–27.

4. An interesting comparison might be made with the history of other monasteries subordinated to Cluny also in the mid- to late eleventh century, including ones even more distant from Cluny. On the monastery of Moissac, for example, see Hourlier, "L'entrée de Moissac"; for Moissac and Lézat, see Magnou-Nortier, *La société laïque*, 498–510; and for the monastery of Marseille, see Soares-Christen, "Saint-Victor de Marseille." Remensnyder (*Remembrance of Kings Past*, chap. 6) describes a general pattern in the late eleventh century of the subordination of previously autonomous monasteries to lay, episcopal, or monastic control.

5. Leclercq, "The Monastic Crisis." See also Cantor, "The Crisis of Western Monasticism"; and for a rejoinder, Van Engen, "The 'Crisis of Cenobitism' Reconsidered." Van Engen notes that "in four crucial areas—recruitment, revenue, quality of personnel, and leadership in the church—the evidence shows that Benedictine houses held their own or even increased in prosperity" in the twelfth century (275–76). The same cannot be said for later in the Middle Ages, as Van Engen admits: "From the late twelfth or early thirteenth century, while never undergoing any sudden crisis or collapse, they [the Benedictine monasteries] assumed a position ever less central to medieval religious life" (304).

6. See Grand (*Les "paix" d'Aurillac*, 81) for a charter from 1284 with the first mention of the "castle of the abbot [*castrum abbatis*]" that probably implies residence.

7. His nickname is said to have been derived from the fact that he was made prior of a dependency of Aurillac by this name, but it cannot be identified, and is perhaps a misreading of Montauban (now in the *département* of Tarn-et-Garonne), since there were several priories belonging to Aurillac near it.

8. *Biographies des troubadours*, ed. Boutière and Schutz, 215–17. See also Hill and Bergin, *Anthology of the Provençal Troubadours*, 137–44. This Villafranca is possibly the one given to the monastery of Aurillac in 1186 by King Fernando II of León (modern Villafranca del Bierzo) and not far from the priory at O Cebreiro; see Gitlitz and Davidson, *The Pilgrimage Road to Santiago*, 305.

9. Ed. and trans. Merwin, "Two Provençal Poems."

10. See his *tenso* 13, ed. Routledge, *Les poésies du moine de Montaudon*, 105–6.

11. See Routledge, ed., *Les poésies du moine de Montaudon*, 70 (*chanson* 6, line 31: "Sainta Fe") and 85 (*enueg* 9, line 1: "Saynt Marsal").

12. Rodez is now in the *département* of Aveyron, Saint-Flour is in Cantal.

13. See Kicklighter, "Les monastères," on the complex maneuverings of monasteries between French and English kings in the border regions.

14. See Grand, *Les "paix" d'Aurillac*, lxii–lxiv, who describes the conflict and also includes a transcription of the agreement between the Count of Toulouse and the abbot of Aurillac ("Documents," 5–6); and de Gournay, *Le Rouergue*, 393.

15. The abbot was Ramnulf or Ralph and the local lord was Astorg III of Conros (in the modern *commune* of Arpajon-sur-Cère); see Joubert, *L'Abbaye bénédictine*, 213, who adds that the circumstances of the event are unclear.

16. On Saint Gerald's guild, see Joubert, *L'Abbaye bénédictine*, 263n9. Charbonnel ("Aurillac, ville romane," 25–26) describes the economic expansion of the region and the growth of the medieval town from archaeological evidence.

17. See Grand, *Les "paix" d'Aurillac*, 318, a charter of 1347.

18. These events are described by Grand, *Les "paix" d'Aurillac*, who includes in appendices transcriptions of the historical documents related to these events. Conflicts continued between abbots and the town councillors—called *consuls*—until 1564, when the king took to himself the right to appoint consuls and a royal governor to lead them. See Grimmer, *Vivre à Aurillac*, 57–70. Such tensions were not unique to Aurillac; see discussions of the development of the town around Cluny in Méhu, "La communauté d'habitants," and the rise of similar conflicts between the monks and townspeople of Cluny in Constable, "The Abbot and Townsmen." Yet the violence that happened at Aurillac seems to be the exception for Auvergne; see Teyssot, "Le mouvement communal," 206. Sadoux ("À propos des reliques") suggests that the relics of Saint Martin mentioned in the *Transitus* (3.3) as having been collected by Saint Gerald were taken from the monastery church at Aurillac at this time and brought to the church at Marcolès, where they are still venerated.

19. See Grand, *Les "paix" d'Aurillac*, 251–54. Another royal charter of Philip VI surviving from 1350 (ibid., 332) shows that the abbots of Aurillac were still resisting royal authority in the matter of judicial appeals; another charter of 1362 (ibid., 334–40) shows that they still appealed to Rome.

20. See Joubert, *L'Abbaye bénédictine*, 295–96; or Charbonnel, "À propos de Saint-Géraud d'Aurillac," 53. Joubert adds (ibid., 300) that in 1335 the next pope withdrew the office of abbot of Aurillac from this individual, although he remained bishop of Saint-Flour, so perhaps the combination of offices proved unworkable.

21. Some indication of what sort of treasure the monks might have collected from wealthy donors may be seen in what survives of the medieval treasury of Conques; see Delmas and Fau, *Conques*, 51–80.

22. See Valiña Sampedro, *El camino de Santiago*, 150; Huidobro y Serna, *Las peregrinaciones jacobeas*, 3: 25; Alvilares, *El Cebrero*, 25; Gitlitz and Davidson, *The Pilgrimage Road to Santiago*, 305; or Beaufrère, *Aurillac et la Haute-Auvergne*, 16.

23. Chaillou, "Les maisons médiévales," 1: 321–22 (Latin text included).

24. See Manry, Sève, and Chaulanges, *L'histoire vue de l'Auvergne*, 140–41. According to the agreement, the Dauphin received the right to build fortifications and a fortified house wherever he saw fit in the town, and received half of the rents from mills and bake ovens and fees for justice; the abbot received all tithes but was forbidden to build a fortified house. Dauzat-sur-Vodable is now in the *département* of Puy-de-Dôme.

25. See Boudet, *Aspres-sur-Buëch*, 22–25, who dates it to 1279 (but adds, 124, that the abbot of Aurillac continued to receive revenues from it); or "Prieuré de St.-Géraud," 52, where it is dated to 1276. Aspres-sur-Buëch is now in the *département* of Hautes-Alpes.

26. "Textes et documents," 11. It is possible that what is called the "vieux château," now in ruins, began as the fortified priory residence, although I could find no support for this suspicion. (On these ruins, including the remnants of a large square tower called the Tour Saint-Géraud, see ibid., 15–17, 23). Salles-Curan is now in the *département* of Aveyron.

27. Mailhet, *Histoire de Saillans*, 60. He notes (98) that the abbots of Aurillac continued to receive payments from the priory. See also Vincent, *Notice historique*. Saillans is now in the *département* of Drôme.

28. See Grand, "Un épisode de la restitution," 228.

29. See Arramond, "L'Église Saint-Pierre-Saint-Géraud"; Chalande, *Histoire des rues de Toulouse*, s.v. "L'Église Saint-Pierre-Saint-Géraud." The abbot's house is now Place Esquirol, no. 4. According to Joubert (*L'Abbaye bénédictine*, 163–64), this house was intended to serve as a residence for monks from Aurillac who were attending the university of Toulouse. Generally on the decline of Benedictine priories in the later Middle Ages, see Foviaux, "De la dépendance."

30. Archives départementales du Tarn-et-Garonne, Montauban, G 462 and G 463, respectively. Cayrac is in the modern *département* of Tarn-et-Garonne.

31. See Denifle, *La guerre de cent ans*, 2: 255 and 2: 415 (on the English mercenaries), 2: 421 (on the French mercenaries), 2: 421n3 (for Latin of quotation), and 2: 422 (on the Navarrese forces). See also Pataki, "Notes sur Aurillac"; and Charbonnel, "Aurillac, ville romane," 28–32.

32. Denifle, *La guerre de cent ans*, 3: 596–97 (with Latin text in n7).

33. On Bournac, see Bedel, *Saint-Affrique*, 21, who notes that the church was first mentioned in 1346 and served as a chapel to the castle there; the castle was destroyed in the Hundred Years' War but rebuilt in 1473 and expanded in 1503. Chaigne, *Le Rouergue*, 152, notes that the so-called castle was actually the medieval priory residence. In contrast, de Gournay, *Le Rouergue*, 196, says that there is evidence for a castle at Bournac already around the year 1000. The existence of castle chapels that were also under the jurisdiction of ecclesiastical authorities is not unique; see Avril, "Églises paroissiales." Both Salles-Curan and Bournac are now in the *département* of Aveyron.

34. See Joubert, *L'Abbaye bénédictine*, 310.

35. See Duby, *L'économie rurale*, 203–30.

36. On the decline and secularization of medieval monasteries, see Racinet, *Crises et renouveaux*; or Le Gall, *Les moines au temps des réformes*.

37. See Ashley and Sheingorn, *Writing Faith*.

38. Quoted in Lauranson-Rosaz, "Peace from the Mountains," 123; see also "Translatio sancti Viviani," 14–16, for the original Latin.

39. The manuscript is Montpellier 142. See above, Chapter 1, on Obazine, now in the *département* of Corrèze.

40. See especially Knowles, "Cistercians and Cluniacs."

41. See Le Goff, "Ordes mendiants." On the mendicants in Aurillac see Joubert (*L'Abbaye bénédictine*, 228n1), who dates the arrival of the Franciscans in Aurillac to 1226.

42. There is no evidence for Cathars in Aurillac, but the limited historical documentation does reveal that they existed in several towns close to the borders of the Auvergne; see Boudet, *Deux épisodes*; and Grand, *Les "paix" d'Aurillac*, lxv. For more on what is known of the Cathars in the south of France in the late twelfth and early thirteenth century see Delaruelle, "Le catharisme en Languedoc."

43. See Baumann, "The Deadliest Sin." More generally, see Vauchez, "La pauvreté volontaire"; or Rosenwein and Little, "Social Meaning." On the eleventh-century origins of these ideas, see Taylor, "The Year 1000," 218.

44. See Bolton, "*Pauperas Christi*," 100.

45. See Bouange (*Saint Géraud d'Aurillac*, 318–22, 553–54) on the possible kinship between Saints Gerald and Robert. See Cantor ("The Crisis of Western Monasticism," 51) on the significance of Robert's rejection of the Cluniac ideal.

46. There are patent problems with the legend as it exists, not least of which are the facts that, though Roch is said to have died of the plague in 1327, it did not strike Italy until 1348, and that, though he is supposed to have received an audience with the pope during his pilgrimage to Rome, from 1309 to 1376 the popes resided in Avignon. Indeed, there is no concrete evidence for the legend of Saint Roch until the late fifteenth century. See Bolle, "Saint Roch: Genèse," who suggests that his cult began with that of the seventh-century bishop Racho of Autun, an argument repeated in Bolle, "Saint Roch de Montpellier"; and resumed in Bolle, "Saint Roch: Une question." Some scholars have questioned various elements of Bolle's thesis, but in general it has become accepted. See the essays in *San Rocco*, ed. Rigon and Vauchez. Among them, Dormeier ("Un santo nuovo") discusses some of the reasons for the popularity of the cult in early modern Europe.

47. Gibson (*A Social History*, 141) and Périé ("Le culte de Saint Roch") both suggest that the cholera epidemics in France of 1832 and 1849 helped to encourage modern devotion to Saint Roch.

48. Grand (*Les "paix" d'Aurillac*, 63–64) includes the transcription of a charter surviving from 1284 that first mentions "the rector of the church of Saint Mary at Aurillac [*rector ecclesie beate Marie de Aureliaco*]." The church was damaged during the Wars of Religion, rebuilt, and then demolished during the period of the French Revolution. It is now the site of the city hall of Aurillac. See Joubert, *Notre-Dame-aux-Neiges*, 12.

49. See Grimmer, *Vivre à Aurillac*, 215, on the shrines of Thiézac and La Font-Sainte. Both are now in the *département* of Cantal. See also Ward, *Miracles and the Medieval Mind*, chap. 8, for more on the establishment of Marian shrines across western Europe in the eleventh and twelfth centuries.

50. Thibout ("Auvergne et Cévennes," 288) notes that most of these statues were based on that of the Virgin Mary at Clermont. Closest to Aurillac (only thirty-seven kilometers from it on modern roads) is the Black Madonna of Quézac, although this sculpture, while said to have been carved in the Middle Ages, was found only in 1826 (Beaufrère, *Le sanctuaire de Quézac*, 17).

51. On the legend see Arias, "El santo milagro del Cebrero"; Alvilares, *El Cebrero*, 40–44; Valiña Sampedro, *El camino de Santiago*, 151–57; Vázques de Parga et al., *Las peregrinaciones a Santiago*, 2: 316–18; Delgado Gómez, *El camino francés*, 27–32. See also Cuende and Izquierdo, *La Virgen María*, on the popularity of devotion to the Virgin Mary along the pilgrimage route to Santiago de Compostela, including the several versions of a *Santa María la Real* (76–82). Miracles related to the blood of Christ were particularly prevalent in the fifteenth century: see Bynum, *Wonderful Blood*, esp. chap. 4 (who mentions very briefly this miracle story, 89).

52. Paris, Bibliothèque Ste.-Geneviève 587, fols. 138r–145v, 165r–171v, a translation of the *Vita prolixior*.

53. It survives only as a fragment containing the days before Gerald's death and the episode in which wine sprang miraculously from the ground. Both elements were derived from the *Vita prolixior*, but in this text they are oddly joined together. It is not a precise translation of the original, then, but it is impossible to know more about it. It is now held at Olot, not far from the church still dedicated to Saint Gerald at Sant Grau d'Entreperes (part of the modern *municipi* of Sales de Llierca), where it may have originated. See Vila, "Un fragment de la vida."

54. Bultot-Verleysen, who has published this text, notes that it is mostly a recopying of the *Vita brevior* and differs only in insignificant ways from it. She speculates that Gui may have included Gerald so that the saints of the south of France would be adequately represented among the saints in his collection, since he himself was from near Limoges and would have known of Saint Gerald from his youth. See Bultot-Verleysen, "Le *Speculum sanctorale*," 371–77 (on the similarities between Gui's text and the *Vita brevior*), 380–81 (on the reasons for which Gui might have included Gerald among the saints whose lives he described), and 384–98 (a critical edition of the text).

55. Biblioteca nazionale di San Marco, Venice, ms. lat. IX 45.

56. On the Protestant era in the southwest of France, see Dubourg, *Les guerres de religion*. On the iconoclasm of the Huguenots in France, see Joblin, "L'attitude des protestants." On the early Protestants of Aurillac, see Joubert, *Les guerres de religion*.

57. Gerbeau ("Dans la tourmente," 68–69) has attempted to reconstruct a list of the various reliquaries into which Gerald's remains were placed, although he admits that insufficient evidence has survived to establish it in a definitive way.

58. Dom Jacques Boyer, *Journal d'un voyage*, written between 1710 and 1714, and quoted in Grimmer, *Vivre à Aurillac*, 83. The bell tower is described by Grand ("La sculpture et l'architecture," 255) and Beaufrère ("L'Église Saint-Géraud d'Aurillac et ses bâtisseurs," 170); the former writes that it was built in 1131; the latter adds that it was demolished in 1794.

59. Archives départementales de Cantal, 3 E 59/6, fol. 182, described by Gerbeau, "Dans la tourmente," 76–77; see also Joubert, *L'Abbaye bénédictine*, 383–93. The murder victim was a consul of the town of Aurillac, and the alleged murderers were servants of the abbot. The convent of Le Buis was investigated at the same time—its abbess was the sister of the abbot, and seems to have lived with her brother in the castle of Aurillac and participated in his scandalous life—but the convent continued in existence until 1792 (Joubert, *La colline inspirée*, 14–15, 36). Similar histories can be seen elsewhere, especially in southern France: in 1537 the monastery of Sainte-Foy in Conques was secularized and canons established there, for example, and in 1568 Protestants sacked it. The monastery of Saint-Martial in Limoges was also secularized in 1535 (de Lasteyrie, *L'Abbaye de Saint-Martial*, 169).

60. Joubert, *L'Abbaye bénédictine*, 333.

61. Ibid., 348–55; see also Charbonnel, "À propos de Saint-Géraud d'Aurillac," 47n47 (who notes the protest made by the consuls of the town of Aurillac at the appointment: Cesare was only about seventeen or eighteen years of age at the time and was not a priest).

62. Cardinal Jean of Lorraine was made abbot of Aurillac in 1524, for example, although he was already archbishop of Narbonne and bishop of Metz and Verdun. He was also later named archbishop of Reims, Albi, and Lyon, bishop of Toul, Agen, and Nantes, as well as abbot of Cluny, Fécamp and Saint-Ouen in Normandy, and Marmoutiers in Alsace. See Joubert, *L'Abbaye bénédictine*, 367–68.

63. Iung, "Autour de Saint-Géraud," 172–76.

64. Grimmer, *Vivre à Aurillac*, 115.

65. Ibid., 140–41. According to Joubert (*Notre-Dame-aux-Neiges*, 69), the hospital was staffed by the Sisters of Charity of Nevers from 1713 although still overseen by the abbot. See also Durand, *Aurillac*, 175–78.

66. Durand, *Aurillac*, 173. In 1762, when the Jesuit order was suppressed in France, the college was given over to professors brought from the University of Paris. See Grimmer, *Vivre à Aurillac*, 220. Joubert (*Notre-Dame-aux-Neiges*, 63) also describes the opening of a school for younger boys in 1777, operated by the Christian Brothers of Saint Jean-Baptiste de la Salle.

67. On the history of this church and town see Thomas, "Histoire de Sieurac," 15, 34, and 37; and Fabre, "Inventaire archéologique," 265–68. It was also restored again in the middle of the nineteenth century, according to Bastié, *Le Languedoc*, 219. Sieurac is in the modern *département* of Tarn.

68. "Les fouilles de février-mars 1954"; see also Allemand, "Actes authentiques," 281n1. This information is also found in otherwise unidentified typed and photocopied documents at the Archives départementales des Hautes-Alpes, identified only as "Documents pour servir a l'histoire des communes des Hautes-Alpes," and listed alphabetically by commune.

69. See Grimmer, *Vivre à Aurillac*, 38–41; or Joubert, *Notre-Dame-aux-Neiges*, 74, 78. Whatever exemptions the monastery of Aurillac might have continued to enjoy were ended in 1623, when Pope Gregory XV decreed that all monasteries, even those like Aurillac under direct papal jurisdiction, were subject to the oversight of their local bishops; see Gaussin, *Huit siècles d'histoire*, 346.

70. Archives départementales de Cantal, 3 E 29/25, described by Gerbeau, "Dans la tourmente," 122–24; see also Grimmer, *Vivre à Aurillac*, 114n16.

71. See Moulier, *Églises romanes*, 2: 45.

72. On Ercole (Hercule) de Manzieri, see Deribier-du-Chatelet, *Dictionnaire statistique*, 1: 128–45, s.v. "Aurillac." Manzieri resided at the French royal court, and had been given the sinecure of Aurillac by Cardinal Mazarin (chief minister to Louis XIV) as a boon, so he may have had little substantial connection to it except as a distant benefactor. A letter of Cardinal Mazarin referred to the abbot Manzieri as the representative of the Duke of Modena in France (*Lettres du Cardinal Mazarin*, 563–64, a letter of 8 August 1658). A letter of Cardinal Fabrizio Spada describes Manzieri as having arranged a marriage between the duke of Modena and Cardinal Mazarin's niece and having been "repaid for it with the abbey of Aurillac in the Auvergne" (letter of 15 August 1674; see *Correspondance du nonce en France*, 303).

73. Dominique de Jésus, *Histoire parænetique*, 1.4bis–2.2; hereafter cited in the text. A copy of this book may be found at the Bibliothèque de l'Arsenal, Paris, no. 8-H-20862. The other two saints included in his collection were Flour (Florus) and Mary (Marius). The three men provided clear complements to each other in a variety of ways: Flour was supposed to have been an early missionary to Auvergne, Mary lived in the sixth century, and Gerald, of course, in the ninth. Moreover, since Flour was a bishop, Mary a monk and abbot, and Gerald a layman, they reflected three forms of the male Christian life. Finally, each was patron of a town—Flour of Saint-Flour, Mary of Mauriac, and Gerald of Aurillac—and so the three also represented the three main towns of Upper Auvergne. The biographical details on Dominique de Jésus are from Moulier, *Églises romanes*, 2: 16, and Joubert, *Notre-Dame-aux-Neiges*, 73–74; see also Hoefer, ed., *Nouvelle biographie générale*, s.v. "Vigier (Gérald)." Bouange ("La divine libératrice," 109) suggested that this Géraud Vigier had been tortured as a Catholic during the Huguenot occupation of the town of Aurillac, which would put his date of birth much earlier than 1596, but I was unable to confirm this information.

74. It is possible that this legend reflects a confusion with the crystal chalice adorned with precious stones that the countess of Narbonne had given to the monastery in the tenth century,

noted in the *Breve chronicon*, and that may still have been kept among the monastery's treasures. See above, Chapter 4.

75. See also 11.7, 15.5, 17.4; 18.1, and 18.5 for other verses quoted from this poem. Neither Maffré nor this other monk are dated in Dominique's text.

76. Dominique may have had the scandalous conduct of the so-called *mignons* of King Henri III (ruled 1574–89) in mind when he wrote of the "petty and perfumed courtier"; see Crawford, "Love, Sodomy, and Scandal," who links anxieties about the king's sexual behavior with the conflicts between Catholics and Protestants in France, as Dominique also seemed to do. See also Stone, "The Sexual Outlaw," on continuing concerns about effeminacy in early seventeenth-century France.

77. See Merrick ("Chaussons in the Streets," 168) for the overwhelming pattern of older men's attraction to younger men in the historical record of homoeroticism in seventeenth-century France.

78. Pascale Moulier ("Iconographie de saint Géraud," 63) and Muzac ("Visages," 401–2) both also describe the image; Moulier also provides information on the artist. On the popularity of wood-cuts such as these in Counter-Reformation Catholic art and their use in religious instruction, see Muchembled, *Popular Culture*, 285–86.

79. Louis Réau (*Iconographie de l'art chrétien*, 1: 426), notes this pattern, saying that it was established already by the late Middle Ages. Réau also notes the crown for royal saints.

80. See Gobillot, "Sur la tonsure," 427–40. On the disappearance of the tonsure in early modern France, see also Trichet, *La tonsure*, chap. 4.

81. See Hall and Uhr, "*Aureola super auream.*"

82. For biographical details on Branche see Prevost and d'Amat, eds., *Dictionnaire de biographie française*, s.v. "Branche (Jacques)." Pébrac is in the modern *département* of Haute-Loire.

83. Branche, *La vie des saincts*, fol. 2r–v; hereafter cited in the text.

84. Three modern stained-glass images of Saint Gerald include his mother with him, but none of them requires or even implies that she should be venerated for her own merits. They are at the church of Saint-Géraud, Aurillac, an image from 1877, at the convent of La Thébaïde (*commune* of Arches, *département* of Cantal), an image from 1894, and at the cathedral of Saint-Flour (*département* of Cantal), and image from 1932. See Moulier, *Sur les pas de saint Géraud*, 11, 80, 82.

85. De Monpalau, *Vida breu de s. Guerau* (hereafter cited in the text). I was unable to find any biographical details about this author.

86. See Beaufrère, "Poèmes liturgiques." Beaufrère includes transcriptions of these poems (200–7), from which the following quotations are taken.

87. Joubert, *Saint Géraud*, 106, describes this statue and dates it to the early nineteenth century, but this seems very unlikely. It also bears a certain stylistic resemblance to the reliquary statue of Saint Robert, founder of the monastery of La Chaise-Dieu that was not far from Aurillac; Joan Evans (*Monastic Iconography in France*, 13–14) notes a preference for new local depictions of the founders of individual Benedictine monasteries in seventeenth-century religious art, and this statue of Saint Gerald might easily fit into such a pattern. Pascale Moulier ("Iconographie de saint Géraud," 64) dates the statue to either the seventeenth or eighteenth century.

88. See Pascale Moulier, "Iconographie de saint Géraud," 61–65; Muzac, "Visages," 398–400; and Joubert, *Saint Géraud*, 105–7.

89. Lempdes-sur-Allagnon is in the modern *département* of Haute-Loire, and Saint-Saturnin in Cantal.

90. It is unknown how early this legend first appeared. It seems, however, a good if much later example of what Amy Remensnyder has described (*Remembering Kings Past*, 57–65): that animals are often remembered as having provided monastic founders with the specific location for their projects.

She suggests that the miraculous event—or one at least beyond human rationale—implies that the monastery exists in sacred space, and hints of special powers to the place.

91. See also Muzac, "Visages," 395–96, who describes the painting and dates it to the first third of the seventeenth century.

92. This painting is described by Pascale Moulier, "Iconographie de saint Géraud," 66, together with another from the same period, from Laroquevieille (in the *département* of Cantal), that shows Gerald a bit more vaguely in prayer before a book, probably the bible, still holding the church he had founded in his hand.

93. Apparently, the name derives from a confusion between the French homonyms *choeur* ("choir"), the part of the church in which the shrine was located, and *coeur* ("heart"); the first evidence for the shrine itself is from 1280. See Moulier, *Églises romanes*, 2: 50.

94. Grimmer, *Vivre à Aurillac*, 204–6; see also Joubert, *Les guerres de religion*, 32–34.

95. See Joubert, "Quelques visites pastorales," 68–69.

96. Archives départementales de Cantal, 4 G 82; see Bouyé, "De la reconstruction," 153n411; or Grimmer, *Vivre à Aurillac*, 216.

97. Quoted in Joubert (*Saint Géraud*, 89–90) from what he called "the Manuscript of Comblat" in the Archives of Aurillac, possibly the municipal archives.

98. See Gibson, *A Social History*, 3–8. Moshe Sluhovsky (*Patroness of Paris*, 153) notes the same factors as diminishing enthusiasm for Saint Geneviève in the eighteenth century.

99. Savènes is in the modern *département* of Tarn-et-Garonne.

100. Compaing, *La vie de saint Géraud*, 3–4 (of the preface, for the dedication and purpose), 19–20 (also of the preface, for the author's discussion of Protestants), 1 (of the translation itself, which is paginated separately, for the author's self-identification), 7–8 (of the final meditations, which are also separately paginated, for the examination of conscience). Compaing seems not to have read the *Vita brevior*, since he quoted the chronicle of Ademar of Chabannes as the source of Gerald's comment that it was better to die without sons than leave wicked heirs (in a marginal note, 74).

101. The two paintings are described by Pascale Moulier, "Iconographie de saint Géraud," 67–68.

102. See Garrigou, "Une ville en révolution," 75–76; Bouyé, "De la reconstruction," 153–56; and Joubert, *La colline inspirée*, 40.

103. See Muzac ("Visages," 433–34), who describes a 1793 map of Aurillac that registers these changes. By 1800, several buildings in one area of the monastery precinct had been demolished and a large rectangular hall had been erected there for use as a wheat market. Joubert ("Le conseil municipal," 515) dates the destruction of the bell tower to 1793. On the sale of the hospice to a private owner, see Quétin, "L'Hôpital d'Aurillac," 520; more generally on the history of the buildings attached to the church of Saint-Géraud in Aurillac during the French Revolution, see Iung, "Autour de Saint-Géraud."

CHAPTER 6

1. See Pierre Moulier ("De saint Géraud à saint Guiral," 101–2), who reprints the letter of request, sent by the parish priest of Saint-Géraud, and the reply from the bishop of Saint-Flour.

2. On these fairs see Durand, *Aurillac*, 133–55, who suggests that they were predominantly for the sale of sheep, and linked with the annual transhumance out of the higher mountains before winter. These fairs of October 13 are first mentioned in a document of 1298 (Grand, *Les "paix" d'Aurillac*, 235) but probably existed well before that date.

3. See Grand, "La sculpture et l'architecture," 250–59; and above, Chapters 4 and 5.

4. See Beaufrère, "L'Église Saint-Géraud d'Aurillac et ses bâtisseurs," 168–60; or Grimmer, *Vivre à Aurillac,* 114n16; and above, Chapter 4.

5. See Joubert, "Le conseil municipal," 514.

6. Ibid.

7. *Bénédiction de la première pierre,* 19–20.

8. The steps in the restoration are outlined by Joubert, "Le conseil municipal," 517–24; and Bouyé, "De la reconstruction," 157–63, 170–81, 187–95. Muzac, "Visages," 435–37, describes the building plans.

9. Durand, *Aurillac,* 222.

10. See Beaufrère, "L'Église Saint-Géraud d'Aurillac et ses bâtisseurs"; and Moulier, *Églises romanes,* 2: 43–50, for the architectural history of the church.

11. See Saunier, "Le bestiaire," 340; and Beaufrère, "L'Église Saint-Géraud d'Aurillac: Découvertes," 375–77. For a comparative perspective on the fate of the church at Cluny see Marquardt, *From Martyr to Monument,* esp. chap. 1.

12. Pascale Moulier ("Iconographie de saint Géraud," 72–74) and Joubert (*Saint Géraud,* 84–85) both provide details about the present day reliquary, which was the work of Thomas-Joseph Armant-Caillat, a renowned maker of religious art in Lyon. On the medieval sculpture of Samson, see Thibout ("Auvergne et Cévennes," 294), or Favreau, Michaud, and Mora (*Corpus des inscriptions,* 39) who date it to the early and late eleventh century, respectively.

13. Muzac, "Visages," 405. He also lists two eighteenth-century urn-shaped reliquaries now held at the church but not displayed.

14. See above, Chapter 4, on the origins of this church. Becquet ("Les débuts de l'Hôpital") says that the first church to Saint Gerald in Limoges, built before the year 1000, was destroyed in about 1080 by the count of Poitiers, but rebuilt by the middle of the twelfth century and reconsecrated in 1180. It was in this rebuilding that the hospice seems to have been added.

15. See above, Chapter 4, for the history of this church. The medieval priory residence still stands nearby but is not identified as such.

16. On this church and its history, see Boudet, *Aspres-sur-Buëch,* 12–22; Dartevelle, *Églises médiévales,* 24; Joubert, *L'Abbaye bénédictine,* 150–52; and Roman, *Dictionnaire topographique,* 6, the last of whom notes that the first reference to *Sanctus Geraldus de Asperis* dates from 1171. Boudet (ibid., 210) says that the priory was founded there in 1061. For a complete listing of the modern churches dedicated to Saint Gerald, see Moulier and Moulier, "Essai de géographie" (with accompanying "Catalogue des sites").

17. On this church, see Bedel, *Rodez-Nord,* 22, who notes that the new church was completed in 1874.

18. See also above, Chapter 4, for Vailhourles, Sieurac, and Aspres-sur-Buëch. Concourès is now in the *département* of Aveyron, and Lédat is in Lot-et-Garonne.

19. It was completed by 1840. On this church, see Fabre, "Inventaire archéologique," 265–68; Thomas, "Histoire de Sieurac"; Bastié, *Le Languedoc,* 219; Roques, *Guide du Tarn,* 455; and Benezech et al., *Communes du Tarn,* 489.

20. Fau (*Rouergue roman,* 76) dates the reconstructed church to between 1884 and 1886 and notes that some of the medieval column capitals were reused in its interior.

21. Jones, "Parish, Seigneurie and the Community," 96–108.

22. On nostalgia for the Middle Ages in nineteenth-century architecture as seen in the abbey of Cluny, see Marquardt, *From Martyr to Monument,* esp. chaps. 2 and 3.

23. See Leniaud, *La révolution des signes*; Emery and Morowitz, *Consuming the Past*; and Emery, *Romancing the Cathedral*.

24. Mérimée, *Notes d'un voyage*, 137.

25. Ibid., 73.

26. On the *art de Saint-Sulpice*, see Savart, "À la recherche"; and Vircondelet, "La dérive du sacré." See also Pirotte, "The Universe of Pious Objects"; and McDannell, *Material Christianity*, 165, 167–73, for broader discussions of modern religious art.

27. Vircondelet (*Le monde merveilleux*, 96) describes typical features of religious art: static postures, open bodies with hands raised in blessing or outstretched in welcome, eyes raised to heaven in ecstasy or lowered in humility, and sorrowful or placid facial expressions. An 1865 letter survives from the sculptor Victor Bariller to Bouange, Gerald's nineteenth-century biographer, asking for advice on whether Saint Gerald might be shown holding a sword instead of a staff; see Pascale Moulier, "Iconographie de saint Géraud," 71.

28. See Pascale Moulier, "Iconographie de saint Géraud," 76–82, on this and other workshops involved in the making of stained-glass depictions of Saint Gerald.

29. Wilson ("Cults of Saints") used *ex-voto* plaques as a means of judging the popularity of the cults of the saints he researched in central Paris.

30. Joubert (*Notre-Dame-aux-Neiges*, 130) notes that an annual procession from the church of Saint Gerald to commemorate the retaking of the town from the Huguenots was suppressed in 1889 by the municipal council of Aurillac. For more on similar practices in modern French Catholicism, see Devlin, *The Superstitious Mind*, 1–42. La Capelle-del-Vern is now part of the modern *commune* of Escandolières, in the *département* of Aveyron, and Monsempron-Libos, in Lot-et-Garonne.

31. See Devlin, *The Superstitious Mind*, 214; see also Cooke, *The Distancing of God*, 271–85.

32. A point also made by Pascale Moulier, "Iconographie de saint Géraud," 71.

33. Saint-Simon is now in the *département* of Cantal.

34. Dutton ("Charlemagne's Mustache," 27–30) notes, for example, that although Charlemagne was remembered in contemporary sources as having sported only a mustache, nineteenth-century depictions of him almost always represent him as bearded.

35. On the date of the stained glass, see de Ribier, *Montvert*, 8n1. Montvert is now in the *département* of Cantal.

36. Banhars is now in the *département* of Aveyron.

37. See above, Chapter 3, for the fourteenth-century seal of the abbots of Aurillac that depicts Gerald's holding a sword, and above, Chapter 4, for two seventeenth-century sculpted images of Gerald's also holding a sword. On the depictions of military saints, see Réau, *Iconographie de l'art chrétien*, 426.

38. See Nye, *Masculinity and Male Codes*, chaps. 7–9. Inhabitants of rural France may not have fenced, although Nye does suggest that both fencing and dueling became popular beyond aristocratic circles, but would probably have been influenced at least by newspaper reports of duels.

39. See Acomb, *The French Laic Laws*. The potent combination of Catholicism and political conservatism in France is found also in the nineteenth-century cult of the Sacred Heart of Jesus; see Jonas, *France and the Cult*, esp. 147–76.

40. Those called Legitimists hoped for the return to royal power of the oldest branch of the Bourbons, who had been restored in 1814 but overthrown in 1830 by a reformist younger branch of the royal family led by the duke of Orléans; the Orleanists preferred a king from this part of the family. These two conservative factions were reconciled in 1883 when the last representative of the older branch of the royal family died and the House of Orléans thereafter represented all Bourbon

aspirations, but it was a halfhearted *rapprochement* at best, the rivalry having become so acrimonious. See Locke, *French Legitimists*, 243, on the involvement of the Catholic clergy in the 1870s and 1880s in advocating the return of the monarchy. Kale (*Legitimism and the Reconstruction*, 210–60) also provides evidence for a strong correlation between Catholics and Legitimists in the second half of the nineteenth century, and for strong rural support for Legitimist politicians, who also tended to support social and economic policies that offered increased benefits for agriculture and that attempted to stem the tide of emigration from rural areas to the industrialized cities. On these political factions in Aurillac, see Estève, "Le souvenir de la Révolution."

41. See Irvine, *The Boulanger Affair Reconsidered*.

42. Ibid., 163, on the importance of the papal encyclical. For a general history of Catholics in nineteenth-century France, see Guillemin, *Histoire des catholiques français*; and Kselman, *Miracles and Prophecies*, esp. chap. 5.

43. See Mauduit and Mauduit, *La France contre la France*.

44. Simon, *Panégyrique de saint Géraud*, 10.

45. The church at La Salette was completed by 1865 and the one at Lourdes by 1876. One writer in 1890 noted that as many as thirty thousand persons arrived at Lourdes each day during the height of the pilgrimage season there; see Thomson, *Troubled Republic*, 161–62. Generally on the revival of pilgrimage in the nineteenth century, see Chelini and Branthomme, *Les chemins de Dieu*, 295–343; Gibson, *A Social History*, 145–51; and Emery and Morowitz, *Consuming the Past*, 143–69. Kselman (*Miracles and Prophecies*, 89) also notes the importance of the papal proclamation of the Immaculate Conception in 1854 in increasing devotion to the Virgin Mary.

46. Gibson (*A Social History*, 137–38) notes the importance of local Marian pilgrimages. See also Beaufrère, *Le sanctuaire de Quézac*, and Moulier, *Églises romanes*, 1: 114, on Quézac in the *département* of Cantal. See Beaufrère (*Le sanctuaire de Quézac*, 16, 43) on the construction of the church.

47. See Ralston, *The Army of the Republic*, 229.

48. See Brosman, *Visions of War in France*, 32 on the Roman *fasces* and Frankish helmets (both also later used by French fascists), and 58 on Roland. See also Elizabeth Emery ("The 'Truth' about the Middle Ages," 106), who notes that there were twenty-six editions of the *Chanson de Roland* printed between 1872 and 1903.

49. See Brosman, *Visions of War*, 49–54. On the political uses of Joan of Arc in the late nineteenth and early twentieth centuries, see Contamine, "Jeanne d'Arc"; and Hanna, "Iconology and Ideology." See also Maurice Aguilhon ("Politics, Images, and Symbols," 186), who suggests that Joan of Arc might have provided a monarchist counterpart to the republican personification of France as the warrior woman "Marianne."

50. Hanna, "Iconology and Ideology," 237.

51. *Bénédiction de la première pierre*, 21–22.

52. Winock, "Joan of Arc"; and Snipes-Hoyt, "Unofficial and Secular Saint." See also Warner, *Joan of Arc*, chap. 12, for a discussion of nineteenth-century depictions of Joan of Arc.

53. See Jonas, *France and the Cult*, 158–60. He adds (168–69) that the Zouaves also fought against republican forces within France, and that they were often compared to Joan of Arc in their defense of monarchist France. See also Cerbelaud-Salagnac, *Les Zouaves pontificaux*; and Faugeras, "Les fidélités en France," on the Papal Zouaves; and Gough, *Paris and Rome*, for more on ultramontanism in nineteenth-century France.

54. Surkis, *Sexing the Citizen*, 69–70.

55. Ibid., 212–42.

56. Cole, *The Power of Large Numbers*; and McLaren, *Sexuality and Social Order*.

57. Rauch, *Le premier sexe*, 121–42.

58. "Lilium inter spinas": *Vita brevior* 7; *Vita prolixior* 2.1. The phrase is taken from the Song of Songs 2.2.

59. See Gibson (*A Social History*, 152–53, 180–90) on the feminization of Catholicism in nineteenth-century France. Compare McDannell, "True Men as We Need Them," on Irish Catholicism in the same period.

60. McDannell (*Material Christianity*, 195) writes: "The masculinization of Christian art is part of a subtle strategy, dating from the mid-nineteenth century, to . . . mak[e] the church a comfortable place for men," adding: "whether ministers and priests knew what made 'men' 'comfortable' is another question."

61. There were many artists and artistic associations in France in the late nineteenth and early twentieth centuries dedicated to reconciling modern trends in art with religion, including individual artists such as Pierre Cécile Puvis de Chavannes (1824–98), Odilon Redon (1840–1916), and Georges Rouault (1871–1958), and groups such as *La société de Saint-Jean pour l'encouragement de l'art chrétien* (founded in 1872), *Les artisans de l'autel* (founded in 1904), *Les Catholiques des Beaux-Arts* (founded in 1909), and *Les ateliers d'art sacré* (founded in 1919). These groups were all were centered in Paris, though, and may not have had much of a presence in other regions of France. Still, it is difficult to believe that the artisans who crafted the images of Saint Gerald were unaware of these artists or the ideas they advocated. On modernism and religious art, see McDannell, *Material Christianity*, 170; or Wilson, *Modern Christian Art*, 51–55. On the art associations, see d'Agnel, *L'art religieux moderne*, 81–88. On a pivotal decade in this movement (the 1890s), see Thomson, *Troubled Republic*, chap. 3. The relationship between these modernist individuals or groups and official Catholicism was always precarious, however, and became more so by the early twentieth century. While the Code of Canon Law of 1917 offered considerable leeway in the expression of religious sentiment in art, the new styles in art were so much associated with anticlericalism and irreligion that in 1932 Pope Pius XI denounced the use of "profane" art forms in churches. See d'Agnel, *L'art religieux moderne*, 73–79. One French art journal, *L'art sacré*, founded in 1937 to promote modernism in religious art, was condemned by Catholic officials in 1954 and ceased publication. See Nichols, "The Dominicans and the Journal."

62. Jacques Maritain, "Discours sur l'art," in *Art et scholastique*, 171, 173.

63. *Abrégé de la vie.*

64. Delzons, *Notice historique sur saint Géraud*. Jean-François-Amédée Delzons (1808–91) was from a family of Aurillac; his father had been ennobled by Napoleon for service during the Revolutionary wars. He was a lawyer by profession and served in the National Assembly during the short-lived Second Republic, but also wrote several works of local history.

65. On Migne and his work, see Bloch, *God's Plagiarist*.

66. Langres is in the *département* of Haute-Marne.

67. See Delmas, *Vie de Monseigneur Bouange*; see also Joubert (*L'Abbaye bénédictine*, 51n4), who says that Bouange knew two canons from the monastery of Aurillac, one of whom gave him a collection of documents relating to it that has since disappeared (and Bouange himself mentioned a fire that consumed some of his research).

68. Bouange published other related writings in his appendices, including the testament attributed to Gerald, though he was skeptical of its authenticity (*Saint Géraud d'Aurillac*, 498–502); the bull of Charles the Simple granting privileges connected to the founding of the monastery of Aurillac, which he considered to be genuine even though it existed only in an eighteenth-century copy (487–93); a handful of papal bulls dating from 1061 to 1107 that had granted privileges to or settled disputes

involving the monastery at Aurillac (557–77); and letters from Pope Sylvester II that mentioned Aurillac (546–53). From Dominique de Jésus, whose biography he had also clearly read, he reprinted the few stanzas that remained of a medieval poetic version of Gerald's life (397–401).

69. Bouange, *Saint Géraud d'Aurillac*, ix; hereafter cited in the text.

70. In 1968 a brief biography of Saint Gerald appeared, also called *Saint Géraud d'Aurillac*, authored by Édouard Joubert, a Catholic priest and curate of Vic-sur-Cère near Aurillac, and also the author of countless articles and small booklets on the religious history of the region, most written between the 1930s and 1970s. Like Bouange, Joubert tried to marry good historical method and pious intention, but with less success. He wrote in his conclusion to this work: "If I have insisted particularly on the devotion rendered to the holy patron of Aurillac . . . it was above all so as to recall to the readers of this biography that the saints lived, suffered, and acquired merits in very human circumstances, and that what they did we can also do, relying greatly on the grace of God" (123). He seems to have relied heavily on Bouange, but where the latter was cautious in presenting uncertainties, Joubert glossed over the limited historical record and presented most of the details of Gerald's life as simple and uncontroversial fact, and all without notes or other information about his sources. For example, he stated without any evidence that Gerald's father died in 879 and his mother shortly thereafter (19–20). He even seems to have invented historical episodes: when describing the charter given to the monastery of Aurillac by Charles the Simple, Joubert imagined a visit by the abbot to the king to receive it (43–44). Where Joubert added something to the knowledge of Gerald is in his incorporation of a growing archaeological record for Aurillac. He noted several studies that had been conducted in the mid-twentieth century beneath and around the church of Saint-Géraud, done by Abel Beaufrère in 1944–45 (71–74, 113). In his chapter 11, he outlined a history of Gerald's relics and the various reliquaries into which they were put. In his chapter 13, he discussed the iconography of Saint Gerald.

71. The image came from the stained-glass workshop of Louis-Victor Gesta at Toulouse; he may have been the artist himself or it might have been someone working there under his direction. See Pascale Moulier, "Iconographie de saint Géraud," 80. Saint-Cirgues is in the *département* of Lot.

72. *Vita prolixior* 4.10. For the legend see also Deribier-du-Chatelet, *Dictionnaire statistique* 5: 141–44, s.v. "Roumégoux."

73. Drugeac is in the *département* of Cantal.

74. See Réau, *Iconographie de l'art chrétien*, 1: 425, on the palm branch symbolizing martyrdom.

75. Estézargues is in the *département* of Gard.

76. Villetelle is in the *département* of Hérault.

77. Mas-de-Londres is now part of the *commune* of Saint-Martin-de-Londres, in the *département* of Hérault.

78. On the 1859 painting by Camille Barnoin, see Breton, *Estézargues*, 33. Breton believes the image to be that of Saint Géri, also known as Gérard de Lunel, on whose legend see below. For another example of confused iconography for a late medieval saint, see Zucker, "Problems in Dominican Iconography."

79. On Saint Guiraud, in the *département* of Hérault, see Aubert, *Dictionnaire d'histoire*, vol. 22, s. v. "Guiraud (Saint)." On the town of Saint Guiraud, see Mestre (*Histoire de la ville de Gignac*, 175), who says that the church there was once the chapel of a fortified manor house built in the tenth or eleventh century, so its dedication may be even earlier. See also Hamlin, *Toponymie de l'Hérault*, 356; or Hamlin, *Les noms de lieux*, 228–29; or Thomas, *Dictionnaire topographique*, 181.

80. See Hamlin, *Les noms de lieux*, 414.

81. See Bougette, *Histoire du Mas-de-Londres*; Germer-Durand, *Dictionnaire topographique*, 207.

82. Soupairac, *Mémoire pour servir à la vie*, 75.

83. Ibid., 99–100, describing an epidemic in Béziers in 1464, when the people of the city went to the cathedral and prayed for deliverance at his tomb.

84. Ibid., 1.

85. See above, Chapter 4.

86. See Girbal, *El santuario*, 5–7.

87. This statue of Saint Gerald does show him wearing black monastic robes underneath his episcopal vestments, which may suggest the appearance of an abbot, but the description of the statue by Casas (*A l'entorn del Puig Segalar*, 125) identifies him as a bishop.

88. Sargatal, *Diccionari dels sants*, 80 (s.v. Grau).

89. Dominique de Jésus, *Histoire paraenetique*, 18.7. He said he found the information in documents then still held at the monastery of Aurillac. Sisteron is now in the *département* of Alpes-de-Haute-Provence.

90. One of these likenesses, in the form of a bust, survived the destruction of the other during the French Revolution and is still at Manosque, but it is disputed which one. Manosque is now in the *département* of Alpes-de-Haute-Provence.

91. On Gerard see Riley-Smith, *The Knights of St. John*, 38–43; on the presence of the relics at Manosque, see Reynaud, *La commanderie*, 195–98; or Luttrell, "The Spiritual Life," 84. Nicholson (*The Knights Hospitaller*, 4) suggests that "it seems likely that this was the body of the Gerard who was master at the time of the First Crusade, and that his body had been taken to the West for safe keeping in response to the threat of Muslim attack on the last European strongholds in the crusader states [ca. 1283]." But why his relics should have been taken to Manosque rather than to the head-quarters of the Hospitallers at Saint-Gilles, near Marseilles, she does not explain. Already in the nineteenth century Feraud (*Histoire civile*, 472) wondered why October 13 served as the local feast day for Blessed Gerard, and he came later (*Les saintes reliques*) to doubt the relics' traditional attribution, although he did not know to whom they belonged. See also Andrieu, "Les reliques de saint Gérard Tenques," who defended the opinion that the relics belonged to Gérard Tenque, although a 1427 document in the Archives communales de Manosque identified the relics as belonging to a "Gérald." On the reliquary bust see de Gérin-Ricard, "Le reliquaire de Gérard Tanques"; and Chambonnet et al., *Le patrimoine religieux*, 74–75.

92. See Bouisson, *Les trois ermites*, who defended the historicity of the legend in the nineteenth century (although his is the earliest account of the legend I have found), while noting that the other brothers are variously identified as Saint Alban, Saint Loup, and Saint Clair, after other mountain peaks in the region. See also Tullou, *Religion populaire en Cévennes*, 35–36 (on the identification of this Saint Guiral with Saint Gerald of Aurillac), and 121 (on the annual fires in the legend).

93. The mutual influence of medieval history and fiction has been noted by other scholars. Remensnyder (*Remembering Kings Past*, 182–201), for example, describes instances in which the narratives of epic poetry became part of monastic foundation legends, sometimes supplementing existing ones entirely. Even this misremembering of a saint's biography is not without parallels. Hedwig Röckelein ("Just de Beauvais") describes how the relics of Saint Just of Beauvais eventually came to be venerated as a Saint Justin of Auxerre, with a life invented for him. The most curious of these saintly metamorphoses is undoubtedly Saint Wilgefortis, also known as Saint Uncumber and Saint Liberata, said to have been a woman who both grew a beard and was crucified, but whose story probably began with misidentified images of Christ crucified (see Friesen, *The Female Crucifix*).

94. See Bouisson, *Les trois ermites*, 105, who describes the painting still hanging in the church of Arrigas. See also Tullou, *Religion populaire en Cévennes*, 19 (on the tomb of Saint Guiral), 41–43

and 152–54 (on the painting in the church at Arrigas), 90–93 (on the eighteenth-century hermit, whose name was Pierre-César Cambassédès), 159 and 161–62 (for an example of a hymn honoring Saint Guiral, composed in 1942). Germer-Durand (*Dictionnaire topographique*, 207, 209) notes that the first mention of the name in this region comes from 1135, and says that the hermitage was built on the ruins of the chapel dedicated to Saint Gerald. See also Aussibal ("La stèle de l'Oratoire") for a description and discussion of a raised stone slab dedicated to Saint Guiral in this region. Arrigas is in the *département* of Gard.

95. Breton, *Estézargues*, 20, 31–34.

96. See Millerot, *Histoire de la ville de Lunel*, 92–95; or Roüet, *Notice sur la ville de Lunel*; or the anonymous *Vie de saint Gérard de Lunel*. All of these works attempt to link Saint Gerald of Lunel both with local nobility and with San Girio or Gerio of Montesanto, canonized in 1760. Roüet notes (216) but dismisses the problems with authenticating this individual. Montesanto has since been renamed Potenza Picena.

97. See Vauchez, "Un modèle hagiographique," who suggests that since the earliest written evidence for Saint Roch's legend dates only to the late fifteenth century, the legend of San Girio may have been a model for the legend of Saint Roch (61–63). Vauchez did not mention and probably did not know about the connection between Gérard of Lunel and Gerald of Aurillac, or that the earliest evidence for the cult of this Saint Gérard dates only from the nineteenth century.

98. Roüet, *Notice sur la ville de Lunel*, 208.

99. Durot (*Histoire de sainte Procule*, 11–12) claimed that she was named already in the mid-fifteenth century by Jean Arfeuilles, a professor at the Sorbonne who had been born at Gannat, but I could not verify this information. Gannat is now in the *département* of Allier.

100. Durot (*Histoire de sainte Procule*, 115–16) claimed that the chapel was built before 1526, but the chapel's exterior is unmistakably modern; I was unable to gain access to its interior.

101. Cornil, *Vie de sainte Procule*.

102. See Emerson, "Two Newly Identified Offices," 37–38. He dates the origins of the cult of Sainte Valerie to at least the early tenth century (40), so it is much older than the cult of Sainte Procule.

103. Cornil, *Vie de sainte Procule*, 13–19.

104. Bouange, *Saint Géraud d'Aurillac*, 429.

105. See Durat, *Histoire de sainte Procule* (including the date of the painting at Rodez, 170).

106. See above, Chapter 5.

107. For more details of this legend, see my "How the Holy Grail." See also Valiña Sampedro, *El camino de Santiago*, 146, 157–58; Alvilares, *El Cebrero*, 33–36; and Huidobro y Serna, *Las peregrinaciones jacobeas*, 3: 26–33.

108. For a comparison, see Hoch, "St. Martin of Tours," on the mixing of visual elements of Saint Martin and Saint Francis of Assisi in Renaissance art.

109. See Dupré, *Symbols of the Sacred*, 8.

110. See Freedberg, *The Power of Images*, 112–28, on the variations in the cult of the Virgin Mary.

CONCLUSION

1. See Valiña Sampedro, *El camino de Santiago*, 172–73 (who is himself the priest in question).

2. *Visitatio capell[a]e sancti Giraldi*, 4G257 (2MI270), fol. 76r/v, Archives départementales de l'Isère, Grenoble.

3. Bouange, *Saint Géraud d'Aurillac*, 101.

4. See Hostache, *Souvenirs des montagnes d'Oisans*, 41.

5. The statue, of an individual likely to appeal to both Catholics and republicans, was apparently intended to symbolize the rapprochement possible between church and state. It was sponsored by the mayor of Aurillac and approved by the municipal council, but paid for with donations authorized by the pope. See Iung, "La statue de Gerbert"; and Estève, "Le souvenir de la Révolution," 359. Iung notes that the sculpture was originally intended to be placed next to the church of Saint-Géraud in Aurillac, either in front of it or on its east side (297–99). The erection of this statue also provides an excellent example of what Stéphane Gerson calls "pride of place" in nineteenth-century France (*Pride of Place*; see also Hargrove, "Shaping the National Image"). On Gerbert, see above, Chapter 4; for other examples of medieval saints who were the subjects of late nineteenth-century French artistic or literary representations, see the various essays in Emery and Postlewate, *Medieval Saints*.

6. Barthélemy (*Chevaliers et miracles*, 4, 16) refers to the "black legend" of the central Middle Ages, and his second chapter analyzes the *Vita prolixior* at length.

7. For a lengthier discussion, see Bull, *Knightly Piety*. Bull generally discounts the impact of the Peace of God movement on notions of the acceptability of violence, but links it to general patterns of noble lay piety. Carl Erdman considers the role of Gerald and other legends of pious Christian knights in the development of the crusader mentality; he also looks at popular devotion to military saints and at precursors in the rhetoric used in such military campaigns as the Ottonian struggles against the pagan Slavs or the early decades of the *Reconquista*, and even the Norman conquest of southern Italy, in describing the intellectual roots of the crusades; Erdman, *Die Entstehung des Kreuzzugsgedankens*, 78–80, 86–123, 253–60. See also Carraz, "Saint Géraud." (Erdman and Carraz both consider Gerald a precocious example of what was an eleventh-century trend, believing that Odo wrote the *Vita prolixior*.) Cluniac intellectual influences on the Crusades have been questioned. Delaruelle ("L'idée de croisade") rejects them; Constable ("Cluny and the First Crusade") is less certain. Still, Urban's message was heard in Auvergne, and one of the men who joined the First Crusade was Richard, viscount of Carlat, just seventeen kilometers east of Aurillac (Gaussin, *Huit siècles d'histoire*, 26).

8. See my *The Manly Eunuch*, chap. 4, on late Roman Christian attitudes toward violence.

9. Lotter ("Das Idealbild," 80) suggests a number of classical and Carolingian examples.

10. On his cult see Duhamel-Amado, "Le *miles conversus*"; Chastang, "La fabrication d'un saint"; Mazel, "Le prince, le saint et le héros"; and Erdman, *Die Entstehung des Kreuzzugsgedankens*, 261. Erdman also considers the cults of other martial saints who might be seen as precursors to Gerald's combination of sanctity and violence, including Maurice, Sebastian, Martin, George, and others (*Die Entstehung des Kreuzzugsgedankens*, 253–60). Another was Arnulf of Metz, who lived in the late sixth and early seventh centuries and whose *vita* was written in the early eighth century, though he abandoned his military lifestyle to become a bishop. Gangulf of Burgundy, who lived in the eighth century and whose *vita* was written in the late ninth or early tenth century, renounced the life of a soldier for that of a hermit and was also martyred. Both Arnulf and Gangulf are compared to Gerald in Airlie, "The Anxiety of Sanctity," 384–85.

11. See Hebers, *Politica y veneración*, who dates the origins of this cult to the twelfth century. Generally on moral themes in Romanesque art, including images of holy violence, see Weisbach, *Reforma religiosa y arte medieval*.

12. Rousset ("L'idéal chevaleresque") has compared Gerald to another lay monastic patron, Bouchard, who refounded Les Fossés (now on the outskirts of Paris), who died in 1005, and whose *vita*, written in 1058, reflects many of the same themes as the *Vita Geraldi*; see also Lauwers, "La vie

du seigneur Bouchard." Lauwers ("La *Vita Wicberti*") describes yet another lay monastic patron, in this instance, of the monastery of Gembloux in the tenth century, whose *vita* was written in about 1100 by Sigebert of Gembloux. Barthélemy (*Chevaliers et miracles*, 267) describes the influence of the *Vita Geraldi* on Helgaud of Fleury's biography of King Robert II of France, and Smyth (*King Alfred the Great*, 187–88, 272–73) sees its influence on the biography of King Alfred of Wessex purported to be that of Asser (but which he believes is a later forgery from around the year 1000).

13. Robinson ("Gregory VII") places the beginnings of militarism put in the service of the Christian religion to the reformist popes of the late eleventh century. It is worth noting that Pope Gregory VII wrote to discourage one Roman layman from becoming a monk, saying that he could do more good in the world than removed from it, and wrote to the abbot of Cluny, criticizing him for admitting the duke of Burgundy to the monastic life for the same reasons, in sentiments echoing the *Vita Geraldi* (see ibid., 189–91). See also Kaeuper, *Chivalry and Violence*, who notes the survival of ambivalence toward the joining of religious and martial roles continuing into the twelfth and thirteenth centuries.

APPENDIX I

1. This is probably a reference to Odo's position as abbot of Aurillac, although he was also abbot of Cluny from 927 until his death in 942.

2. See above, Chapter 2, on the dating of Gerald's death.

3. Odo shifts between first-person singular and first-person plural here, but it is not uncommon for early medieval hagiographers to refer to themselves with the plural. I have tried to use common sense in translating with "we" or "I."

4. The unnamed Queen of Sheba is said to have visited King Solomon because of his wisdom; see 1 Kings 10:1–13 and 2 Chron. 9:1–12. She is referred to simply as the Queen of the South in Matt. 12:42 and Luke 11:31.

5. See Rom. 13:1.

6. See Acts 10:44–48.

7. See 1 Kings 2:30.

8. In Chapter 1, above, I suggest that Vailhourles might have been Gerald's birthplace. It is about halfway between Cahors and Albi, and was an estate belonging to the monastery of Aurillac that might have been among the properties given over by Gerald from his family's holdings.

9. Caesarius, bishop of Arles, and Aredius, abbot of a monastery near Limoges (later called after him Saint-Yrieix), both lived in the sixth century.

10. See Ps. 13:6. If Aimon and Turpin to whom this *vita* was dedicated were indeed related to Saint Gerald (see my discussion in Chapter 1, above), these comments might be interpreted as praise of them, too, or even as flattery.

11. There are of course echoes of the prediction of the birth of Jesus to Joseph, as described in Matt. 1:20–21.

12. See Wisd. 6:1.

13. This is my addition for clarity's sake: Odo did not name "the ancient enemy."

14. Odo neglected to mention the involuntary seminal emission that must have followed these images, but it is clear from the rest of the sentence.

15. See Ecclus. 32:1.

16. The opposite sentiment is expressed with the same expression in Ecclus. 35:11.

17. See Job 29:24.

18. See Eccles. 12:11.

19. See Job 31:18.

20. The Latin is unclear, but the sentence might better be understood as "Great respect was maintained by him at mealtimes."

21. See 2 Thess. 3:12.

22. Literally, "before terce," using the monastic reckoning.

23. See Eccles. 10:17.

24. Odo presumably was contrasting the active life of a layman to the contemplative or cloistered one of a monk.

25. See Cant. 2:2.

26. See Ps. 132:1.

27. See Gen. 8:9.

28. Here Odo seemed to imply (and I have intensified that notion with my addition) that Gerald did not normally live near Aurillac. This would make sense, of course, since there was probably nothing there except the monastery in Gerald's day (see above, Chapter 1, for this argument). In the final section of the *Vita brevior*, Odo seemed to suggest that Gerald lived at Capdenac (modern Capdenac-le-Haut; see below).

29. See Ps. 11:2.

30. There is a negative here, found in all of the manuscripts, but that seems to be misplaced.

31. Ps. 140:3.

32. See Col. 3:17.

33. As noted above in Chapter 2, this is a liturgical phrase.

34. See 1 Kings 2:30.

35. Solignac was a monastery founded in the seventh century south of Limoges.

36. Lucca was a popular stopping point on the medieval pilgrimage road south from the Alps to Rome, called the *via Francigena*.

37. Argentat is not far to the northwest of Aurillac.

38. This might be Asti instead of Aosta—the Latin is Asta—since both lay along the *via Francigena*, and both had several church buildings.

39. Here and further down in this passage at "marveled" the text slips into present tense.

40. The Latin is a bit unclear, but *eulogiae* (here, "holy gifts") is elsewhere used to refer to food given to monks or hermits, including in the *Regula sancti Benedicti* 54.

41. Modern Capdenac-le-Haut, in the *département* of Lot, southwest of Aurillac.

BIBLIOGRAPHY

UNPUBLISHED SOURCES

Albi, Bibliothèque municipale, ms. 34.

Aurillac, Archives départementales du Cantal, mss. 3 E 29/25, 3 E 59/6, 4 G 9, 4 G 82, and 101 F 32.

Braga, Arquivo municipal, ms. fragment 12.

Clermont-Ferrand, Bibliothèque municipale, ms. 149.

Dijon, Bibliothèque municipale, ms. 660.

El Escorial, Real biblioteca del Escorial, ms. H III 11.

Évreux, Bibliothèque municipale, ms. 101.

Gap, Archives départementales des Hautes-Alpes, "Documents pour servir à l'histoire des communes des Hautes-Alpes."

Grenoble, Archives départementales de l'Isère, ms. 4 G 257 (2 MI 270).

Mantova [Mantua], Biblioteca Teresiana, ms. 455.

Montauban, Archives départementales du Tarn-et-Garonne, mss. G 462 and G463.

Montpellier, Bibliothèque de la Faculté de Médecine, ms. 142.

Paris, Bibliothèque de l'Arsenal, mss. 162 and 8 H 20862.

Paris, Bibliothèque nationale de France, collection latine, mss. 776, 944, 2826, 3783 t. II, 3809, 3820, 5298, 5301, 5315, 5353, 5365, 5399, 11749, 12601, 15149, 15436, 16733, 17006, collection latine, nouvelles acquisitions, mss. 1497, 2246, 2261, 2663.

Paris Bibliothèque Sainte-Geneviève, ms. 587.

Rouen, Bibliothèque municipale, ms. 1389.

Toledo, Biblioteca capitular, ms. 44.2.

Toulouse, Bibliothèque municipale, ms. 478.

Tours, Bibliothèque municipale, ms. 156.

Vaticano [Vatican], Biblioteca Vaticana, Registra latina, ms. 517.

Venezia [Venice], Biblioteca nazionale di San Marco, ms. lat. IX 45.

PUBLISHED SOURCES

A arquitectura do camiño de Santiago: Descrición gráfica do camiño francés en Galicia. Ed. Xunta de Galicia. A Coruña: Universidade da Coruña, 1999.

Abou-El-Haj, Barbara. "The Audiences for the Medieval Cult of Saints." *Gesta* 30, no. 1 (1991): 3–15.

———. *The Medieval Cult of Saints: Formations and Transformations.* Cambridge: Cambridge University Press, 1994.

Abrégé de la vie de saint Géraud, comte d'Aurillac. Aurillac: Picut, 1837.

Acomb, Evelyn Martha. *The French Laic Laws (1879–1889): The First Anti-Clerical Campaign of the Third French Republic.* New York: Octagon, 1967.

Ademar de Chabannes. *Chronicon. Corpus Christianorum Continuatio Medieualis*, 129. Ed. Pascale Bourgain, Richard Landes, and Georges Pon. Turnhout: Brepols, 1999.

———. *Commemoratio abbatum basilicae sancti Marcialis.* In *Chroniques de Saint-Martial de Limoges.* Ed. H. Duplès-Agier. Paris: Jules Renouard, 1874.

———. *Epistula de apostolatu sancti Martialis. PL* 141: 87–112.

Ainaud de Lasarte, Juan. "Moissac et les monastères catalans, de la fin du Xe au début du XIIe siècle." In *Moissac et l'occident au XIe siècle*, ed. Édouard Privat. Actes du colloque international de Moissac, 3–5 mai 1963. Toulouse: Centre national de la recherche scientifique/Université de Toulouse, 1964.

Airlie, Stuart. "The Anxiety of Sanctity: St. Gerald of Aurillac and His Maker." *Journal of Ecclesiastical History* 43, no. 3 (1992): 372–95.

Agulhon, Maurice. "Politics, Images, and Symbols in Post-Revolutionary France." In *Rites of Power: Symbolism, Ritual, and Politics since the Middle Ages*, ed. Sean Wilentz. Philadelphia: University of Pennsylvania Press, 1985, 177–205.

Alibert, Pierre. "Le maître de Varen: Sculpteur rouergat vers 1050." *Revue du Rouergue*, n.s., 36 (1993): 497–522.

Allemand, F. "Actes authentiques de la translation des reliques de Saint Pélade en 1485 et 1764." *Bulletin de la Société d'études des Hautes-Alpes*, no. 32 (1909): 271–86.

Alvilares, José. *El Cebrero.* Santiago de Compostela: Porto, 1956.

Andrade Cernadas, José Miguel. *Monxes e mosteiros na Galicia medieval.* Santiago de Compostela: Universidade de Santiago de Compostela, 1995.

Andrieu, Auguste. "Les reliques de saint Gérard Tenques à Manosque." *Annales des Basses-Alpes* 5 (1891–92): 381–92.

Arias, Plácido. "El santo milagro del Cebrero y los abades del monasterio de San Benito el Real de Valladolid." *Boletín de la comisión de monumentos de Lugo* 31–32 (1949): 316–18.

Arramond, Jean-Charles et al. "L'Église Saint-Pierre-Saint-Géraud de la Pierre à Toulouse." Toulouse: privately printed, 1993.

Ashley, Kathleen M., and Pamela Sheingorn. "An Unsentimental View of Ritual in the Middle Ages or, Sainte Foy Was No Snow White." *Journal of Ritual Studies* 6, no. 1 (1992): 63–85.

———. *Writing Faith: Text, Sign, and History in the Miracles of Sainte Foy.* Chicago: University of Chicago Press, 1999.

Ashton, Gail. *The Generation of Identity in Late Medieval Hagiography: Speaking the Saint.* London: Routledge, 2000.

Aubel, François. "Les comtes de Quercy (fin VIIIe–début Xe siècle)." *Annales du Midi* 109 (1997): 309–35.

Aubert, R. *Dictionnaire d'histoire et de géographie ecclésiastiques.* Paris: Letouzey, 1988.

Aubrun, Michel. *L'ancien diocèse de Limoges des origines au milieu du XIe siècle.* Clermont-Ferrand: Institut d'études du Massif Central, 1981.

Augry, Gwenaëlle. "Reliques et pouvoir ducal en Aquitaine (fin Xe s.–1030)." In *Reliques et sainteté dans l'espace médiéval*, ed. Jean-Luc Deuffic. Saint-Denis: PECIA Ressources en médiévistique, 2006, 261–80.

Aussibal, Robert. "La stèle de l'Oratoire St.-Guiralet." *Revue du Rouergue*, no. 128 (1978): 321–24.

Avril, Joseph. "Églises paroissiales et chapelles de châteaux aux XIIe–XIIIe siècles." In *Seigneurs et seigneuries au moyen âge*. Actes du 117e congrès national des sociétés savantes, Clermont-Ferrand, 1992. Paris: CTHS, 1993, 461–79.

Bachrach, Bernard. "The Northern Origins of the Peace Movement at Le Puy in 975." *Historical Reflections/Réflexions historiques* 14, no. 3 (1987): 405–21.

———. "'*Potius rex quam esse dux putabatur*': Some Observations Concerning Ademar of Chabannes' Panegyric on Duke William the Great." *Haskins Society Journal* 1 (1989): 11–21.

———. "Toward a Reappraisal of William the Great, Duke of Aquitaine (995–1030)." *Journal of Medieval History* 5, no. 1 (1979): 11–21.

Baker, Derek. "*Vir Dei*: Secular Sanctity in the Early Tenth Century." In *Popular Belief and Practice: Studies in Church History* 8, ed. C. J. Cuming and Derek Baker. Papers Read at the Ninth Summer Meeting and the Tenth Winter Meeting of the Ecclesiastical History Society. Cambridge: Cambridge University Press, 1972, 41–53.

Baraldés, Marissa, Bartolomeu Casas, and Josep M. Costa. *Una petjada per la Vall del Llierca: Passat i present del seu patrimoni religiós*. Vall del Llierca: Ajuntaments de la Vall del Llierca, 2008.

Barone, Giulia. "Une hagiographie sans miracles: Observations en marge de quelques vies du Xe siècle." In *Les fonctions des saints dans le monde occidental (IIIe–XIIIe siècle)*, ed. Jean-Yves Tilliette et al. Rome: École française de Rome, 1991, 435–46.

Barral Iglesias, Alejandro, and Ramón Yzquerido Perrín. *Santiago Cathedral: A Guide to Its Art Treasures*. Trans. Gordon Keitch. León: Edilesa, 2004.

Barthélemy, Dominique. *Chevaliers et miracles: La violence et le sacré dans la société féodale*. Paris: Armand Colin, 2004.

———. "The 'Feudal Revolution.'" *Past and Present*, no. 152 (1996): 196–205.

———. *La mutation de l'an mil a-t-elle eu lieu? Servage et chevalerie dans la France des Xe et XIe siècles*. Paris: Fayard, 1997.

———. "La paix de Dieu dans son contexte (989–1041)." *Cahiers de civilisation médiévale* 40 (1997): 3–35.

Bastié, Maurice. *Le Languedoc, première partie: Description complète du département du Tarn*. Albi: Nouguiès, 1875.

Baumann, Priscilla. "The Deadliest Sin: Warnings against Avarice and Usury on Romanesque Capitals in Auvergne." *Church History* 59, no. 1 (1990): 7–18.

Bautier, Anne-Marie. "De 'prepositus' à 'prior,' de 'cella' à 'prioratus': Évolution linguistique et genèse d'une institution (jusqu'à 1200)." In *Prieurs et prieurés dans l'occident médiéval*, ed. Jean-Loup Lemaître. Geneva: Droz, 1987, 1–21.

Beaufrère, Abel. *Aurillac et la Haute-Auvergne sur les chemins de Compostelle*. Paris: Centre d'Études Compostellanes, 1978.

———. "Découverte de peintures romanes à l'Église Saint-Géraud d'Aurillac." *Revue de la Haute-Auvergne* 42 (1971): 241–49.

———. "L'Église Saint-Géraud d'Aurillac: Découvertes récentes et compléments d'information." *Revue de la Haute-Auvergne* 55 (1993): 369–79.

———. "L'Église Saint-Géraud d'Aurillac et ses bâtisseurs de l'époque préromane aux siècles classiques." *Revue de la Haute-Auvergne* 54 (1992): 156–99.

———. "Poèmes liturgiques en l'honneur de Saint Géraud, comte d'Aurillac." *Revue de la Haute-Auvergne* 47 (1979): 191–207.

———. *Le sanctuaire de Quézac (Cantal)*. Aurillac: Gerbert, 1981.

———. "San Grau: Le bon comte Géraud d'Aurillac et la Catalogne." *Revue de la Haute-Auvergne* 57 (1995): 5–38.

———. "Sur la sépulture de saint Géraud." *Revue de la Haute-Auvergne* 30/31 (1939–44): 234–38.

———. "Sur les pas quotidiens du bon comte Géraud." *Revue de la Haute-Auvergne* 43 (1972): 197–210.

Becquet, Jean. "Le concile de Limoges de 1031." *Bulletin de la Société archéologique et historique du Limousin* 128 (2000): 23–64.

———. "Les débuts de l'Hôpital Saint-Géraud de Limoges (XIIe–XIIIe siècles)." *Bulletin de la Société archéologique et historique du Limousin* 114 (1987): 38–58.

———. "Les évêques de Limoges aux Xe, XIe et XIIe siècles." *Bulletin de la Société archéologique et historique du Limousin* 104 (1977): 63–90.

———. "Les saints dans le culte en Limousin au Moyen âge." *Bulletin de la Société archéologique et historique du Limousin* 119 (1991): 26–59.

Bedel, Christian-Pierre. *Rignac/Rinhac: Al canton.* Rodez: Mission départementale de la Culture de l'Aveyron, 1991.

———. *Rodez-Nord/Rodes-Nord: Al canton.* Rodez: Mission départementale de la Culture de l'Aveyron, n.d.

———. *Saint-Affrique/Sent-Africa: Al canton.* Rodez: Mission départementale de la Culture de l'Aveyron, 2002.

———. *Salles-Curan/Las Salas: Al canton.* La Primaube: Mission départementale de la Culture de l'Aveyron, 1997.

Bedel, Christian-Pierre, and Jean-Pierre Gaffier. *Vailhourles.* Rodez: Centre culturel occitan du Rouergue, 1988.

Bénédiction de la première pierre des nouvelles constructions de Saint-Géraud (15 décembre 1857). Aurillac: Picut et Bonnet, 1858.

Benezech, Francine, et al., eds. *Communes du Tarn: Dictionnaire de géographie administrative, paroisses, étymologie, blasons, bibliographie.* Albi: Archives et patrimoine, 1990.

Berman, Constance Hoffman. *The Cistercian Evolution: The Invention of a Religious Order in Twelfth-Century Europe.* Philadelphia: University of Pennsylvania Press, 2000.

Bernard Itier. *Chronicon armarii monasterii s. Marcialis.* In *Chroniques de Saint-Martial de Limoges,* ed. H. Duplès-Agier. Paris: Jules Renouard, 1874.

Besseyre, Marianne, and Marie-Thérèse Gousset. "Le scriptorium de Saint-Martial de Limoges: De l'héritage carolingien au roman aquitain." In *Saint-Martial de Limoges: Ambition politique et production culturelle (Xe–XIIIe siècles),* ed. Claude Andrault-Schmitt. Actes du colloque tenu à Poitiers et Limoges du 26 au 28 mai 2005. Limoges: Presses universitaires de Limoges, 2006, 337–44.

Bibliotheca hagiographica latina antiquae et mediae aetatis. 2 vols. Brussels: Société des Bollandistes, 1898–1901.

Biographies des troubadours: Textes provençaux des XIIIe et XIVe siècles, ed. Jean Boutière and A.-H. Schutz. New York: Burt Franklin, 1950. Trans. Margarita Egan, *The Vidas of the Troubadours.* New York: Garland, 1984.

Bisson, Thomas. "The 'Feudal Revolution.'" *Past and Present,* no. 142 (1994): 6–42.

———. "Unheroed Pasts: History and Commemoration in South Frankland before the Albigensian Crusades." *Speculum* 65, no. 2 (1990): 281–308.

Bitel, Lisa. *Landscape with Two Saints: How Genovefa of Paris and Brigit of Kildare Built Christianity in Barbarian Europe.* Oxford: Oxford University Press, 2009.

Blanc, Colette. "Les pratiques de piété des laïcs dans les pays du Bas-Rhône aux XIe et XIIe siècles." *Annales du Midi* 72 (1960): 137–47.

Blanks, David R. "Islam and the West in the Age of the Pilgrim." In *The Year 1000: Religious and Social Response to the Turning of the First Millennium*, ed. Michael Frassetto. New York: Palgrave Macmillan, 2002, 257–71.

Blanton, Virginia. *Signs of Devotion: The Cult of St. Æthelthryth in Medieval England, 695–1615*. University Park: Pennsylvania State University Press, 2007.

Bloch, R. Howard. *God's Plagiarist: Being an Account of the Fabulous Industry and Irregular Commerce of the Abbé Migne*. Chicago: University of Chicago Press, 1994.

Boehm, Barbara Drake. "Medieval Head Reliquaries of the Massif Central." 2 vols. Ph.D. diss., New York University, 1990.

Boglioni, Pierre. "La scène de la mort dans les premières hagiographies latines." In *Le sentiment de la mort*, ed. Claude Sutto. Études présentées au Ve colloque de l'Institut d'études médiévales de l'Université de Montréal. Montreal: Univers, 1979, 183–210.

———. "Les animaux dans l'hagiographie monastique." In *L'animal exemplaire au moyen âge (Ve–XVe siècle)*, ed. Jacques Berlioz and Marie Anne Polo de Beaulieu. Rennes: Presses Universitaires de Rennes, 1999, 51–79.

Bolle, Pierre. "Saint Roch de Montpellier, doublet hagiographique de saint Raco d'Autun: Un apport décisif de l'examen approfondi des incunables et imprimés anciens." In *"Scribere sanctorum gesta": Recueil d'études d'hagiographie médiévale offert à Guy Philippart*, ed. Étienne Renard et al. Turnhout: Brepols, 2005, 525–72.

———. "Saint Roch: Genèse et première expansion d'un culte au XVe siècle." Thèse de doctorat, Université libre de Bruxelles, 2001.

———. "Saint Roch: Une question de méthodologie." In *San Rocco: Genesi e prima espansione di un culto*, ed. Antonio Rigon and André Vauchez. Brussels: Société des Bollandistes, 2006, 9–56.

Bolton, Brenda M. "*Paupertas Christi*: Old Wealth and New Poverty in the Twelfth Century." In *Renaissance and Renewal in Christian History*, ed. Derek Baker. Oxford: Basil Blackwell, 1977, 95–103.

Bonnassie, Pierre. *From Slavery to Feudalism in Southwestern Europe*. Trans. Jean Birrell. Cambridge: Cambridge University Press, 1991.

———. *Les sociétés de l'an mil: Un monde entre deux âges*. Brussels: De Boeck Université, 2001.

Bonnassie, Pierre, and Frédéric de Gournay. "Sur la datation du *Livre des miracles de Sainte Foy de Conques*." *Annales du Midi* 107 (1995): 457–73.

Booker, Courtney. *Past Convictions: The Penance of Louis the Pious and the Decline of the Carolingians*. Philadelphia: University of Pennsylvania Press, 2009.

Bouange, G.-M.-F. "La divine libératrice d'Aurillac" (1880). In *Notre-Dame-aux-Neiges*, ed. Édouard Joubert. Aurillac: Moderne, 1964, 105–30.

———. *Saint Géraud d'Aurillac et son illustre abbaye*. Aurillac: L. Bonnet-Picut, 1881.

Bouchard, Constance B. "The Origins of the French Nobility: A Reassessment." *American Historical Review* 86, no. 3 (1981): 501–32.

———. *Sword, Miter, and Cloister: Nobility and the Church in Burgundy, 980–1198*. Ithaca, N.Y.: Cornell University Press, 1987.

Boudet, Marcellin. *Aspres-sur-Buëch et ses chartes de coûtumes (1276–1439)*. Grenoble: Allier, 1903.

———. *Deux épisodes des guerres albigeoises en Haute-Auvergne d'après les textes contemporains (1223–1226)*. Aurillac: E. Bancharel, 1904.

Bougette, Émile. *Histoire du Mas-de-Londres* (1909). In *Histoire du pays de Londres (Hérault, Languedoc)*. Montpellier: S. A. Dumons, 1991.

Bouisson, E. *Les trois ermites: Légende languedocienne.* 1890; Ferrières: Decoopman, 2007.

Bourgain, Pascale. "La culture et les procédés littéraires dans les sermons d'Adémar de Chabannes." In *Saint-Martial de Limoges: Ambition politique et production culturelle (Xe–XIIIe siècles),* ed. Claude Andrault-Schmitt. Actes du colloque tenu à Poitiers et Limoges du 26 au 28 mai 2005. Limoges: Presses universitaires de Limoges, 2006, 411–28.

Bouyé, Édouard. "De la reconstruction à la paroisse Saint-Géraud d'Aurillac (XVIIe siècle–début XXIe siècle)." In *Saint-Géraud d'Aurillac: Onze siècles d'histoire,* ed. Édouard Bouyé et al. Aurillac: Association des amis du patrimoine de Haute-Auvergne, 2009, 127–201.

Bouyssou, Léonce. "La chronique des premiers abbés d'Aurillac." *Revue de la Haute-Auvergne* 43 (1972): 323–28.

Boyer, Jean-François. "Reliquaires et orfèvrerie à Saint-Martial." In *Saint-Martial de Limoges: Ambition politique et production culturelle (Xe–XIIIe siècles),* ed. Claude Andrault-Schmitt. Actes du colloque tenu à Poitiers et Limoges du 26 au 28 mai 2005. Limoges: Presses universitaires de Limoges, 2006, 39–57.

Bozóky, Edina. "Les miracles de saint Martial et l'impact politique de son abbaye." In *Saint-Martial de Limoges: Ambition politique et production culturelle (Xe–XIIIe siècles),* ed. Claude Andrault-Schmitt. Actes du colloque tenu à Poitiers et Limoges du 26 au 28 mai 2005. Limoges: Presses universitaires de Limoges, 2006, 60–69.

———. "La politique des reliques des premiers comtes de Flandre (fin du IXe–fin du XIe siècle)." In *Les reliques: Objets, cultes, symboles,* ed. Edina Bozóky and Anne-Marie Helvétius. Actes du colloque international de l'Université du Littoral-Côte d'Opale (Boulogne-sur-Mer) 4–6 septembre 1997.Turnhout: Brepols, 1999.

Braga, Gabriella. "Problemi di autenticità per Oddone di Cluny: L'epitome dei 'Moralia' di Gregorio Magno." *Studi medievali,* ser. 3, 18 (1977): 45–145.

Brakke, David. "The Problematization of Nocturnal Emissions in Early Christian Syria, Egypt, and Gaul." *Journal of Early Christian Studies* 3, no. 4 (1995): 419–60.

Branche, Jacques. *La vie des saincts et sainctes d'Auvergne et du Velay.* Le Puy[-en-Velay]: Philippe Guynand, 1652.

Bremond, Alphonse. "Le Prieuré de Saint-Géraud à Toulouse." *La semaine catholique de Toulouse,* 25 April 1869.

Breton, René. *Estézargues: Village du Gard rhodanien.* Nîmes: Christian Lacour, 1989.

Breve chronicon Auriliacensis abbatiae. In G.-M.-F. Bouange, *Saint Géraud d'Aurillac et son ilustre abbaye,* unfinished second volume. Aurillac: L. Bonnet-Picut, 1889. Trans. Léonce Bouyssou, "La brève chronique de l'abbaye d'Aurillac." *Revue de la Haute-Auvergne* 43 (1973): 323–28.

Brisset, Françoise. "Guillaume le Grand et l'église." *Bulletin de la Société des antiquaires de l'ouest et des musées de Poitiers,* 4th ser., 12 (1972): 441–60.

Brooke, Christopher N. L. "Approaches to Medieval Forgery." *Journal of the Society of Archivists* 3 (1968): 377–86.

Brosman, Catharine Savage. *Visions of War in France: Fiction, Art, Ideology.* Baton Rouge: Louisiana State University Press, 1999.

Brousse, J.-R. "Une découverte archéologique: Les derniers restes de l'Église Saint-Géraud, Place Esquirol." *L'express du Midi,* 3 November 1932.

Brown, Elizabeth A. R. "Georges Duby and the Three Orders." *Viator* 17 (1986): 51–64.

Bruand, Olivier. "Géraud d'Aurillac, chevalier modèle, chevalier réel." *Revue de la Haute-Auvergne* 72 (2010): 3–21.

Bull, Marcus. *Knightly Piety and the Lay Response to the First Crusade: The Limousin and Gascony, c. 970–c. 1130.* Oxford: Clarendon, 1993.

Bulles, Bénédicte. "Saint Amadour: Formation et évolution de sa légende (XIIe–XXe siècle)." *Annales du Midi* 107 (1995): 437–55.

Bultot-Verleysen, Anne-Marie. "Le dossier de saint Géraud d'Aurillac." *Francia* 22, no. 1 (1995): 173–206.

———. "L'évolution de l'image de Géraud d'Aurillac († 909), seigneur laïque et saint, au fil de ses trois *vitae*." In *"In principio erat verbum": Mélanges offerts en hommage à Paul Tombeur par des anciens étudiants à l'occasion de son éméritat*, ed. B.-M. Tock. Turnhout: Brepols, 2005, 45–92.

———. "Des *Miracula* inédits de saint Géraud d'Aurillac († 909)." *Analecta Bollandiana*, no. 118 (2000): 47–141.

———. *Odon de Cluny: Vita sancti Geraldi Aureliacensis.* Brussels: Société des Bollandistes, 2009.

———. "Le *Speculum sanctorale* de Bernard Gui, témoin d'un intérêt pour la *Vita* de saint Géraud d'Aurillac au XIVe siècle. In *"Scribere sanctorum gesta": Recueil d'études d'hagiographie médiévale offert à Guy Philippart*, ed. Étienne Renard et al. Turnhout: Brepols, 2005, 367–98.

———. "Saint Géraud d'Aurillac: De la *vita* au culte; Jalons d'une recherche." *Revue de la Haute-Auvergne* 72 (2010): 71–89.

Bynum, Caroline Walker. *Wonderful Blood: Theology and Practice in Late Medieval Northern Germany and Beyond.* Philadelphia: University of Pennsylvania Press, 2007.

Cabanes, Marie-Louise, and Pierre Cabanes. *Panorama du Rouergue.* Rodez: Subervie, 1978.

Caillet, Jean-Pierre. "Reliques et architecture religieuse aux époques carolingienne et romane." In *Les reliques: Objets, cultes, symboles*, ed. Edina Bozóky and Anne-Marie Helvétius. Actes du colloque international de l'Université du Littoral-Côte d'Opale (Boulogne-sur-Mer) 4–6 septembre 1997. Turnhout: Brepols, 1999, 169–98.

Caitucoli, Christiane. "Nobles et chevaliers dans le *Livre des miracles de sainte Foy*." *Annales du Midi* 107 (1995): 401–16.

Callahan, Daniel. "Adémar de Chabannes et la paix de Dieu." *Annales du Midi* 89 (1977): 21–43.

———. "The Peace of God and the Cult of the Saints in Aquitaine in the Tenth and Eleventh Centuries." In *The Peace of God: Social Violence and Religious Response in France around the Year 1000*, ed. Thomas Head and Richard Landes. Ithaca, N.Y.: Cornell University Press, 1992, 165–83.

———. "The Sermons of Ademar of Chabannes and the Cult of St. Martial of Limoges." *Revue bénédictine* 86 (1976): 251–95.

———. "William the Great and the Monasteries of Aquitaine." *Studia monastica* 19 (1977): 321–42.

Calzada i Oliveras, Josep. *Sant Gregori: Fulls d'història de la parròquia i el poble.* Girona: Ajuntament de Sant Gregori, 1986.

Camille, Michael. *The Gothic Idol: Ideology and Image-Making in Medieval Art.* Cambridge: Cambridge University Press, 1989.

Cantor, Norman F. "The Crisis of Western Monasticism, 1050–1130." *American Historical Review* 66, no. 1 (1960): 47–67.

Carraz, Damien. "Saint Géraud et le culte des saints guerriers en France méridionale (Xe–XIIe siècle)." *Revue de la Haute-Auvergne* 72 (2010): 91–114.

Cartulaire de l'Abbaye de Vabres au diocèse de Rodez: Essai de reconstitution d'un manuscrit disparu, ed. Étienne Fournial. Saint-Étienne: Reboul, 1989.

Casas, Josep, Sebastià Balateu, and Victòria Soler. *A l'entorn del Puig Segalar: Albons, Garrigoles, La Tallada d'Empordà, Viladamat.* Girona: Disputació de Girona, 2007.

Catalogus codicum hagiographicorum latinorum antiquorum saeculo xvi qui asserrantur in bibliotheca nationali Parisiensis. Paris: Bibliothèque nationale, 1890.

Cerbelaud-Salagnac, Georges. *Les Zouaves pontificaux.* Paris: France-Empire, 1963.

Chaigne, Louis. *Le Rouergue: Province vivante.* Paris: Fernand Lanore, 1969.

Chaillou, Melanie. "Les maisons médiévales de Puycelsi (XIIIe, XIVe, XVe siècles)." 2 vols. Mémoire de maîtrise, Université de Toulouse-Le Mirail, 2001.

Chalande, Jules. *Histoire des rues de Toulouse: Monuments, institutions, habitants.* Toulouse: Douladoure, 1919.

———. "Une vieille église disparue." *Journal de Toulouse,* 2 January 1921.

Chambon, Jean-Pierre. "*Icitus,* nom de rivière dans les *Miracles de S. Géraud d'Aurillac.*" *Analecta Bollandiana* 121 (2003): 103–7.

Chambonnet, J., et al. *Le patrimoine religieux de la Haute Provence: Manosque.* N.p.: Bulletin de l'Association pour l'étude et la sauvegarde du patrimoine religieux de la Haute Provence, 1994.

Charbonnel, Nicole. "À propos de Saint-Géraud d'Aurillac et de son rayonnement." In *Sur les pas de Géraud d'Aurillac en France et en Espagne: Histoire, culte et iconographie,* ed. Pierre Moulier. Saint-Flour: Cantal patrimoine, 2010, 41–55.

———. "Aurillac, ville romane." *Revue de la Haute-Auvergne* 61 (1999): 21–59.

———. "La ville de Gerbert, Aurillac: Les origines." In *Gerbert l'européen,* ed. Nicole Charbonnel and Jean-Eric Iung. Acts du colloque d'Aurillac, 4–7 juin 1996. Aurillac: Gerbert, 1997, 53–78.

Charbonnel, Nicole, and Jean-Eric Iung, eds. *Gerbert l'européen.* Acts du colloque d'Aurillac, 4–7 juin 1996. Aurillac: Gerbert, 1997.

Chastang, Pierre. "La fabrication d'un saint: La *Vita Guillelmi* dans la production textuelle de l'Abbaye de Gellone au début du XIIe siècle." In *Guerriers et moines: Conversion et sainteté aristocratiques dans l'occident médiéval (IXe–XIIe siècle),* ed. Michel Lauwers. Antibes: APDCA, 2002, 429–47.

Cheirézy, Céline. "Hagiographie et société: L'exemple de Saint Léonard de Noblat." *Annales du Midi* 107 (1995): 417–35.

Chelini, Jean, and Henry Branthomme. *Les chemins de Dieu: Histoire des pèlerinages chrétiens des origines à nos jours.* Paris: Hachette, 1982.

Chevalier, C.-U.-J., ed. *Visites pastorales et ordinations des évêques de Grenoble de la maison de Chissé publiées d'après les registres originaux.* Lyon: Auguste Brun, 1874.

Cochelin, Isabelle. "Quête de liberté et réécriture des origines: Odon et les portraits corrigés de Baume, Géraud et Guillaume." In *Guerriers et moines: Conversion et sainteté aristocratiques dans l'occident médiéval (IXe–XIIe siècle),* ed. Michel Lauwers. Antibes: APDCA, 2002, 183–215.

Cole, Joshua. *The Power of Large Numbers: Population, Politics, and Gender in Nineteenth-Century France.* Ithaca, N.Y.: Cornell University Press, 2000.

Compaing, M. *La vie de s. Géraud, comte d'Aurillac, écrite en latin par s. Odon, second abbé de Cluny, et traduite en françois par M. Compaing.* Aurillac: Leonard Viallanes, 1715.

Conant, Kenneth John. *Carolingian and Romanesque Architecture 800 to 1200.* 1959; Harmondsworth: Penguin, 1966.

Constable, Giles. "The Abbot and Townsmen of Cluny in the Twelfth Century." In *Church and City, 1000–1500: Essays in Honor of Christopher Brooke,* ed. David Abulafia et al. Cambridge: Cambridge University Press, 1992, 151–71. Reprinted in *Cluny from the Tenth to the Twelfth Centuries.* London: Ashgate, 2000.

———. "Baume and Cluny in the Twelfth Century." In *Tradition and Change: Essays in Honor of Marjorie Chibnall presented by her Friends on the Occasion of Her Seventieth Birthday,* ed. Diana Greenway et al. Cambridge: Cambridge University Press, 1985, 35–61. Reprinted in *Cluny from the Tenth to the Twelfth Centuries.* London: Ashgate, 2000.

———. "Cluny and Rome." In *The Abbey of Cluny: A Collection of Essays to Mark the Eleven-Hundredth Anniversary of Its Foundation*. Münster: LIT, 2010, 19–41.

———. "Cluny and the First Crusade." In *Le concile de Clermont de 1095 et l'appel à la croisade*. Actes du colloque universitaire internationale de Clermont-Ferrand (23–25 juin 1995) organisé et publié avec le concours du Conseil Régional d'Auvergne. Rome: École française de Rome, 1997, 179–93. Reprinted in *Cluny from the Tenth to the Twelfth Centuries*. London: Ashgate, 2000.

———. "Cluny in the Monastic World of the Tenth Century." In *Il secolo di ferro: Mito e realtà del secolo X*. Spoleto: Centro italiano di studi sull'allto medioevo, 1991, I: 391–437. Reprinted in *Cluny from the Tenth to the Twelfth Centuries*. London: Ashgate, 2000.

———. "Forgery and Plagiarism in the Middle Ages." *Archiv für Diplomatik, Schriftgeschichte, Siegel, und Wappenkunde* 29 (1983): 1–41.

———. "Les listes de propriétés dans les privilèges pour Baume-les-Messieurs aux XIe et XIIe siècles." *Journal des Savants* 5 (1986): 97–131. Reprinted in *Cluny from the Tenth to the Twelfth Centuries*. London: Ashgate, 2000.

———. "Monasteries, Rural Churches and the *Cura animarum* in the Early Middle Ages." In *Settimane di studio del Centro italiano di studi sull'alto medioevo*, 28: *Cristianizzazione ed organizzazione ecclesiastica delle campagne nell'alto medioevo: espansione e resistenze (Spoleto, 10–16 aprile 1980)*. Spoleto: Centro italiano di studi sull'alto medioevo, 1982. Reprinted in *Monks, Hermits and Crusaders in Medieval Europe*. London: Variorum, 1988.

———. "The Orders of Society." In *Three Studies in Medieval Religious and Social Thought*. Cambridge: Cambridge University Press, 1995.

Contamine, Philippe. "Jeanne d'Arc dans la mémoire des droites." In *Histoire des droites en France*, ed. Jean-François Sirinelli. Paris: Gallimard, 1992, 399–435.

Cooke, Bernard J. *The Distancing of God: The Ambiguity of Symbol in History and Theology*. Minneapolis: Fortress, 1990.

Cornil, M. C. *Vie de sainte Procule: Patronne de Gannat*. Moulins: A. Ducroix et Gourjon Dulac, 1865.

Correspondance du nonce en France: Fabrizio Spada (1674–1675), ed. Ségolène de Dainville-Barbiche. Rome: École française de Rome, 1982.

Crawford, Katherine B. "Love, Sodomy, and Scandal: Controlling the Sexual Reputation of Henry III." *Journal of the History of Sexuality* 12, no. 4 (2003): 513–42.

Crozet, René. "Le voyage d'Urbain II en France (1095–1096) et son importance au point de vue archéologique." *Annales du Midi* 49 (1937): 42–69.

Cruvellier, Jean-François. "Note sur l'expulsion des Sarrasins au Xe siècle." *Bulletin de la Société d'études des Hautes-Alpes*, no. 1 (1882): 247–53.

Cuende, María, and Darío Izquierdo. *La Virgen María en las rutas jacobeas: Camino francés*. Santiago de Compostela: Xunta de Galicia/Consellería de Cultura e Comunicación social, 1997.

D'Agnel, G. Arnaud. *L'art religieux moderne*. Grenoble: B. Arthaud, 1936.

Dahl, Ellert. "Heavenly Images: The Statue of St. Foy of Conques and the Signification of the Medieval 'Cult-Image' in the West." *Acta ad archaeologiam et artium historiam pertinentia* 8 (1978): 175–91.

Dalarun, Jacques. "La mort des saints fondateurs: De Martin à François." In *Les fonctions des saints dans le monde occidental (IIIe–XIIIe siècle)*, ed. Jean-Yves Tilliette et al. Rome: École française de Rome, 1991, 193–215.

Darlington, Oscar G. "Gerbert, the Teacher." *American Historical Review* 52, no. 3 (1947): 456–76.

Dartevelle, Guylaine. *Églises médiévales des Hautes-Alpes.* Taulignan: Plein-Cintre, 1990.

De Gérin-Ricard, Henri. "Le reliquaire de Gérard Tenque à Manosque." *Bulletin de la Société scientifique et littéraire des Basses-Alpes* 24 (1932–33): 179–81.

Degoul, Geneviève. "Les châteaux seigneuriaux dans la région d'Aurillac." *Revue de la Haute-Auvergne* 42 (1970): 49–62.

———. "Découverte d'un temple gallo-romain à Aurillac." *Revue de la Haute-Auvergne* 46 (1978): 272–318.

De Gourgues, M. le Vicomte. *Dictionnaire topographique du département de la Dordogne.* Paris: Imprimerie nationale, 1873.

De Gournay, Frédéric. *Le Rouergue au tournant de l'an mil: De l'ordre carolingien à l'ordre féodal (IXe–XIIe siècle).* Toulouse: Société des lettres, sciences et arts de l'Aveyron, 2004.

De Labriolle, Roger. "Insertion monastique dans la moyenne vallée de la Durance aux XIe et XIIe siècles." *Bulletin de la Société d'études des Hautes-Alpes,* nos. 48–49 (1970–71): 60–67.

De Lahondes, Jules. "L'Église Saint-Géraud." *L'express du Midi,* 12 October 1913.

De la Roncière, Charles. "De la mémoire vécue à la tradition, perception et enregistrement du passé." In *Temps, mémoire, tradition au moyen âge.* Actes du XIIIe congrès de la Société des historiens médiévalistes de l'enseignement supérieur public (Aix-en-Provence, 4–5 juin 1982). Aix-en-Provence: Université de Provence, 1983, 267–79.

Delaruelle, Étienne. "Le catharisme en Languedoc vers 1200: Une enquête." *Annales du Midi* 72 (1960): 149–67.

———. "L'idée de croisade dans la littérature clunisienne du XIe siècle et l'Abbaye de Moissac." *Annales du Midi* 75 (1963): 419–39.

De Lasteyrie, Charles. *L'Abbaye de Saint-Martial de Limoges: Étude historique, économique et archéologique précédée de recherches nouvelles sur la vie du saint.* Paris: Alphonse Picard, 1901.

Delgado Gómez, Jaime. *El camino francés de Santiago en su tramo lucense.* N.p.: Hércules/Xunta de Galicia/Consellería de Relacións Institucionais e Portavoz do Goberno, 1993.

Delisle, Léopold. "Les manuscrits de Saint-Martial de Limoges: Réimpression textuelle du catalogue publié en 1730." *Bulletin de la Société archéologique et historique du Limousin* 43 (1895): 1–60.

Delmas, Claire, and Jean-Claude Fau. *Conques.* Millau: du Bellroi, 1989.

Delmas, Ernest. "Une découverte archéologique: La façade de l'Hôpital Saint-Géraud." *Revue de la Haute-Auvergne* 30 (1937–38): 190–92.

Delmas, Guillaume. *Vie de Monseigneur Bouange (Guillaume-Marie-Frédéric), évêque de Langres.* Auch: G. Foix, 1885.

Delzons, Jean-François-Amédée. *Notice historique sur saint Géraud, fondateur de la ville et du monastère d'Aurillac.* Clermont-Ferrand: Perol, 1845.

———. *Origine de la ville d'Aurillac.* Clermont-Ferrand: Ferdinand Thibaud, 1862.

De Mérindol, Christian. "Le soin des malades dans un monastère de fondation franque: Corbie en Picardie (VIIe–XIVe siècles)." In *Fondations et oeuvres charitables au moyen âge,* ed. Jean Dufour and Henri Platelle. Paris: CTHS, 1999, 185–203.

De Monpalau, Josep. *Vida breu de s. Guerau* (1664). In Enric Claud Girbal, *El santuario de San Geraldo (Sant Grau) del término de la villa de Tossa.* Girona: Paciano Torres, 1884.

Denifle, Henri. *La guerre de cent ans et la désolation des églises, monastères et hôpitaux en France.* 3 vols. Paris: Alphonse Picard, 1899.

De Ribier, Louis. *Montvert: Essai de monographie communale.* Paris: Édouard Champion, 1925.

Deribier-du-Châtelet, Jean-Baptiste. *Dictionnaire statistique, ou histoire, description et statistique du département du Cantal.* 5 vols. Aurillac: V. Picut, 1852.

Devlin, Judith. *The Superstitious Mind: French Peasants and the Supernatural in the Nineteenth Century.* New Haven, Conn.: Yale University Press, 1987.

Diem, Albrecht. *Das monastische Experiment: Die Rolle der Keuschheit bei der Entstehung des westlichen Klosterwesens.* Münster: LIT, 2005.

Dierkens, Alain. "Du bon (et du mauvais) usage des reliquaires au Moyen Âge." In *Les reliques: Objets, cultes, symboles*, ed. Edina Bozóky and Anne-Marie Helvétius. Actes du colloque international de l'Université du Littoral-Côte d'Opale (Boulogne-sur-Mer) 4–6 septembre 1997. Turnhout: Brepols, 1999.

———. "Les funerailles royales carolingiennes." In *La sacralisation du pouvoir: Images et mises en scène*, ed. Alain Dierkens and Jacques Marx. Brussels: Université libre de Bruxelles, 2003, 45–58.

———. "Martial, Sernin, Trophime et les autres: À propos des évangelisateurs et des apôtres en Gaule. In *Saint-Martial de Limoges: Ambition politique et production culturelle (Xe–XIIIe siècles)*, ed. Claude Andrault-Schmitt. Limoges: Presses universitaires de Limoges, 2006, 25–37.

Diesenberger, Maximilian. "How Collections Shape the Texts: Rewriting and Rearranging *Passions* in Carolingian Bavaria." In *Livrets, collections et textes: Études sur la tradition hagiographique latine*, ed. Martin Heinzelmann. Ostfildern: Jan Thorbecke, 2006, 195–224.

Dolbeau, François. "Les hagiographes au travail: Collecte et traitement des documents écrits (IXe–XIIe siècles)." In *Manuscrits hagiographiques et travail des hagiographes*, ed. Martin Heinzelmann. Sigmaringen: Jan Thorbecke, 1992, 49–76.

Dominique de Jésus [Géraud Viguier]. *Histoire parænetique des trois saincts protecteurs du Haut Auvergne.* Paris: Chez Claude Sonnius, 1635.

Dormeier, Heinrich. "Un santo nuovo contro la peste: Cause del successo del culto di san Rocco e promotori della sua diffusione al Nord delle Alpi." In *San Rocco: Genesi e prima espansione di un culto*, ed. Antonio Rigon and André Vauchez. Brussels: Société des Bollandistes, 2006, 225–43.

Dubois, Jacques. "La vie quotidienne dans les prieurés au moyen âge." In *Prieurs et prieurés dans l'occident médiéval*, ed. Jean-Loup Lemaître. Geneva: Droz, 1987, 95–114.

Dubourg, Jacques. *Les guerres de religion dans le sud-ouest.* Luçon: Sud-ouest, 1992.

Dubourg-Noves, Pierre. "Eglise de Monsempron." *Congrès archéologique de France, 127e session, 1969, Agen.* Paris: Société française d'archéologie, 1969, 242–58.

Dubreucq, Alain. "La littérature des *specula*: Délimitation du genre, contenu, destinataires et réception.'" In *Guerriers et moines: Conversion et sainteté aristocratiques dans l'occident médiéval (IXe–XIIe siècle)*, ed. Michel Lauwers. Antibes: APDCA, 2002, 17–39.

Duby, Georges. *The Early Growth of the European Economy: Warriors and Peasants from the Seventh to the Twelfth Century.* Trans. Howard B. Clarke. Ithaca, N.Y.: Cornell University Press, 1974.

———. *L'économie rurale et la vie des campagnes dans l'occident médiéval.* 1962; Paris: Flammarion, 1977.

———. "The Origins of Knighthood." In *The Chivalrous Society*. Trans. Cynthia Postan. London: Edward Arnold, 1977, 158–70.

———. "The Structure of Kinship and Nobility: Northern France in the Eleventh and Twelfth Centuries." In *The Chivalrous Society*. Trans. Cynthia Postan. London: Edward Arnold, 1977, 134–48.

———. *The Three Orders: Feudal Society Imagined.* Trans. Arthur Goldhammer. Chicago: University of Chicago Press, 1980.

Duckett, Eleanor. *Death and Life in the Tenth Century.* Ann Arbor: University of Michigan Press, 1967.

Dufour, Jean. *La bibliothèque et le scriptorium de Moissac.* Geneva: Droz, 1972.

———. "Essai de simplification de la liste épiscopale de Rodez pour les IXe et Xe siècles." *Revue du Rouergue* n.s. 10 (1987): 163–74.

Duhamel-Amado, Claudie. "Le *miles conversus et fundator:* De Guillaume de Gellone à Pons de Léras." In *Guerriers et moines: Conversion et sainteté aristocratiques dans l'occident médiéval (IXe–XIIe siècle),* ed. Michel Lauwers. Antibes: APDCA, 2002, 419–27.

Dunbabin, Jean. *France in the Making, 843–1180.* Oxford: Oxford University Press, 1985.

Duplès-Agier, Henri, ed. *Chroniques de Saint-Martial de Limoges.* Paris: Jules Renouard, 1874.

Dupré, Louis. *Symbols of the Sacred.* Grand Rapids, Mich.: William B. Eerdmans, 2000.

Durand, Alfred. *Aurillac: Géographie urbaine.* Aurillac: Moderne, 1946.

Durliat, Marcel. "Saint-Géraud d'Aurillac aux époques preromane et romane." *Revue de la Haute-Auvergne* 43 (1973): 329–42.

Durot, J.-Henri. *Histoire de sainte Procule et de son culte.* Gannat: F. Marion, 1888.

Dutton, Paul Edward. "Charlemagne's Mustache." In *Charlemagne's Mustache and Other Cultural Clusters of a Dark Age.* New York: Palgrave Macmillan, 2004, 3–42.

Emerson, John A. "Two Newly Identified Offices for Saints Valeria and Austriclinianus by Ademar de Chabannes (Ms. Paris, Bibl. Nat., Latin 909, Fols. 79–85v)." *Speculum* 40, no. 1 (1965): 31–46.

Emery, Elizabeth. *Romancing the Cathedral: Gothic Architecture in Fin-de-Siècle French Culture.* Albany: State University of New York Press, 2001.

———. "The 'Truth' about the Middle Ages: *La Revue des Deux Mondes* and Late Nineteenth-Century French Medievalism." In *Medievalism and the Quest for the "Real" Middle Ages,* ed. Clare A. Simmons. London: Frank Cass, 2001, 99–114.

Emery, Elizabeth, and Laura Morowitz. *Consuming the Past: The Medieval Revival in Fin-de-siècle France.* London: Ashgate, 2003.

Emery, Elizabeth, and Laurie Postlewate, eds. *Medieval Saints in Late Nineteenth Century French Culture: Eight Essays.* Jefferson, N.C.: McFarland, 2004.

Erdman, Carl. *Die Entstehung des Kreuzzugsgedankens.* Stuttgart: W. Kohlhammer, 1935.

Esteban i Darder, Vicenç. "Tota una història: Sant Grau." *Turissa,* no. 13 (1993): 3–5.

Estève, Christian. "Le souvenir de la Révolution et la vie politique au XIXe siècle dans le Cantal: L'exemple de la deuxième république." *Revue de la Haute-Auvergne* 55 (1993): 341–68.

Evans, Joan. *Monastic Iconography in France: From the Renaissance to the Revolution.* Cambridge: Cambridge University Press, 1970.

Fabre, Geraldine. "Inventaire archéologique du canton de Réalmont." Memoire de maîtrise, Université de Toulouse-Le Mirail, 1987–88.

Facciotto, Paolo. "Moments et lieux de la tradition manuscrite de la *Vita Geraldi.*" In *Guerriers et moines: Conversion et sainteté aristocratiques dans l'occident médiéval (IXe–XIIe siècle),* ed. Michel Lauwers. Antibes: APDCA, 2002, 217–33.

———. "Il *Sermo de festivitate s. Geraldi* di Oddone di Cluny." *Hagiographica* 3 (1996): 113–36.

Farmer, Sharon. *Communities of Saint Martin: Legend and Ritual in Medieval Tours.* Ithaca, N.Y.: Cornell University Press, 1991.

Fau, Jean-Claude. *Rouergue roman.* Paris: Zodiaque, 1990.

Faugeras, Marius. "Les fidelités en France au XIXe siècle: Les Zouaves pontificaux (1860–1870)." *Enquêtes et documents* 11 (1986): 275–303.

Favreau, Robert, Jean Michaud, and Bernadette Mora, eds. *Corpus des inscriptions de la France médiévale.* Vol. 18, *Allier, Cantal, Loire, Haute-Loire, Puy-de-Dôme.* Paris: CNRS, 1995.

Féraud, J.-J.-M. *Histoire civile, politique, religieuse et biographique de Manosque.* Digne[-les-Bains]: Repos, 1848.

———. *Les saintes reliques de la Chapelle du Château de Manosque.* Digne-les-Bains: Barbaroux, Chaspoul et Constans, 1885.

Ferreira, Manuel Pedro. "Two Offices for St. Gerald: Braga and Aurillac." In *Commemoration, Ritual and Performance: Essays in Medieval and Early Modern Music,* ed. Jane Morlet Hardie. Ottawa: Institute of Medieval Music, 2006, 37–47.

Fini, Maria Luisa. "L'*Editio minor* della '*Vita*' di Oddone di Cluny e gli apporti dell'*Humillimus*: Testo critico e nuovi orientamenti." *L'archiginnasio: Bolletino della Biblioteca communale di Bologna* 63–65 (1968–70): 132–259.

———. "Studio sulla *Vita Odonis* reformata di Nalgodo: Il *fragmentum mutilum* del Codice latino n.a. 1496 della Bibliothèque nationale di Parigi." *Atti della Accademia delle Scienze dell'Istituto di Bologna* 63, no. 2 (1975): 33–147.

Fletcher, R. A. *Saint James's Catapult: The Life and Times of Diego Gelmirez of Santiago de Compostela.* Oxford: Clarendon, 1984.

Flodoard of Rheims. *Annals.* Trans. Steven Fanning and Bernard S. Bachrach. Peterborough: Broadview, 2004.

Flohic, Jean-Luc, ed. *Le patrimoine des communes de la méridienne verte.* Paris: Flohic, 2000.

Flori, Jean. *L'idéologie du glaive: Préhistoire de la chevalerie.* Geneva: Droz, 1983.

Forsyth, Ilene. *The Throne of Wisdom: Wood Sculptures of the Madonna in Romanesque France.* Princeton, N.J.: Princeton University Press, 1972.

Forth, Christopher E. *The Dreyfus Affair and the Crisis of French Manhood.* Baltimore, Md.: Johns Hopkins University Press, 2004.

"Les fouilles de février-mars 1954 au prieuré de Saint-Géraud de Montgardin." Unidentified newspaper clipping from the archives of the church of Montgardin, 1954.

Fouracre, Paul. "Merovingian History and Merovingian Hagiography." *Past and Present,* no. 127 (1990): 3–38.

Fouracre, Paul, and Richard A. Gerberding, eds. *Late Merovingian France: History and Hagiography, 640–720.* Manchester: Manchester University Press, 1996.

Fournier, Gabriel. "Saint Géraud et son temps." *Revue de la Haute-Auvergne* 43 (1973): 342–53.

Foviaux, Jacques. "De la dépendance à l'autonomie: Prieurs et prieurés de 1285 a 1392." In *Prieurs et prieurés dans l'occident médiéval,* ed. Jean-Loup Lemaître. Geneva: Droz, 1987, 137–60.

Fraïsse, Chantal. "Un traité des vertus et des vices illustré à Moissac dans la première moitié du XIe siècle." *Cahiers de civilisation médiévale* 42 (1999): 221–42.

Frassetto, Michael. "The Art of Forgery: The Sermons of Ademar of Chabannes and the Cult of St. Martial of Limoges." *Comitatus* 26 (1995): 11–26.

———. "Heresy, Celibacy, and Reform in the Sermons of Ademar of Chabannes." In *Medieval Purity and Piety: Essays on Medieval Clerical Celibacy and Religious Reform,* ed. Michael Frassetto. New York: Garland, 1998, 131–48.

———. "Heretics, Antichrists, and the Year 1000: Apocalyptic Expectations in the Writings of Ademar of Chabannes." In *The Year 1000: Religious and Social Responses to the Turning of the First Millenium,* ed. Michael Frassetto. New York: Palgrave Macmillan, 2002, 73–84.

———. "Violence, Knightly Piety and the Peace of God Movement in Aquitaine." In *The Final Argument: The Imprint of Violence on Society in Medieval and Early Modern Europe,* ed. Donald J. Kagay and L. J. Andrew Villalon. Woodbridge: Boydell, 1998, 13–26.

Fray, Sébastien. "Le véritable fondateur de Saint-Géraud d'Aurillac: Odon ou Géraud?" *Revue de la Haute-Auvergne* 72 (2010): 23–45.

Freedberg, David. *The Power of Images: Studies in the History and Theory of Response*. Chicago: University of Chicago Press, 1989.

Fried, Johannes. "Endzeiterwartung um die Jahrtausendwende." *Deutsches Archiv für Erforschung des Mittelalters* 45 (1989): 381–473.

Friesen, Ilse E. *The Female Crucifix: Images of St. Wilgefortis since the Middle Ages*. Waterloo: Wilfrid Laurier University Press, 2001.

Frontón, Isabel. *El arte románico en el camino de Santiago: El arte de viajar*. Madrid: Jaguar, n.d.

Fumagalli, Vito. "Note sulla 'Vita Geraldi' di Odone di Cluny." *Bolletino dell'Istituto storico italiano per il medio evo e Archivio Muratoriano* 76 (1964): 217–40.

Gaborit-Chopin, Danielle. *La décoration des manuscrits à Saint-Martial de Limoges et en Limousin du IXe au XIIe siècle*. Mémoires et documents publiés par la Société de l'École des Chartes, 18. Paris: Librairie Droz, 1969.

———. "Les dessins d'Adémar de Chabannes." *Bulletin archéologique*, n.s. 3 (1968): 163–225.

Gajano, Sofia Boesch. "Uso e abuso del miracolo nella cultura altomedioevale." In *Les fonctions des saints dans le monde occidental (IIIe–XIIIe siècle)*, ed. Jean-Yves Tilliette et al. Rome: École française de Rome, 1991, 109–22.

Gaposchkin, M. Cecilia. *The Making of Saint Louis: Kingship, Sanctity, and Crusade in the Later Middle Ages*. Ithaca, N.Y.: Cornell University Press, 2008.

Garrigoux, Alice. "Une ville en révolution: Les Jacobins d'Aurillac (1790–1795)." *Revue de la Haute-Auvergne* 52 (1989): 37–85.

Garver, Valerie L. *Women and Aristocratic Culture in the Carolingian World*. Ithaca, N.Y: Cornell University Press, 2009.

Gaussin, Pierre-Roger. *Huit siècles d'histoire: L'Abbaye de la Chaise-Dieu, 1043–1790*. Brioude: Almanach, 1967.

Geary, Patrick. *Aristocracy in Provence: The Rhône Basin at the Dawn of the Carolingian Age*. Philadelphia: University of Pennsylvania Press, 1985.

———. *Living with the Dead in the Middle Ages*. Ithaca, N.Y.: Cornell University Press, 1994.

———. "The Ninth-Century Relic Trade: A Response to Popular Piety?" In *Religion and the People, 800–1700*, ed. James Obelkevich. Chapel Hill: University of North Carolina Press, 1979, 8–19.

———. *Phantoms of Remembrance: Memory and Oblivion at the End of the First Millennium*. Princeton, N.J.: Princeton University Press, 1994.

———. "Sacred Commodities: The Circulation of Medieval Relics." In *Commodities and Cultures*, ed. Arjun Appadurai. Cambridge: Cambridge University Press, 1986, 169–91.

Gerbeau, Lucien. "Dans la tourmente: Décadence, guerres de religion, réforme catholique (XVIe–début XVIIe siècle)." In *Saint-Géraud d'Aurillac: Onze siècles d'histoire*, ed. Édouard Bouyé et al. Aurillac: Association des amis du patrimoine de Haute-Auvergne, 2009, 47–125.

Germer-Durand, M. E. *Dictionnaire topographique du département du Gard*. Paris: Imprimerie nationale, 1868.

Gerson, Stéphane. *The Pride of Place: Local Memories and Political Culture in Nineteenth-Century France*. Ithaca, N.Y.: Cornell University Press, 2003.

Gibson, Ralph. *A Social History of French Catholicism, 1789–1914*. London: Routledge, 1989.

Girbal, Enric Claudi. *El santuario de San Gerardo (Sant Grau) del término de la villa de Tossa*. Girona: Paciano Torres, 1884.

Gitlitz, David M. and Linda Kay Davidson. *The Pilgrimage Road to Santiago: The Complete Cultural Handbook*. New York: St Martin's Griffin, 2000.

Gobillot, Philippe. "Sur la tonsure chrétienne et ses prétendues origines païennes." *Revue d'histoire ecclésiastique* 21 (1925): 399–454.

Goetz, Hans-Werner. "Protection of the Church, Defense of the Law, and Reform: On the Purposes and Character of the Peace of God, 989–1038." In *The Peace of God: Social Violence and Religious Response in France around the Year 1000*, ed. Thomas Head and Richard Landes. Ithaca, N.Y.: Cornell University Press, 1992, 259–79.

González Bueno, Antonio. *El entorno sanitario del camino de Santiago*. Madrid: Cátedra, 1994.

Gough, Austin. *Paris and Rome: The Gallican Church and the Ultramontane Campaign, 1848–1853*. Oxford: Clarendon, 1986.

Grafton, Anthony. *Forgers and Critics: Creativity and Duplicity in Western Scholarship*. Princeton, N.J.: Princeton University Press, 1990.

Grand, Roger. "Un épisode de la restitution des biens d'église usurpés par les laïques dans le haut moyen age." *Revue historique de droit français et étranger* 29 (1934): 219–75.

———. *Les "paix" d'Aurillac: Étude et documents sur l'histoire des institutions municipales d'une ville à consulat (XIIe–XVe siècle)*. Paris: Société d'histoire du droit, 1901.

———. "La sculpture et l'architecture romanes à Saint-Géraud d'Aurillac: Nouvelles recherches, nouveaux aperçus." In *Mélanges en hommage à la mémoire de Fr. Martroye*. Paris: C. Klincksieck, 1941, 239–67.

Grier, James. *The Musical World of a Medieval Monk: Ademar de Chabannes in Eleventh-Century Aquitaine*. Cambridge: Cambridge University Press, 2006.

Grimmer, Claude. *Vivre à Aurillac au XVIIIe siècle*. Aurillac: Gerbert, 1983.

Guillaume, Paul. "Règlement des Prieurés de Saillans et d'Aspres-sur-Buëch." *Bulletin de la Société d'études des Hautes-Alpes*, no. 4 (1885): 382–94.

Guillemin, Henri. *Histoire des catholiques français au XIXe siècle (1815–1905)*. Geneva: Milieu du monde, 1947.

Guillot, Olivier. "Formes, fondements et limites de l'organisation politique en France au Xe siècle." In *Il secolo di ferro: Mito e realtà del secolo X*. Spoleto: Centro italiano di studi sull'alto medioevo, 1991, 1: 57–116.

Hahn, Cynthia. "Picturing the Text: Narrative in the Life of the Saints." *Art History* 13, no. 1 (1990): 1–33.

———. "Seeing and Believing: The Construction of Sanctity in Early-Medieval Saints' Shrines." *Speculum* 72, no. 4 (1997): 1079–1106.

Hall, Edwin, and Horst Uhr. "*Aureola super Auream*: Crowns and Related Symbols of Special Distinction for Saints in Late Gothic and Renaissance Iconography." *Art Bulletin* 67, no. 4 (1985): 567–603.

Hallinger, Kassius. "The Spiritual Life of Cluny in the Early Days." In *Cluniac Monasticism in the Central Middle Ages*, ed. Noreen Hunt. Hamden, Conn.: Archon, 1971, 29–55.

Hamlin, Frank R. *Les noms de lieux du département de l'Hérault: Nouveau dictionnaire topographique et étymologique*. Mèze: privately printed, 1983.

———. *Toponymie de l'Hérault: Dictionnaire topographique et étymologique*. Millau: Bellfroi, 2000.

Hanna, Martha. "Iconology and Ideology: Images of Joan of Arc in the Idiom of the *Action française*, 1908–1931." *French Historical Studies* 14, no. 2 (1985): 215–39.

Hargrove, June. "Shaping the National Image: The Cult of Statues to Great Men in the Third Republic." In *Nationalism in the Visual Arts*, ed. Richard A. Etlin. Hanover, N.H.: University Press of New England, 1991, 49–63.

Hauréau, Jean-Barthélemy. *Histoire littéraire du Maine*. 10 vols. 1870–77; Geneva: Slatkine, 1969.

Head, Thomas. "The Cult of Relics in the Eleventh Century." In *Medieval Hagiography: An Anthology*, ed. Thomas Head. New York: Garland, 2000.

———. "The Development of the Peace of God in Aquitaine (970–1005)." *Speculum* 74, no. 3 (1999): 656–86.

———. *Hagiography and the Cult of Saints: The Diocese of Orléans, 800–1200.* Cambridge: Cambridge University Press, 1990.

———. "Letaldus of Micy and the Hagiographic Traditions of the Abbey of Nouaillé: The Context of the *Delatio corporis s. Juniani.*" *Analecta Bollandiana* 115 (1997): 253–67.

Hebers, Klaus. *Política y veneración de santos en la península ibérica: Desarollo del "Santiago político."* Trans. Rafael Vazquez Ruano. Pontevedra: Fundación cultural Rutas de románico, 1999.

Heene, Katrien. "*Audire, legere, vulgo*: An Attempt to Define Public Use and Comprehensibility of Carolingian Hagiography." In *Latin and the Romance Languages in the Early Middle Ages,* ed. Roger Wright. London: Routledge, 1991, 146–63.

Heinzelmann, Martin. "Manuscrits hagiographiques et travail des hagiographes: L'exemple de la tradition manuscrite des Vies anciennes de Sainte Geneviève de Paris." In *Manuscrits hagiographiques et travail des hagiographes,* ed. Martin Heinzelmann. Sigmaringen: Jan Thorbecke, 1992, 9–16.

———. "Sanctitas und 'Tugendadel': Zu Konzeptionen von 'Heiligkeit' im 5. und 10. Jahrhundert." *Francia* 5 (1977): 741–52.

Helgaud of Fleury. *Vie de Robert le Pieux (Epitoma vitae regis Roberti Pii).* Ed. Robert-Henri Bautier and Gillette Labory. Paris: Centre national de la recherche scientifique, 1965.

Helvétius, Anne-Marie. "Le récit de vengeance des saints dans l'hagiographie franque (VIe–IXe siècle)." In *La vengeance, 400–1200,* ed. Dominique Barthélemy et al. Rome: Collection de l'École française de Rome, 2006, 421–50.

Herrick, Samantha Kahn. *Imagining the Sacred Past: Hagiography and Power in Early Normandy.* Cambridge, Mass.: Harvard University Press, 2007.

———. "Studying Apostolic Hagiography: The Case of Fronto of Périgueux, Disciple of Christ." *Speculum* 85, no. 2 (2010): 235–70.

Hill, Raymond Thompson, and Thomas Goddard Bergin. *Anthology of the Provençal Troubadours: Texts, Notes, and Vocabulary.* New Haven, Conn.: Yale University Press, 1941.

Hoch, Adrian S. "St. Martin of Tours: His Transformation into a Chivalric Hero and Franciscan Ideal." *Zeitschrift für Kunstgeschichte* 50, no. 4 (1987): 471–82.

Hoefer, M., ed. *Nouvelle biographie générale: Depuis les temps les plus reculés jusqu'à nos jours.* Paris: Firmin Didot, 1866.

Hooreman, Paul. "Saint-Martial de Limoges au temps de l'abbé Odolric (1025–1040)." *Revue belge de musicologie* 3 (1949): 5–36.

Hostache, Marius. *Souvenirs des montagnes d'Oisans.* Grenoble: Roche, 1975.

Hourlier, Dom Jacques. "L'entrée de Moissac dans l'ordre de Cluny." In *Moissac et l'occident au XIe siècle,* ed. Édouard Privat. Actes du colloque international de Moissac, 3–5 mai 1963. Toulouse: Centre national de la recherche scientifique/Université de Toulouse, 1964, 25–33.

Howe, John. "The Nobility's Reform of the Medieval Church." *American Historical Review* 93, no. 2 (1988): 317–39.

Hubert, Jean, and Marie-Clothilde Hubert. "Piété chrétienne ou paganisme? Les statues-reliquaires de l'Europe carolingienne." In *Cristianizzazione ed organizzazione ecclesiastica delle campagne nell'alto medioevo: Espansione e resistenze.* Spoleto: Centro italiano di studi sull'alto medioevo, 1982, 235–75.

Huidobro y Serna, Luciano. *Las peregrinaciones jacobeas.* Vol. 3. Madrid: Instituto de España, 1951.

Innes, Matthew. "'A Place of Discipline': Carolingian Courts and Aristocratic Youth." In *Court Culture in the Early Middle Ages*, ed. Catherine Cubitt. Proceedings of the First Alcuin Conference. Turnhout: Brepols, 2003, 59–76.

Iogna-Prat, Dominique. "Le 'baptême' du schéma des trois ordres fonctionnels: L'apport de l'école d'Auxerre dans la seconde moitié du IXe siècle." *Annales: Économies, sociétés, civilisations* 41 (1986): 101–26.

———. "Cluny comme 'système ecclésial.'" In *Die Cluniazenser in ihrem politisch-sozialen Umfeld*, ed. Giles Constable et al. Münster: LIT, 1998, 7–92.

———. *Études clunisiennes*. Paris: Picard, 2002.

———. "Hagiographie, théologie et théocratie dans le Cluny de l'an mil." In *Les fonctions des saints dans le monde occidental (IIIe–XIIIe siècle)*, ed. Jean-Yves Tilliette et al. Rome: École française de Rome, 1991, 241–57.

———. "La Madeleine du *Sermo in veneratione sanctae Mariae Magdalenae* attribué à Odon de Cluny." *Mélanges de l'École française de Rome: Moyen âge* 104 (1992): 37–70.

———. "Panorama de l'hagiographie abbatiale clunisienne (v. 940–v. 1140)." In *Manuscrits hagiographiques et travail des hagiographes*, ed. Martin Heinzelmann. Sigmaringen: Jan Thorbecke, 1992, 77–118.

———. "La place idéale du laïc à Cluny (v. 930–v. 1150): D'une morale statutaire à une éthique absolue?" In *Guerriers et moines: Conversion et sainteté aristocratiques dans l'occident médiéval (IXe–XIIe siècle)*, ed. Michel Lauwers. Antibes: APDCA, 2002, 291–316.

———. "La *vita Geraldi* d'Odon de Cluny: Un texte fondateur?" In *Guerriers et moines: Conversion et sainteté aristocratiques dans l'occident médiéval (IXe–XIIe siècle)*, ed. Michel Lauwers. Antibes: APDCA, 2002, 143–55.

Irvine, William D. *The Boulanger Affair Reconsidered: Royalism, Boulangism, and the Origins of the Radical Right in France*. Oxford: Oxford University Press, 1989.

Iung, Jean-Eric. "Autour de Saint-Géraud d'Aurillac au temps des derniers chanoines." *Revue de la Haute-Auvergne* 58 (1996): 167–86.

———. "Des prieurés lointains de Saint-Géraud d'Aurillac: Saint-Géraud de Saillans et Saint-Pierre de Varen." *Revue de la Haute-Auvergne* 64 (2002): 305–15.

———. "La statue de Gerbert à Aurillac." In *Gerbert l'européen*, ed. Nicole Charbonnel and Jean-Eric Iung. Acts du colloque d'Aurillac, 4–7 juin 1996. Aurillac: Gerbert, 1997, 285–305.

Jacobsen, Werner. "Saints' Tombs in Frankish Church Architecture." *Speculum* 72, no. 4 (1997): 1107–43.

Jacomet, Humbert. "Pèlerinage et culte de saint Jacques en France: Bilan et perspectives." In *Pèlerinages et croisades*. Actes du 118e congrès national annuel des sociétés historiques et scientifiques (Pau, 1993). Paris: CTHS, 1995, 83–199.

Jaeger, C. Stephen. *The Envy of Angels: Cathedral Schools and Social Ideals in Medieval Europe, 950–1200*. Philadelphia: University of Pennsylvania Press, 1994.

Jestice, Phyllis G. "A New Fashion in Imitating Christ: Changing Spiritual Perspectives around the Year 1000." In *The Year 1000: Religious and Social Responses to the Turning of the First Millenium*, ed. Michael Frassetto. New York: Palgrave Macmillan, 2002, 165–85.

———. "Why Celibacy? Odo of Cluny and the Development of a New Sexual Morality." In *Medieval Purity and Piety: Essays on Medieval Clerical Celibacy and Religious Reform*, ed. Michael Frassetto. New York: Garland, 1998, 81–115.

Joblin, Alain. "L'attitude des protestants face aux reliques." In *Les reliques: Objets, cultes, symboles*, ed. Edina Bozóky and Anne-Marie Helvétius. Actes du colloque international de l'Université du Littoral-Côte d'Opale (Boulogne-sur-Mer) 4–6 septembre 1997. Turnhout: Brepols, 1999.

John of Salerno. *Vita sancti Odonis. PL* 133: 43–86. Gerard Sitwell, trans., *St. Odo of Cluny: Being the Life of St. Odo of Cluny by John of Salerno and the Life of St. Gerald of Aurillac by St. Odo*. London: Sheed and Ward, 1958.

Jonas, Raymond. *France and the Cult of the Sacred Heart: An Epic Tale for Modern Times*. Berkeley: University of California Press, 2000.

Jones, Anna Trumbore. "Discovering the Aquitanian Church in the Corpus of Ademar of Chabannes." *Haskins Society Journal* 19 (2007): 82–98.

———. "Lay Magnates, Religious Houses, and the Role of the Bishop in Aquitaine (877–1050)." In *The Bishop Reformed: Studies of Episcopal Power and Culture in the Central Middle Ages*, ed. John S. Ott and Anna Trumbore Jones. London: Ashgate, 2007, 21–39.

———. *Noble Lord, Good Shepherd: Episcopal Power and Piety in Aquitaine, 877–1050*. Leiden: Brill, 2009.

———. "Pitying the Desolation of Such a Place: Rebuilding Religious Houses and Constructing Memory in Aquitaine in the Wake of the Viking Incursions." *Viator* 37 (2006): 85–102.

Jones, Christopher A. "Monastic Identity and Sodomitic Danger in the *Occupatio* by Odo of Cluny." *Speculum* 82, no. 1 (2007): 1–53.

Jones, P. M. "Parish, Seigneurie and the Community of Inhabitants in Southern Central France During the Eighteenth and Nineteenth Centuries." *Past and Present*, no. 91 (1981): 74–108.

Joubert, Édouard. *L'Abbaye bénédictine de Saint-Géraud d'Aurillac (894–1561)*. Aurillac: Moderne, 1981.

———. *La colline inspirée d'Aurillac: L'Abbaye bénédictine de Saint-Jean-du-Buis (1289–1792)*. Aurillac: Moderne, 1966.

———. "Le conseil municipal d'Aurillac et la restauration de l'Église Saint-Géraud au XIXe siècle." *Revue de la Haute-Auvergne* 39 (1965): 513–24.

———. *Les guerres de religion à Aurillac (1569–1610)*. Aurillac: Moderne, 1984.

———. *Notre-Dame-aux-Neiges*. Aurillac: Moderne, 1964.

———. "Quelques visites pastorales en Haute Auvergne au XVIIe et XVIIIe siècles." *Revue de la Haute-Auvergne* 46 (1977): 61–70.

———. *Saint Géraud d'Aurillac*. Aurillac: Gerbert, 1968.

Juillet, Jacques. "Les domaines du comte Géraud au pays des quatre rivières." *Revue de la Haute-Auvergne* 43 (1973): 353–76.

Kaeuper, Richard W. *Chivalry and Violence in Medieval Europe*. Oxford: Oxford University Press, 1999.

Kaiser, Reinhold. *Bischofsherrschaft zwischen Königtum und Fürstenmacht: Studien zur bischöflichen Stadtherrschaft im westfränkisch-französischen Reich im frühen und hohen Mittelalter*. Bonn: Ludwig Röhrscheid, 1981.

Kale, Steven D. *Legitimism and the Reconstruction of French Society, 1852–1883*. Baton Rouge: Louisiana State University Press, 1992.

Kicklighter, Joseph A. "Les monastères de Gascogne et le conflit franco-anglais (1270–1327)." *Annales du Midi* 91 (1979): 121–33.

Knapp, Vincent J. *Disease and Its Impact on Modern European History*. Lewiston, Md.: Edwin Mellen, 1989.

Knicely, Carol. "Food for Thought in the Souillac Pillar: Devouring Beasts, Pain and the Subversion of Heroic Codes of Violence." *RACAR: Revue d'art canadienne/Canadian Art Review* 24, no. 2 (1997): 14–37.

Knowles, David. "Cistercians and Cluniacs: The Controversy Between Saint Bernard and Peter the Venerable." In *The Historian and Character*. Cambridge: Cambridge University Press, 1963, 50–75.

Kselman, Thomas A. *Miracles and Prophecies in Nineteenth-Century France*. New Brunswick, N.J.: Rutgers University Press, 1983.

Kubach, Hans Erich. *Romanesque Architecture*. Milan: Electa, 1978.

Kuchenbuch, Ludolf. "*Opus feminile*: Das Geschlechterverhältnis im Spiegel von Frauenarbeiten im früheren Mittelalter." In *Weibliche Lebensgestaltung im früheren Mittelalter*, ed. Hans-Werner Goetz. Cologne: Böhlau, 1991, 139–75.

Kuefler, Mathew. "Dating and Authorship of the Writings about Saint Gerald of Aurillac." *Viator* 44, no. 2 (2013): 49–98.

———. "How the Holy Grail Ended up in O Cebreiro, Galicia." *Brocar: Cuadernas de investigación histórica*, no. 36 (2012): 53–64.

———. "Les histoires de Géraud d'Aurillac." In *Sur les pas de Géraud d'Aurillac en France et en Espagne: Histoire, culte et iconographie*, ed. Pierre Moulier. Saint-Flour: Cantal patrimoine, 2010, 21–40.

———. *The Manly Eunuch: Masculinity, Gender Ambiguity, and Christian Ideology in Late Antiquity*. Chicago: University of Chicago Press, 2001.

Labande, Edmond-René. "La formation de Gerbert à St-Géraud d'Aurillac. In *Gerberto: Scienza, storia e mito*, ed. Michele Tosi. Bobbio: Archivi Storici Bobiensi, 1985, 21–34.

Lambert, Malcolm. *Medieval Heresy: Popular Movements from the Gregorian Reform to the Reformation*. 3rd ed. Oxford: Blackwell, 2002.

Landes, Richard. "Autour d'Ademar de Chabannes († 1034): Précisions chronologiques au sujet du Limousin vers l'an mil." *Bulletin de la Société archéologique et historique du Limousin* 122 (1994): 23–54.

———. "Between Aristocracy and Heresy: Popular Participation in the Limousin Peace of God, 994–1033." In *The Peace of God: Social Violence and Religious Response in France around the Year 1000*, ed. Thomas Head and Richard Landes. Ithaca, N.Y.: Cornell University Press, 1992, 184–218.

———. "The Dynamics of Heresy and Reform in Limoges: A Study of Popular Participation in the 'Peace of God' (994–1033)." *Historical Reflections/Réflexions historiques* 14 (1987): 467–511.

———. "A *Libellus* from St. Martial of Limoges Written in the Time of Ademar of Chabannes (989–1034): Un faux à retardement." *Scriptorium* 37 (1983): 178–204.

———. *Relics, Apocalypse, and the Deceits of History: Ademar of Chabannes, 989–1034*. Cambridge, Mass.: Harvard University Press, 1995.

Landes, Richard, and Catherine Paupert. *Naissance d'apôtre: La vie de saint Martial de Limoges*. Turnhout: Brepols, 1991.

Lauranson-Rosaz, Christian. "Entre deux mondes: L'Auvergne de Gerbert." In *Gerbert l'européen*, ed. Nicole Charbonnel and Jean-Eric Iung. Acts du colloque d'Aurillac, 4–7 juin 1996. Aurillac: Gerbert, 1997, 33–52.

———. "L'Auvergne au Xe siècle: Terre de 'romanité.'" *Revue de la Haute-Auvergne* 61 (1999): 9–20.

———. *L'Auvergne et ses marges (Velay, Gévaudan) du VIIIe au XIe siècle: La fin du monde antique?* Le Puy-en-Velay: Les cahiers de la Haute-Loire, 1987.

————. "Les origines d'Odon de Cluny." *Cahiers de civilisation médiévale* 37 (1994): 255–67.

————. "Peace from the Mountains: The Auvergnat Origins of the Peace of God." In *The Peace of God: Social Violence and Religious Response in France around the Year 1000*, ed. Thomas Head and Richard Landes. Ithaca, N.Y.: Cornell University Press, 1992, 104–34.

————. "La vie de Géraud d'Aurillac: Vecteur d'une certaine conscience aristocratique dans le midi de la Gaule." In *Guerriers et moines: Conversion et sainteté aristocratiques dans l'occident médiéval (IXe–XIIe siècle)*, ed. Michel Lauwers. Antibes: APDCA, 2002, 157–81.

Lauwers, Michel. "La 'vie du seigneur Bouchard, comte vénérable': Conflits d'avouerie, traditions carolingiennes et modèles de sainteté à l'Abbaye des Fosses au XIe siècle." In *Guerriers et moines: Conversion et sainteté aristocratiques dans l'occident médiéval (IXe–XIIe siècle)*, ed. Michel Lauwers. Antibes: APDCA, 2002, 371–418.

————. "La *Vita Wicberti* de Sigebert de Gembloux: Modèles ecclésiologiques et revendications locales en Lotharingie à la fin du XIe siècle." In *Guerriers et moines: Conversion et sainteté aristocratiques dans l'occident médiéval (IXe–XIIe siècle)*, ed. Michel Lauwers. Antibes: APDCA, 2002, 493–500.

Leclercq, Jean. "The Monastic Crisis of the Eleventh and Twelfth Centuries." In *Cluniac Monasticism in the Central Middle Ages*, ed. Noreen Hunt. Hamden, Conn.: Archon, 1971, 217–37.

————. "Recherches sur d'anciens sermons monastiques." *Revue Mabillon* 36 (1946): 1–14.

Le Gall, Jean-Marie. *Les moines au temps des réformes (1480–1560)*. Seysell: Champ Vallon, 2001.

Le Goff, Jacques. "Ordres mendiants et urbanisation dans la France médiévale: État de l'enquête." *Annales: Économies, sociétés, civilisations* 25 (1970): 924–46.

Lemaître, Jean-Loup. *Mourir à Saint-Martial: La commémoration des morts et les obituaires à Saint-Martial de Limoges du XIe au XIIIe siècle*. Paris: Boccard, 1989.

Lemarignier, Jean-François. "Structures monastiques et structures politiques dans la France de la fin du Xe et des débuts du XIe siècle." In *Il monachismo nell'alto medioevo e la formazione della civiltà occidentale*. Spoleto: Centro italiano di studi sull'alto medioevo, 1957, 357–400.

Leniaud, Jean-Michel. *La révolution des signes: L'art à l'église (1830–1930)*. Paris: Cerf, 2007.

Leroquais, V. *Les sacramentaires et les missels manuscrits des bibliothèques publiques de France*. 3 vols. Paris, 1924.

Lettres du Cardinal Mazarin pendant son ministère recueillies. Ed. G. d'Avenal. Vol. 8 (July 1657–August 1658). Paris: Imprimerie Nationale, 1894.

Levillain, Léon. "Adémar de Chabannes, généalogiste." *Bulletin de la Société des antiquaires de l'ouest*, 3rd ser., 10 (1934): 237–63.

Leyser, Conrad. "Masculinity in Flux: Nocturnal Emission and the Limits of Celibacy in the Early Middle Ages." In *Masculinity in Medieval Europe*, ed. D. M. Hadley. London: Longman, 1999, 103–20.

Lifshitz, Felice. "Beyond Positivism and Genre: 'Hagiographical' Texts as Historical Narrative." *Viator* 25 (1994): 95–113.

Lobrichon, Guy. "Le culte des saints, le rire des hérétiques, le triomphe des savants." In *Les reliques: Objets, cultes, symboles*, ed. Edina Bozóky and Anne-Marie Helvétius. Actes du colloque international de l'Université du Littoral-Côte d'Opale (Boulogne-sur-Mer) 4–6 septembre 1997. Turnhout: Brepols, 1999.

Locke, Robert R. *French Legitimists and the Politics of the Moral Order in the Early Third Republic*. Princeton, N.J.: Princeton University Press, 1974.

Lotter, Friedrich. "Das Idealbild adliger Laienfrömmigkeit in den Anfängen Clunys: Odos Vita des Grafen Gerald von Aurillac." In *Benedictine Culture, 750–1050*, ed. W. Lourdaux and D. Verhelst. Louvain: Leuven University Press, 1983, 76–95.

Luces de peregrinación. Madrid: Museo arqueológico national/Santiago de Compostela: Museo diocesano y Monasterio de San Martiño Pinario, 2003–4.

Luttrell, Anthony. "The Spiritual Life of the Hospitallers of Rhodes." In *The Hospitaller State on Rhodes and Its Western Provinces, 1306–1462*. Aldershot: Ashgate Variorum, 1999, sec. 9, 75–96.

Lyman, Thomas W. "The Politics of Selective Eclecticism: Monastic Architecture, Pilgrimage Churches, and 'Resistance to Cluny.'" *Gesta* 27, nos. 1–2 (1988): 83–92.

Magnou-Nortier, Élisabeth. "The Enemies of the Peace: Reflections on a Vocabulary, 500–1100." In *The Peace of God: Social Violence and Religious Response in France around the Year 1000*, ed. Thomas Head and Richard Landes. Ithaca, N.Y.: Cornell University Press, 1992, 58–79.

———. "Ombres féminines dans l'histoire de Languedoc, aux Xe et XIe siècles." *Cahiers de civilisation médiévale* 34 (1991): 51–56.

———. *La société laïque et l'église dans la province ecclésiastique de Narbonne (zone cispyrénéenne) de la fin du VIIIe à la fin du XIe siècle*. Toulouse: Université de Toulouse-Le Mirail, 1974.

Mailhet, André. *Histoire de Saillans*. 1892; Paris: Livre d'histoire, 2003.

Mâle, Émile. *Religious Art from the Twelfth to the Eighteenth Century*. Trans. unknown. New York: Pantheon, 1949.

Manry, André-Georges, Roger Sève, and Martial Chaulanges. *L'histoire vue de l'Auvergne: Choix de documents concernant la Basse-Auvergne et le Puy-de-Dôme*. Clermont-Ferrand: G. de Bussac, 1959.

Manselli, Raoul. *Il soprannaturale e la religione popolare nel medio evo*. 1985; Rome: Studium, 1993.

Marboutin, Y.-R. "Monsempron: Le Prieuré, la paroisse, l'Église." *Revue de l'Agenais* 57 (1930): 3–28.

Maritain, Jacques. *Art et scholastique*. 3rd ed. Paris: Louis Rouart, 1935.

Marquardt, Janet T. *From Martyr to Monument: The Abbey of Cluny as Cultural Patrimony*. Newcastle: Cambridge Scholars, 2007.

Marrier, Martin, ed. *Biblioteca cluniacensis in qua ss. patrum abbatum Cluniacensis vitae, miracula, scripta, . . . omnia*. Paris: Protat, 1614.

Martindale, Jane. "The French Aristocracy in the Early Middle Ages." *Past and Present*, no. 75 (1977): 5–45.

———. "Peace and War in Early Eleventh-Century Aquitaine." In *Medieval Knighthood IV*, ed. Christopher Harper-Bill and Ruth Harvey. Papers from the Fifth Strawberry Hill Conference 1990. Woodbridge: Boydell, 1992, 147–76.

Martínez Pizarro, Joaquín. "On Nið against Bishops." *Medieval Scandinavia* 11 (1982): 149–53.

Mauduit, Anne-Marie, and Jean Mauduit. *La France contre la France: La séparation de l'église et de l'état, 1902–1906*. Paris: Plon, 1984.

Maury, André. "Le rayonnement de Saint-Victor de Marseille en Rouergue." *Revue du Rouergue*, no. 82 (1967): 121–27.

Mazel, Florian. "Le prince, le saint et le héros: Guilhem de Baux (1173–1218) et Guillaume de Gellone alias Guillaume d'Orange." In *Guerriers et moines: Conversion et sainteté aristocratiques dans l'occident médiéval (IXe–XIIe siècle)*, ed. Michel Lauwers. Antibes: APDCA, 2002, 449–65.

McDannell, Colleen. *Material Christianity: Religion and Popular Culture in America*. New Haven, Conn.: Yale University Press, 1995.

———. "True Men as We Need Them: Catholicism and the Irish Male." *American Studies* 27 (1986): 19–36.

McKitterick, Rosamond. "Latin and Romance: An Historian's Perspective." In *Latin and the Romance Languages in the Early Middle Ages*, ed. Roger Wright. London: Routledge, 1991, 130–45.

McLaren, Angus. *Sexuality and Social Order: The Debate over the Fertility of Women and Workers in France, 1770–1920.* New York: Homes and Meier, 1983.

McLaughlin, Megan. "Secular and Spiritual Fatherhood in the Eleventh Century." In *Conflicted Identities and Multiple Masculinities,* ed. Jacqueline Murray. New York: Garland, 1999, 25–43.

McNeill, John T. "Asceticism versus Militarism in the Middle Ages." *Church History* 5, no. 1 (1936): 3–28.

Meckler, Michael. "Wolves and Saracens in Odilo's *Life of Mayeul.*" In *Latin Culture in the Eleventh Century,* ed. Michael W. Herren et al. Proceedings of the Third International Conference on Medieval Latin Studies, Cambridge, September 9–12, 1998. Turnhout: Brepols, 2002, 2: 116–28.

Méhu, Didier. "La communauté d'habitants de Cluny et l'*ecclesia Cluniacensis* (fin Xe–début XIIIe siècle)." In *Die Cluniazenser in ihrem politisch-sozialen Umfeld,* ed. Giles Constable et al. Münster: LIT, 1998, 165–88.

Mérimée, Prosper. *Notes d'un voyage en Auvergne,* ed. Pierre-Marie Auzas. Paris: Adam Biro, 1989.

Merrick, Jeffrey. "Chaussons in the Streets: Sodomy in Seventeenth-Century Paris." *Journal of the History of Sexuality* 15, no. 2 (2006); 167–203.

Merwin, W. S. "Two Provençal Poems." *Hudson Review* 8, no. 2 (1955): 208–11.

Mestre, Jacques. *Histoire de la ville de Gignac et des communes de son canton des origines à 1900.* Millau: La Société des imprimeries Maury Saint-Georges-de-Luzençon, 1988.

Migne, Jacques-Paul, ed. *Patrologiae Cursus completus: Series Latina.* Paris: Garnier, 1844–55.

Miles, Margaret R. *Image as Insight: Visual Understanding in Western Christianity and Secular Culture.* Boston: Beacon, 1985.

Millerot, Thomas. *Histoire de la ville de Lunel: Depuis son origine jusqu'en 1789.* Nîmes: Christian Lacour, 1993.

Mills, Robert. "The Signification of the Tonsure." In *Holiness and Masculinity in the Middle Ages,* ed. P. H. Cullum and Katherine J. Lewis. Cardiff: University of Wales Press, 2004, 109–26.

Moulier, Pascale. "Iconographie de saint Géraud du moyen âge à nos jours." In *Sur les pas de Géraud d'Aurillac en France et en Espagne: Histoire, culte et iconographie,* ed. Pierre Moulier. Saint-Flour: Cantal patrimoine, 2010, 57–89.

Moulier, Pascale, and Pierre Moulier. "Essai de géographie du culte géraldien." In *Sur les pas de Géraud d'Aurillac en France et en Espagne: Histoire, culte et iconographie,* ed. Pierre Moulier. Saint-Flour: Cantal patrimoine, 2010, 113–18.

Moulier, Pierre. "De saint Géraud à saint Guiral, et retour: Acclimation, appropriation, oblitération d'un culte." In *Sur les pas de Géraud d'Aurillac en France et en Espagne: Histoire, culte et iconographie,* ed. Pierre Moulier. Saint-Flour: Cantal patrimoine, 2010, 91–111.

———. *Églises romanes de Haute-Auvergne.* Vol. 1. *Le Mauriacois.* Nonette: Créer, 1999.

———. *Églises romanes de Haute-Auvergne.* Vol. 2. *La région d'Aurillac.* Nonette: Créer, 2000.

———. "Le 'jet de pierres,' une tradition de l'an mil à Aurillac." *Patrimoine en Haute-Auvergne* 6 (2005): 57–61.

———, ed. *Sur les pas de Géraud d'Aurillac en France et en Espagne: Histoire, culte et iconographie.* Saint-Flour: Cantal patrimoine, 2010.

Mouzat, Jean. "Visite à une fondation de l'Abbaye de Tulle sur le chemin de Saint-Jacques-de-Compostelle: Hornillos del Camino." *Société des lettres, sciences et arts de la Corrèze* 74 (1970): 91–100.

Muchembled, Robert. *Popular Culture and Elite Culture in France, 1400–1750.* Trans. Lydia Cochrane. Baton Rouge: Louisiana State University Press, 1985.

Murray, Jacqueline. "Masculinizing Religious Life: Sexual Prowess, the Battle for Chastity and Monastic Identity." In *Holiness and Masculinity in the Middle Ages*, ed. P. H. Cullum and Katherine J. Lewis. Cardiff: University of Wales Press, 2004, 24–42.

Muzac, André. "Visages d'Aurillac dans le passé: Catalogue de l'exposition." *Revue de la Haute-Auvergne* 43 (1973): 377–475.

Nalgod of Cluny. *Vita sancti Odonis. PL* 133: 85–104.

Nelson, Janet. "Monks, Secular Men and Masculinity, c. 900." In *Masculinity in Medieval Europe*, ed. D. M. Hadley. London: Longman, 1999, 121–42.

Nichols, Aidan. "The Dominicans and the Journal *L'art sacré.*" *New Blackfriars* 88 (2007): 25–45.

Nicholson, Helen. *The Knights Hospitaller.* Woodbridge: Boydell, 2001.

Noble, Thomas F. X. *Images, Iconoclasm, and the Carolingians.* Philadelphia: University of Pennsylvania Press, 2009.

———. "Secular Sanctity: Forging an Ethos for the Carolingian Nobility." In *Lay Intellectuals in the Carolingian World*, ed. Patrick Wormald and Janet L. Nelson. Cambridge: Cambridge University Press, 2007, 8–36.

Noble, Thomas F. X., and Thomas Head, eds. *Soldiers of Christ: Saints and Saints' Lives from Late Antiquity and the Early Middle Ages.* University Park: Pennsylvania State University Press, 1995.

Nora, Pierre, ed. *Realms of Memory: The Construction of the French Past*, trans. Arthur Goldhammer. 3 vols. New York: Columbia University Press, 1996–98.

Nye, Robert A. *Masculinity and Male Codes of Honor in Modern France.* Oxford: Oxford University Press, 1993.

Odilo of Cluny. *Vita Maioli. PL* 142: 943–62.

Odo of Cluny. *Occupatio*, ed. Antonius Swoboda. Leipzig: Teubner, 1900.

Pataki, Tibor. "Notes sur Aurillac et ses glacis défensifs au début de la guerre de cent ans (1345–1362)." *Bulletin de la Société des études littéraires, scientifiques et artistiques du Lot* 121 (2000): 83–98.

Paxton, Frederick S. "Forgetting Hathumoda: The Afterlife of the First Abbess of Gandersheim." In *History in the Comic Mode: Medieval Communities and the Matter of Person*, ed. Rachel Fulton and Bruce W. Holsinger. New York: Columbia University Press, 2007, 15–24.

———. "History, Historians, and the Peace of God." In *The Peace of God: Social Violence and Religious Response in France around the Year 1000*, ed. Thomas Head and Richard Landes. Ithaca, N.Y.: Cornell University Press, 1992, 21–40.

Périé, Jean-Marie. "Le culte de Saint Roch en Rouergue." *Revue du Rouergue*, n.s. 53 (1998): 63–69.

Perrel, Jean. "Le bas Limousin et le chemin de Compostelle." *Bulletin de la Société des lettres, sciences et arts de la Corrèze* 67 (1963): 49–54.

Peter the Venerable. *De miraculis. PL* 189: 851–954.

Peters, Edward. "Mutations, Adjustments, Terrors, Historians, and the Year 1000." In *The Year 1000: Religious and Social Responses to the Turning of the First Millenium*, ed. Michael Frassetto. New York: Palgrave Macmillan, 2002, 9–28.

Philippart, Guy. "L'hagiographie comme littérature: Concept récent et nouveaux programmes?" *Revue des sciences humaines*, no. 251 (1998): 11–39.

———. "Le manuscrit hagiographique latin comme gisement documentaire: Un parcours dans les *Analecta Bollandiana* de 1960 à 1989." In *Manuscrits hagiographiques et travail des hagiographes*, ed. Martin Heinzelmann. Sigmaringen: Jan Thorbecke, 1992, 17–48.

———. "Le saint comme parure de Dieu, héros séducteur et patron terrestre d'après les hagiographes lotharingiens du Xe siècle." In *Les fonctions des saints dans le monde occidental (IIIe–XIIIe siècle)*, ed. Jean-Yves Tilliette et al. Rome: École française de Rome, 1991, 123–42.

Philippart, Guy, ed. *Hagiographies: Histoire internationale de la littérature hagiographique, latine et vernaculaire, de l'occident des origines à 1550*. 5 vols. Turnhout: Brepols, 1994–2012.

Philippart, Guy, and Michel Trigalet. "L'hagiographie latine du XIe siècle dans la longue durée: Données statistiques sur la production littéraire et sur l'édition médiévale." In *Latin Culture in the Eleventh Century*, ed. Michael W. Herren et al. Proceedings of the Third International Conference on Medieval Latin Studies, Cambridge, September 9–12, 1998. Turnhout: Brepols, 1998, 2: 281–301.

Pirotte, Jean. "The Universe of Pious Objects: Use and Evolution of the Pious Object from the Sixteenth to the Twentieth Century." *Lumen Vitae* 41 (1986): 410–25.

Piva, Paolo. *Da Cluny a Polirone: Un recupero essenziale del romanico europeo*. San Benedetto Po: Museo Civico Polironiano, 1980.

———. "Il monasterio di S. Benedetto di Polirone." In *Monasteri benedettini in Lombardia*, ed. Giorgio Picasso. Milan: Silvana, 1980, 195–206.

Platelle, Henri. "Le problème du scandale: Les nouvelles modes masculines aux XIe et XIIe siècles." *Revue belge de psychologie et de pédagogie* 53 (1975): 1071–96.

Poble, Pierre-Éric. "Les structures territoriales en Auvergne méridionale au temps de Géraud d'Aurillac." *Revue de la Haute-Auvergne* 72 (2010): 47–69.

Pohl, Walter. "History in Fragments: Montecassino's Politics of Memory." *Early Medieval Europe* 10, no. 3 (2001): 343–74.

Poly, Jean-Pierre, and Eric Bournazel. *The Feudal Transformation, 900–1200*. Trans. Caroline Higgitt. London: Holmes and Meier, 1991.

———. "Que faut-il préférer au 'mutationisme'? Ou le problème du changement social." *Revue historique de droit français et étranger* 72 (1994): 401–12.

Poeck, Dietrich W. "Abbild oder Verband: Cluny und seine Klöster." In *Die Cluniazenser in ihrem politisch-sozialen Umfeld*, ed. Giles Constable et al. Münster: LIT, 1998, 93–120.

Pon, Georges. "La culture d'Adémar à la lumière de sa vie de saint Amant de Boixe." In *Saint-Martial de Limoges: Ambition politique et production culturelle (Xe–XIIIe siècles)*, ed. Claude Andrault-Schmitt. Actes du colloque tenu à Poitiers et Limoges du 26 au 28 mai 2005. Limoges: Presses universitaires de Limoges, 2006, 391–410.

Poncelet, Albert. "La plus ancienne vie de s. Géraud d'Aurillac († 909)." *Analecta Bollandiana* 14 (1895): 89–107.

Poulin, Joseph-Claude. *L'idéal de sainteté dans l'Aquitaine carolingienne d'après les sources hagiographiques (750–950)*. Laval: Presses de l'Université de Laval, 1975.

———. "Les *libelli* dans l'édition hagiographique avant le XIIe siècle." In *Livrets, collections et textes: Études sur la tradition hagiographique latine*, ed. Martin Heinzelmann. Ostfildern: Jan Thorbecke, 2006, 15–193.

———. "Un élément négligé de critique hagiographique: Les titres de chapitres." In *"Scribere sanctorum gesta": Receuil d'études d'hagiographie médiévale offert à Guy Philippart*, ed. Étienne Renard et al. Turnhout: Brepols, 2005, 309–42.

Powell, Timothy. "The 'Three Orders' of Society in Anglo-Saxon England." *Anglo-Saxon England* 23 (1994): 103–32.

Prevost, M., and d'Amat, Roman, eds. *Dictionnaire de biographie française*. Paris: Letouzey, 1956.

"Prieuré de St.-Géraud d'Aspres-sur-Buëch." N.p., n.d. Among papers at the church of Saint-Géraud in Aspres-sur-Buëch.

Quétin, Michel. "L'Hôpital d'Aurillac de 1649 à la révolution." *Revue de la Haute-Auvergne* 40 (1966): 517–21.

Quintard, Alain. *Monsempron-Libos: De la légende à l'histoire.* Brive: Chastrusse, 1989.

Ralston, David B. *The Army of the Republic: The Place of the Military in the Political Evolution of France, 1871–1914.* Cambridge, Mass.: MIT Press, 1967.

Racinet, Philippe. *Crises et renouveaux: Les monastères clunisiens à la fin du moyen âge (XIIIe–XVIe siècles): De la Flandre au Berry et comparisons méridionales.* Arras: Artois Presses Université, 1997.

Ralph Glaber. *Rodulfi Glabri historiarum libri quinque/Rodulfus Glaber, The Five Books of the Histories.* Ed. and trans. John France. Oxford: Clarendon, 1989.

Rauch, André. *Le premier sexe: Mutations et crise de l'identité masculine.* Paris: Hachette, 2000.

Réau, Louis. *Iconographie de l'art chrétien.* 3 vols. Paris: Presses universitaires de France, 1955.

Remensnyder, Amy. "Legendary Treasure at Conques: Reliquaries and Imaginative Memory." *Speculum* 71, no. 4 (1996): 884–906.

———. "Un problème de cultures ou de culture? La statue-reliquaire et les *joca* de sainte Foy de Conques dans le *Liber miraculorum* de Bernard d'Angers." *Cahiers de civilisation médiévale* 33, no. 4 (1990): 351–79.

———. *Remembering Kings Past: Monastic Foundation Legends in Medieval Southern France.* Ithaca, N.Y.: Cornell University Press, 1995.

Répertoire des monuments historiques et des sites: Lot-et-Garonne, ed. Association départementale de développement culturel et service départemental de l'architecture. Agen: Blanchard, 1987.

Reuter, Timothy. "The 'Feudal Revolution.'" *Past and Present,* no. 155 (1997): 177–95.

Reynaud, Félix. *La commanderie de l'Hôpital de Saint-Jean de Jérusalem de Rhodes et de Malte à Manosque (XIIe siècle–1789).* Gap: Société d'études des Hautes-Alpes, 1981.

Reynolds, Susan. *Fiefs and Vassals: The Medieval Evidence Reinterpreted.* Oxford: Oxford University Press, 1994.

Riché, Pierre. *Gerbert d'Aurillac: Le pape de l'an mil.* Paris: Fayard, 1987.

Rigon, Antonio, and André Vauchez, eds. *San Rocco: Genesi e prima espansione di un culto.* Brussels: Société des Bollandistes, 2006.

Rigaux, Dominique. "Le dossier iconographique de Saint Roch: Nouvelles images, nouvelle chronologie." In *San Rocco: Genesi e prima espansione di un culto,* ed. Antonio Rigon and André Vauchez. Brussels: Société des Bollandistes, 2006, 245–68.

Riley-Smith, Jonathan. *The Knights of St. John in Jerusalem and Cyprus, c. 1050–1310.* Vol. 1 of *A History of the Order of the Hospital of St. John of Jerusalem,* ed. Lionel Butler. London: Macmillan, 1967.

Robinson, I. S. "Gregory VII and the Soldiers of Christ." *History,* no. 58 (1973): 169–92.

Röckelein, Hedwig. "Just de Beauvais alias Justin d'Auxerre: L'art de dédoubler un saint." In *Livrets, collections et textes: Études sur la tradition hagiographique latine,* ed. Martin Heinzelmann. Ostfildern: Jan Thorbecke, 2006, 323–60.

Roman, M. J. *Dictionnaire topographique du département des Hautes-Alpes.* Paris: Imprimerie nationale, 1884.

Romig, Andrew. "The Common Bond of Aristocratic Masculinity: Monks, Secular Men and St. Gerald of Aurillac." In *Negotiating Clerical Masculinities: Priests, Monks and Masculinity in the Middle Ages,* ed. Jennifer Thibodeaux. Houndmills: Palgrave Macmillan, 2010, 39–56.

Roques, Jean. *Guide du Tarn.* Albi: Revue du Tarn, 1981.

Rosé, Isabelle. *Construire une société seigneuriale: Itinéraire et ecclésiologie de l'abbé Odon de Cluny (fin du IXe–milieu du Xe siècle).* Turnhout: Brepols, 2008.

———. "La *Vita Gregorii Turonensis* d'Odon de Cluny: Un texte clunisien?" *Memini: Travaux et documents* 9–10 (2005–6): 191–277.

Rosenwein, Barbara. "The Family Politics of Berengar I, King of Italy (888–924)." *Speculum* 71 (1996): 247–89.

———. "Piety and Power: Cluniac Spirituality in the Time of St. Odo (926–942)." Ph.D. diss., University of Chicago, 1974.

———. *Rhinoceros Bound: Cluny in the Tenth Century.* Philadelphia: University of Pennsylvania Press, 1982.

———. "Saint Odo's Saint Martin: The Uses of a Model." *Journal of Medieval History* 4 (1978): 317–331.

———. *To Be the Neighbor of Saint Peter: The Social Meaning of Cluny's Property, 909–1049.* Ithaca, N.Y.: Cornell University Press, 1989.

Rosenwein, Barbara, Thomas Head, and Sharon Farmer. "Monks and Their Enemies: A Comparative Approach." *Speculum* 66, no. 4 (1991): 764–96.

Rosenwein, Barbara, and Lester K. Little. "Social Meaning in the Monastic and Mendicant Spiritualities." *Past and Present*, no. 63 (1974): 4–32.

Roüet, Adolphe. *Notice sur la ville de Lunel au moyen-âge: Et vie de saint Gérard, seigneur de cette ville au XIIIe siècle.* 1878; Nîmes: Christian Lacour, 1994.

Rousset, Paul. "L'idéal chevaleresque dans deux *Vitae* clunisiennes." In *Études de civilisation médiévale (IXe–XIIe siècles): Mélanges offerts à Edmond-René Labande à l'occasion de son départ à la retraite et du XXe anniversaire du C.E.S.C.M. part ses amis, ses collègues, ses élèves.* Poitiers: Centre d'études supérieures de civilisation médiévale, 1974, 623–33.

Routledge, Michael J., ed. *Les poésies du moine de Montaudon.* Montpellier: Centre d'études occitanes de l'Université Paul Valéry, 1977.

Rubenstein, Jay. "Biography and Autobiography in the Middle Ages." In *Writing Medieval History,* ed. Nancy Partner. London: Hodder Arnold, 2005, 22–41.

Ruiz de la Peña Solar, Juan Ignacio. *Foncebadón y la asistencia hospitaliaria en los puertos de las montañas Astur-Galaico-Leonesas durante la edad media.* Astorga: Centro de Estudios Astorganos "Marcelo Macías," 2003.

Sadoux, Jacques. "À propos des reliques de Marcolès: Saint Géraud d'Aurillac et saint Martin de Tours." *Revue de la Haute-Auvergne* 36 (1958): 343–45.

Saltet, Louis. "Un cas de mythomanie historique bien documenté: Adémar de Chabannes (988–1034)." *Bulletin de littérature ecclésiastique* 32 (1931): 149–65.

———. "Une discussion sur Saint Martial entre un lombard et un limousin en 1029." *Bulletin de littérature ecclésiastique* 26 (1925): 161–86, 278–302.

———. "Les faux d'Adémar de Chabannes: Prétendues décisions sur Saint Martial au Concile de Bourges du 1er novembre 1031." *Bulletin de littérature ecclésiastique* 27 (1926): 145–60.

———. "Une prétendue lettre de Jean XIX sur Saint Martial fabriquée par Adémar de Chabannes." *Bulletin de littérature ecclésiastique* 27 (1926): 117–39.

Sargatel i Pellicer, Ramon. *Diccionari dels sants.* Barcelona: Edicions 62, 1996.

Saunier, Francine. "Le bestiaire dans la sculpture romane de Haute-Auvergne (archiprêtré de Mauriac): Sources et filiations." *Revue de la Haute-Auvergne* 55 (1993): 289–340.

Savart, Claude. "À la recherche de l'"art' dit de Saint-Sulpice." *Revue d'histoire de la spiritualité* 52, nos. 3–4 (1957): 265–82.

Savigni, Raffaele. "Les laïcs dans l'ecclésiologie carolingienne: Normes statuaires et idéal de 'conversion.'" In *Guerriers et moines: Conversion et sainteté aristocratiques dans l'occident médiéval (IXe–XIIe siècle),* ed. Michel Lauwers. Antibes: APDCA, 2002, 41–92.

Schmitt, Jean-Claude. "Les reliques et les images." In *Les reliques: Objets, cultes, symboles*, ed. Edina Bozóky and Anne-Marie Helvétius. Actes du colloque international de l'Université du Littoral-Côte d'Opale (Boulogne-sur-Mer) 4–6 septembre 1997. Turnhout: Brepols, 1999, 145–68.

Schneider, Jean. "Aspects de la société dans l'Aquitaine carolingienne d'après la *Vita Geraldi Auriliacensis*." *Académie des inscriptions et belles-lettres, Comptes rendus des séances de l'année*. Paris: Klincksieck, 1973.

Schulenburg, Jane Tibbetts. *Forgetful of Their Sex: Female Sanctity and Society, ca. 500–1100*. Chicago: University of Chicago Press, 1998.

Schwarzmaier, Hansmartin. "The Monastery of St. Benedict, Polirone, and its Cluniac Associations." In *Cluniac Monasticism in the Central Middle Ages*, ed. Noreen Hunt. Hamden, Conn.: Archon, 1971, 123–42.

Segl, Peter. "Die Cluniacenser in Spanien: Mit besonderer Berücksichtigung ihrer Aktivitäten im Bistum León von der Mitte des 11. bis zur Mitte des 12. Jahrhunderts." In *Die Cluniazenser in ihrem politisch-sozialen Umfeld*, ed. Giles Constable et al. Münster: LIT, 1998, 537–58.

Settipani, Christian. *La noblesse du midi carolingien: Études sur quelques grandes familles d'Aquitaine et du Languedoc du IXe au XIe siècles: Toulousain, Périgord, Limousin, Poitou, Auvergne*. Oxford: Prosopographica et Genealogica, 2004.

Shahar, Shulamith. "The Old Body in Medieval Culture." In *Framing Medieval Bodies*, ed. Sarah Kay and Miri Rubin. Manchester: Manchester University Press, 1994, 160–86.

Sheingorn, Pamela, ed. *The Book of Sainte Foy*. Philadelphia: University of Pennsylvania Press, 1995.

Sigal, Pierre-André. "Le déroulement des translations de reliques principalement dans les regions entre Loire et Rhin aux XIe et XIIe siècles." In *Les reliques: Objets, cultes, symboles*, ed. Edina Bozóky and Anne-Marie Helvétius. Actes du colloque international de l'Université du Littoral-Côte d'Opale (Boulogne-sur-Mer) 4–6 septembre 1997. Turnhout: Brepols, 1999.

———. "Le travail des hagiographes aux XIe et XIIe siècles: Sources d'information et méthodes de rédaction." *Francia* 15 (1987): 149–82.

Silvestre, Hubert. "Le problème des faux au moyen âge." *Le moyen âge* 66 (1960): 351–70.

Simon, Adrien. *Panégyrique de saint Géraud, le bon comte d'Aurillac, prononcé dans l'ancienne église abbatiale le 14 octobre 1906 devant Mgr Lecoeur, évêque de Saint-Flour, par M. l'abbé Adrien Simon, Vicaire à N.-D. aux Neiges, directeur de l'Echo religieux d'Aurillac*. Aurillac: Imprimerie moderne, 1906.

Sinding-Larsen, Staale. *Iconography and Ritual: A Study of Analytical Perspectives*. Oslo: Universitetsforlaget AS, 1984.

Sitwell, Gerard, ed. and trans. *St. Odo of Cluny: Being the Life of St. Odo of Cluny by John of Salerno and the Life of St. Gerald of Aurillac by St. Odo*. London and New York: Sheed and Ward, 1958.

Skinner, Patricia. *Family Power in Southern Italy: The Duchy of Gaeta and Its Neighbours, 850–1139*. Cambridge: Cambridge University Press, 2003.

Sluhovsky, Moshe. *Patroness of Paris: Rituals of Devotion in Early Modern France*. Leiden: Brill, 1998.

Smith, Julia M. H. "Gender and Ideology in the Early Middle Ages." In *Gender and Christian Religion*, ed. R. N. Swanson. Papers Read at the 1996 Summer Meeting and the 1997 Winter Meeting of the Ecclesiastical History Society. Woodbridge: Boydell, 1998, 51–73.

———. "The Problem of Female Sanctity in Carolingian Europe, c. 780–920." *Past and Present*, no. 146 (1995): 3–37.

Smith, Katherine Allen. "Saints in Shining Armor: Martial Asceticism and Masculine Models of Sanctity, ca. 1050–1250." *Speculum* 83, no. 3 (2008): 572–602.

————. *War and the Making of Medieval Monastic Culture*. Woodbridge: Boydell, 2011.

Smith, L. M. *Cluny in the Eleventh and Twelfth Centuries*. London: Philip Allan, 1930.

————. *The Early History of the Monastery of Cluny*. Oxford: Oxford University Press, 1920.

Smyth, Alfred P. *King Alfred the Great*. Oxford: Oxford University Press, 1995.

Snipes-Hoyt, Carolyn. "Unofficial and Secular Saint in Integral Nationalist Discourse: Maurice Barrès' Literary Jeanne d'Arc." In *Medieval Saints in Late Nineteenth Century French Culture: Eight Essays*, ed. Elizabeth Emery and Laurie Postlewate. Jefferson, N.C.: McFarland, 2004, 195–221.

Soares-Christen, Eliana Magnani. "Saint-Victor de Marseille, Cluny et la politique de Grégoire VII au nord-ouest de la Méditerranée." In *Die Cluniazenser in ihrem politisch-sozialen Umfeld*, ed. Giles Constable et al. Münster: LIT, 1998, 321–47.

Sohn, Andreas. *Der Abbatiat Ademars von Saint-Martial de Limoges (1063–1114): Ein Beitrag zur Geschichte des cluniacensischen Klösterverbandes*. Münster: Aschendorff, 1989.

Solt, Claire Wheeler. "Romanesque French Reliquaries." *Studies in Medieval and Renaissance History* 9 (1987): 167–236.

Soupairac, V. *Mémoires pour servir à la vie de saint Guiraud, second prieur de Cassan, évêque de Béziers*. Montpellier: Jean Martel, 1884.

Souter, Alexander, ed. *A Glossary of Later Latin (to 600 A.D.)*. Oxford: Clarendon, 1949.

Stalley, Roger. *Early Medieval Architecture*. Oxford: Oxford University Press, 1999.

Stone, Donald. "The Sexual Outlaw in France, 1605." *Journal of the History of Sexuality* 2, no. 4 (1992); 597–608.

Stopford, J. "Some Approaches to the Archeology of Christian Pilgrimage." *World Archeology* 26 (1994): 57–72.

Surkis, Judith. *Sexing the Citizen: Morality and Masculinity in France, 1870–1920*. Ithaca, N.Y.: Cornell University Press, 2006.

Taylor, Claire. "Royal Protection in Aquitaine and Gascony by c. 1000: The Public, the Private, and the Princely." In *Peace and Protection in the Middle Ages*, ed. T. B. Lambert and David Rollason. Durham: Durham University Press, 2009, 36–59.

————. "The Year 1000 and Those Who Labored." In *The Year 1000: Religious and Social Response to the Turning of the First Millennium*, ed. Michael Frassetto. New York: Palgrave Macmillan, 2002, 187–236.

Terelliac, A.-L. "Églises et chapelles disparues: Saint-Pierre-Saint-Géraud." *La croix du Midi*, 20 August 1950.

"Textes et documents pour mieux connaître Salles-Curan et son histoire: Et l'histoire associée des Canabières, de Bouloc et des Faux." N.p.: privately printed by the Association des amis d'Eugène Viala et du Levézou, 2001.

Teyssot, Josiane. "Le mouvement communal en Auvergne, XIIe–XVe siècles." *Annales du Midi* 109 (1997): 201–10.

Thibout, Marc. "Auvergne et Cévennes." In *L'art roman en France*, ed. Michel Aubert. Paris: Flammarion, 1961, 257–320.

Thomas, Émile. "Histoire de Sieurac, canton de Réalmont (Tarn)." Typed manuscript, n.d.

Thomas, Eugène. *Dictionnaire topographique du département de l'Hérault*. Paris: Imprimerie nationale, 1865.

Thomson, Richard. *The Troubled Republic: Visual Culture and Social Debate in France, 1889–1900*. New Haven, Conn.: Yale University Press, 2004.

Töpfer, Bernhard. "The Cult of Relics and Pilgrimage in Burgundy and Aquitaine at the Time of the Monastic Reform." In *The Peace of God: Social Violence and Religious Response in France around the Year 1000*, ed. Thomas Head and Richard Landes. Ithaca, N.Y.: Cornell University Press, 1992, 41–57.

Touati, François-Olivier. "Un dossier à rouvrir: L'assistance au moyen âge." In *Fondations et oeuvres charitables au moyen âge*, ed. Jean Dufour and Henri Platelle. Paris: CTHS, 1999, 23–38.

"Translatio sancti Viviani episcopi in coenobium Figiacense et eiusdem ibidem miracula." *Analecta Bollandiana* 8 (1889): 256–77.

Treffort, Cécile. "Le comte de Poitiers, duc d'Aquitaine, et l'église aux alentours de l'an mil (970–1030)." *Cahiers de civilisation médiévale* 43 (2000): 395–445.

Trichet, Louis. *La tonsure: Vie et mort d'une pratique ecclésiastique*. Paris: Cerf, 1990.

Tullou, Adrienne Durand. *Religion populaire en Cévennes: Le culte à Saint-Guiral*. Béziers: Annales du Midi rural, 1981.

Valiña Sampedro, Elias. *El camino de Santiago: Estudio histórico-jurídico*. Lugo: Disputacion provincial, 1971.

Van Engen, John. "The 'Crisis of Cenobitism' Reconsidered: Benedictine Monasticism in the Years 1050–1150." *Speculum* 61, no. 2 (1986): 269–304.

Van Meter, David C. "Eschatological Order and the Moral Arguments for Clerical Celibacy in Francia around the Year 1000." In *Medieval Purity and Piety: Essays on Medieval Clerical Celibacy and Religious Reform*, ed. Michael Frassetto. New York: Garland, 1998, 149–75.

———. "The Peace of Amiens-Corbie and Gerard of Cambrai's Oration on the Three Functional Orders: The Date, the Context, the Rhetoric." *Revue belge de philologie et d'histoire/Belgisch tijdschrift voor philologie en geschiedenis* 74 (1996): 633–57.

Van Uytfanghe, Marc. "The Consciousness of a Linguistic Dichotomy (Latin-Romance) in Carolingian Gaul: The Contradictions of the Sources and of their Interpretation." In *Latin and the Romance Languages in the Early Middle Ages*, ed. Roger Wright. London: Routledge, 1991, 114–29.

Vauchez, André. *The Laity in the Middle Ages: Religious Beliefs and Devotional Practices*. Trans. Margery Schneider. Notre Dame, Ind.: University of Notre Dame Press, 1993.

———. "Un modèle hagiographique et culturel en Italie avant Saint Roch: Le pèlerin mort en chemin." In *San Rocco: Genesi e prima espansione di un culto*, ed. Antonio Rigon and André Vauchez. Brussels: Société des Bollandistes, 2006, 56–69.

———. "La pauvreté volontaire au moyen âge." *Annales: Économies, sociétés, civilisations* 25 (1970): 1566–73.

Vázquez de Parga, Luis et al. *Las peregrinaciones a Santiago de Compostela*. 3 vols. 1948; Pamplona: Gobierno de Navarra/Departamento de Educación y Cultura, 1992.

Verdon, Jean. "Recherches sur les monastères féminins dans la France du sud aux IXe–XIe siècles." *Annales du Midi* 88 (1976): 117–38.

Veyrard-Cosme, Christiane. "Problèmes de réécriture des textes hagiographiques latins: La *Vita Richarii* d'Alcuin et ses réécritures." In *Latin Culture in the Eleventh Century*, ed. Michael W. Herren et al. Proceedings of the Third International Conference on Medieval Latin Studies, Cambridge, September 9–12, 1998. Turnhout: Brepols, 1998, 2: 476–502.

Vie de saint Gérard de Lunel. Montpellier: Auguste Seguin, 1837.

Vigié, Albert. *Histoire de Belvès*. Paris: Res Universis, 1990.

Vila, Pep. "Un fragment de la vida de sant Grau." *Patronat d'Estudis Històrics d'Olot i Comarca* (1996–98): 225–39.

Vincent, Abel. *Notice historique sur Saillans*. Valence: Imprimerie Valentinoise, 1855.

Vircondelet, Alain. "La dérive du sacré dans l'imagerie saint-sulpicienne." *Revue de l'Institut catholique de Paris* 30 (1989): 57–72.

———. *Le monde merveilleux des images pieuses*. Paris: Hermé, 1988.

"Vita s. Amantii auctore, ut videtur, Hugone episcopo Engolismensi, ex. cod. Parisino lat. 3784." *Analecta Bollandiana* 8 (1889): 329–55.

Ward, Benedicta. *Miracles and the Medieval Mind: Theory, Record and Event, 1000–1215*. Philadelphia: University of Pennsylvania Press, 1982.

Warner, Marina. *Alone of All Her Sex: The Myth and the Cult of the Virgin Mary*. New York: Vintage Books, 1976.

———. *Joan of Arc: The Image of Female Heroism*. Berkeley: University of California Press, 1981.

Weinstein, Donald, and Rudolph M. Bell. *Saints and Society: The Two Worlds of Western Christendom, 1000–1700*. Chicago: University of Chicago Press, 1982.

Weisbach, Werner. *Reforma religiosa y arte medieval: La influencia de Cluny en el románico occidental*. Trans. Helmut Schlunk and L. Vásquez de Parga. Madrid: Espasa-Calpe, 1949.

Werner, Karl Ferdinand. "Liens de parenté et noms de personne: Un problème historique et méthodologique." In *Famille et parenté dans l'occident médiéval*, ed. Georges Duby and Jacques Le Goff. Rome: École française de Rome, 1977, 13–18 and 25–34.

White, Stephen D. "The 'Feudal Revolution.'" *Past and Present*, no. 152 (1996): 205–23.

Wickham, Chris. "The 'Feudal Revolution.'" *Past and Present*, no. 155 (1997): 196–208.

Wilson, Stephen. "Cults of Saints in the Churches of Central Paris." *Comparative Studies in Society and History* 22, no. 4 (1980): 548–75.

Wilson, Winefride. *Modern Christian Art*. New York: Hawthorn Books, 1965.

Winoch, Michel. "Joan of Arc." In *Realms of Memory: The Construction of the French Past*. Ed. Pierre Nora. Trans. Arthur Goldhammer. Vol. 3. New York: Columbia University Press, 1998, 433–80.

Winter, Jay. "Historians and Sites of Memory." In *Memory in Mind and Culture*, ed. Pascal Boyer and James V. Wertsch. Cambridge: Cambridge University Press, 2009, 252–71.

Wollasch, Joachim. "Königtum, Adel und Klöster im Berry während des 10. Jahrhunderts." In *Neue Forschungen über Cluny und die Cluniacenser*, ed. Joachim Wollasch et al. Freiburg: Herder, 1959, 19–165.

———. "Parenté noble et monachisme réformateur: Observations sur les 'conversions' à la vie monastique aux XIe et XIIe siècles." *Revue historique* 535 (1980): 3–24.

Wormald, Patrick, and Janet L. Nelson, eds. *Lay Intellectuals in the Carolingian World*. Cambridge: Cambridge University Press, 2007.

Zaballos, Yannick. "Monsempron-Libos: Ancien prieuré." *Aquitaine: Direction régionale des affaires culturelles/Service régional de l'archéologie* 3 (1993): 90–92.

Zanichelli, Giuseppa. "La produzione libraria e la sua illustrazione (961–1125)." In *Storia di San Benedetto Polirone: Le origine (961–1125)*, ed. Paolo Golinelli. Bologna: Patron, 1998, 173–87.

Zimmermann, Michel. "La Catalogne de Gerbert." In *Gerbert l'européen*, ed. Nicole Charbonnel and Jean-Eric Iung. Acts du colloque d'Aurillac, 4–7 juin 1996. Aurillac: Gerbert, 1997, 79–101.

Ziolkowski, Jan. "The *Occupatio* by Odo of Cluny: A Poetic Manifesto of Monasticism in the Tenth Century." *Mittellateinisches Jahrbuch* 24–25 (1989–90): 559–67.

Zucchitello, Mario. *Tossa: La formació d'une vila, el comte, l'abat, els tossencs (segles IX–XII)*. Tossa [de Mar]: Quaderns d'estudis tossencs, 1998.

Zucker, Mark J. "Problems in Dominican Iconography: The Case of St. Vincent Ferrer." *Artibus et Historiae* 13, no. 25 (1992): 181–93.

ACKNOWLEDGMENTS

I have benefited from the generous help of many, including in France at the Bibliothèque nationale de France, the Institut des recherches et d'histoire des textes, the Bibliothèque de l'Arsenal, and the Bibliothèque Sainte-Geneviève, all in Paris; the Archives départementales across France in Alpes-de-Haute-Provence (at Digne-les-Bains), Aude (Carcassonne), Aveyron (Rodez), Cantal (Aurillac), Drôme (Valence), Haute-Garonne (Toulouse), Hautes-Alpes (Gap), Haute-Vienne (Limoges), Hérault (Montpellier), Isère (Grenoble), Lot-et-Garonne (Agen), Puy-de-Dôme (Clermont-Ferrand), Rhône (Lyon), Tarn (Albi), and Tarn-et-Garonne (Montauban), the Bibliothèques municipales in Aurillac, Limoges, Lyon, Rodez, Toulouse, and Tours, and the Bibliothèque de la faculté de médecine in Montpellier; in Spain, the Biblioteca nacional de España and the Real academia de la historia in Madrid, the libraries of the Consejo superior de investigaciones científicas and of the Casa de Galicia (also in Madrid), the Biblioteca nacional de Catalunya in Barcelona, the Arxiu històric municipal de Tossa de Mar, the Archivos históricos provinciales in Lugo and in León, the Biblioteca intercentros de Lugo, the Archivo histórico diocesano de Santiago de Compostela, and the Real biblioteca del monasterio de El Escorial; in Italy, the Archivio comunale di Mantova, the Biblioteca Teresiana in Mantua, and the Biblioteca nazionale Marciana in Venice. I am grateful to the staff at these institutions and to the many other individuals—municipal and museum officials, church staff and caretakers, and local history experts—across southern France and northern Spain. Funding for research was provided in part by the Mellon Foundation, the Society for French Historical Studies, the National Endowment for the Humanities, and the College of Arts and Letters at San Diego State University.

I am also grateful to those scholars who have read and commented on parts of this book over the years or offered helpful advice: Robert Babcock, Isabelle Cochelin, Patrick Geary, Richard Landes, John Ott, Joseph-Claude

Poulin, Barbara Rosenwein, Julia M. H. Smith, Katherine Allen Smith, Anna Trumbore Jones, and especially Thomas Head. I have been delighted to make the "virtual" acquaintance of Pierre and Pascale Moulier of Saint-Flour, France, who generously shared their findings with me and invited me to contribute to their book *Sur les pas de saint Géraud en France et en Espagne* (my "Les histoires de Géraud d'Aurillac"). I am also grateful to them for permission to reprint many of the images in this book, and also to Josep Casas i Genover of Albons, Spain, Miquel Palomeras i Anglada of Sales de Llierca, Spain, Gilbert Coudon of Parlan, France, and Sylvie L'Hostis of Saint-Martin-du-Londres, France. Images were also given to me by the Musée d'art et d'archéologie of Aurillac and the Office du Tourisme of Conques. I thank Ruth Mazo Karras, Jerome Singerman, Caroline Winschel, and Erica Ginsburg for their editorial help, and Melodie Tune at San Diego State University, who created the maps. Saint Gerald has received much recent academic interest, including from Anne-Marie Bultot-Verleysen, Paolo Facciotto, Dominique Iogna-Prat, and Isabelle Rosé, and while I disagree with some of their conclusions, especially about Odo of Cluny's authorship of most of the writings about Saint Gerald, I am grateful for the quality of their scholarship. A more detailed version of Chapter 1 appeared as an article published in *Viator* in 2013 (my "Dating and Authorship").

I am grateful to my family, Joe Elliott and Brian Giguere, who traveled with me to many of the churches dedicated to Saint Gerald—and to Brian again for some of the photos included in the book. My friends Maria Rybakova and Oliva Espín read the whole of the manuscript. They and Don Dale, Sarah Elkind, and Beth Holmberg, and also my sisters, Janet Bishop, Phyllis Kelly, Laurie Plomp, and Frances Josey, have provided attentive audiences for my stories about Saint Gerald. This book is dedicated to my mother, Aimée Kuefler (née Lamoureux), who sadly did not live to see it.